The Human Tradition
in the Civil Rights
Movement

The Human Tradition in America

CHARLES W. CALHOUN
Series Editor
Department of History, East Carolina University

The nineteenth-century English author Thomas Carlyle once remarked that "history is the essence of innumerable biographies." In this conception of the past, Carlyle came closer to modern notions that see the lives of all kinds of people, high and low, powerful and weak, known and unknown, as part of the mosaic of human history, each contributing in a large or small way to the unfolding of the human tradition. This idea forms the foundation for this series of books on the human tradition in America. Each volume is devoted to a particular period or topic in American history and each consists of minibiographies of persons whose lives shed light on that period or topic.

By bringing the study of history down to the level of the individual, these sketches reveal not only the diversity of the American people and the complexity of their interaction but also some of the commonalities of sentiment and experience that Americans have shared in the evolution of their culture. Our hope is that these explorations of the lives of "real people" will give readers a deeper understanding of the human tradition in America.

Charles W. Calhoun, ed., *The Human Tradition in America from the Colonial Era through Reconstruction*

Charles W. Calhoun, ed., *The Human Tradition in America: 1865 to the Present*

Nancy L. Rhoden and Ian K. Steele, eds., *The Human Tradition in Colonial America*

Nancy L. Rhoden and Ian K. Steele, eds., *The Human Tradition in the American Revolution*

Michael A. Morrison, ed., *The Human Tradition in Antebellum America*

Steven E. Woodworth, ed., *The Human Tradition in the Civil War and Reconstruction*

Ballard C. Campbell, ed., *The Human Tradition in the Gilded Age and Progressive Era*

Donald W. Whisenhunt, ed., *The Human Tradition in America between the Wars, 1920–1945*

Malcolm Muir Jr., ed., *The Human Tradition in the World War II Era*

David L. Anderson, ed., *The Human Tradition in America since 1945*

David L. Anderson, ed., *The Human Tradition in the Vietnam Era*

Nina Mjagkij, ed., *Portraits of African American Life since 1865*

Kriste Lindenmeyer, ed., *Ordinary Women, Extraordinary Lives: Women in American History*

Roger Biles, ed., *The Human Tradition in Urban America*

Eric Arnesen, ed., *The Human Tradition in American Labor History*

Benson Tong and Regan A. Lutz, eds., *The Human Tradition in the American West*

Ty Cashion and Jesús F. de la Teja, eds., *The Human Tradition in Texas*

Clark Davis and David Igler, eds., *The Human Tradition in California*

James C. Klotter, ed., *The Human Tradition in the Old South*

James C. Klotter, ed., *The Human Tradition in the New South*

Susan M. Glisson, ed., *The Human Tradition in the Civil Rights Movement*

The Human Tradition in the Civil Rights Movement

Edited by Susan M. Glisson

ROWMAN & LITTLEFIELD PUBLISHERS, INC.
Lanham • Boulder • New York • Toronto • Oxford

ROWMAN & LITTLEFIELD PUBLISHERS, INC.

Published in the United States of America
by Rowman & Littlefield Publishers, Inc.
A wholly owned subsidary of The Rowman & Littlefield Publishing Group, Inc.
4501 Forbes Boulevard, Suite 200, Lanham, Maryland 20706
www.rowmanlittlefield.com

PO Box 317
Oxford
OX2 9RU, UK

British Library Cataloguing in Publication Information Available

Library of Congress Cataloging-in-Publication Data

The human tradition in the civil rights movement / edited by Susan M. Glisson.
    p. cm. — (The human tradition in America)
  ISBN-13: 978-0-7425-4408-6 (cloth : alk. paper)
  ISBN-10: 0-7425-4408-7 (cloth : alk. paper)
  ISBN-13: 978-0-7425-4409-3 (pbk. : alk. paper)
  ISBN-10: 0-7425-4409-5 (pbk. : alk. paper)
  1. African American civil rights workers—United States—Biography. 2. Civil
rights workers—United States—Biography. 3. African Americans—Civil
rights—History—19th century. 4. African Americans—Civil rights—History—
20th century. 5. Minorities—Civil rights—United States—History—20th
century. 6. Civil rights movements—United States—History—19th century. 7.
Civil rights movements—United States—History—20th century. 8. Social
change—United States—History—19th century. 9. Social change—United
States—History—20th century. 10. United States—History—(1865–)—
Biography. I. Glisson, Susan M., 1967– II. Series.

E185.96.H86 2006
323.092'273—dc22
[B]   2006015180

Printed in the United States of America

⊗™ The paper used in this publication meets the minimum requirements of
American National Standard for Information Sciences—Permanence of Paper
for Printed Library Materials, ANSI/NISO Z39.48-1992.

For June Glisson,
who taught me to value everyone

Contents

Part III: Awakenings

Part IV: Freedom Is a Constant Struggle

Part V: The Borning Movement

Introduction:
The Human Tradition
and Civil Rights

Susan M. Glisson

On March 2, 1955, fifteen-year old Claudette Colvin, an eleventh grader at Booker T. Washington High School, boarded a bus in Montgomery, Alabama. Later, a white man boarded but all the seats were full. The white driver, as was custom and law, asked Colvin, an African American, to give up her seat. She refused and was arrested, having violated Section 10 of the Montgomery City Code. Section 10 mandated the "separation of races" on bus lines. Specifically, it stated that "any employee in charge of a bus operated in the city shall have the powers of a police officer." In short, passengers had to obey any orders of the bus driver as if he or she were an officer of the law. In practice, the City Code meant that bus drivers had free rein to enforce segregation. Drivers forced black passengers to enter the front of the bus, pay their fee, then exit and reenter at the back of the bus. Whites seated themselves from front to back, while blacks had to seat themselves from back to front. If a white passenger got on the bus and all the seats were full, the bus driver would order black passengers to stand to provide a seat for the white passenger.

Most African Americans in Montgomery worked in service jobs or as laborers with little access to private transportation. More than half of black women were employed as domestic servants in white homes. Buses, therefore, provided crucial transportation for many African Americans throughout the city. The indignities of bus travel, reflective of the larger system of segregation, had long incensed black Montgomerians. Bus drivers were often none too gentle when ordering blacks to move. These and other abuses of segregation created a firm commitment in the black community to secure more fair treatment. As early as the 1880s and 1890s, agricultural workers in the surrounding area had joined the Colored Farmers Alliance to try to alleviate racial prejudice. As segregation hardened over the early twentieth century, blacks petitioned the state legislature not to disenfranchise black voters. Though they were unsuccessful, they continued to press for political rights, encouraged in 1944 by the Supreme Court decision in *Smith v. Allright*, which outlawed the South's all-white primary.

Such resistance manifested itself in protest against abusive treatment on buses as well. Whether rich or poor, from professors at the local black college to domestic servants in white homes, members of a diverse black community were united by ill treatment on buses. Spurred by the democratic promises of World War II, which mocked fighting fascism abroad without changing it at home, citizens of Montgomery began to organize against the abuses suffered by blacks on city buses. In 1949, faculty at nearby all-black Alabama State University formed the Women's Political Caucus (WPC). In the early 1950s, when WPC chair Jo Ann Robinson experienced her first abusive incident on a bus, she guided the group's focus primarily to ways to improve the transportation system. The group began planning a one-day boycott of the buses, contingent on having an appropriate incident of abuse to energize the black community.

Claudette Colvin was arrested nine months before Rosa Parks. At her hearing, the court seemed shocked that a black eleventh-grade girl could challenge white authority and queried Colvin as to the leaders who had prompted her actions. She replied with ungrammatical wisdom: "Our leaders is just we ourself." Colvin's arrest offered an opportunity to the Women's Political Caucus to put its one-day boycott of the buses into effect. Colvin was a member of the National Association for the Advancement of Colored People (NAACP) Youth Council. Initially her arrest seemed the perfect catalyst, but then local leaders noted her family's poor economic status, and there were rumors that she was pregnant. Ultimately, the group decided that Colvin was not an appropriate representative to prod the community and the nation to action. It would take the arrest of Parks, an older, well-respected secretary who had been trained in organizing, to catalyze the boycott in December 1955.

Colvin's story is representative of several themes in this volume. First, she is more than likely unknown to the general reader. Most of the personalities generally associated with civil rights movement activity were male heads of well-known organizations. Lesser known but equally important are the grassroots, local people who fought for change outside of the glare of newspaper headlines. If Martin Luther King Jr. was an architect of the civil rights movement, then the unknown participants like Colvin are the bricks and mortar of the edifice the movement built.

Second, many of the foot soldiers of the black struggle for freedom were women, and their involvement shaped the struggle in profound ways. Unlike the more charismatic, hierarchical leadership style of the well-known King, women evolved a cooperative, consensus-oriented, grassroots example of leadership that empowered the poor and marginalized to fight for themselves rather than relying on a "savior." Perhaps most associated with Ella Baker, a cofounder of King's Southern Christian Leadership Conference (SCLC) and beloved adviser to the radical Student Nonviolent Coordinating Committee (SNCC), this leadership style rejected the more authoritarian models in large organizations like the SCLC, the NAACP, and others and sought instead to empower and train organizers on the local level to seek social change in their communities.

Third, while the more recognized period of civil rights activity occurred in the 1950s and 1960s, that activism grew from a strong history of resistance to slavery and segregation. Thus, though it is important to understand what might be distinctive about the more well-known period of movement work in the mid-twentieth century, it is crucial to understand the connections between that period and earlier black efforts to seek equity. Social change can come immediately, with cataclysmic events that disrupt the status quo. But more often, it comes slowly, in the everyday, unrewarded, unglamorous organizing that occurs over decades. As SNCC member Julian Bond once said of Ella Baker's work, "She paved the way for us without us ever knowing that she did."[1] Many movement organizers have always understood the deep connections that exist between activists of decades ago and today. The young militants of SNCC borrowed strategies, avoided similar pitfalls, and inherited a shared vision of a just society in ways that reinforced the links between organizations, initiatives, and generations.

Fourth, there was very often an internal tension among participants in the movement about the best strategies for accomplishing their goals. Indeed, there could even be disagreements about what those objectives should be. Accommodation versus resistance, the participation of whites, nonviolence as a strategy versus nonviolence as a way of life, civil rights or economic parity, leadership from the middle class instead of from the poor and outcast— all of these issues shaped movement efforts in profound ways and, at times, have torn it apart. And yet, such conflicts also created a dynamic movement for social change that so transformed race relations in this country that many students today cannot conceive of a society in which blacks and whites were separated by law. But this amnesia is dangerous, for it not only erases an understanding of a racist system that still operates today, albeit in more subtle and structural forms, but it also renders the strategies for attacking such a system inaccessible.

Fifth, using the tactics and ideals crafted by the civil rights movement, other individuals and organizations sought to improve their own circumstances in the 1970s. As SNCC member and Freedom Singer Bernice Johnson Reagon has explained, "The movement was the borning struggle" for social change.[2] The accomplishments and challenges of black movement veterans inspired other movements for social change including the women's movement, the Latino struggle that resulted in *La Raza*, and activists of the American Indian Movement, as well as gay activists in the aftermath of Stonewall, the 1969 rebellion of gays against police repression in New York. And in turn, they employed lessons that had been handed down to SNCC members from earlier activists like Amzie Moore, Ella Baker, and others.

Although we might begin much earlier in the story of resistance to racism, this volume enters into the narrative of struggle roughly during the post-Reconstruction period, at a time when the notion of "whiteness" developed in response to the racial and social dislocation at the end of Reconstruction. As white Southerners no longer had the mechanism of slavery to control blacks and as Union forces retreated from the region, supremacists reinforced their previous control of the social order using first de facto or customary segregation and then codifying such traditions into law. White skin, rather than being free or slave, became the entry ticket to participation in American democracy. In 1890 the state of Mississippi passed a new state constitution, becoming the first state to do so after Reconstruction. It disenfranchised the hard-won right to vote of African Americans in the state, and other Southern states soon followed Mississippi's lead. But from the onset of this new system of racism, blacks resisted these efforts. The ongoing American racial conversation revolved around the efforts of blacks to secure the freedoms promised at the nation's founding, which blacks had been able to borrow during Reconstruction, but which were quickly repossessed. The range of white supremacy was far and wide, stretching beyond sharecropping plantations in the South to migrant fields on the West Coast to ethnic enclaves in urban centers. The treatment and exclusion of people of color has tested the limits of American democracy. And the experience of black Americans has been the bellwether of those restrictions. The volume concludes with the stories of those who were deeply influenced by the civil rights movement in their own work in the 1970s, but it could continue to the present day in antiglobalization, antiwar, and ongoing racial justice efforts. Each chapter describes the life of overlooked figures during the freedom struggle stretching from the 1880s into the 1970s. The chapters address variously the ideal of integration; the roles of violence and nonviolence in civil rights efforts; and grassroots, local, action-oriented social change.

While traditional understandings of the black struggle for freedom reflect the primary aims of political participation sought during the 1950s and 1960s, the efforts to secure freedom by blacks encompassed a much broader agenda. Social parity, economic opportunity, and educational equity joined with the dream of political power to delineate the goals of African Americans for full citizenship rights in the American democracy. Thus, activists created labor unions, sought entry into white schools, and sat in at lunch counters, in addition to attempting to register to vote. And they were aided at times by progressive whites who understood that their freedom was entangled with the freedom of others. But they also met fierce resistance from a power structure determined to keep them subservient and oppressed. Indeed, as historian Timothy Tyson has pointed out, the post-Reconstruction fervor to cement white supremacy was a response to black power and interracial cooperation of the postwar period. So, any story of the black struggle for freedom must engage these various issues in order to understand the complicated nature of the efforts. In the end, what emerges from more thorough explorations of the subject is a dynamic, organic movement that has ebbed and flowed over time but has always tried to move forward. And it is a portrait that is more accessible to us because it shares the power of ordinary people to transform their lives.

Part I explores the early black empowerment and interracial organizing characteristic of the Reconstruction and post-Reconstruction period. "Abraham Galloway: Prophet of Biracial America" chronicles the life and times of Abraham H. Galloway, the fiery young slave rebel, radical abolitionist, and Union spy who rose out of bondage to become one of the most significant and stirring black leaders in the American South during the Civil War. "Homer Plessy: Unsuccessful Challenger to Jim Crow" examines the hope for civil liberties that blacks experienced after the Civil War and the eventual erosion of their rights after Reconstruction. James K. Vardaman successfully intertwined his oppression of blacks with an effort to improve the lives of poor whites. His life reflects the backlash of white supremacists against increasing black political strength at the turn of the century and showcases the decreasing opportunities of black Americans as the veil of legal segregation descended across the region.

Part II examines the ways in which black Americans and, at times, their white allies tested and stretched the limits of segregation and violence. Ida B. Wells directly challenged the Southern legal establishment. Embittered by her treatment in court, Wells inaugurated a campaign against lynching, confronting the system that had denied her justice. A. Philip Randolph participated in and decisively influenced numerous movements for social change in twentieth-century America. In many ways, Randolph's contributions to twentieth-century black political and social movements constitute a crucial link between an earlier civil rights tradition based in black unions and the broader civil rights tradition of the 1960s. Lucy Randolph Mason was the first Southern organizer for the Congress of Industrial Organizations (CIO). Through moral suasion and an active campaign of publicity that used her access to an elite white base of power, Lucy Randolph Mason was able, for a time, to aid the cause of labor and racial justice in the South. But it would fall to a new generation to enforce the truth of Mason's prediction that whites and blacks could work together.

Part III looks at an individual who helped create the co-optable networks of activism later used to create a more cohesive movement, as well as two activists who both used and expanded those networks, infusing them with strategies of nonviolent direct action to challenge the white supremacist system. Amzie Moore was one of the key leaders of the black freedom struggle in Mississippi in the years prior to what we understand as the civil rights movement. With decades of organizing experience under his belt, it was Moore who would introduce the young activists from SNCC to an older generation of black freedom fighters in the Delta. He helped insure that the leadership of the movement in Mississippi would no longer reflect just the black middle class, but rather the full range of black experience in the state.

Students trained by James Lawson launched protests in Nashville that ended segregation at the downtown lunch counters by May 1960. It was this group who were among the core leaders of the student activists who founded SNCC. SNCC's Charles Sherrod employed nonviolence to spur the grassroots efforts aimed at overthrowing all aspects of Jim Crow in the southwest Georgia city of Albany. Despite internal tension between SNCC and King's SCLC, as well as the surprising and often effective strategy of the local police chief to respond to the nonviolence of activists with nonviolent tactics, the Albany Movement laid the foundations to undermine Jim Crow there and provided important lessons for the rest of the civil rights movement.

Part IV takes a deeper look at two women, one a student and the other a sharecropper, who employed a more collective, nonhierarchical leadership style despite a difference in economic status. Civil rights activist Diane Nash's middle-class Catholic upbringing and notions of female respectability and racial uplift influenced her decision to become involved in the civil rights movement. "Mae Bertha Carter: These Tiny Fingers" tells the story of clear-eyed determination, down-home grit, and sweet triumph of the Carter family of Sunflower County, Mississippi—African American sharecroppers who, in 1965, sent their children to desegregate the previously all-white school system. It illustrates how local people, in spite of intimidation, harassment, and threats of violence, were the ones truly responsible for the implementation of civil rights legislation. The third chapter in Part IV examines the life of Robert F. Williams, which suggests that violence and nonviolence, civil rights and Black Power, are more complicated—and more closely intertwined—than traditional accounts portray them. Williams's life disrupts much of what we associate with Black Power, suggesting that the factors that define it were already present in the American South in the 1950s, long before anyone chanted "Black Power."

Part V takes a closer look at those movements in the 1970s inspired by and reflective of the strategies employed in the black struggle for freedom. Judith Benninger Brown's first movement experiences were in the fight for black civil rights in the Black Belt South. Those lessons, not a reaction to male chauvinism or a flight from it, impelled and emboldened Brown to organize for women's freedom. As a graduate student, José Angel Gutiérrez studied the poverty and inequality of his hometown of Crystal City, Texas. He then worked with community leaders to establish a new political party that was a revolutionary political transformation, creating a new government under the control of the city's Mexican American majority. Leonard Peltier exemplifies a brand of civil rights activism defined by a relationship to an indigenous community and contextualized by the historical treatment of Native Americans in the United States. Emulating black activists of the 1960s, Peltier put his thoughts into action by participating in large-scale protests. Such high-profile activism made him a target for law enforcement seeking to quell social unrest and culminated in his arrest and conviction of the murder of two FBI agents on an Indian reservation in 1975. In spite of his continued imprisonment, Peltier still insists on working for Indian rights. Sylvia Lee Rivera was an activist for the rights and visibility of gay, lesbian, and transgender people, gender nonconformists, and homeless street youth. Through her role in the 1969 Stonewall Rebellion, she became a pivotal figure in and an icon of two movements: gay liberation and transgender rights.

Lawrence Guyot, who chaired the Mississippi Freedom Democratic Party, the parallel political institution created by movement activists in that state, once said that he was a chauvinist before the movement. He credited Ella Baker with changing him. His assertion is instructive for it reveals what the black struggle for freedom ultimately sought. The struggle was not simply about freeing blacks; instead it was an effort to free all of us. It was not just an effort to secure political power for blacks. Rather, it was a quest to achieve the freedom of all individuals, black, white, or brown, unfettered by any prejudice, oppression, fear, or hate. As contemporary measurements in education, housing, health care, and criminal justice indicate that racism and exclusion are still with us, this work is a modest attempt to share those efforts that have been successful at resisting and dismantling discrimination. Too often, we have been taught that Rosa Parks was just too tired to get up from her seat that day in Montgomery or that Martin Luther King Jr. saved America from itself. Rather, as Ella Baker asserted, "The movement made Martin rather than Martin making the movement."[3] From across a broad spectrum of experience, economic status, and region, ordinary individuals have accomplished extraordinary victories against oppression. And they did so through persistent, organized, bottom-up work. They can do so again. As Claudette Colvin reminded us long ago, our leaders are we ourselves. We are the people we have been waiting for.

NOTES

I would like to thank April Grayson for helping me find photographs for this book. A special thank you goes to D. Allan "Chip" Mitchell for being my second pair of eyes. Thanks also to Kris Gilliland and Amy Schmidt for help with indexing.

1. Julian Bond, personal interview by author, Oxford, Miss., February 7, 1998.

2. Bernice Johnson Reagon, "The Borning Struggle," in Dick Cluster, ed., *They Should Have Served That Cup of Coffee* (Cambridge, Mass.: South End Press, 1979).

3. David Garrow, *Bearing the Cross: Martin Luther King, Jr., and the Southern Christian Leadership Conference* (New York: Vintage Books, 1986).

SUGGESTED READING

D'Angelo, Raymond. *American Civil Rights Movement: Readings and Interpretations.* New York: McGraw-Hill, 2001.

Evers-Williams, Myrlie, and Mark Bauerlein, editors. *Civil Rights Chronicle: The African-American Struggle for Freedom.* Lincolnwood, Ill.: Publications International, 2003.

Fairclough, Adam. *Better Day Coming: Blacks and Equality, 1890–2000.* New York: Penguin, 2002.

Forman, James. *The Making of Black Revolutionaries.* Seattle: University of Washington Press, 1997.

Morris, Aldon D. *The Origins of the Civil Rights Movement: Black Communities Organizing for Change.* New York: The Free Press, 1984.

Sitkoff, Harvard. *The Struggle for Black Equality.* New York: Hill and Wang, 1993.

I

HOPE IS BORN

1

{ꝣ}

Abraham Galloway: Prophet of Biracial America

David S. Cecelski

"Abraham Galloway: Prophet of Biracial America" chronicles the life and times of Abraham H. Galloway, the fiery young slave rebel, radical abolitionist, and Union spy who rose out of bondage to become the most significant and stirring black leader in the American South during the Civil War. Born in slavery and apprenticed to the brickmason's trade, he sought neither fame nor fortune and lived only thirty-three years (1837–1870). And yet he became the cherished leader of the South's freedpeople, organized one of the first regiments of ex-slaves to fight in the war, led a historic delegation of recently freed slaves that met with President Lincoln, founded the first civil rights groups in American history below the Mason-Dixon Line, convened two landmark political conventions of former slaves, led a black militia that fought the Ku Klux Klan, and was one of the first black men elected to his home state's legislature. Above all, he burned with a passion against tyranny and injustice. He was a freedom fighter in what he called "a Second American Revolution."

Galloway was the revolutionary leader in the freedpeople's Civil War. Historians are far more likely to remember other black leaders of the era, mainly Northern free blacks like Frederick Douglass, Henry Highland Garnett, and John Mercer Langston. Few of those black leaders, however, had any direct involvement in the struggle against slavery within the South. None of them captured the heart and soul of the South's slaves or embodied the collective vision of freedom that had emerged out of slavery like Galloway. This chapter takes seriously Galloway's intellectual, cultural, and political life and offers a new understanding of the slaves of the South and of the Civil War itself.

In the spring of 1863, a recruiting agent for the Union army walked the streets of New Bern, North Carolina, looking for Abraham H. Galloway. The seaport was usually a town of 5,500 inhabitants, but at that moment it was overflowing with thousands of fugitive slaves who had escaped from the Confederacy. The setting was one of excess in all things: hardship, disarray, fear, heartbreak, joy. Federal troops crowded into colonial homes and antebellum manors. Downtown buildings lay in charred ruins: retreating Confederates had burned some of them, and a Union general torched the others after snipers shot at his sentries. The Confederates had fled so quickly that they left doors banging in the wind, family portraits in front yards, a piano in the middle of a street. The murmur of sawmills could be heard across the Trent River, the sound of the former slaves building a new city. The days clattered noisily by, and even the stillness of evening was broken by short bursts of ecstasy: slave sisters reunited after a lifetime apart or a slave family that had survived a journey of 150 miles. No one breathed easy. New Bern was a sliver of sanctuary for African Americans in the slave South, and the Confederate army could have recaptured the city at any time.[1]

Edward W. Kinsley, the recruiting agent, had not come to New Bern with the intention of looking for Galloway. He had arrived there as an emissary of Governor John Albion Andrew of Massachusetts, an abolitionist leader seeking to recruit an African American regiment. Kinsley had expected the former slaves to throng into the army's ranks; instead, they avoided him nearly to a man. "Something was wrong," he realized, "and it did not take [me] long to find out the trouble." All pointed him to one individual, the man whom the slave refugees considered their leader. "Among the blacks," he learned, "was a man of more than ordinary ability, a coal black negro named Abraham Galloway."[2]

In 1863 Galloway was only twenty-six years old, a prodigy who had already lived three men's lives. Born into enslavement by the Cape Fear River, Galloway had grown up in Wilmington. He had become a fugitive slave, an abolitionist leader, a Union spy. He was tall, strong, and handsome, with long wavy hair and flashing eyes. He was not, as Kinsley remembered, "coal black," but light-skinned. He consented to see Kinsley but even after several meetings refused to help recruit former slaves into the Union army. Then, for unknown reasons, Galloway changed his mind. He sent a message to Kinsley to meet him at the home of a black leader named Mary Ann Starkey. When the New England abolitionist arrived that night at midnight, somebody blindfolded him and led him into an attic room. When the blindfold came off, as Kinsley later recounted, "he could see by the dim light of the candle that the room was nearly filled with blacks, and right in front of him stood Abraham Galloway and another huge negro, both armed with revolvers."[3]

That night the convocation of liberated slaves did not mince words. If the Union intended to make the war a crusade for black freedom, then Kinsley would find no shortage of recruits in New Bern. But if the Federal army

HON. ABRAM GALLOWAY.

Abraham Galloway (Image courtesy of North Carolina Archives and History.)

planned to use black men like chattel and wage a war merely for the preservation of the Union, that was another story. Kinsley had to know that Galloway was serving the Union army—wild rumors of his exploits as a Union spy were whispered on every street corner—and must have wondered, was Galloway really willing to hurt the Union cause by withholding black troops or was this merely a negotiating tactic to improve the lot of black soldiers and their families? Galloway and his lieutenants did not let Kinsley know, and we will probably never know either. Instead, they bluntly listed their demands: equal pay, provisions for black soldiers' families, schooling for soldiers' children, and assurances that the Union would force the Confederacy to treat captured blacks as prisoners of war rather than execute them as traitors.

Kinsley later described the next few moments as the most harrowing of his life. Galloway had not brought him to that dark attic to negotiate terms, but to guarantee them. Holding a revolver to Kinsley's head, he compelled the Union recruiter to swear a personal oath that the Federal army would meet these conditions. After Kinsley did so, the former slaves released him into the night air. "The next day," he remembered later, "the word went forth, and the blacks came to the recruiting station by [the] hundreds and a brigade was soon formed."[4] The more than five thousand African Americans eventually recruited in New Bern, most of them former slaves, became the core of the 35th, 36th, and 37th Regiments, United States Colored Troops, known originally as the African Brigade.[5]

Rarely have we glimpsed what the tens of thousands of black Southerners who found asylum in Federal territory during the Civil War did with their new freedom. Instead, historians have tended to see the "freedpeople," or "contrabands" (as the Union army called blacks under Federal occupation), either as if through the eyes of so many New England missionaries, as downtrodden, helpless souls entirely reliant on white goodwill, or, just as misleadingly, as patriotic "good soldiers" blindly devoted to the Union cause and serving unquestionably under the terms and conditions that Union commanders offered them. This scene in New Bern hints at a different story: instead of docility, we see militancy; instead of unquestioning loyalty to the Union cause, we see former slaves attempting to shape the Union cause; instead of imbibing the politics of white abolitionists or Republicans, we see black Carolinians charting their own political course; instead of the contrabands looking to Northern blacks for political guidance, we glimpse a new politics emerging out of the struggle against slavery in the South.

For all of the story's broader implications about the former slaves and the Civil War, the center of its intrigue is Kinsley's portrayal of that "man of more than ordinary ability . . . named Abraham Galloway." The young black leader comes to mind particularly now, as we contemplate the various meanings of the Wilmington "race riot" a hundred years ago. Galloway spent most of his life in Wilmington, but he has been utterly forgotten there, as elsewhere. He became arguably the most important black leader in North Carolina during the Civil War and Reconstruction. Yet, except for brief entries in a few biographical dictionaries and short passages in broader scholarly works about Reconstruction, this mercurial figure has received little notice, having never been the subject of a book, a journal article, or a magazine feature.[6] The white supremacists of 1898 drew a veil of forgetfulness over the black militancy and political radicalism that Galloway embodied. They revised the history of the Civil War and Reconstruction into a fable of "Negro domination" and black sexual predation. In the history books they replaced black radicals such as Galloway with images of shiftless, deferential, and primitive blacks, so unable to recognize their own best interests that they needed white guidance at every step.[7] Galloway and the black insurgents who followed in his footsteps were purged from the Southern past, victims of the white supremacists of the post-Reconstruction generation no less than those who died in Wilmington in 1898. Galloway, son of Wilmington, personified a different path into the twentieth century, a democratic politics that was sown in slavery, grew into first light during the Civil War, and flowered in Reconstruction. Here, then, is the story of Abraham H. Galloway: slave, fugitive, abolitionist, Union spy, special agent, leader of the freedpeople, women's suffragist, state senator.

Galloway was born on February 13, 1837, in Smithville (later Southport), the seat of Brunswick County, North Carolina, twenty-five miles south of Wilmington at the mouth of the Cape Fear River.[8] His mother, Hester Hankins, was a slave born in 1820.[9] His father, John Wesley Galloway, the son of a Brunswick County planter, was white.[10] Relatively little is known about Abraham's mother: she was likely, but not certainly, owned by planter William Hankins of Town Creek, and she married Amos Galloway, one of John Wesley's slaves, in or about 1846.[11] As we will see later, she and her son remained close throughout his life. Not surprisingly, the life of Abraham's father is better documented. The Galloways included some of the wealthiest planters and merchants in Brunswick County, but John Wesley was only a small farmer, later a ship's pilot and, sometime after 1850, captain of the federal lightship off Frying Pan Shoals. He seems to have shared the aristocratic values of his wealthier cousins, but he never owned much property beyond four African Americans.[12] The circumstances of his relationship with Abraham's mother are altogether murky. We know only that Abraham later recalled that John Wesley "recognized me as his son and protected me as far as he was allowed so to do."[13]

A well-off railroad mechanic in Wilmington named Marsden Milton Hankins owned Galloway from infancy.[14] How the mulatto child came into the Hankins household is not clear; Hankins may have owned Abraham's mother, or, if she was owned by John Wesley Galloway, Abraham may have been sold for discretion's sake when John Wesley first married in 1839. Galloway later recalled that Hankins "was a man of very good disposition who always said he would sell before he would use a whip." His wife, Mary Ann, evidently was not so even-tempered; Galloway remembered her as a "very mean woman" who "would whip contrary to his orders."[15] Trained as a brickmason, young Galloway was hiring out his own time before his twentieth birthday, a common practice for slave artisans in antebellum Wilmington. Hankins, a skilled laborer himself, could not supervise a slave closely. He left Galloway to seek out brickmasonry jobs when, where, and how he pleased so long as the slave continued to bring into the Hankins household a steady $15 a month.[16]

In 1857 Galloway escaped from Wilmington. He later explained that he fled the port city because he could no longer earn the $15 a month that Hankins required of him. This may seem a rather uncompelling motivation for such a risky undertaking, especially if we take his word that Hankins was not a malicious master. But if the failure to earn money might lead to Galloway's sale in the local slave market—a fate that could have marooned him on one of the rice fields or turpentine orchards of the Lower Cape Fear—then it makes sense. No matter his gentle nature, Hankins clearly saw Galloway primarily as a financial investment—and every investor sometimes has to cut his losses. At any rate, Galloway and a friend, a slave named Richard Eden, found a schooner captain willing to conceal them among the turpentine barrels in his cargo hold.[17]

An abolitionist underground of free and slave residents of Wilmington helped fugitive slaves to escape by ship throughout the 1850s.[18] The seaport's political leaders seemed to find solace in blaming free black sailors from ports outside of the South for such antislavery activity. "They are of course," wrote the *Wilmington Aurora*'s editor, "all of them, from the very nature of their position, abolitionists."[19] Local whites seemed reluctant to acknowledge subversive elements within the local slave community. Typically, when copies of David Walker's *Appeal to the Coloured Citizens of the World*— one of the primary documents in American antislavery thought—appeared in Wilmington in 1830, the town's leaders struck out brutally at black sailors, but they apparently did not consider the fact that Walker had been born and raised a free black in Wilmington. Though Walker had traveled extensively after leaving the South, his call for armed resistance to slavery had its roots in the intellectual culture of African Americans in the Cape Fear. Sustained by strong linkages to maritime black communities across the Western Hemisphere, this intellectual culture was grounded in the egalitarian ideals of the Enlightenment, an evangelical theology that stressed the "natural rights" of all peoples before God, and a particular brand of abolitionism born of African American slavery. Slave literacy had been outlawed in North Carolina in 1830, but this political vision was preserved among a predominantly illiterate people in song, sermon, and saying, eventually, with David Walker and others, to make its way onto the page at first flush of formal learning.[20] Galloway left Wilmington, as Walker had, with a political vision far more defiantly egalitarian than that of most of the abolitionists he would meet north of the Mason-Dixon Line.

Galloway arrived in Philadelphia in June of 1857. Perhaps with the help of black sailors, he and Eden reached the Vigilance Committee of Philadelphia. They met with William Still, an African American coal merchant who was the committee's executive secretary, and they were soon forwarded to its contacts in Canada in order to evade the fugitive slave laws of the United

States. On July 20, 1857, Eden wrote one of the committee's directors that he and Galloway had arrived in Kingston, Ontario, in "good health" and that Galloway had found employment, presumably as a brickmason, at $1.75 a day.[21] Over the next four years, Galloway immersed himself in the abolitionist movement and quite likely in aiding other African Americans to flee the South. As the nearest part of Canada for most fugitive slaves who fled the South, Ontario had a large African American community with a strong stake in the abolitionist cause. The black fugitives founded relief societies, newspapers, political groups, and even secret militias that supported the "Underground Railroad" in the United States and helped black refugees get established in Canada.[22] Galloway seems to have devoted himself to the abolitionist cause in a serious way. Several newspaper reports later indicated that he left Canada and gave antislavery speeches in the United States and was especially active in the abolitionist movement in Ohio, which, if true, he did at risk of being prosecuted under the Fugitive Slave Act of 1850.[23] During these years, Galloway also built extensive ties among the abolitionist leaders of Boston, though the exact character of his relationship with the Bird Club and other Boston antislavery groups remains uncertain.

Whatever else Galloway accomplished in the abolitionist movement or the Underground Railroad, he convinced George L. Stearns, the Boston industrialist who bankrolled John Brown's military raids in Kansas and sponsored the 54th Regiment, Massachusetts Volunteers (the black regiment featured in the 1989 movie *Glory*), that he would serve the Union army well as a spy. This is the single most compelling reason for believing that Galloway was involved in covert activities in the abolitionist movement. Stearns was a serious man who recruited thousands of black soldiers from Maine to Texas, and Galloway would have made a fine Union enlistee. By the outbreak of the Civil War, however, Stearns had seen something in Galloway that suggested a far more decisive role.[24]

Galloway returned south at the beginning of the Civil War. Stearns had brought the young mulatto to the attention of a Boston acquaintance, Colonel Edward A. Wild, who evidently introduced Galloway to General Benjamin F. Butler at Fortress Monroe, Virginia. Galloway was soon recruited into the Union's secret service under Butler. Working out of Fortress Monroe, Galloway undertook special missions in the coastal portions of Virginia and North Carolina that had been captured by Federal troops during General Ambrose E. Burnside's campaign of 1861–1862.[25] We will probably never know more than a hint of what Galloway did in his capacity as an intelligence agent for the Union army. Mystery shrouds much of his life, and none more than his service under Butler.[26] He reportedly answered directly to Butler and was said to "possess the fullest confidence of the commanding General."[27] It is quite likely that Galloway returned to North Carolina even prior to the Federal occupation; a Union corporal stationed in the occupied seaport of Beaufort, North Carolina, later noted in his diary that Galloway was "in the detective service of Gen. Butler" and had scouted marine landings for Union troops, presumably during the Burnside campaign.[28] That is quite plausible. Union commanders depended heavily on local slaves to identify landing sites during the Burnside expedition. Somebody had to recruit the slave pilots or somehow elicit the necessary piloting knowledge from African American watermen. One report indicated that Galloway also investigated claims of Union sympathy among Confederate prisoners of war near Norfolk and recruited white Unionists into a military regiment.[29]

Galloway began working out of New Bern soon after its capture by Federal forces in March 1862. The colonial-era port became the headquarters of the Federal regiments in North Carolina and the Union blockading fleet. During the remainder of the war, the Union kept a precarious hold on the city, using it as a base for military raids into eastern North Carolina and for a nasty war with Confederate guerrillas. Thousands of runaway slaves poured into the city. One can only imagine the different ways that Galloway might have been, as a Northern journalist later wrote of him, "of some service to the Union army." The slaves who flocked to New Bern brought with them a wealth of information about the Confederacy that had to be culled. Guides for reconnaissance missions and raids into the state's interior had to be recruited, as did spies willing to move across Confederate lines on espionage and intelligence-gathering missions. Familiar with the terrain, Confederate defenses, and local slave communities, the former slaves were especially well situated to perform these challenging tasks. "Upwards of fifty volunteers of the best and most courageous," wrote Vincent Colyer, superintendent of Negro affairs in New Bern in 1862–1863, "were kept constantly employed on the perilous but important duty of spies, scouts, and guides." Colyer reported that the black operatives "were invaluable and almost indispensable. They frequently went from thirty to three hundred miles within the enemy's lines; visiting his principal camps and most important posts, and bringing us back important and reliable information."[30] More than likely, Galloway was the chief intelligence agent working among the fugitive slaves in North Carolina. He worked closely with the Union commanding officers in New Bern, including Brigadier General Edward A. Wild (promoted from colonel in 1863), Brigadier General John J. Peck, and Major General John C. Foster.[31]

Whatever duties Galloway carried out as a spy for the Union army, they gave him a unique vantage point to organize among the great crowds of former slaves congregating behind Federal lines. As soon as New Bern had fallen in March 1862, the city was, in Burnside's words, "overrun with fugitives from the surrounding towns and plantations."

Hundreds, then thousands, of African American men, women, and children fled from bondage in Confederate territory to freedom in New Bern. "It would be utterly impossible . . . to keep them outside of our lines," an overwrought Burnside reported to the secretary of war, "as they find their way to us through woods and swamps from every side."[32]

Situated in New Bern, Galloway built strong contacts among the fugitives there as well as among the smaller, outlying contraband camps in Beaufort, Plymouth, and Washington and on Roanoke Island. In these camps congregated the most ardent radicals, the most incorrigible troublemakers, the most militant artisans, the most defiant slave preachers—in short, the black Carolinians who had most ardently dared to defy or deceive slavery. Inevitably, these insurgents saw the nature of power in the slave South with the clarity characteristic of outlaws. They saw its inherent violence, its paternalist veneer, its pathological foundations in ideas of racial purity, sexual domination, and social hierarchy. They bore scars that they had acquired the hard way, as they negotiated plantation discipline and eluded slave patrols and the Home Guard. It was no accident that Galloway emerged as a leader among this self-selected assembly of liberated slaves. Many, including Galloway himself, moved back and forth between occupied and Confederate territory, venturing into the latter even as far as Wilmington, working as Union agents or searching for families and friends still in bondage. Out of New Bern's contraband camps, then, black men and women extended lifelines deep into Confederate territory, expanding and informing the radical political culture that was emerging in New Bern.

By the spring of 1863, Galloway had become more than a Union spy. He had become the most important political leader among the more than ten thousand former slaves who resided in the contraband camps and seaports occupied by the Federal army. The liberated slaves had erected their largest shanty towns along the outskirts of New Bern. Out of those rough-hewn villages arose a great revival of African American political culture, a ferment comparable in ways to the black freedom movement that would come a century later. Unfettered by slavery, the black multitude exulted in the free expression of worship, family life, even music. Moreover, they looked to politics both as a weapon against their outlandishly racist treatment by the Union occupying forces and as a tool to shape their destiny after the Civil War.[33] They organized schools, relief societies, self-help associations, and churches, including St. Peter's, the first African Methodist Episcopal Zion church in the South.[34] These institutions became cornerstones of black political life.

Confronted by the dangers of Confederate guerrillas and the depredations of Union soldiers, they also organized a black militia. William H. Singleton, the only black veteran who wrote a memoir of the New Bern occupation, indicated that the refugees had been drilling on their own during the early spring of 1862, well before President Lincoln permitted African Americans to serve in the army. Singleton suggests, in fact, that this militia formed the heart of the black brigades recruited in New Bern in the summer of 1863. If that is true, then on the night that Galloway negotiated the terms of black enlistment, he had a stronger hand than merely the revolver aimed at Edward

Kinsley's head; he had a fighting force of at least several hundred black soldiers anxiously waiting to join the fray.[35] The fact that hundreds of black men showed up almost instantly at a word from their leader certainly suggests a high degree of existing organization. Galloway had also clearly begun to mark an independent political course that placed his first loyalty to the former slaves, not the Union army.

This was the milieu in which Galloway grew into political prominence. No matter how much his radical politics had been shaped by his own life in slavery, in the abolitionist movement, or as a Union spy, Galloway was home. He was of this society, knew its people, knew its horrors. He could scarcely help but play a leadership role in the black political movements emerging within New Bern, and he developed a close relationship to the black women organizing support for the slave refugees. He worked especially closely with Mary Ann Starkey, at whose home Edward Kinsley met Galloway that night. Starkey had turned her home into a meeting place for a small adult "reading school" and a Bible school class. She also led a black women's relief society that solicited funds and supplies among both the former slaves and Northern abolitionists for refugee families and, later, for black soldiers.[36]

Working with black groups like Mary Ann Starkey's relief society and William Singleton's militia, Galloway seems to have discovered a new maturity. Prior to this moment, the twenty-six-year-old had lived the kind of rebel's life that required talents for subterfuge: guile, restraint, dissemblance, patience, the ability to act boldly but carefully under pressure and in solitude. These gifts served Galloway well as a fugitive, an abolitionist, and a spy. Now Galloway developed a genius for politics. He became a grassroots organizer, a coalition builder, and an inspiring orator. As a secret agent and political leader, he seemed to pop up everywhere in Federal territory—and he struck quite a figure. He was already renowned for a severe sense of honor and a fearless readiness to defend it, a trait that could only have endeared him to former slaves, for whom honor had always been a white man's prerogative. Galloway may already have gotten into the habit that he developed later of always carrying a pistol where people could see it in his belt. Yet he could not have seemed reckless or foolhardy. For all his bravado, there was a disarming quiet about Galloway; patience, tact, and wariness had helped him to survive too many dangers not to be a part of him. Still, he laughed loud and often, and he must have had a sweet side, for everywhere the young man went black Carolinians crowded around him as if he were a prophet.[37]

The recruitment of North Carolina's former slaves into the Union army began in May of 1863. In the seaport of Beaufort, thirty-five miles east of New Bern, a Confederate sympathizer named Levi Pigott groused in his diary that "the black traitors are gathering in considerable numbers" to join the army. Pigott described the "horror, or the fiery indignation that burns in [the rebels'] bosoms . . . when they think of their husbands and brothers and sons who may fall at the hands of the black savages."[38] Galloway did nothing to allay such Confederate hostility. Prior to President Lincoln's approval for former slaves to join the Union army, Galloway had made black military service the issue about which he was most outspoken. He not only recruited black soldiers when the time came, but he also articulated a political rationale for armed struggle that unnerved die-hard rebels such as Pigott. At black political rallies held during the Federal occupation, Galloway argued that the former slaves would fight harder and better than white Union soldiers. At one point, he was quoted as saying that although McClellan "failed to take Richmond with 200,000 white soldiers, Butler would soon take it *with twenty thousand negroes.*"[39]

More fervently, Galloway contended that the black regiments would compel a victorious Union to grant the former slaves both freedom and political equality—that is, the right to vote, serve on juries, and run for elected office, all issues around which no political consensus had yet been reached, even in the North. Galloway's linkage of military service and political equality reflected a growing accord among African American leaders. "Once let the black man get upon his person the brass letters U.S., let him get an eagle on his button and a musket on his shoulder and bullets in his pocket," Frederick Douglass had said, "and there is no power on earth which can deny that he has earned the right to citizenship in the United States."[40] Galloway shared Douglass's conviction. During a speech at a rally celebrating the first anniversary of the Emancipation Proclamation, Galloway told Beaufort's freed men and women, as Levi Pigott remembered it, "that their race would have not only their personal freedom, but political equality, and if this should be refused them at the ballot box[,] they would have it at the cartridge box!"[41]

With more than fifty thousand blacks fighting in the Union army by the end of 1863, Galloway shifted his priorities toward the achievement of black political equality after the Civil War.[42] He was still seen frequently among the liberated slaves in North Carolina: he moved to Beaufort and married Martha Ann Dixon, the eighteen-year-old daughter of two former slaves, on December 29, 1863.[43] He was active with pro-Union political groups and local organizations that defended the rights of black soldiers in Beaufort and New Bern. He spoke frequently at the black churches that had become the heart of political education and community organizing in the contraband camps, as well as at the mass rallies held by the freedpeople on Independence Day and the anniversary of Emancipation Day. He assisted Union officers in recruiting black soldiers in Beaufort and New Bern, and probably over a much wider area.[44] Brigadier General Wild referred to him at this point not as a Union spy but as his "confidential recruiting agent," a term that suggests that Galloway was recruiting former slaves for special missions, presumably in Confederate territory. Galloway's contacts among slaves even in the most heavily fortified cities of the Confederacy were extensive by the fall of 1863. Their extent can be measured by his success that November, in Wild's words, at "manag[ing] to get his *mother* sent out of Wilmington, N.C." Wilmington was one of the most heavily guarded cities in the Confederacy, yet Galloway somehow arranged for his slave mother to escape to New Bern. Three Union generals—Wild, Peck, and Foster—felt so beholden to Galloway that they promised their former spy and "confidential recruiting agent" that they would play a part in getting his mother from New Bern to the home of one of Galloway's contacts in Boston. "I would like to do all I can for Galloway, who has served his country well," Wild wrote Edward Kinsley on November 30, 1863.[45]

The scope of Galloway's political leadership grew as he represented the liberated slave communities of North Carolina at the national level. In May of 1864, he was part of a five-man delegation of black leaders who met with President Lincoln to urge him to endorse suffrage for all African Americans. He also began to travel extensively to Boston and New York, where he met with abolitionist leaders about the political fate of former slaves after the war.[46] In addition, Galloway was one of 144 black leaders who answered the call to "the strong men of our people" and attended the National Convention of Colored Citizens of the United States, on October 4, 1864, in Syracuse, New York. Presided over by Frederick Douglass, the convention was the most important gathering of American black leaders during the Civil War. Skeptical of the commitment to racial equality in both the Democratic and Republican parties, the convention delegates articulated a black political agenda that called for the abolition of slavery, the end of racial discrimination, and political equality.[47] They also founded the National Equal Rights League and pledged themselves to organize state chapters to advocate political equality. Though his political organizing in the freedpeople's camps must have tailed off at the end of 1864—many of his most militant lieutenants were fighting with Grant in Virginia, and a yellow fever epidemic had swept New Bern and Beaufort—Galloway had organized a state chapter and five local chapters of the Equal Rights League in North Carolina by January 1865.[48]

New Bern and Beaufort remained the central points for black political organizing in North Carolina immediately after the Civil War. New Bern and its adjacent freedpeople's camp, James City, were especially important. The Federal forces had compelled the state's other contraband camps to disband and return the lands on which they were situated to their antebellum owners, but the former slaves in James City had refused to surrender their new homes. They and other black residents of the Federal occupation area had developed political, educational, and religious institutions that gave them a long head start in confronting postwar life. For all its hardships (or perhaps because of its hardships), the Federal occupation had been a very effective "rehearsal for Reconstruction," to borrow the title of Willie Lee Rose's land-mark study of black freedpeople in South Carolina.[49] While former slaves elsewhere struggled to disentangle themselves from the web of slavery, fit-fully trying out new rights and testing their new limits for the first time, the freedpeople whom Galloway had helped to politicize during the Federal oc-cupation of the North Carolina coast moved steadfastly to make an impact on Reconstruction politics. Galloway remained in the thick of this political ferment, exhibiting, as one journalist said, an "exceedingly radical and Ja-cobinical spirit" that resonated deeply among African Americans.[50] When, in 1865, more than two thousand former slaves celebrated the Fourth of July with a Beaufort parade organized by the Salmon P. Chase Equal Rights League, Galloway delivered the keynote address, calling for "all equal rights before the law, and nothing more."[51]

Not surprisingly, a few weeks later, on August 28, Galloway emerged, as a correspondent for the *New York Times* put it, as the "leading spirit" of a mass meeting of New Bern's black citizens, organized to shape a political agenda for the postwar era. It was the first such gathering of former slaves held in the South. In a long keynote address, Galloway called for voting rights and public schooling. "We want to be an educated people and an in-telligent people," he told the crowd. In a double-edged declaration that echoed his words of two years before, he also declared that "if the negro knows how to use the cartridge box, he knows how to use the ballot box."[52]

Beyond endorsing black suffrage, the mass meeting in New Bern ad-dressed the white backlash against the freedpeople and the violent, unde-mocratic nature of the postwar society that had emerged during Presidential Reconstruction. The black New Bernians, led by Galloway, resolved "that the many atrocities committed upon our people in almost every section of our country . . . clearly demonstrate the immense prejudice and hatred on the part of our former owners toward us." They protested "the enforcement of the old code of slave laws that prohibits us from the privileges of schools, that deny us the right to control our families, that reject our testimony in courts of justice, that after keeping us at work without pay till their crops are laid by and then driving us off, [refuse] longer to give us food and shelter." In great detail, the delegates described white terrorism—"whipping, thumb-screwing and not infrequently murdering us in cold blood"—against blacks who challenged the antebellum racial code. "In our judgement," they con-cluded, with something more than a measure of understatement, North Car-olina "comes far short of being a republican form of government and needs to be remodeled."[53]

The New Bern assembly appointed Galloway and two other men, John Randolph and George W. Price, to head the call for a statewide freedpeople's convention in Raleigh on September 29. The organizers appealed to the state's black citizens soon thereafter with newspaper announcements under the banner "Freedmen of North Carolina, Arouse!" The three New Bern leaders instructed black Carolinians to assemble in every township to "speak their views" and to organize district meetings where delegates would be nominated to the freedpeople's convention in Raleigh.[54] On the same day that Governor William Holden called to order a state constitutional convention dominated by the antebellum aristocracy, Galloway called to order 117 black delegates representing forty-two counties at an African Methodist Episcopal church in Raleigh. Few dressed so finely as their white counterparts across town, some had passed the collection plate to obtain a railroad ticket, and many had slipped out of their hometowns quietly in order to avoid violence at the hands of local white conservatives.[55] While the white conservatives drafted the so-called Black Codes to bar African Americans from political life, the black delegates articulated a profoundly more democratic vision of Southern society. They demanded the full rights of citizenship, public schools, equal protection under the law, regulation of working hours, and the abolition of all laws "which make unjust discriminations on account of race or color."[56]

The black delegates represented a wide range of political views, from strident nationalists to fearful accommodationists, but the more radical delegates from New Bern, Beaufort, and Roanoke Island dominated the convention in large part because they had refined their political ideology and gained practical experience in political argument and strategy during the years of Federal occupation. Several black leaders from the Federal occupation shone with special brilliance in Raleigh. The Reverend James W. Hood, an AME Zion leader in New Bern, was elected chairman of the convocation, for instance. His moderate willingness to appeal to white goodwill and his cautious advice for the freedpeople to move slowly carried a great deal of influence. But none of the delegates made a deeper impression on the black participants or white observers than Galloway. "Perhaps the most remarkable person among the delegates," a Northern journalist, John Richard Dennett, observed, was "a light-yellow man whose features seemed to indicate that there was a cross of Indian blood in his veins." In Dennett's description of Galloway one can imagine why white conservatives found the former slave so unsettling and why he held so powerful an appeal for so many freedpeople. The ex-slaves had been born into a Southern society that upheld white supremacy and tried to deny the existence of interracial sex, that associated blackness with ugliness, that compelled black men to carry themselves with great deference, and that punished any black who dared to challenge a white man's superior intelligence. Politically and personally, Galloway would have none of it. "His hair was long and black and very curly," Dennett wrote.

> He appeared to be vain of its beauty as he tossed it carelessly off his forehead, or suffered it to fall heavily and half conceal his eyes. These were twinkly and slippery, and nearly always half shut, for he laughed much, and then they partly

closed of themselves, and at other times he had a way of watching from under his dropped lids. He was a wellshaped man, but it was hardly to be discovered as he lolled in his seat, or from the insufferably lazy manner of his walking. When he spoke, however, he stood erect, using forcible and graceful gestures. His voice was powerful, and, though an illiterate man, his speaking was effective.

We can hear Dennett trying to fit Galloway into an antebellum racial stereotype—"the insufferably lazy manner of his walking," his "slippery" eyes—but neither Galloway's force of will nor Dennett's grudging admiration allows him to do it. "His power of sarcasm and brutal invective," Dennett conceded, "and the personal influence given him by his fearlessness and audacity, always secured him a hearing."[57] Galloway's defiance of white authority alarmed more cautious black delegates, and the freedpeople's convention as a whole struck a more conciliatory posture when they presented their demands to the white convention. But few would forget Galloway or fail to tell stories about him when they returned to homes besieged by white terror. He may have frightened them, for they knew how white conservatives might react to such an insurgent, but he also gave voice to the vision of freedom born in bondage.

Galloway left New Bern for Wilmington late in 1866 or early in 1867. He may have moved to rejoin his mother—she probably returned to Wilmington soon after the Civil War (she was definitely there by 1870)—or he may have returned home because he recognized that Wilmington would again become the capital of African American political life in North Carolina.[58] Wilmington was the state's largest city and had a majority-black population; its large number of black artisans and maritime laborers formed the core of a politically militant class that would have attracted Galloway. By January 3, 1866, the North Carolina office of the Equal Rights League had also conspicuously opened in downtown Wilmington. Galloway's relocation to Wilmington and the opening of the Equal Rights League's office may not have been unrelated.[59]

Galloway tried to give his life a semblance of normalcy in Wilmington. He and his wife went about raising their two sons and attended St. Paul's Episcopal Church, while he joined the Masons. Reconstruction was not an ordinary time, however, and a quiet life was not his destiny. The Wilmington that Galloway returned to was in the throes of a violent conflict over the shape of postwar society. Nothing was guaranteed—certainly not the freedpeople's right to vote, to own land, to receive schooling, to earn decent wages, to enjoy the normal privileges of civil society, and to have equal protection under the law. These issues were all being worked out on the streets of towns like Wilmington just as surely as in the halls of the U.S. Congress. Every encounter between a black person and a white person was fraught with danger. "They perceive insolence in a tone, a glance, a gesture, or failure to yield enough by two or three inches in meeting on the sidewalk," a visitor noted of Wilmington's white citizens.[60] Cape Fear conservatives sought to reestablish their antebellum power at the same time that blacks sought to assert their new rights of freedom and citizenship. The talents for covert organizing and self-defense that Galloway had honed as a runaway slave, a fugitive abolitionist, and a Union spy would be put to good use in Reconstruction Wilmington.

By the beginning of 1866, conservatives had regained power in Wilmington, in large part due to Union military commanders who sympathized more with the Cape Fear aristocrats than with former slaves. "The true soldiers, whether they wore the gray or the blue are now united in their opposition . . . to negro government and negro equality," gloated a local newspaper, adding, "Blood is thicker than water."[61] Nightriders and white militias brutally beat, killed, and otherwise terrorized African Americans who dared to act like free citizens, and they strove to reimpose control over the freedpeople's lives—including control over whom they worked for, what wages they commanded, where they lived, and how they raised their children. The presence of black troops among the Federal occupying force in Wilmington had momentarily restrained conservative violence, but Union commanders showed a lack of resolve in supporting the black troops, even refusing to intervene when Confederate militia groups targeted them. Increasingly, the black troops realized that they were on their own in postwar Wilmington. They mutinied against their white officers in September 1865, and in February 1866 they laid siege to the city jail in order to halt the public whipping of black prisoners convicted in a trial in which the conservative judge had not allowed black testimony. After that, Union commanders withdrew all black troops from the Lower Cape Fear and replaced them with white soldiers.[62] White terror reigned throughout the Cape Fear. "The fact is," a freedman reported, "it's the first notion with a great many of these people, [that] if a Negro says anything or does anything that they don't like, [they] take a gun and put a bullet into him."[63] Not far from Wilmington, in Duplin County, a police captain named J. N. Stallings gave orders to shoot without trial blacks who had been accused of minor theft.[64]

With passage of the Reconstruction Acts by the Radical Congress of 1867, Wilmington blacks gained a crucial new political opportunity. The Reconstruction Acts restored federal military authority in the South and required states in the former Confederacy to pass a constitution that guaranteed universal male suffrage before they could be readmitted to the Union. The acts also opened the polls to black voters while banning from political life any antebellum officeholder who had taken an oath to uphold the U.S. Constitution but sided with the Confederacy. Galloway was soon looking toward the constitutional convention that would occur in Raleigh early in 1868. On September 4, 1867, he addressed a mass meeting of the state's Republican Party at Tucker Hall in Raleigh, delivering a conciliatory address aimed at building broad, biracial support for the Republicans. He exhorted his audience to "go everywhere there is a black man or a poor white man and tell him the true condition of the Republican Party."[65] Later that month, "after loud calls for 'Galloway,'" he addressed a torchlit procession of black citizens from the top of Wilmington's market house. "My people stand here tonight fettered, bound hand [and] foot by a Constitution that recognizes them as chattel," Galloway exclaimed.[66] That fall he was elected one of thirteen delegates from seven Cape Fear counties to serve at the constitutional convention.

Galloway was, in the words of historian W. McKee Evans, one of "a small group of active delegates who largely dominated the life of the convention."[67] During the constitutional convention, which ran from January to March of 1868, Galloway served on the judiciary committee, and alongside white reformer Albion Tourgee on the committee for local government. As one of only 13 blacks among the 120 persons elected to the constitutional convention, however, he felt a special responsibility to represent the political concerns of the state's African American population. At one point, on February 20, Galloway explained his support for the popular election of the judiciary by saying, in a reporter's paraphrase, that "the Judiciary in New Hanover was a bastard, born in sin and secession." "In their eyes, it was a crime to be a black or a loyal man," he continued, and he denounced conservative judges who had allegedly imprisoned blacks solely to keep them from voting.[68] At another point, Galloway vehemently opposed public support of a railroad that, in his words, "did not employ a single colored man," and he also refused to support a YMCA request to use the convention hall unless "no distinction be made between the races."[69]

Galloway routinely endured arguments about black inferiority from conservative delegates and their newspaper editors, as he would later in the state senate. Every day that he spent in Raleigh, he heard comments such as the *Sentinel*'s, that true North Carolinians would blush "that a set of apes and hybrids should be holding a brutal carnival in her halls of legislation."[70] Much to their dismay, conservative delegates discovered that such remarks inspired Galloway's most cutting rhetoric. Following one harangue on the unfitness of blacks for suffrage, Galloway responded by saying "that the best blood in Brunswick County flowed in [my] veins," a reference to his own mixed-race heritage, "and if [I] could do it, in justice to the African race, [I] would lance [my]self and let it out."[71] Despite the rancor, conservatives were a small minority at the constitutional convention. On March 16, 1868, the delegates signed a new state constitution that introduced universal male suffrage, removed all religious and property qualifications for officeholding, endorsed the popular election of county officials, increased public school support, and made the state's penal code more humane.[72]

When he returned to Wilmington, Galloway discovered that the conservatives had launched a vicious campaign to intimidate black voters from ratifying the new constitution or electing Radical leaders in the upcoming April election. Galloway himself was running for the state senate, in the first election in which blacks were eligible to hold state office. Under the leadership of Colonel Roger Moore, one of Cape Fear's most celebrated aristocrats, the Ku Klux Klan attempted to frighten blacks away from the polls. Klan terrorism prevailed in other parts of North Carolina but collided with a stubborn militancy among African Americans in Wilmington. Black men patrolled the city's streets, firing their guns in the air and wielding fence rails to intimidate Klansmen. Shots and scuffles shattered the evening quiet on the downtown streets repeatedly on the nights between April 18 and 21 in 1868, and while exactly what happened in the darkness is unknown, after that the Ku Klux Klan was never a force in Wilmington during Reconstruction.[73] Even without documentary proof, one feels confidant that Galloway was not sitting quietly at home with his family. In the spring 1868 election the Republicans carried two-thirds of the electorate in New Hanover County, and voters chose Galloway to represent New Hanover and Brunswick counties in the state senate. That fall, he was also voted the first black elector to a presidential convention in North Carolina history.[74]

Galloway realized that armed self-defense was crucial to political survival in Wilmington. Conservative leaders held him in contempt, Democratic editors parodied him mercilessly, and the threat of assassination followed his every step. Wherever he went in the port city, Galloway conspicuously wore a pistol in his belt, a noteworthy symbol of defiance only two years after Wilmington conservatives had organized house searches to disarm the black population. The rise of the Republican Party helped to back up Galloway's lone firearm. Later in 1868, a local militia, one of several organized by Wilmington blacks to defend themselves against white terrorists, elected Galloway their commander. Led most commonly by Union veterans, the black militias—like their ubiquitous white counterparts—supposedly existed to fight off foreign invasion or to quell insurrections, but they acted during Reconstruction as a military wing of the Republican Party.[75] Nobody understood better than former slaves and Union veterans that a constitution was only as strong as the military power available to defend it. The Klan would rage out of control in the Carolina Piedmont from 1868 to 1870 but remained prudently quiet in Wilmington.[76]

Galloway was one of three black senators, joined by seventeen black representatives, in the North Carolina General Assembly of 1868. He was only thirty-one years old, poor, and still could not read or write.[77] He was, however, an extraordinary orator and an influential legislator. He was an intelligent, ferocious debater, the kind of man whose biting sense of humor and sharp eye for hypocrisy inspired most of the senate conservatives to steer away from a direct argument with him. Few of his fellow senators had ever been compelled to confront a black man as an equal, much less a black man as fearless and battle-tested as Galloway. The *Wilmington Daily Journal*, a

Democratic newspaper that was apparently still squeamish about Galloway's mixed-race parentage, once referred to him as "the pugilistic 'Indian Senator.'"[78] On one occasion, after a white senator from Craven County had insulted him in the midst of a floor debate over the racial makeup of New Bern's city council, Galloway declared "that he would hold the Senator from Craven responsible for his language, outside of this Hall; and . . . that, if hereafter, the Senator from Craven insulted him, he would prove to him the blood of a true Southron."[79] That was by no means the only incident in which Galloway reminded conservative Democrats that he was at least as aristocratic by birth as them. He not only claimed to be "a true Southron," but he also brazenly touted his parentage by a black woman and a white man.[80] No senate floor debate could examine the "color line" or anti-black laws without Galloway taunting his Democratic colleagues for their hypocrisy in language that reminded them that they were ultimately talking about family. Repeatedly, when a conservative called black men sexual predators posing threats to "white womanhood," Galloway reminded the senators how commonly white men pursued black women—and, knowing Galloway, he was probably well enough acquainted with the conservative Democrats' private lives to make more than a few of them nervous with a wink or a whisper. No wonder Galloway attracted venomous editorials in Democratic newspapers. The *Wilmington Journal* referred to Galloway's flaunting of his "bastardy" as "disgusting vulgarity [that is] a disgrace to any civilized community." Another time, the *Daily Journal*'s editors could barely bring themselves to acknowledge Galloway's having mentioned his parentage and interracial sex, referring obliquely to "some indelicate remarks [by Galloway] in regard to . . . white men mingling with negroes which we omit for the sake of decency."[81]

The codifying of a new color line occupied the senate repeatedly during Galloway's first term. This was true even with respect to the conduct of the General Assembly itself. On July 8, 1868, as a typical example, Galloway successfully amended a proposal to segregate the senate galleries by race to allow for a middle section that could be occupied voluntarily by blacks and whites.[82] Such a racial "middle ground" would become unthinkable after the Wilmington massacre of 1898, but for a generation black activists such as Galloway drew a more fluid boundary between black and white North Carolinians. It required constant diligence, however, as can be seen from a floor debate over racial segregation in public schools on February 26, 1869. When a Senator Love introduced an amendment requiring that no black teacher be employed in a school that had white students, a Senator Hayes, with Galloway's support, moved to amend Love's amendment to say, "or employ white teachers to serve in any school wherein colored children are to be instructed." This second amendment unnerved conservatives, who feared the political implications of black control over black schooling. To make the point stronger, Galloway moved next to amend Love and Hayes's amendment, facetiously adding a provision "that no white Democrat should teach any colored girl." Ruled out of order, Galloway had won the day if not the war. The full senate rejected Love's amendment and later created a state board of education and the first statewide system of public schooling. Yet not even white Republicans supported the call by Galloway and his fellow black legislators for racially integrated public schools or for equal funding of black schools.[83]

Much of Galloway's brief senate career addressed the most fundamental rights of the freed men and women. He voted for the Fourteenth and Fifteenth Amendments to the U.S. Constitution, introduced a successful bill to help former slaves hold onto land and homes given them while in bondage, and supported several measures to curtail the Ku Klux Klan, including a bill to create a state militia to combat white terrorism. Galloway strongly supported Governor Holden's ill-fated attempts to crack down on the Ku Klux Klan in the Piedmont, where by mid-1870 at least 260 KKK terrorist acts had been documented. He also pushed to guarantee that blacks serve on juries, a right granted by the 1868 constitution, but one that Galloway contended was often ignored by county commissioners.[84]

More than any other elected leader in North Carolina, Galloway also fought for women's rights. The rights of women had become an important political issue in the Reconstruction South, with Radicals and suffragists briefly finding common cause in an advocacy of universal suffrage. Black Southerners supported women's suffrage far more strongly than whites, perhaps a sign of the relatively higher status that black women had held in slave families and of a more collective sensibility toward voting among the ex-slaves.[85] Twice Galloway introduced bills to amend the state's constitution to allow women's suffrage, once in 1868 and again in 1869. Outraged by an 1868 state supreme court ruling that men had a right to beat their wives, he sought unsuccessfully to force the senate judiciary committee to report a bill against domestic violence. He also supported a bill that gave women a greater right to sign deeds, and another to protect married women from willful abandonment or neglect by their husbands.[86] Women's suffrage and many of the other pioneering women's rights measures advocated by Galloway would not become law in North Carolina for half a century.

With respect to his support for women's suffrage, as for most issues for which he fought, we should resist the temptation to see Galloway as ahead of his time. The fiery young activist had emerged out of a politically vibrant slave culture deeply committed to egalitarian democracy and communitarian values in the Cape Fear. His years as a fugitive slave, Northern abolitionist, and Union spy had strengthened his commitment to the African American men and women among whom he had grown up. He had also been deeply influenced by his experience in the freedpeople's camps of North Carolina. Galloway embodied the black radicalism that emerged in the Cape Fear during Reconstruction, but he did not invent it; this tradition grew from a collective experience. To his credit, he found within himself the strength of spirit and the raw courage to carry that collective vision of racial justice and political equality out into a world that was not ready for it.

Galloway died unexpectedly of fever and jaundice on September 1, 1870, at his mother's home in Wilmington.[87] He was only thirty-three years old. He had just been reelected to the state senate, still held together a fragile biracial coalition in the local Republican Party, and had recently survived an assassination attempt.[88] He died on the cusp of a conservative resurgence that would prevail across North Carolina between 1870 and 1877. Racial violence, official corruption, and the Republican Party's own internal divisions paved the way for the Democratic triumph. Compared to the rest of North Carolina, however, Wilmington remained a stronghold of African American political power and working-class militancy. W. McKee Evans has argued, in fact, that the unique ability of Wilmington Republicans to maintain significant numbers of black policemen and militia units preserved the relative peace of Cape Fear society from 1868 to 1877. At one point, in 1875, the *Wilmington Journal* even alleged that "there are now nearly, or quite as many negro [militia] companies in this city, as there are white companies throughout the limits of North Carolina."[89] This was an exaggeration, but it does suggest that Wilmington blacks continued to embrace the political militancy personified by Galloway long after his death.

Though he died a pauper, an estimated 6,000 mourners gathered at Galloway's funeral on September 3, 1870. They came from every Wilmington neighborhood and from the countryside for many miles around. The funeral procession stretched half a mile through a downtown Wilmington draped with American flags at half-mast. The Masons in their finery, the black firemen's brigades, the political and fraternal societies, a hundred carriages, and throngs of people on horseback and on foot marched down Market Street to St. Paul's Episcopal Church. The multitude could not fit into the church and crowded the streets nearby. One newspaper called it the largest funeral in the state's history.[90] As the vast mass of black men, women, and children accompanied Galloway's coffin to the cemetery, they could not possibly have imagined that his life would so quickly seem like a half-forgotten dream. Indeed, Galloway's story is a familiar saga, and one that cuts across the ages. It is the oft-told story of the rebel hero who lives a life so deeply unreconciled to tyranny that it inspires even the most downtrodden and despised to suspect, at least for a brief instant, that freedom and justice may not be just a dream. That we have forgotten him says as much about our day as his.

NOTES

I would like to express my deepest gratitude to the following individuals for their help in researching and writing this essay: Tim Tyson, Paige Raibmon, George Stevenson,

Richard Reid, Margaret Rogers, Beverly Tetterton, John David Smith, John Haley, Glenda Gilmore, Peter Wood, Laura Edwards, Kelly Navies, Stephen Kantrowitz, Jeffrey Crow, Rev. Vernon Tyson, William Harris, Laura Hanson, and Raymond Gavins.

1. The broad picture that I have drawn of occupied New Bern and the specific incidents that I have mentioned are derived from a variety of primary and secondary sources. See John Barrett, *The Civil War in North Carolina* (Chapel Hill: University of North Carolina Press, 1963), 93–113; Joe A. Mobley, *James City: A Black Community in North Carolina, 1863–1900* (Raleigh: North Carolina Department of Cultural Resources, Division of Archives and History, 1981), 1–25; and David Cecelski, "A Thousand Aspirations," *Southern Exposure* 18, no. 1 (Spring 1990): 22–25. Among the most interesting of the many published reminiscences and diaries written by Union soldiers in New Bern, see W. P. Derby, *Bearing Arms in the Twenty-seventh Massachusetts Regiment of Volunteer Infantry during the Civil War, 1861–1865* (Boston: Wright & Potter, 1883), esp. 94–95; James A. Emmerton, *A Record of the Twenty-third Regiment Mass. Vol. Infantry in the War of the Rebellion, 1861–1865 . . .* (Boston: William Ware & Co., 1886); "Corporal" [Z. T. Haines], *Letters from the Forty-fourth Regiment M.V.M.: A Record of the Experience of a Nine Months Regiment in the Department of North Carolina in 1862–3* (Boston: Herald Job Office, 1863); Vincent Colyer, *Report of the Services Rendered by the Freed People to the United States Army, in North Carolina, in the Spring of 1862, After the Battle of New Bern* (New York: Vincent Colyer, 1864); J. Waldo Denny, *Wearing the Blue in the 25th Mass. Volunteer Infantry* (Worcester, Mass.: Putnam & Davis, 1879); Thomas Kirwan, *Soldiering in North Carolina* (Boston: n.p., 1864); John J. Wyeth, *Leaves from a Diary, Written While Serving in Co. #44 Mass. From September, 1862, to June, 1863* (Boston: L. F. Lawrence & Co., 1878); J. Madison Drake, *The History of the Ninth New Jersey Veteran Vols.* (Elizabeth, N.J.: Journal Printing House, 1889); Herbert E. Valentine, *Story of Co. F, 23d Massachusetts Volunteers in the War for the Union, 1861–1865* (Boston: W. B. Clarke & Co., 1896); D. L. Day, *My Diary of Rambles with the 25 Mass. Volunteer Infantry, with Burnside's Coast Division: 18th Army Corp and Army of the James* (Milford, Mass.: King and Billings, 1884); and Albert W. Mann, *History of the Forty-fifth Regiment Massachusetts Volunteer Militia* (Jamaica Plain, Mass.: 1908).

2. Mann, *History of the Forty-fifth Regiment*, 446–49.

3. Mann, *History of the Forty-fifth Regiment*, 446–49.

4. Mann, *History of the Forty-fifth Regiment*, 301–2, 446–49. Kinsley later related this story to a reunion of the 45th Regiment, Massachusetts Volunteer Infantry, which had been stationed in New Bern in 1863. The essential parts of Kinsley's story—including his role in the recruitment of African American soldiers in New Bern, his acquaintance with Galloway and Starkey, Galloway's involvement in Union recruitment despite his devotion to independent black organizing, and Starkey and Galloway's having worked together—are confirmed in a series of letters among Kinsley, Brigadier General Edward A. Wild, and Mary Ann Starkey in the Edward W. Kinsley Papers, 1862–1889, Special Collections Library, Duke University, Durham, N.C. (hereafter, DU).

5. For an excellent overview of the recruitment of the African Brigade in New Bern, and for references to more general works on the recruitment of black soldiers into the Union army, see Richard Reid, "Raising the African Brigade: Early Black Recruitment in Civil War North Carolina," *North Carolina Historical Review* 70, no. 3 (July 1993): 266–97.

6. The few published works that discuss Galloway refer mainly to his political life during Reconstruction. See W. McKee Evans, *Ballots and Fence Rails: Reconstruction on the Lower Cape Fear* (Chapel Hill: University of North Carolina Press, 1966), 87–91; Leonard Bernstein, "The Participation of Negro Delegates in the Constitutional Convention of 1868 in North Carolina," *Journal of Negro History* 34, no. 4 (October 1949): 391–409; Elizabeth Balanoff, "Negro Legislators in the North Carolina General Assembly, July, 1868–February, 1872," *North Carolina Historical Review* 49, no. 1 (January 1972): 23–24, 27; William S. Powell, ed., *Dictionary of North Carolina Biography* (Chapel Hill: University of North Carolina Press, 1979–96), 2:271–72; 67; and Eric Foner, *Freedom's Lawmakers: A Directory of Black Officeholders during Reconstruction* (New York: Oxford University Press, 1993), 81–82.

7. For background on this literature of the "Age of Reaction" in North Carolina, see David S. Cecelski, "Oldest Living Confederate Chaplain Tells All? Or, James B. Avirett and the Rise and Fall of the Rich Lands," *Southern Cultures* 3, no. 4 (Winter 1997/98): 5–24.

8. *New National Era*, September 4, 1870.

9. Martha A. Little deposition, September 22, 1927, Celie Galloway Pension Application File (1927), U.S. Department of the Interior: Bureau of Pensions, Veterans Administration Hospital, Winston-Salem, N.C. (hereafter, VA); October 15, 1866, entry, New Hanover County: Record of Cohabitation, 1866–1868, North Carolina State Archives, Raleigh (hereafter, NCSA); Ninth Federal Census: New Hanover County, North Carolina, Population Schedule, 1870, National Archives, Washington, D.C. (hereafter, NA). In 1927 Celie Galloway, the widow of another Abraham (or Abram) Galloway, also of Brunswick County, applied for veterans benefits based on her husband's military service in the Union army. To establish that her husband was not the better-known Abraham H. Galloway, the subject of this essay, her attorney visited Beaufort, North Carolina, to take depositions from the surviving family of Abraham H. Galloway in order to ascertain details about his personal appearance, military career, and death that would distinguish the two men and justify the widow's claims for pension benefits. The attorney interviewed Abraham H. Galloway's widow, Martha Ann Little, who still lived in her native Beaufort; she had remarried in 1887.

10. William Still, *The Underground Railroad: A Record of Facts, Authentic Narratives, Letters, etc., Narrating the Hardships, Hair-Breadth Escapes, and Death Struggles of the Slaves in their Efforts for Freedom* (Philadelphia: Porter & Coates, 1872), 150–52; Petition of Lewis A. Galloway for Division of Negroes (March 1837), Lewis A. Galloway Estate Record, Brunswick County Estate Records, NCSA; Lewis Galloway Will (1826), Brunswick County Wills, 1765–1912, NCSA.

11. William Hankins is the only member of the Hankins family in Brunswick County or New Hanover County who owned slaves in 1850. In that year, he owned twenty-four slaves, including two female slaves of Hester's age. The 1850 census does not list slaves by name, only by age and gender. Seventh Federal Census: Brunswick County, North Carolina, Population and Slave Schedules, 1850, and New Hanover County, Population and Slave Schedules, 1850, NA. Amos Galloway belonged to Lewis Galloway at the time of his death in 1826 and was apportioned to his son John Wesley legally by 1837 and in practice some time before that date. Amos and Hester Hankins considered themselves married as of April 1846, though it is doubtful that they shared a household at that time. They were living together in Wilmington as of the 1870 federal census. See Petition of Lewis A. Galloway for Division of

Negroes (March 1837), Lewis Galloway Estate Record, Brunswick County Estate Records, NCSA; October 15, 1866, entry, New Hanover County Record of Cohabitation, 1866–1868, NCSA; Ninth Federal Census: New Hanover County, North Carolina, Population Schedule, 1870, NA.

12. Sixth, Seventh, and Eighth Federal Censuses: Brunswick County, North Carolina, Population and Slave Schedules for 1840, 1850, and 1860, NA; Seventh and Eighth Federal Censuses: New Hanover County, North Carolina, Population and Slave Schedules for 1850 and 1860, NA; John W. Galloway (1864), Brunswick County Estate Records, NCSA; John W. Galloway died at the age of fifty-three of yellow fever, evidently while serving in the Confederate coast guard in Bermuda on September 27, 1864. See *Wilmington Daily Journal*, October 15, 1864. Cited in Helen Moore Sammons, *Marriage and Death Notices from Wilmington, North Carolina Newspapers, 1860–1865* (Wilmington, N.C.: North Carolina Room, New Hanover County Public Library, 1987), 76.

13. Quoted in Still, *Underground Railroad*, 150–52.

14. William Still indicates that a Milton Hawkins owned Galloway, but the deposition of Galloway's wife and the listings of a locomotive mechanic named Milton Hankins in the 1860 and 1870 federal censuses confirm his owner as Milton Hankins. The mistake was presumably a typographical error. See Martha A. Little deposition, Celie Galloway pension file, VA; Still, *Underground Railroad*, 150–52; Eighth and Ninth Federal Censuses: New Hanover County, North Carolina, Population Schedules for 1860 and 1870.

15. Still, *Underground Railroad*, 150–52; Fugitive Slave Ledger, William Still Papers, Historical Society of Philadelphia, Philadelphia, Pa.; *Wilmington Daily Journal*, July 20, 1869.

16. Still, *Underground Railroad*, 150–52. For background on slave life in antebellum Wilmington, see esp. Peter P. Hinks, *To Awaken My Afflicted Brethren: David Walker and the Problem of Antebellum Slave Resistance* (University Park: Pennsylvania State University Press, 1997), 1–21; David S. Cecelski, "The Shores of Freedom: The Maritime Underground Railroad in North Carolina, 1800–1861," *North Carolina Historical Review* 71, no. 2 (April 1994): 174–206; Alan D. Watson, *Wilmington: Port of North Carolina* (Columbia: University of South Carolina Press, 1992), 46–52; and James Howard Brewer, "Legislation Designed to Control Slavery in Wilmington and Fayetteville," *North Carolina Historical Review* 30, no. 2 (April 1953): 155–66. There are also two indispensable autobiographies written by former slaves who grew up in Wilmington. See Rev. William H. Robinson, *From Log Cabin to the Pulpit; or, Fifteen Years in Slavery*, 3rd ed. (Eau Claire, Wis.: James H. Tifft, 1913); and Thomas H. Jones, *The Experience of Thomas H. Jones, Who Was a Slave for Forty-Three Years* (Boston: Bazin & Chandler, 1862).

17. Still, *Underground Railroad*, 150–52.

18. For a detailed examination of slave runaways and maritime culture in antebellum Wilmington, see Cecelski, "The Shores of Freedom," 174–206.

19. Guion Griffis Johnson, *Ante-Bellum North Carolina: A Social History* (Chapel Hill: University of North Carolina Press, 1937), 577–78.

20. Hinks, *To Awaken My Afflicted Brethren*, 1–21, 173–236; Julius S. Scott, "The Common Wind: Currents of Afro-American Communication in the Era of the Haitian Revolution" (PhD diss., Duke University, 1986); W. Jeffrey Bolster, *Black Jacks: African*

American Seamen in the Age of Sail (Cambridge, Mass.: Harvard University Press, 1997), esp. 190–214; David Walker, *Appeal to the Coloured Citizens of the World, But in Particular, and Very Expressly, to Those of the United States of America*, rev. ed. with intro. by Sean Wilentz (New York: Hill & Wang, 1995).

21. Still, *Underground Railroad*, 151–52.

22. David G. Hill, *The Freedom-Seekers: Blacks in Early Canada* (Agincourt: Book Society of Canada, 1981), 24–61; Ken Alexander and Aris Glaze, *Towards Freedom: The African-Canadian Experience* (Toronto: Umbrella Press, 1996), 51.

23. The abolitionist movement in Ohio seems a likely field for Galloway's labors. Secret, militant black abolitionist groups with strong ties to Canada operated out of Ohio throughout the 1850s, among them a military group known as the Liberators that had close ties to John Brown. There is some evidence that these clandestine groups served the Union army in an intelligence capacity in the early stages of the Civil War, which, if true, makes it an enticing possibility that it was from one of these groups that Galloway was recruited into the spy service. See Richard Hinton, *John Brown and His Men* (New York: Funk & Wagnalls, 1894), 171–75; and William Cheek and Aimee Cheek, *John Mercer Langston and the Fight for Black Freedom, 1829–65* (Urbana: University of Illinois Press, 1989), 350–52.

24. Wild to Kinsley, November 30, 1863, Edward W. Kinsley Papers, DU; *National Cyclopaedia of American Biography* (New York: James T. White & Co., 1898), 8:231; Frank P. Stearns, *The Life and Times of George Luther Stearns* (Philadelphia: J. B. Lippincott Co., 1907), esp. 276–320; Charles E. Heller, *Portrait of an Abolitionist: A Biography of George Luther Stearns, 1809–1867* (Westport, Conn.: Greenwood Press, 1996), 123–59.

25. Wild to Kinsley, November 30, 1863, Edward W. Kinsley Papers, DU; *New National Era*, September 4, 1870.

26. Union military records occasionally refer to spying activities, but no official records have yet been found that discuss Galloway's duties as an intelligence agent. The following National Archives records have been consulted for mention of Galloway without success: RG 110, Scouts, Guides, Spies, and Detectives; Secret Service Accounts; RG 109, Union Provost Marshal's Files of Papers Relating to Citizens or Business Firms (M345); RG 92, index to scouts in Reports of Persons and Articles Hired and the index to Quartermaster Claims; RG 59, Letters of Application and Recommendation During the Administrations of Abraham Lincoln and Andrew Johnson; RG 94, indexes to Letters Received by the Adjutant General's Office, 1861–1865 (M725); and General Information Index.

27. *Raleigh Weekly Standard*, September 7, 1870.

28. Edmund Cleveland diary, November 24, 1864, Southern Historical Collection, University of North Carolina Library, Chapel Hill.

29. *New National Era*, September 22, 1870.

30. Colyer, *Report of the Services Rendered by the Freed People*, 9–10. Colyer describes a number of intelligence missions conducted by former slaves in Confederate territory. See pp. 10–22.

31. Wild to Kinsley, November 30, 1863, Edward W. Kinsley Papers, DU.

32. Gen. Ambrose E. Burnside to Hon. E. M. Stanton, Secretary of War, March 21, 1862, U.S. War Department, *The War of the Rebellion: A Compilation of the Official Records of the Union and Confederate Armies* (Washington, D.C.: Government Printing Office, 1880–1901), ser. 1, vol. 9, 199–200.

33. The racist conduct of the Union army is one of the strongest themes in both the private papers and published works by Federal soldiers stationed in North Carolina during the Civil War. See, among many others, Arthur M. Schlesinger, ed., "Letter of a Blue Bluejacket," *New England Quarterly* 1, no. 4 (October 1928): 562, 565; Emmerton, *A Record of the Twenty-Third Regiment, Mass. Vol. Infantry*, 135–36; Levi W. Pigott diary, August 15, 1863, August 17, 1864, Levi W. Pigott Papers, NCSA.

34. See esp. Colyer, *Report of the Services Rendered*, 29–51; Mobley, *James City*, 5–13, 29–46; Cecelski, "A Thousand Aspirations," 22–25.

35. William H. Singleton, *Recollections of My Slavery Days* (New York: n.p., 1922), 8–9. Copy in the New York Public Library, New York, N.Y.

36. Andrew J. Wolbrook to Edward W. Kinsley, September 3, 1863, and Wolbrook to Kinsley, September 12, 1863, Edward W. Kinsley Papers, DU. Starkey and Galloway worked closely throughout the Civil War, and Starkey clearly held Galloway in great esteem. After the war, however, the two seem to have had at least a momentary falling out over financial matters. See Mary Ann Starkey to Edward W. Kinsley, July 27, 1865, Edward W. Kinsley Papers, DU.

37. Evans, *Ballots and Fence Rails*, 111–12; John Richard Dennett, *The South As It Is: 1865–1866*, ed. Henry M. Christman (New York: Viking, 1965), 151–53.

38. Pigott diary, May 30, June 1, June 18, 1863, L. W. Pigott Papers, NCSA.

39. Pigott diary, January 1, 1864, L. W. Pigott Papers, NCSA; Proceedings of the National Convention of the Colored Citizens of the United States, 1864, reprinted in Herbert Aptheker, *A Documentary History of the Negro People in the United States* (New York: Citadel Press, 1951), 1:511–13.

40. Aptheker, *Documentary History*, 1:522–23.

41. Pigott diary, January 1, 1864, L. W. Pigott Papers, NCSA.

42. The Lincoln administration first considered the use of black troops in mid-1862. "Limited and unauthorized" use of black troops had actually occurred in at least Kansas, Louisiana, and South Carolina before August 1862, when the War Department finally authorized the recruitment of the first slave regiment—the 1st South Carolina Volunteers, recruited from the occupied portion of the Sea Islands—into the Union army. In September 1862, Lincoln issued a "Preliminary Proclamation of Emancipation" that stated that as of January 1, 1863, slaves in the Confederate states would be "forever free." Once the proclamation went into effect, blacks were recruited on a mass scale. Six months later, thirty black regiments had been organized. More than 186,000 blacks enlisted in the Union army, and roughly one-third of them would eventually be listed as dead or missing. See Leon F. Litwack, *Been in the Storm So Long: The Aftermath of Slavery* (New York: Knopf, 1979), 69–71, 98.

43. Galloway married Martha Ann Dixon at the Beaufort home of her parents, Napoleon and Massie Dixon. Martha A. Little deposition, Celie Galloway pension file, VA; Marriage Register: Carteret County, N.C., 1850–1981, NCSA; Eighth Federal Census: Carteret County, N.C., Population and Slave Schedules, 1860.

44. Pigott diary, August 4, 1863, L. W. Pigott Papers, NCSA; Cleveland diary, November 24, 1864, Southern Historical Collection, University of North Carolina Library, Chapel Hill.

45. Wild to Kinsley, November 30, 1863, Edward W. Kinsley Papers, DU. In this letter, Wild refers to Galloway's Boston contact as a "Mr. Stevenson of 7 Hull St." This was presumably John Hubbard Stephenson (1820–1888) of 9 Hull Street, of the millinery firm of Stephenson & Plympton. He is not known to have been a part of the

city's abolitionist movement. See *Boston Directory* (Boston: George Adams, 1862); and *Boston Evening Transcript*, December 22, 1888.

46. *North Carolina Times* (Raleigh, N.C.), May 21, 1864; Mary Ann Starkey to Edward W. Kinsley, May 21, 1864, Edward W. Kinsley Papers, DU.

47. *The Liberator*, September 9, 1864, reprinted in Aptheker, *Documentary History*, 1:511, 516.

48. Horace James, *Annual Report of the Superintendent of Negro Affairs in North Carolina, 1864, With an Appendix, Containing the History and Management of the Freedmen in this Department up to June 1st, 1865* (Boston: W. P. Brown, n.d.), 6–18; *Old North State* (Beaufort, N.C.), January 7, 1865; John Niven, ed., *The Salmon P. Chase Papers*, vol. 1, *Journals, 1829–1872* (Kent, Ohio: Kent State University Press, 1993), 542–44.

49. Willie Lee Rose, *Rehearsal for Reconstruction: The Port Royal Experiment* (Indianapolis: Bobbs-Merrill, 1964).

50. Sidney Andrews, *The South Since the War; As Shown by Fourteen Weeks of Travel and Observation in Georgia and the Carolinas* (Boston: Ticknor & Fields, 1866), 125.

51. Roberta Sue Alexander, *North Carolina Faces the Freedmen: Race Relations during Presidential Reconstruction, 1865–67* (Durham, N.C.: Duke University Press, 1985), 16; Pigott diary, July 4, 1865, L. W. Pigott Papers, NCSA.

52. *New York Times*, September 17, 1865.

53. *New York Times*, September 17, 1865.

54. *Wilmington Herald*, September 8, 1865.

55. Evans, *Ballots and Fence Rails*, 87–91.

56. Aptheker, *Documentary History*, 1:546.

57. Dennett, *The South As It Is*, 151–53.

58. *New National Era*, September 22, 1870. Galloway is not listed in the city directories of New Bern or Wilmington in 1865–1866. See Frank D. Smaw Jr., *Smaw's Wilmington Directory* (Wilmington, N.C.: Frank D. Smaw Jr., ca. 1866); and R. A. Shotwell, *New Bern Mercantile and Manufacturers' Business Directory and North Carolina Farmers Reference Book* (New Bern, N.C.: W. I. Vestal, 1866).

59. Evans, *Ballots and Fence Rails*, 93.

60. Dennett, *The South As It Is*, 42.

61. Quoted in Litwack, *Been in the Storm So Long*, 271.

62. Evans, *Ballots and Fence Rails*, 64–81; Litwack, *Been in the Storm So Long*, 289.

63. Dennett, *The South As It Is*, 110.

64. Evans, *Ballots and Fence Rails*, 83–85.

65. *Tri-Weekly Standard* (Raleigh, N.C.), September 7, 1867.

66. Wilmington *Evening Star*, September 25, 1867; *New National Era*, September 22, 1870.

67. Evans, *Ballots and Fence Rails*, 95–97.

68. *Wilmington Journal*, February 21, 1868.

69. *The Standard* (Raleigh, N.C.), January 25, February 17, 1868, cited in Bernstein, "The Participation of Negro Delegates," 399, 407.

70. Quoted in Evans, *Ballots and Fence Rails*, 98.

71. *Wilmington Weekly Journal*, February 28, 1868.

72. Evans, *Ballots and Fence Rails*, 95–97.

73. Evans, *Ballots and Fence Rails*, 98–102.

74. Linda Gunter, "Abraham H. Galloway: First Black Elector," *North Carolina African-American Historical and Genealogical Society Quarterly* (Fall 1990): 9–10.

75. *The Christian Recorder*, September 24, 1870. For background on the black militias in the Reconstruction South, see Otis A. Singletary, *Negro Militia and Reconstruction* (Austin: University of Texas Press, 1957).

76. Allen W. Trelease, *White Terror: The Ku Klux Klan Conspiracy and Southern Reconstruction* (Baton Rouge: Louisiana State University Press, 1971), 189–225; Evans, *Ballots and Fence Rails*, 101–2, 145–48; William C. Harris, *William Woods Holden: Firebrand of North Carolina Politics* (Baton Rouge: Louisiana State University Press, 1987), 287–307.

77. Balanoff, "Negro Legislators," 23–24, 27.

78. *Wilmington Daily Journal*, July 20, 1869.

79. *Wilmington Weekly Journal*, April 2, 1869.

80. See, for example, *New York Times*, September 17, 1865.

81. *Wilmington Daily Journal*, July 20, 1869; *Wilmington Journal*, August 4, 1870, 72. Bill Reaves Collection, New Hanover County Public Library, Wilmington, N.C. (hereafter, NHCPL).

82. *Senate and House Journals, 1868*, 41–42.

83. *Senate and House Journals, 1869*, 360–61; Balanoff, "Negro Legislators," 34–36.

84. Balanoff, "Negro Legislators," 41–42, 44–48; *North Carolina Standard* (Raleigh, N.C.), January 21, 1868, February 10, 1870; *Laws of North Carolina, 1868–69–70*, chap. 77; A. H. Galloway to George Z. French, and J. S. W. Eagles to Governor Holden, August 10, 1869, Governors Letter Book 60, NCSA.

85. For an informative discussion of the collective outlook on voting held by Reconstruction blacks, see Elsa Barkley Brown, "Negotiating and Transforming the Public Sphere: African American Political Life in the Transition from Slavery to Freedom," *Public Culture* 7 (1994): 107–46.

86. *Senate and House Journals, 1868–1869*, 209, 223, 648; *1869–70*, 466; *Wilmington Journal*, February 1869, Bill Reaves Collection, NHCPL; Balanoff, "Negro Legislators," 42–44.

87. Galloway grew ill so suddenly that his wife and two young sons, John L. and Abraham Jr., were not able to return from a trip to New Bern before his death. "Widow's Declaration of Pension for Martha A. Little," January 29, 1894, Celie Galloway pension file, VA.

88. *Raleigh Weekly Standard*, September 7, 1870; *Wilmington Daily Journal*, 2–4, September 10, 1870, April 23, 1871, Bill Reaves Collection, NHCPL; *The Christian Recorder*, September 24, 1870.

89. Evans, *Ballots and Fence Rails*, 137–41.

90. *The Christian Recorder*, September 24, 1870; *Wilmington Journal*, September 2–4, 1870, Bill Reaves Collection, NHCPL; *Raleigh Weekly Standard*, September 17, 1870.

2

Homer Plessy: Unsuccessful Challenger to Jim Crow

Minoa Uffelman

"Homer Plessy: Unsuccessful Challenger to Jim Crow" places the famous Louisiana segregation test case in the historical and social context of the late nineteenth century. Exploring the conditions of African Americans in the South in general and New Orleans in particular, this chapter chronicles the hopes for civil liberties that people of color experienced after the Civil War and the eventual erosion of their rights. In the 1896 eight-to-one ruling by the Supreme Court, the "separate but equal" concept seemed to confirm what most white Americans accepted as normal and what was already common practice. In 1896 the case received little white press coverage. The black press, however, railed against the ruling, and African Americans eventually developed long-term protest strategies led by the NAACP to overturn Plessy v. Ferguson. *The reversal happened in 1954 with* Brown v. Board of Education.

On June 7, 1892, a New Orleans shoemaker, Homer Adolph Plessy, bought a first-class ticket and took a seat on a New Orleans train. Plessy was seven-eighths white and perhaps might have ridden unmolested, except that he *wanted* to be arrested. Plessy was part of a well-planned and organized test case to prove the unconstitutionality of the recent series of segregation laws on public conveyances passed by several state legislatures. For the next four years, the case wound its way through the legal system until it was heard by the United States Supreme Court. In 1896 the court heard *Plessy v. Ferguson* and ruled firmly on the side of legal segregation, using the famous phrase "separate but equal." Once legitimized by the highest court in the

31

land, the concept was readily applied to many aspects of Southern society without impunity. Eventually there would be separate waiting rooms, bathrooms, drinking fountains, seating in places of entertainment, cemeteries, hospitals, and schools. How could eight of the nine Supreme Court judges justify what modern Americans see as blatant discrimination based entirely on the color of one's skin? To understand this case it is essential to place the decision in the context of events and ideologies in American culture during the waning days of the nineteenth century.

The Civil War ended slavery but did not solve many of the monstrous problems facing the postwar South. Slaves needed assistance from the federal government as they transitioned from chattel to free people. Many had hoped for "forty acres and a mule" to help establish their new lives. They were sorely disappointed. Congress established the Freedman's Bureau in March of 1865 to provide freed slaves with food, clothes, and shelter. Another important task was to help freedmen negotiate labor contracts with their employers. This was especially important given that slaves had been forbidden to learn to read. One of the most daunting yet vital tasks of the bureau was to establish schools and colleges for African Americans who were eager to learn. The Freedman's Bureau often coordinated with Northern voluntary associations in its efforts to improve the lives of Southern blacks. While many African Americans benefited tremendously from the bureau's efforts, particularly concerning education, it was underfunded and not always effective.

White Southerners were desperate to maintain their cheap labor source and keep African Americans in subservient positions. Communities passed series of laws called Black Codes, which effectively limited the freedoms of African Americans. Black Codes included vagrancy and apprentice laws, sometimes assigning freedmen to guardians who happened to be their former owners. The laws prohibited interracial marriage, enacted curfews, and provided for a pass system limiting mobility of African Americans. Whites wanted to ensure that the freedmen would stay where whites thought they belonged. Some states established different punishments for the same crime depending on the race of the convicted person. For instance, housebreaking was a capital offense in South Carolina for blacks but not for whites. Some whites used violence and intimidation to impede African Americans from voting. The most violent Southerners formed hate groups such as the White Caps and the Ku Klux Klan to systematically terrorize local blacks.

Northern politicians were determined to circumvent the South's blatant attempts to undermine black civil liberties. The First Civil Rights Bill was passed in March 1866, guaranteeing freedmen the right to own and rent property, make contracts, and have access to court. Federal authorities could bring suit against violators. The country passed three amendments to the Constitution. The Thirteenth Amendment prohibited slavery in the United States. The Fourteenth Amendment gave freed slaves citizenship but did not explicitly give African Americans suffrage. To encourage states to give the vote to blacks, the amendment reduced representation proportionally if voters were disfranchised. To further buttress the African American right to vote, the Fifteenth Amendment stated explicitly that franchise could not be denied because of race, color, or past servitude.

Radical Reconstruction began in March 1867. It replaced the Presidential Reconstruction under Andrew Johnson and divided the Southern states that refused to ratify the Fourteenth Amendment into five military districts, each to be governed by a major general in the U.S. Army. Military governors were to register all adult black men to vote and were given considerable discretion in registering former Confederates. The governors were to supervise the election of constitutional conventions that were required to include black suffrage. When state legislatures passed the Fourteenth Amendment, then the state could reenter the Union. By 1870, all Southern states were once again part of the United States.

It was during this tumultuous period that Homer Plessy was born free in 1863 to Creole parents. In 1864 thousands of jubilant African Americans gathered in New Orleans's Congo Square to celebrate Louisiana's passage of an emancipation ordinance. It is unknown if young Homer's parents took him there to celebrate that day, but it would have been a time of great expectations for people of color. The passage of the Thirteenth, Fourteenth, and Fifteenth Amendments would have given African Americans great hope and optimism about the future. Blacks were further overjoyed when in 1867 New Orleans desegregated streetcars. Then two years later, New Orleans became the only Southern city to experiment with integrated public schools. Plessy grew up seeing black men vote, hold political office in both local and state capacities, and sit on juries. In New Orleans, black policemen earned the same wages as their white counterparts. Louisiana even took the dramatic step of legalizing interracial marriages. In the early 1870s a remarkable biracial organization called for political equality and the end to racial discrimination. The Unification Movement may have been short lived, but remarkably 1,800 blacks and whites signed their names to a document calling for racial equality. The Crescent City was moving forward with improved civil rights, and Homer Plessy would have benefited.

There are no known surviving papers left by Plessy, but public records give us some facts of his life. Homer was born on St. Patrick's Day in 1863 to Adolphe and Rosa Plessy. His Creole ancestry gave him a light complexion. He lived in a racially mixed middle-class suburb and attended a Catholic church that held mass in French and Latin. In 1869 Adolphe died at age forty-six. Two years later his mother married Victor M. Dupart, who later become one of the 1,800 signers of the Unification document. Plessy followed in family tradition to become a cobbler when he was seventeen. In 1888 he married Louise Bordenave, and the young couple rented a home on North Claibourne Avenue in the Faubourg Treme district. Many musicians and

Supreme Court of the United States,

No. 210, October Term, 1895.

Homer Adolph Plessy
Plaintiff in Error,

vs.

J. H. Ferguson, Judge of Section "A"
Criminal District Court for the Parish
of Orleans.

In Error to the Supreme Court of the State of
Louisiana

This cause came on to be heard on the transcript of the
record from the Supreme Court of the State of Louisiana,
and was argued by counsel.

On consideration whereof, It is now here ordered and
adjudged by this Court that the judgment of the said Supreme
Court, in this cause, be, and the same is hereby, affirmed
with costs.

Per Mr. Justice Brown,
May 18, 1896.

Dissenting:
Mr. Justice Harlan

Court Document from Homer v. Plessy (Image courtesy of the National Archives and Records Administration.)

artists lived in this neighborhood, and they tended to be radical and egalitarian. Active in local affairs, Plessy was an officer of a benevolent religious society that provided medical and burial expenses for members.

The future might have looked bright for people of color in New Orleans, but several major cultural, political, and ideological changes were conspiring to roll back improved civil rights and replace color-blind opportunities with discriminatory laws and segregation. Specifically, the presidential election of 1876 proved disastrous for Southern equality. Samuel J. Tilden, a Democrat, won the popular vote; however, he did not win the electoral vote. Several states had disputed electoral votes, and a commission was established to determine the outcome of the election. The electoral commission held a Republican majority and awarded all the disputed votes to the Republican candidate, Rutherford B. Hayes. President Hayes immediately ordered the remaining Federal troops guarding Republican-controlled statehouses removed. By 1877, every Southern state had been "Redeemed" by the Democrats. In short order the Redeemers began to undo the progress of Radical Reconstruction. Simultaneously, Northerners lost interest in the plight of African Americans. Additionally, during the last part of the nineteenth century, the Supreme Court became much more conservative and legally eviscerated a great deal of civil rights legislation.

Historians have plumbed public records, newspapers, diaries, and copies of speeches to determine how white Americans of the late nineteenth century thought. Among many topics, W. J. Cash explores the concept of white Southern womanhood in *The Mind of the South*. White men seized upon fears of black rapists to justify segregation and even violence against perceived threats. Indeed, just the accusation of rape could and often did result in a lynching. White Southern society condoned this type of vigilante justice, and perpetrators did not fear arrest.[1] Joel Williamson in *A Rage for Order* further describes the psychological fear whites felt at having thousands of black men suddenly freed without the constraints of slavery to guarantee social order. He argues that lynching began as a reaction to the "black beast" but once implemented could be extended to practically any offense "real or imagined."[2] The white newspapers in New Orleans in the 1890s reflected the racial attitudes described by historians.

In *The Strange Career of Jim Crow*, C. Vann Woodward describes how Southern society created legal segregation. He proves that Jim Crow laws were a product of a particular historical period and had not existed in time immemorial as Southern apologists suggested. The first Jim Crow law for railroads was passed by Florida in 1887. Mississippi passed a similar law in 1888; Texas did so in 1889; Louisiana did so in 1890; Alabama, Arkansas, Georgia, and Tennessee did so in 1891; and Kentucky did so in 1892. By the turn of the century, North and South Carolina as well as Virginia had also passed segregation laws for railroad cars.[3]

With the impetus of Jim Crow laws in transportation came another sinister trend in Southern governments. States wrote new constitutions to exclude black franchisement. White Southerners knew that blacks voted Republican and implemented a number of different techniques to prevent black participation in elections. Some states passed "grandfather clauses." If a voter's grandfather had never voted, then he could not vote, effectively disfranchising all freedmen. Other states established literacy tests where it was up to the local electoral commission to determine the reading standard. Blacks attempting to vote were given more difficult tests than whites. Some states used poll taxes to prevent poor African Americans from voting. This had the added benefit of sifting out poor whites who at times had joined forces to work against the white power structure. In particular, the Populist Movement saw some interracial cooperation between poor farmers that upset white elites.

Additionally, other factors contributed to this conservative backlash. A new generation of post-slavery African Americans had reached adulthood. They did not remember the "peculiar institution" and were unwilling to defer to whites. Newspapers of the period are replete with accounts of "uppity" blacks who did not know their place in polite society. The scientific community struggled to make sense of what they viewed as a racial problem. Social scientists armed with tape measures, calipers, charts, and new pseudoscientific theories argued that people of African descent were inferior to Caucasians. This concept of white superiority fit in nicely with the imperialistic impulses of European nations. It justified European and American domination of their "little brown brothers." Certainly Southerners eagerly embraced these theories espoused by late-nineteenth-century scientists because they confirmed white superiority, and they also felt a certain sense of vindication.

Therefore, legal segregation did not develop in a social vacuum but against a backdrop of white anxieties and changing ideologies. Homer Plessy was not the first and only person to challenge the newly developing racist laws. Several other African Americans did so earlier. Within two years of the end of the Civil War, New Orleans attempted to segregate the mule-powered streetcars. One-third of the cars were painted with huge black stars to indicate to African Americans that these were the proper streetcars to ride. Black Union soldiers could ride the cars either with or without stars; all other blacks were to ride only the designated starred cars. Whites could ride whichever cars were most convenient. The black newspaper *New Orleans Crescent* called for the black community to protest. One black rider challenged the new segregated system and was arrested, but the streetcar company attempted to de-escalate the situation by dropping the charges. Denied a test case, the protesters tried another tactic. A group confronted a "whites only" car a block from Plessy's home. The company instructed streetcar drivers that if blacks boarded unstarred streetcars they were not to move. Protesters across the city used this company policy to immobilize the entire system. With business halted, the streetcar companies abandoned the segregated star system, and integrated public transportation continued. Plessy was a young boy of four when this successful protest of segregation happened in his neighborhood. Perhaps he had no personal memory of it, but it is likely he would have heard of the success as he matured, having to confront the railroad and the new strategies to segregate riders of public transportation.

Railroad construction exploded in the South after the war, and different states developed different systems of separation. The initial segregation of railroad cars was not delineated along racial lines but along class and gender ones. African American women often protested this new classification. Originally the first-class cars were for "ladies." Several cultural assumptions contributed to this classification. Foremost was the ideology of white Southern womanhood and that women needed to be protected spatially from associating with the rougher aspects of society; that is, lower-class men who might be drinking, cussing, and smoking. Ladies' cars were safer, nicer, quieter, and cleaner, with air unpolluted by smoke. Indeed, the second-class cars were often called "smoking" cars. Importantly, Southerners also wanted to prevent white women from having to share a train with African American men. This true motive is revealed almost unintentionally by some laws permitting black servants, escorts, and nurses to sit in first-class accommodations with the whites with whom they traveled. Therefore, railroads allowed black employees to travel with their white employers but did not want autonomous people of color tainting the ladies' carriages. This exclusion reveals the true intention of segregation, and the message was clear. Black servants were welcome; free people of color were not.

There was no uniform system of segregation. Laws varied from state to state and from rail company to rail company, and were often enforced irregularly by conductors. Firsthand accounts of white travelers from the period reveal the schizophrenic application of Jim Crow laws. In some areas, particularly New Orleans, where the racially mixed population was quite high, conductors did not relish having to determine who was white and who was not. In practicality the system was somewhat self-segregating because many blacks could not afford the higher cost of a first-class ticket. If, however, a well-dressed, properly behaved African American bought a first-class ticket and no white passenger complained, the African American was often left alone. Remember, Plessy himself was one-eighth black and probably could have "passed" as white if he had wanted, but instead he wanted to challenge the law and told the conductor he was black.

Surprisingly, more African American women than men brought suits to challenge racial segregation. Between 1855 and 1890 the Interstate Commerce Commission published twenty-four cases from state and federal courts. Men filed only five suits. The women who filed suit tended to be educated and were often teachers. The married women who brought suit were usually married to professional men. This suggests a certain class consciousness of the women who considered themselves part of the "better class." Whereas these women saw class trumping race, rail companies and conductors saw it differently. In 1883 a conductor on the Chesapeake, Ohio & Southwestern Railroad asked a young Ida B. Wells to remove herself from the Ladies' car. She refused and was forcefully ejected by the conductor with the assistance of two male passengers. Wells managed to bite a plug out of the conductor's hand in the process. She found the whole episode humiliating and filed suit. The case eventually made it all the way to the Tennessee Supreme Court, on which sat several former Confederate officers. The court ruled in favor of the railroad, and the injustice Wells felt contributed to her desire to right social injustices. She later became one of the most famous antilynching activists in the world.

In 1890 when a Jim Crow transportation bill was proposed in Louisiana, the African American and mixed population protested. A group formed, naming itself "A Protest of the American Citizens' Equal Rights Association of Louisiana Against Class Legislation." They stated that the passage was "unconstitutional, un-American, unjust, dangerous and against sound public policy." Ominously, it declared it would "be a free license to the evilly-disposed that they might with impunity insult, humiliate, and otherwise maltreat inoffensive persons, and especially women and children who happen to have a dark skin."[4] These concerned citizens certainly understood the long-term implications of this segregation law. One of the members, L. A. Martinet, edited the New Orleans *Crusader*, which he used as an organ of protest. As one of the main contributors, Rodolphe L. Desdunes used his pen to furiously defend the civil rights that he saw eroding. He was particularly furious with the sixteen Louisiana African American representatives who he felt could have prevented passage of the Jim Crow legislation. Imitating past protest strategies and anticipating Montgomery, Alabama, in 1955, Desdunes proposed a boycott of the railroads. The group rejected this idea in favor of attempting to legally overturn the Jim Crow laws constitutionally.

In September of 1891 the protesters formed a new group to fight segregation in the courts and to devise a coordinated strategy. Reflecting the French heritage of Lousiana, they named their group "Comité des Citoyens," or the "Citizens' Committee to Test the Constitutionality of the Separate Car Law." They determined that first they needed funds to finance the fight. Soon they raised the substantial sum of $3,000. Next, Martinet set out to find a good civil rights attorney, and he began corresponding with a famous carpetbagger known for his liberal attitudes, Albion Winegar Tourgee. (*Carpetbagger* was a term of derision Southerners gave Northerners who moved to the South to exploit the region after the Civil War. Supposedly the transplanted Northerner arrived with all his possessions in cheap luggage made of carpets.) Of French Huguenot stock, Tourgee had served in the Union army and emigrated to North Carolina after the war to practice law. As a Radical Republican, he helped write North Carolina's Radical Constitution. Later he served on the bench of the North Carolina Superior Court. At the time he was perhaps best known as the author of six novels about the Reconstruction South. Tourgee brought prestige and zeal into the battle against Louisiana's Jim Crow system.

Tourgee and the Citizens' Committee considered several strategies to test the law. One scenario was to have a light-skinned mulatto woman buy a ticket in the first-class car, thereby testing the arbitrariness of race. Another option was to have an African American man book a seat from out of state and then as the train entered Louisiana refuse to move to the segregated car. This plan had the advantage of creating an interstate commerce issue. The Committee considered a third possibility: to have an African American attempt to buy a sleeper ticket and be refused while white passengers obtained tickets. Significantly, Martinet discovered that the rail companies themselves did not support Jim Crow cars for financial reasons. It would prove costly to provide the extra carriages that would be necessary to comply with the law. When the Louisiana and Nashville Railroad agreed to be a part of the test case, the Committee decided to have someone buy a ticket from New Orleans to Mobile, Alabama, challenging the constitutional right for the federal government to regulate interstate commerce.

On February 24, 1892, Daniel F. Desdunes, the twenty-one-year-old son of Rodolphe, was arrested. Just as with Homer Plessy, this young man was chosen because of his extremely light skin. He might have been left alone had this not been a test case. In May the Louisiana Supreme Court ruled that Jim Crow laws were unconstitutional when *interstate* travel was involved. The court recognized that only the federal government had power to regulate travel between states. Because most Southern states had Jim Crow laws, this was a hollow victory. It was incumbent on the Committee to test *intrastate* travel to achieve the constitutional victory they desired. The next man who volunteered to be arrested was Homer Adolph Plessy.

Plessy bought a first-class ticket on June 7, 1892, walked past the "Colored Only" sign, and sat in the carriage reserved for whites. The conductor asked him if he was a "colored" man, and Plessy replied in the affirmative. "If you are colored you should go into the car set apart for your race. The law is plain and must be obeyed," replied the conductor. After refusing to move, Plessy was taken to the Fifth Precinct Station, where he was booked and released on $500 bail. Judge John Howard Ferguson, originally from Massachusetts, presided over the case. One of Plessy's lawyers used the Fourteenth Amendment to argue that his civil rights had been violated. In simple language the amendment reads, "no state shall make or enforce any law which shall abridge the privileges or immunities of any citizen of the United States." As an American citizen, Plessy had had his liberty violated. Judge

Ferguson disagreed. He ruled that the state had the legal right to regulate intrastate transportation. Ferguson wrote, "He was simply deprived of the liberty of doing as he pleased, and of violating a penal statue with impunity."[5] Plessy appealed, and the Louisiana Supreme court ruled in favor of the state. Now the case headed to the highest court in the country under the name *Plessy v. Ferguson*.

The black and white newspaper accounts perfectly illustrate the polarized racial attitudes toward Plessy's arrest and the social implications of the judicial outcome. The *Daily Crescent* is the most often quoted because of its stereotypical racial language:

IN THE WRONG COACH,
A Snuff-Colored Descendant of Ham Kicks Against the 'Jim Crow' Law,
And Takes the Jail End of It Rather
Than Comply With Its Distinctive Provisions[6]

By using the benign and disingenuous term "distinctive provisions," the white writer never acknowledged the discriminatory racial policies that Plessy had protested. By contrast, the African American writer of the *Crusader* stressed that the civil rights that all Americans should enjoy were being denied to Plessy by the new segregation policies. The article stated that after the conductor asked him to retire to the colored coach, "Plessy determinedly told him that he was an American citizen and proposed to enjoy his rights as such. . . ." Later the article reads, "Plessy said he would go to jail first before relinquishing his right as a citizen."[7] The incident in the white papers dealt with "distinctive provisions"; the same incident in the *Crusader* was portrayed as being about an American's liberty.

The intervening six years between passage of Louisiana's Jim Crow law and the Supreme Court hearing witnessed a conservative backlash toward civil rights. Southern states had begun to disfranchise African American voters. Congress in 1892 defeated the Lodge Bill, a bill that would have extended occupation of Federal troops to protect against election fraud. The same year Louisiana reinstated a ban on interracial marriage and established segregated waiting rooms in railroad stations. In 1894 Congress rescinded several Reconstruction laws that protected black rights. Then in 1895 one of the most famous black men of the time, Booker T. Washington, made a speech that became known as the Atlanta Compromise. The head of the Tuskegee Institute seemingly accepted segregation as long as it was equal. He argued that African Americans should attend segregated schools and get an industrial education. Other African American leaders highly criticized Washington, but Southern whites took comfort in what appeared to be a famous black ally.

When the Citizens' Committee organized this test case by recruiting a person willing to be arrested, finding a railroad company willing to participate, and committing lawyers to prosecute the case, they felt they had a chance at victory. However, even as early as 1893 the correspondence between Martinet and Tourgee reflected the realization that if the case made it to the Supreme Court, the chances of victory were exceedingly slim. In a letter dated October 31, 1893, Tourgee discussed each of the justices and concluded that there would be "five who are against us."[8] Despite the dismal assessment by the two lead attorneys concerning *Plessy v. Ferguson*, the local activists in New Orleans stepped up protests against increased segregation in their city. The *Crusader* went from a weekly to a daily newspaper and relentlessly railed against both old and new erosions of civil liberties.

In the fall of 1895, Plessy's lawyers Tourgee, S. F. Phillips, and F. D. McKenny filed the final papers. Louisiana Attorney General M. J. Cunningham, Lionel Adams, and Alexander Porter Morse argued the state's case. The case was heard the following April. In his brief to the Supreme Court, Tourgee made a two-prong argument. The first was that Plessy was deprived of his property. The property in question was his "reputation of being white." Tourgee argued that in American society whiteness was "the master-key that unlocks the golden door of opportunity."[9] The court ignored this argument. More significantly, Tourgee maintained that this segregation law violated the Thirteenth and Fourteenth Amendments.

On May 18 Justice Henry Billings Brown, writing for the majority of eight, said the segregation law did not violate the Fourteenth Amendment. Citing as precedents the segregated schools in Washington, D.C., and the ban on interracial marriages, Brown maintained that regulations were legal as long as they were reasonable. He wrote that state legislatures could determine reasonableness because each "is at liberty to act with reference to the established usages, customs, and traditions of the people, and with a view to the promotion of their comfort, and the preservation of the public peace and good order." He went on further to theorize that legislation could not resolve racial differences. "Legislation is powerless to eradicate racial instincts, or to abolish distinctions based on physical differences. . . . If one race be inferior to the other socially, the constitution of the United States cannot put them on the same plane."[10] Justice Brown of Massachusetts had no faith that the constitution could guarantee social equality.

Ironically, the lone dissenter was John Marshall Harlan, a former Kentucky slaveholder who had opposed emancipation and the passage of civil rights legislation. Shocked by the terrorism of the Ku Klux Klan, Harlan had a change of heart and became a Republican as well as an advocate of racial equality. He argued that the segregation laws were unconstitutional. "The arbitrary separation of citizens, on the basis of race, while they are on a public highway, is a badge of servitude wholly inconsistent with the civil freedom and the equality before the law established by the Constitution. It can not be justified upon any legal grounds." Furthermore, he wrote, "Our Constitution is color-blind, and neither knows nor tolerates classes among citizens. In respect of civil rights, all citizens are equal before the law. . . . The thin disguise of 'equal' accommodations for passengers in railroad coaches will not mislead any one, nor atone for the wrong of this day." Portending the future, he asked the rhetorical question of where the segregation would end, "the use of the streets . . . [the] courtroom, the jury box, the legislative hall, or to any other place of public assembly?"[11] Eventually, his rhetorical question would be answered yes.

The reaction of the press and the American public is revealing of the dominant attitude in white America concerning civil rights. White media gave *Plessy v. Ferguson* very little coverage, and there was virtually no editorializing except in the black press. Most white Americans agreed with the seven justices who had upheld the state's right to regulate. In 1922 black historian Carter G. Woodson identified *Plessy* as one of the most important cases concerning African American citizenship.[12] His white counterparts, however, failed to grasp the magnitude for decades. Charles Warren's 1922 history of the Supreme Court did not mention it,[13] and in his revision four years later, he at least listed it in a footnote with twenty-four other cases concerning African Americans.[14] Carl Brent Swisher's 1943 survey of constitutional history omitted *Plessy*.[15] Even the esteemed historian Henry Steele Commager did not include the *Plessy* decision in his canonical *Documents of American History*.[16]

While historians missed the historical significance of the case, black Americans started living with the reality of a legally segregated country. On January 11, 1897, Plessy returned to a Louisiana court for sentencing. He pleaded guilty and paid the $25 fine, and the case was closed. The Committee had disbanded, and publication of the *Crusader* had ceased. The next year the Redeemers drew up a new state constitution that made integrated school illegal, funded pensions for relatives of Confederate soldiers, made the redundant decision to declare the Democratic party for "whites only," and disfranchised African American voters. Between the elections of 1896 and 1900, 120,000 black voters were removed from the register. There would not be another black legislator in Louisiana until 1967.

Plessy v. Ferguson illustrates the complexities of understanding history. It is impossible to fully grasp the huge significance of this case without understanding the historical context. The *Plessy* decision established a legal precedent that all Southern states used to defend the passage of a variety of segregation laws. On the other hand, the case can be seen as confirming what most Americans including legal authorities in the late nineteenth century saw as conventional wisdom. This is evidenced by the eight-to-one ruling of the justices. Only Justice Harlan argued for a "color-blind" Constitution. Also, the media basically reported the proceedings as a matter of course with no debates or commentary. Importantly, this decision of legalized segregation led to the development of an organization determined to legally attack Jim Crow, the National Association for the Advancement of Colored People (NAACP).

The NAACP formed in 1909. It developed a long-term strategy of attacking segregation. The *Plessy* decision never stated that African Americans were second-class citizens. It said that the facilities must be "separate but equal." The cases the NAACP pursued in the 1930s and 1940s concentrated on guaranteeing that equality was actually achieved. The organization won several cases using this argument. World War II helped change the climate of racism in a several important ways. First, many Americans saw the irony of defending Jews from the Nazis while maintaining legal segregation in the South. There were strong parallels between anti-Semitism and racial discrimination that could not be ignored. Second, many blacks fought in American uniforms and were loath to come home and be treated as second-rate citizens. As veterans they were entitled to housing benefits and the educational opportunities made possible by the GI Bill, creating a larger middle class. This group of African Americans joined and contributed financially to the NAACP. By the 1950s the group thought it was time to challenge legal segregation in the school system.

In *Brown v. Board of Education of Topeka, Kansas* (1954) the NAACP's lead lawyer, Thurgood Marshall, argued that even when educational facilities were equal, it created a feeling of inferiority for minority children. One day before the fifty-eighth anniversary of *Plessy v. Ferguson*, the Supreme Court of the United States unanimously reversed its decision. *Brown v. Board of Education* was the legal wrecking ball that would be used to destroy the segregated wall created by Jim Crow. Still, the debate of the legality of racial classifications has not been resolved. *Plessy* determined that legal racial classifications are not inherently unconstitutional. The Supreme Court is still grappling with this thorny question. The whole argument of affirmative action is based on this very concept. Is the U.S. Constitution color-blind? The jury is still out.

Little is known of Homer Plessy after 1896. It appears he carried on his life working, attending church, and being loved by his family. His obituary simply read, "Plessy—on Sunday March 1, 1925, at 5:10 a.m. beloved husband of Louise Bordenave."[17] Ironically, while he was denied the right to sit in an integrated train car, he was interred in the two-hundred-year-old interracial cemetery of his maternal family.

NOTES

1. W. J. Cash, *The Mind of the South* (New York: Vintage Books, 1969), 116–20.

2. Joel Williamson, *A Rage for Order* (New York: Oxford University Press, 1986), 121.

3. C. Vann Woodward, "Plessy v. Ferguson: The Birth of Jim Crow." *American Heritage* 15, no. 3 (1964): 52.

4. Woodward, "Plessy v. Ferguson." 53.

5. Keith Weldon Medley, "The Sad Story of How 'Separate but Equal' was Born." *Smithsonian* 24, no. 11 (1994): 114.

6. *Daily Crescent*, June 8, 1892.

7. *Crusader*, June 1892.

8. Keith Weldon Medley, *We as Freemen: Plessy v. Ferguson* (Gretna, La.: Pelican, 2003). Quoted and the first page of the letter reproduced in.

9. Brook Thomas, ed., *Plessy v. Ferguson: A Brief History with Documents* (Boston: Bedford Books, 1997).

10. Thomas, *Plessy v. Ferguson*, 31–34.

11. Thomas, *Plessy v. Ferguson*, 34–35; Medley, *We as Freemen*, 203–5; C. Vann Woodward, "*Plessy v. Ferguson:* The Birth of Jim Crow," *American Heritage* 15, no. 3 (1964): 52–55, 100–103.

12. Carter G. Woodson, *The Negro in Our History* (Washington D.C.: The Associated Publishers, 1922): 419.

13. Charles Warren, *The Supreme Court in the United States History* (Boston: Little, Brown, 1922).

14. Warren, *The Supreme Court in the United States, Volume 2* (Boston: Little, Brown, 1926): 621.

15. Carl Brent Swisher, *American Constitutional Development* (Boston: Houghton Mifflin, 1943).

16. Henry Steel Commanger and Milton Canton, eds., *Documents of American History, Volume 1* Englewood Cliffs, NJ: Prentice Hall, 1968).

17. *New Orleans Times-Picayune*, March 3, 1925.

SUGGESTED READING

Klarman, Michael J. *From Jim Crow to Civil Rights: The Supreme Court and the Struggle for Racial Equality*. New York: Oxford University Press, 2004.

Medley, Keith Weldon. "The Sad Story of How 'Separate but Equal' Was Born." *Smithsonian* 24, no. 11 (1994): 105–17.

———. *We as Freemen: Plessy v. Ferguson*. Gretna, La.: Pelican, 2003.

Thomas, Brook, editor. *Plessy v. Ferguson: A Brief History with Documents*. Boston: Bedford Books, 1997.

Welke, Barbara Y. "When All the Women Were White, and All the Blacks Were Men: Gender, Class, Race, and the Road to *Plessy*, 1955–1914." *Law and History Review* 13, no. 2 (1995): 261–316.

Woodward, C. Vann. "*Plessy v. Ferguson*: The Birth of Jim Crow." *American Heritage* 15, no. 3 (1964): 52–55, 100–103.

———. *The Strange Career of Jim Crow*. New York: Oxford University Press, 2002.

3

𝓔

James K. Vardaman: "A Vote for White Supremacy" and the Politics of Racism

Paul R. Beezley

The exclusion of certain groups from politics and society, the denial of their basic civil rights, and their forced segregation into second-class citizenship are basic facts of American history. What is often surprising to today's student is the bottom-up nature and popularity of campaigns among white Americans to deny minorities their full rights. From discrimination and exclusion of the Chinese on the Pacific coast to the segregation of African Americans, these movements received mass popular support from the white male voters of the time. James K. Vardaman rode the popularity of racism to great political success. His life reveals the great popularity of racism and the mind-set behind the effort to severely restrict the rights of African Americans at the end of the nineteenth century. In the South at that time, the superiority of the white race was never questioned. What made Vardaman stand out was his aggressive rhetoric of white superiority. Few men, then or since, have so plainly stated their belief in the fundamental inequality of white and black Americans. Vardaman successfully intertwined his oppression of blacks with an effort to improve the lives of common whites. Together, these issues made him the most powerful man in Mississippi, if only briefly.

On June 28, 1930, thousands of white Mississippians filed quietly by the flag-draped coffin of James K. Vardaman beneath the dome of the state's new capitol building. Despite Vardaman's being out of the public eye for nearly a decade, an outpouring of grief by the public convinced the family to allow this state funeral for their father and husband. Vardaman lost his

45

last two runs for public office in 1918 and 1922. He then retired and spent his final years in Birmingham, Alabama. Yet thousands stood in line, braving the late-June heat and humidity to bid farewell to this man. This reflected the strong bond that Vardaman created between himself and the common white folks of Mississippi, a bond that remained despite his political miscues and electoral losses. These people came out to pay their last respects to their great "White Chief," who represented a fundamental change in the state's political structure twenty-five years earlier. Here lay the man who embodied and represented the hopes and ideas of the small white farmers of the state, who fought for them against the powerful planters of the Delta, the corporations of the North, and the business elite of the state's cities. Most importantly, he gave voice to their hatred of African Americans. His progressive policies and demands for reform appealed to the common white men of the state, but the racist feelings that he proudly and openly voiced vaulted Vardaman to his position as a political icon, the "White Chief." He embodied a potent combination of populist rhetoric and racism that became intertwined and inseparable, and he represents a powerful force in Southern politics that helped to ensure the survival of racial discrimination for more than sixty years. The themes that Vardaman brought together reappeared repeatedly over the next few decades. For these reasons it is important to look at Vardaman's life and his views to understand how common whites, often in the same economic situation as their fellow black Southerners, became so politically motivated by racism.

Vardaman did not invent this appeal to either the small farmer's causes or white supremacy. Both issues were well-established themes of Mississippi politics dating back to the Reconstruction era and earlier. But Vardaman brought a new, deeper commitment to the economic concerns of the common white, and a more aggressive and virulent determination to secure permanent white supremacy. By the time he reached the apex of his power in 1911, his rhetoric on both issues reached a level rarely surpassed before or since in Southern politics.

James Kimbal Vardaman was born on July 26, 1861, in Jackson County, Texas. His parents had arrived in Texas three years earlier from Mississippi. Along with a partner, Vardaman's father owned several thousands acres of land and several dozen slaves. Shortly after Vardaman's birth, his father joined the Confederate Army and fought for the duration of the Civil War. Following the war and the freeing of their slaves, the family fell into hard financial times. In 1868, the land was sold to cover debts, and the Vardaman family made the long trek back to Mississippi.

The Vardamans never regained the financial wealth they enjoyed prior to the Civil War. Vardaman grew up on a small farm as the family worked hard, never starving but never getting ahead. Vardaman's ability to help on the family's farm was hampered when his right arm got caught in a corn-shelling machine shortly after the family's return to Mississippi. He could write and

James K. Vardaman (Image courtesy of the Library of Congress Prints and Photographs Division.)

lift light objects, but the mangled arm severely limited his ability to do heavy work. In part because of his physical limitations, Vardaman turned to books at an early age and determined to make a career out of politics.

He received a limited formal education. At eighteen he moved in with an uncle, in part to take advantage of his relative's large collection of books. Over the next three years he read everything he could, from literature to history to law. He maintained this habit for the rest of his life. While living with his uncle, he also clerked for a local lawyer. This apprenticeship was the common way for young men to learn the law. In 1882 he took and passed the bar examination and became certified to practice law in Mississippi.

At twenty-one, Vardaman set out on his own. He moved to the small crossroads county seat of Winona, Mississippi, to begin practicing law. There Vardaman met a man who became a lifelong friend and mentor, Dr. B. F. Ward. Ward, a veteran of the Confederate Army, remained unreconstructed and unapologetic about the Confederacy or the South's antebellum past. He regularly denounced the leaders of the New South movement. These men pushed the region to adopt Northern ways including industrialization and small farms. Ward publicly branded them as traitors to the South's heritage. He argued that Jefferson Davis was a superior leader compared to Abraham Lincoln. Finally, he was an unrelenting foe of equality for black Americans. He believed those of African descent were an inferior race that needed to be confined to the lowest caste of society. Ward argued that the lynching of black men accused of raping white women was the only appropriate punishment. From Ward, the twenty-one-year-old Vardaman learned the righteousness of the Confederate cause, the nightmare that Reconstruction had been, and an undying devotion to the supremacy of the white race.

If Ward helped to shape the young Vardaman's outlook on Southern history and race relations, his cousin Hernando DeSoto Money helped to shape his career. Money was a wealthy lawyer in Winona who represented the district in the U.S. House of Representatives. As a young man beginning his career, Vardaman greatly admired his successful cousin. Five months after his arrival in Winona, Money bought a local paper and asked his own son and Vardaman to become coeditors. The paper was short-lived. It went broke, and Money sold it. But this brief experience as a newspaper editor opened the door to a career that occupied the majority of Vardaman's life.

In 1884, Vardaman married a young widow with an infant son. Her husband had died and left them a large plantation in the Delta region in the western portion of the state. Vardaman gave up his career and moved with his new family to the plantation shortly after their marriage. Farming did not suit Vardaman, and the family soon rented the land and moved nearby to the growing town of Greenwood, Mississippi. The Delta region of the state was just being opened up to settlement in this time period, thanks to the construction of massive levees to hold back both the Mississippi and Yazoo rivers. The deep soil made the Delta one of the most fertile areas in the world. While the Winona region's population was overwhelmingly white, the Delta was the inverse, being overwhelmingly black. Greenwood was the market center of the area, and it became Vardaman's home for the next twenty years.

In Greenwood, Vardaman bought a large house and began again to practice law. Vardaman cut a fine figure in Greenwood. Tall, with dark skin and broad shoulders, his most striking feature was his shoulder-length black hair that he maintained till his death. He took great pride in his dress and regularly took more than an hour each morning getting himself ready for the day. An easy man to be around, he was a gifted story- and joke teller and a good listener. He made and kept friends easily, remembering the names of people he met weeks or months earlier. He filled his home regularly with long-term guests and those he brought home for lunch on a daily basis. Despite his convivial nature, his law practice struggled. Soon after his move to Greenwood, he again ventured into journalism. In May of 1890, he bought the Greenwood *Enterprise*. For the next five years, the paper occupied his time as its owner and editor.

As the editor of the *Enterprise*, Vardaman promoted the ideas of civic progress that he held for the rest of his life. He had true faith that education of the common man and reforms by the elite could vastly improve the lives of all people. In Greenwood itself, he promoted a range of civic projects from a city water system to an electric street car system and the construction of a brick high school. For the state as a whole, he tried to rally his readers to abolish the corrupt and inhuman convict-leasing system, and he even backed halting the death penalty. While he clearly stated that African Americans should have no political rights, he felt that whites had a responsibility to ensure their humane treatment. This opposition to capital punishment did not extend to black men who raped white women. While he felt society needed to attempt to rehabilitate most criminals, black men who committed what he considered the most heinous of crimes forfeited all claims to humanity, becoming simply beasts. The only acceptable course of action in those cases was immediate lynching. Vardaman did repeatedly call for the lynching to be done quickly, and condemned the numerous cases where accused black men were tortured for hours before finally being put to death.

Indeed, Vardaman's liberal views on civic action were balanced by his absolute belief in white supremacy. Without question, Vardaman was "a hardshelled racist."[1] Vardaman came of age as white Mississippi struggled to throw off the Reconstruction government imposed by the victorious Union after the Civil War. Two pillars of those Reconstruction governments were the Republican party and political equality for the recently freed African Americans. Thus, opposition to Reconstruction became centered in the Democratic party, which portrayed itself as the "white man's party" in opposition to the "black Republicans." By the 1880s the political victory was complete, but not secured. Blacks still voted in great numbers in Mississippi, particularly in the Delta region where Vardaman lived. For Vardaman and men of his generation, securing permanent white supremacy was a driving force in their politics and social outlook. At all costs, blacks needed to be kept in a place of inferiority to whites. The *Enterprise* repeatedly supported and bolstered the argument that African Americans needed to be banned from both the polling place and political office, as they were incapable of self-government. Vardaman happily pointed to the failure of Haiti to govern itself since its revolution in the 1790s as evidence of African incompetence.

But during these early years in Greenwood, Vardaman maintained a measured tone in all things, whether promoting progressive reforms or supporting white supremacy. He tempered his clear disdain toward African

Americans by his use of the term "Negro" in his writings. He also championed the cause of abused convict laborers. He repeatedly argued that as long as blacks accepted their inferior place and did not strive to rise above what he saw as their natural position in society, whites would treat them well.

This deep commitment to white supremacy came to play a major role in Vardaman's political life, and it was fully developed by 1890. In this attitude he hardly stood out for the time. Whites throughout the United States, and indeed the world, held the simple belief that God intended the white race to dominate all of mankind. Both the theories of social Darwinism and the example of the world around them demonstrated this. While Charles Darwin intended to apply his theory of the survival of the fittest only to animals, scholars in both the United States and Britain took Darwin's theory and applied it to mankind. In this view, the Anglo-Saxon race was fittest, thus destined to rule. All other races fell in line behind the Anglo-Saxons of England, and to a lesser extent the United States: the Germans, then the French, on down the line through Europe, spreading out east and west, until one reached the end of the line, the darkest-skinned peoples of the earth, the Africans. Proof of this theory seemed to surround people of the day. The British Empire ruled more than a third of the globe. Great technological advances during the 1800s created a modern lifestyle for many Europeans and Americans that dramatically separated them from the other preindustrial cultures of the world. Whites ruled the world. Reality and science combined to make this a seemingly unquestionable fact.

The presence of such a large population of people of African descent made whites in the southern United States acutely aware that this fact was not necessarily a reality. To the large white landowners of the Delta who looked out across fields of black labor toiling away as they sat on porches being served by black servants, white supremacy seemed natural and secure. But the majority of Mississippians were small farmers. For these whites, in the hill counties of eastern and northern Mississippi, the rhetoric of white superiority often clashed with their day-to-day reality. The period following Reconstruction until the start of World War I was one of great struggle on the farms. For many struggling farmers, the entire families, including wives and daughters, often toiled in the fields, often beside hired black labor. Many more lost their land and became tenant farmers, finding themselves in exactly the same economic position as blacks. These whites seethed with resentment both toward blacks as a race and toward the whites who seemed to have left them behind. Vardaman picked up these twin resentments of race and class and used them to propel his political career.

Vardaman's political career began soon after his arrival in Greenwood. He quickly found a spot on the county's Democratic Party committee and shortly thereafter became its chairman. In the system of the day, the committee picked nominees for county offices and elected delegates with instructions on how to vote at the state convention that picked the ticket for state offices. Vardaman won election to the state House of Representatives in 1889, and in 1894 he was elected Speaker of the House. During this period he supported the conservatives within the Democratic Party, a wing of the party dominated in part by his cousin Hernando Money.

In 1895 he made his first run for governor. At this time Vardaman began to break with the conservatives. He came out for a wide range of reforms and issues that were important to the small farmers, the agrarians, of the state. During this campaign Vardaman also began discussing the reform of the state's public school funding. Mississippi distributed money according to population, which supported both white and black schools. The heavily populated Delta received a great deal of this revenue. However, black children went to school in far fewer numbers than whites. This allowed the Delta counties to spend a great deal more money on the white schools. The less-populated hill counties received much less funding and thus could afford only a few weeks of school in bare-bones conditions for their overwhelmingly white students. Vardaman proposed to distribute school funding according to the taxes each race paid. This would dramatically decrease the funding for the Delta while raising the funding for the hill counties.

In every speech he gave that year, Vardaman argued that educating blacks was a waste of time and money, and worse, dangerous. In Vardaman's view, blacks were incapable of truly learning. But what they did learn made them dissatisfied with their positions in society. Education wrecked good field hands and made them believe they deserved both the right to vote and the right to hold political office. Since whites could never tolerate either of these things, black education would lead to a race war. The crowds Vardaman spoke to loved this. Not only did it boost support for white schools, it hammered at blacks and took a dig at the rich whites of the Delta. He spoke across the state, sometimes three or four speeches a day. At every stop the crowds erupted in approval for his race and class-based arguments. Already an accomplished and dynamic speaker, Vardaman discovered a message the people wanted to hear.

But the public did not vote for the gubernatorial nomination; instead, the county committees and the state convention picked the candidate. As the convention drew near, it became clear Vardaman lacked enough support, and he withdrew from the race. He returned to Greenwood and bought a new paper, the Greenwood *Commonwealth*, and returned to editing. His time on the campaign trail changed him. His attacks on national and state leaders became sharper and more personal. He also greatly increased his hostility toward blacks. The word "nigger" began to appear freely throughout his editorials and articles.

The rousing response to Vardaman's race-baiting on the campaign trail certainly encouraged him to continue it on the pages of his newspaper. While he was not out of step with the prevailing view of the time, he became increasingly strident and proud of his bold declarations in favor of white supremacy and black inferiority. He said what many white men thought but few polite men would say in public. To him it became a badge of honor. By this time, he was aware of Ben Tillman of South Carolina. Tillman rode a wave of unvarnished racism to the United States Senate, and constructed a political machine on the foundations of progressive policies for small white farmers while stroking the flames of racial hatred. In Tillman, Vardaman saw a man who dared to speak what everyone knew, a true man who said what he thought regardless of how polite society recoiled back from it. This was the type of man Vardaman aspired to become, both in rhetoric and in political success.

One of the things that hampered Vardaman's political career was his lack of military experience. He got his chance to change that with the outbreak of the Spanish-American War in 1898. Vardaman ended up with a desk job, working for the Judge Advocate General's Corps in Santiago, overseeing claims hearings and one court-martial. The closest he got to combat was a trip out to the San Juan Hill battlefield. Still, this was honorable service, and he proudly promoted it the rest of his life. From Santiago in November 1898, Vardaman wrote home to Mississippi and declared himself a candidate for governor in 1899. Vardaman returned home just a few weeks before the state convention met. With multiple candidates vying for the nomination, Vardaman became lost in the crowd. With really no time to canvass the state, and scant attention from the press, his candidacy never got off the ground.

Vardaman again returned home to Greenwood and to newspaper editing. His paper continued to provide a platform to launch attacks on what were now his favorite enemies: trusts, the robber barons, Republicans, and, of course, blacks. His straightforward, often harsh remarks made the paper a popular one. Other papers quoted Vardaman's editorials often, and his paid circulation grew quickly. As his popularity and notoriety rose, so did his political prospects. In 1903, after years of fighting over the issue, the state Democratic party finally switched to a primary election for statewide offices. At last Vardaman's popularity among the common white man seemed about to pay off.

The campaign for the 1903 election began more than a year before the primary, and Vardaman was one of the first to announce his candidacy again for governor. The central theme again was the futility of funding black education. Over the previous ten years this theme repeatedly proved its popularity on the campaign stump, and Vardaman rode the issue hard. His other issues all revolved around progressive reforms to the state's political and economic system. Many of his positions contradicted votes and pronouncements he made as a legislator earlier in his career. His opponents for the Democratic nomination repeatedly pointed to these contradictions, but many Mississippians had moved politically the same way as Vardaman over the previous ten years. They did not see these past votes as problematic.

Whatever questions were raised in voters' minds about his political transformation on reform were overshadowed by his appeal to their racism. In
the end, white supremacy trumped everything.

Vardaman effectively framed the debate in 1903. It became an issue of how
committed each man was to white supremacy, and how far each was willing
to go to defend and ensure that. Not only did Vardaman want to redistrib-
ute the state education funding so that it favored white counties, he also proposed repealing the Fifteenth Amendment, which gave black men the right
to vote, and severely restricting the Fourteenth Amendment, which guaranteed all people, but especially blacks, equal protection under the law and
due process. These were pure folly, truly impossible goals, but ones his audience loved and cheered wildly when he announced them. With the debate
framed, his opponents struggled to match him on the race issue. Here was a
man willing to battle the federal government and the rest of the nation in order to ensure white supremacy. Anything less made one's commitment to
white men suspect. Vardaman's state slogan made it clear: "A vote for Vardaman is a vote for white supremacy. . . ."[2]

Vardaman's racist platform found such a receptive audience in 1903 in
part because of the ongoing struggle over the post office in Indianola, Mississippi, which inflamed whites' negrophobia in the state. Mrs. Minnie Cox
was appointed postmistress of Indianola during Republican Benjamin Harrison's administration and was reappointed under William McKinley. Cox
was a college graduate and the wife of a successful businessman. Local
whites initially accepted her in this position. When Theodore Roosevelt appointed a white Democrat to oversee his patronage appointments, locals expected all the federal positions to revert to whites. Roosevelt had no intention of replacing blacks with white Democrats, but locals in Indianola began
a movement to remove Cox. They framed their opposition to her not in par-
tisan terms, but in racial ones, warning of the threat of black officeholders,
the desire of blacks to dominate whites, and the insult of white women asking a black woman for their mail. Momentum grew, and Vardaman took up
the issue in his paper in 1902 and on the campaign trail the next year. Pressure became so great on Cox that she resigned at the start of 1903, and she
and her husband fled the state. In retaliation, Roosevelt ordered the Indianola post office closed. This action caused the issue to explode statewide as
whites raged against Roosevelt's support of a black woman against the
wishes of the white citizens.

It was against this background of whites struggling to dominate blacks
and Mississippi's struggle with the Republican-dominated federal government that Vardaman's campaign gained such traction. He was not alone. His
cousin Hernando Money ran for the United States Senate that year. A conservative politically, and a moderate on race issues through his twenty-plus-
year career, in 1903 Money adopted a platform of white supremacy that mirrored Vardaman's. Again, Vardaman's views on white supremacy did not

stand out or indeed lead the white voters of Mississippi. What distinguished Vardaman was his commitment to these views, and his aggressive and bold pronunciations of them at every opportunity.

Money easily won the Democratic nomination, which ensured his election by the legislature to the U.S. Senate. Vardaman came in first in a crowded field but did not win a majority, leading to a runoff. During the few weeks leading up to the runoff, the rhetoric became more intense. Vardaman's opponent denounced his racism as dangerous and his platform of limiting school funding, repealing the Fifteenth Amendment, and modifying the Fourteenth Amendment unobtainable. Vardaman simply stepped up his racist appeals. In the end, he won a narrow 6,000-vote victory out of 96,000 votes cast.

Vardaman effectively led a coalition of white farmers, progressives, and racists to victory in 1903. A number of factors combined to bring Vardaman victory beyond his overt appeal to white supremacy. They included a pent-up frustration with the small group of wealthy men who ran the state government. There was a widespread feeling of wanting to turn all the old politicians out and bring in someone new. Vardaman represented that fresh start. He also rode the tide demanding political reform, from electing the state judges to cleaning up the corrupt prison system. Finally, Vardaman's own personal magnetism helped him win this election. His striking long black hair, often offset by a white suit, his booming voice, his easy nature with people, his quick wit—all of these traits played well with the mass audiences he spoke before in town and court squares throughout Mississippi. In the first election in which Mississippi voters got to pick their candidates, Vardaman presented a man who looked, acted, and spoke like a leader. His overjoyed supporters chartered trains that brought hundreds of men to Greenwood who marched about the town and celebrated Vardaman's victory as their victory.

Vardaman's four-year term as governor was generally a success. He got many of his reform programs through the legislature, most importantly an overhaul of the prison system that included an end to convict leasing. He proved himself an able administrator. On many of his anti-black programs, he found himself forced to backtrack. He made no progress on attacking the Fourteenth and Fifteenth Amendments, and he gave up on his plan to divide school funding according to how each race paid into the fund. This did not mean he stepped away from his rhetoric of negrophobia. The governor took every chance to discuss the black race as the single greatest threat facing the United States. To help establish this view, he publicly discussed every violent crime committed by an African American, especially rapes of white women.

Many racial moderates, who were just as committed to white supremacy but believed in more moderate rhetoric, feared Vardaman's strident language would spark an upsurge in white attacks on blacks. In the weeks just after his inauguration, there was an upsurge in violence, and Vardaman moved quickly to end this extralegal violence. Nine times over the course of his administration, he intervened to stop mobs from lynching an accused black man. Twice he made direct appeals to the mobs himself. He also hired the Pinkerton Detective Agency to investigate the Whitecaps in the southern part of the state. These men, akin to the Klu Klux Klan, were terrorizing and murdering blacks in Lincoln and Franklin counties. Vardaman pushed the investigation and saw several men brought to trial for murder. In the end, the groups were smashed. Overall, whites' attacks on blacks subsided during his term.

In 1905, Senator Money announced that he would not seek reelection in 1907. Almost immediately, Vardaman jumped into the race. Throughout 1906 Vardaman campaigned for the nomination. Again, traveling throughout the state, Vardaman deepened his ties to the small farmers. His rhetoric gave voice to the small farmers' hopes of economic and political reform, and to their desire for racial supremacy if nothing else. He lost a close nomination race by only slightly more than one thousand votes. While he did not move on to the Senate, it clearly established his popularity with the common man and as a force in Mississippi politics.

After his term as governor ended in January of 1908, he settled his family in Jackson. He returned to editing, this time with a paper called *The Issue*. It did not provide so much news as a platform for Vardaman to remain in the public eye. It acted more as a magazine of opinion, publishing articles on progressive reform and white supremacy. In an era when white supremacy publications appeared on every corner, *The Issue* stood out for its aggressive attacks on any hint of black equality. Vardaman also began touring the country as an orator, perhaps his greatest skill. Over the next few years, his speaking tours provided most of the family's income.

Vardaman developed a well-thought-out speech that he called "The Impending Crisis," which he delivered throughout the South, the Southwest, the Midwest, and the Great Plains states. In it he argued that black and white children shared equal mental abilities from birth up until puberty. At that time, while white children's minds continued to develop, black mental growth halted. Thus, advanced education for blacks wasted time and money. In addition, he believe that blacks lacked an innate, natural sense of right and wrong, leading naturally to their criminal nature. To allow political and social equality for African Americans would, in his view, lead to the intermarriage of blacks and whites, with the degradation of the white race. This miscegenation would cause a decline in the intellectual activity and progress that made the United States such a great nation. This was the impending crisis that Vardaman wanted to prevent. To do so, he believed in the total destruction of any hope for political and social equality between the races. Only the repeal of the Fourteenth and Fifteenth Amendments could ensure this. His continuous bookings throughout large parts of the country between

1908 and 1916 demonstrate both the appeal of this message and Vardaman's ability as an orator.

But Vardaman wanted to be a politician, and in 1910 another Senate seat opened up. The sitting senator, Anselm McLaurin, died suddenly in office in December of 1909. Vardaman was an unshakable foe of McLaurin and had intended to run against him in 1911. The struggle to fill the remainder of the term pitted Vardaman against a broad anti-Vardaman faction. The opposition to Vardaman disliked him for a number of reasons. His populism offended conservatives, he lacked the formal education needed for the highest body in the nation, men disliked him for both personal and political reasons, and many were offended by his racial pronouncements.

Those who objected to Vardaman's brash and open attacks on blacks rejected them not because the objectors supported black equality, but because they believed he used the attacks simply to bolster his own political career. They argued that black equality, particularly in the South, was an impossibility. Vardaman's rhetoric constituted a cheap political trick that bolstered his position while encouraging violent attacks on blacks by whites. Worse, they feared that his white-hot verbal attacks on blacks would provoke a backlash by Northern whites, which might better the position of blacks in Southern society. For these men, continuing quiet disfranchisement and segregation were the best policies to ensure white supremacy.

It fell to the state legislature to fill the remainder of McLaurin's term. The anti-Vardaman opposition put forward a number of candidates in order to muddy the field so badly that no one could get a majority until they could find a candidate who could defeat Vardaman. For two months the legislature debated the issue before LeRoy Percy emerged as the consensus candidate. Percy defeated Vardaman in the final tally by a mere five votes. Immediately Vardaman's supporters cried foul and began making charges of bribery. Both chambers of the legislature investigated the bribery charges but took no action, so the charges hung in the air and dominated the run-up to the primary in 1911 for the full Senate term.

Just as the debate over the black postmistress of Indianola created the atmosphere that allowed Vardaman to sweep to the governorship, now the scandal over Percy's appointment opened the door for him to move into the Senate. In this election, however, class dominated the debate. Percy was a wealthy planter from the Delta. Well educated, but not charming, he represented to many voters the elite of the state. The widespread belief that he got his Senate seat through a conspiracy of the state's corrupt elite determined to stop the people's champion, Vardaman, only further weakened Percy's position. Vardaman exploited his ability to connect with the common man. In this race, his humble beginnings and his lack of a formal education became his greatest asset.

Percy faced hecklers at every campaign stop. At one stop, in frustration he called the crowd "cattle." Vardaman's supporters seized on this insult and made it their own. Throughout the state, Vardaman supporters proudly declared themselves cattle, rednecks, and hillbillies as the class divisions between whites in Mississippi became the driving force in the election. The racism that dominated Vardaman's previous elections fell to the side. During this campaign, Vardaman appeared only in a white suit. His supporters soon began calling him "the White Chief." The nickname stuck. When the vote came, Vardaman defeated Percy by more than fifty thousand votes, and every supporter of Vardaman running for state office won.

In a huge celebration in Jackson, the state capital, immediately following the vote, thousands of Vardaman supporters wore red neckties and red bandanas. This election marked the peak of Vardaman's popularity and power. The size of the victory shocked many in Mississippi and folks around the nation, most of whom knew Vardaman only from his racist pronouncements. Vardaman rode this huge victory to his seat in the Senate.

In the Senate, Vardaman showed himself to be an aggressive champion of the little man. He supported a wide range of progressive causes, from the income tax to child labor laws to women's suffrage. His drive to restrict blacks to inferior positions also reappeared openly and aggressively. Vardaman supported President Woodrow Wilson's effort to segregate all federal workplaces. He also spoke openly about his desire to disfranchise blacks throughout the nation. His efforts to repeal the two constitutional amendments went nowhere, but he continued to speak out. Even in a nation full of outspoken racists, as the United States was in these years, Vardaman stood out. Vardaman was fully in step with white attitudes, but his voice remained one of the most open and vocal on this issue.

Vardaman's downfall was not his racial positions. It was the coming of the First World War. As the United States slowly found itself being dragged into the European war, Vardaman opposed all of President Wilson's proposals to prepare the nation for war. Vardaman held to the progressive viewpoint that the arms manufacturers and the banks created wars in an effort to drive up their profits. As war fever gripped the nation and Mississippi, Vardaman steadfastly refused to back down from his principle. His popularity shrank. When a special session of Congress was called to declare war on Germany, a friend warned Vardaman that voting against the war would cost him the 1918 election. Vardaman refused to change his position. He was one of only six senators to vote against the war in April of 1917.

In the 1918 election, Vardaman ran a disorganized campaign. His own ill health and the need to be in Washington for congressional meetings also hampered his reelection effort. His opponent, Congressman Pat Harrison, defined the election as a choice between support of President Wilson and the war or Vardaman. Throughout the campaign, Vardaman struggled to run on his record of support for the common man. But he faced hostile crowds for the first time in his career. In several towns he found his speaker's platform painted yellow. Vardaman returned to the issue that worked so well in the past, blatant racist appeals. He warned of the dangers the black men fighting in Europe would pose when they returned home, the demands for equality they would make, and the feelings of equality they were learning in Europe. But even this did not change the public debate. The war remained the only issue on the public's mind.

Vardaman lost the election by twelve thousand votes. Just six years after reaching the peak of his power, he found himself out of office, his seemingly insurmountable popularity shattered. He came back to Jackson and again began editing a weekly paper. He ran for the Senate again in 1922 and made a good showing, leading in the first round of voting. But he failed to win a majority, and in the runoff he lost. This ended his political and public careers. Shortly thereafter, he and his wife moved to Birmingham to live with their daughters. His only income came from his Spanish-American War pension. On June 25, 1930, after a long decline of several months, James Vardaman died.

On June 26, newspapers around the country announced the death of a former Mississippi senator. The obituaries called him a fighter, a "picturesque political figure," the "White Chief." Few mentioned his virulent racism directly. The *Birmingham News* called him a forceful character who "attracted the attention of the entire nation by some of his utterances and activities." The paper mentioned the numerous progressive reforms he helped enact and even mentioned the origins of his nickname, his white suit, and the long black hair. There was no mention of his racial positions at all.[3] The *New York Times* headline led with his vote against the war with Germany. It did mention his racial views, but only to say they were often inaccurately reported. While Vardaman would not discuss political or social equality, he did see lynchings decrease while he was governor, and "it is said that all Negroes who knew him admired him."[4] The easy acceptance of Vardaman's racial rhetoric by obituary writers in 1930 demonstrates that he was not out of step with the bulk of public opinion even at that late date. At the time of his death, Vardaman was remembered for his actions opposing the war and his work for the common man.

Today Vardaman's views on race are so far out of the mainstream that they define his legacy. A modern judgment on Vardaman certainly cannot overlook his aggressive racism. To most his rabid race-baiting is repulsive. Indeed, he should be vilified for stirring up hatred among any groups of people. But a historian should attempt to take a dispassionate view of the past and attempt to judge people against the context of the times in which they lived. This means that while his racism should be discussed and recognized, it should not completely overshadow the positive accomplishments that he achieved as a champion of the little guy. In truth, Vardaman was a complicated man. He fought hard for the small farmers and the working man against the larger planters and corporate titans. He worked tirelessly throughout much of his life to promote the common good. His commitment to white supremacy was an integral part of both his thinking and his political success. For a man committed to such forward-thinking polices as banning child labor and reforming prisons to hold such outright racist views is difficult to understand from a modern perspective. What it reflects and teaches us today is as much about how complicated human beings are as it is about how deeply committed to racial superiority all of white America was at the turn of the century. Few challenged what Vardaman said on race, or the positions he took. Certainly no one in Mississippi thought he was wrong in his views. All whites agreed on white superiority and black inferiority. Instead his opponents argued against his aggressiveness and his rabid rhetoric. James Vardaman was a radical in his progressive politics and his rhetoric of white supremacy. While his political views were often out of step with many white Americans, his views on race were notable only for the aggressive language and emotion he used to express them.

NOTES

1. William F. Holmes, *The White Chief: James Kimble Vardaman* (Baton Rouge: Louisiana State University Press, 1970), 34.
2. Holmes, *The White Chief*, 105.
3. *Birmingham News*, June 26, 1930, 1.
4. *New York Times*, June 26, 1930, 23.

SUGGESTED READING

Holmes, William F. *The White Chief: James Kimble Vardaman*. Baton Rouge: Louisiana State University Press, 1970.

McMillen, Neil. *Dark Journey: Black Mississippians in the Age of Jim Crow*. Chicago and Urbana: University of Illinois Press, 1990.

Strickland, William M. "James Kimble Vardaman: Manipulation Through Myths in Mississippi." In *The Oratory of Southern Demagogues*, edited by Cal M. Logue and Howard Dorgan. Baton Rouge: Louisiana State University Press, 1981.

II

&

SHOULD WE STAY OR SHOULD WE GO?

4

&

Ida B. Wells:
Higher Law and
Community Justice

Christopher Waldrep

As an African American and a woman, Ida B. Wells had two formidable liabilities that prevented access to the domain of white males in the Gilded Age South. She further underscored her exclusion by directly challenging the Southern legal establishment. Born a slave in 1862, Wells lost her parents to yellow fever when she was fourteen but managed to finish her education and become a schoolteacher in Tennessee. On a trip to Memphis in 1883 she was ejected from the "ladies'" passenger car, which the railroad company reserved for whites only. Wells sued and lost on appeal to the Tennessee Supreme Court, which was loaded with former Confederates.

Embittered by her treatment in court, Wells inaugurated a campaign confronting the system that had denied her justice. Her greatest passion was the elimination of lynching, the most radical means of maintaining the South's caste system. Crusading to eradicate this evil, she challenged the mythology that black men frequently raped white women.

When Gilded Age journalist Ida B. Wells launched her crusade against Southern lynching, she took on a tradition hundreds of years old. Long before the beginnings of American history, rioters had used violence to defend community values. The most sophisticated articulation of this "doctrine of vigilance" came in 1887 when historian Hubert Howe Bancroft defined law as the will of the community as a whole, the voice of the people. Bancroft did not define community, but he must have meant a neighborhood of shared values within a limited geographic space where residents had reached consensus on law and justice, right and wrong. According to Bancroft, a lynching really represented the ultimate provincial assertion that a small group of neighbors can best set the bounds of moral conduct without guidance from the broader polity or a higher authority. Many white people shared Bancroft's views.

Wells's campaign against lynching, then, amounted to an attack on ideas firmly entrenched in nineteenth-century white constitutionalism, an ethic of decentralized government. She began her career committed to the ideal of a higher law at a time when whites reiterated their dedication to local sovereignty. Wells's campaign against lynching coincided with her realization that she could not realistically expect whites to apply a color-blind law to race relations. Indeed, nearly a century of research into the workings of law shows that this expectation was hopelessly naive. A wide variety of social, economic, and political forces shape lawmaking and law enforcement. But the fictions societies choose to believe do influence governing. Mythology is the vehicle by which citizens learn the values and beliefs that inform the allocation of power and distribution of rights. Myths preserve and present the collective ideology in a narrative form. For a time, Wells favored a particular myth about law, one that she hoped would make a truly biracial society possible. Her insight that neutrally enforced law was an impossibility changed her life. She began to favor self-help for African Americans over preparation for life in an integrated society. But she never ceased to attack localism.

In 1862, when Wells was born a slave in Holly Springs, Mississippi, white Southerners mythologized law as truly neutral. The common law, one judge insisted, "is not the result of the wisdom of any one man or society of men, in any one age, but of the wisdom and experience of many ages of wise and discreet men."[1] At the same time Southern whites paid homage to higher law, they also believed that states and neighborhoods were best suited to interpreting and enforcing that law. Many also believed that throughout history republics thrived when they governed only a small territory such as a state or a county. Only in a limited space could neighbors build the consensus necessary to set boundaries between right and wrong. At its most extreme, this rhetoric of popular sovereignty could mutate into a justification for vigilantes and lynch mobs. When mobs formed they inevitably claimed to speak for the whole people. American revolutionaries took to the streets against British authority, insisting they represented the people against a government no longer legitimate.

In the 1850s, San Francisco lynchers claimed to act for the people in place of an impotent government. Their partisans insisted the people had the right and the duty to maintain a perpetual vigil over anything related to their own governance. When the servants of the people proved unfaithful, the people were obliged to "rise in their sovereign privilege" and overthrow their governors.[2] Since a vigilance committee acted for the people, it could not act unlawfully; to the contrary, it was acting in accordance with the "true" law.

Wells's challenge to this localism followed the Civil War, emancipation, and Reconstruction. Abraham Lincoln had found within the Constitution precepts that expanded national power. His party passed laws local-minded Democrats had thwarted for years, including laws providing for a national income tax, a central bank, federal support for a transcontinental railroad, and the abolition of slavery. The United States ended slavery with the 1865 Thirteenth Amendment and then enacted the Civil Rights Act of 1866. These measures challenged the states' powers. The 1866 law defined national citizenship for the first time and articulated the rights associated with that citizenship. Two years later the principles legislated in the 1866 Civil Rights Act became part of the Constitution as the Fourteenth Amendment. Republicans espoused a new nationalism, one that promised to define and defend the rights of American citizens.

Laws passed to protect the rights of black citizens reached even the little Mississippi village of Holly Springs, where Ida B. Wells began life. Holly Springs had a population of just three thousand, of which slaves had made up one-third. Wells's parents were artisans and had enjoyed that degree of independence common to slaves who had advanced skills. Wells's father, Jim, was a carpenter, the son of his master and a slave woman named Peggy. Jim's owner and father never put his son on the auction block; Wells wrote that her father did not know the worst horrors of slavery. Wells's mother, Elizabeth Warrenton, by contrast, had been sold and resold and had lost track of her original family. Like her husband, she had a skill prized by Holly Springs whites. Wells later described her mother as a famous cook.

The independence that Wells's parents enjoyed as slaves probably encouraged them to assert themselves after emancipation. But Reconstruction also encouraged Wells's father to claim political rights that he believed were guaranteed by the federal government; he refused to vote Democratic even when pressed to do so by his white employer. Jim Wells followed his political aspirations until he was cut down by a yellow fever epidemic. His wife died at the same time.

News of her parents' deaths reached Wells at Shaw University, now known as Rust College. She wanted to rush to the side of her six sisters and brothers, now orphans, but friends urged her not to set foot in disease-ridden Holly Springs. No passenger trains ran because no one wanted to go into a town ravaged by yellow fever. Wells, though, demonstrated the determination and stalwart courage for which she later became famous. Only fourteen years old, she took a freight train into Holly Springs and helped nurse her family. After the epidemic abated, Wells insisted on keeping her siblings together, finding work as a schoolteacher to support them.

Like most African Americans in the years after the Civil War, Wells embraced the notion of national citizenship rights. In this era, African Americans

*Ida B. Wells, c. 1917 (Image courtesy of the Special Collections Research Center,
University of Chicago Library.)*

used whites' own universal-rights discourse to make demands. They de-
ployed patriotic icons and quoted the Declaration of Independence. They
wanted to participate in a society administered by laws enforced fairly. Wells
condemned the racial segregation enforced by local authorities as a sin and
aimed harsh criticism at those African Americans "tacitly conniving at it by
assenting to their caste arrangements."[3] In an article published in 1886 she exhorted black schoolteachers to cultivate strong character in their students.

With a noble character marked by "quiet deportment and manly indepen-dence," blacks could hope to "convince the world that worth and not color made the man."[4] In an article published a year later, Wells lashed out at African Americans willing to accept separate fraternal lodges and labor or-ganizations. In these early writings, Wells envisioned a color-neutral, if not color-blind, society.

Wells understood that law had to be the backbone of such a society. In her diary, she recorded that she "firmly believed" that the law would protect her rights.[5] Whites had relied on race to allocate resources and maintain order; blacks such as Wells wanted to substitute law. In 1875, Congress enacted a new civil rights law requiring that "all persons within the jurisdiction of the United States shall be entitled to the full and equal enjoyment of the accom-modations, advantages, facilities, and privileges of inns, public conveyances on land or water, theaters, and other places of public amusement."[6] The statute represented an attempt by Congress to throw out old informal neigh-borhood rules and patriarchies, creating a new society ruled by abstract, na-tional standards.

Southern whites did what they could to thwart congressional efforts to end discrimination. In Tennessee, the legislature tried to forestall state suits inspired by the 1875 civil rights law by abolishing the common-law right of victims of discrimination to sue. The new statute gave proprietors of public facilities "perfect and complete" power to exclude persons from their estab-lishments. After passage of this law, the railroads routinely charged blacks first-class fares but assigned them seats in shabby smoking cars. On some trains baggage cars doubled as smoking cars. In these cars, blacks and whites mingled, and conductors made no effort to control foul language and drinking.

In Tennessee, African American voters put into office legislators they thought would support laws protecting their rights. The four African Amer-icans serving in the Tennessee state legislature in 1881 vigorously fought against racial discrimination. Thomas A. Sykes urged repeal of the 1875 state statute. Newspapers praised Sykes as "a fluent speaker," and he adroitly steered his controversial bill into the legislature, where it lost only narrowly, 31–29.

Beaten on that front, Tennessee blacks tried another approach. State rep-resentative Isaac F. Norris proposed a ban on racial discrimination by rail-roads, but white lawmakers prevented his bill from coming to a vote. In-stead, the legislature considered a compromise measure requiring separate but equal facilities for the races on railroad cars. Though a far cry from what blacks had proposed and though intended to guarantee segregation, the compromise bill was an effort to impose a statewide legal standard on local practices. Discrimination varied from railroad to railroad, and propo-nents of the bill claimed it would "clarify a rather confused legal situa-tion."[7] Black legislators cast the only votes against the bill, which was passed by an overwhelming majority. The law mattered little, though, because railroads ignored it.

Railroad companies sometimes called their first-class coaches "ladies' cars." Gentlemen rode with their ladies in these cars. Lower-class men and blacks of both genders rode the integrated cars. White Victorians regarded African American females not as "ladies" but as "women" and, as such, easily shunted them into less-well-supervised second-class cars. Several courts had upheld this practice, ruling that railroad companies had considerable power to seat passengers where they wished.

In 1880 a black correspondent for the *New York Age* reported that trains serving Nashville segregated passengers by race. The next year blacks challenged segregation by purchasing first-class tickets and sitting in the first-class cars reserved for whites. The railroad companies feared the courts might rule against them and played a game of cat and mouse with protesters. On one train the railroad moved all the white passengers from the first-class car to another car and locked the doors. On another train the company steered whites onto a car normally reserved for blacks to avoid seating them with early-arriving black passengers. In none of these incidents did the company have the nerve to forcibly remove blacks from seats reserved for whites.

The railroads understood that the courts had given them considerable authority to police their own trains, but this authority had limits. State supreme courts agreed that the railroads had a duty to enforce order and maintain peace on their cars, and separating the races was a reasonable way to do so. The state courts could overrule unreasonable regulations or the caprice of railway employees, but the duty of maintaining order lay with the company. And maintaining order meant segregated facilities. The state supreme court in Pennsylvania showed itself almost obsessed with maintaining the boundary between black and white Americans. "From social amalgamation," the judges warned, "it is but a step to illicit intercourse, and but another to intermarriage."[8]

On September 15, 1883, Wells, now twenty-one years old, traveled by train from Memphis to Shelby County, Tennessee, where she had a teaching job. The train she rode had three cars: a baggage car behind the train engine and two first-class cars, one for black men and women and white male passengers and one for whites only. Since the train company switched the cars, using one car for blacks and whites on one trip and the same car for whites only the next, the two cars offered equal physical accommodations.

But a rougher class of people rode in the mixed car. As Wells boarded the train, she glimpsed a drunken man among the passengers on the integrated car and boarded the ladies' car, as she had done before without incident. When the conductor found Wells riding in the ladies' car, he told her she would have to ride in the mixed car. Wells refused, and the conductor tried to physically drag her from her seat. She still refused to go, biting the conductor on the hand, bracing her feet against the seat in front, and gripping the seat behind. It took three men to eject her from the car. Whites in the car stood on their seats to watch the show and applauded when the trainmen finally succeeded in removing her.

Wells hired a lawyer and sued the railroad. Under the Civil Rights Act of 1875 she could have gone to federal court and claimed the railroad had violated her Fourteenth Amendment rights. Starting in 1873, however, the Supreme Court had begun to restore the localism prevalent before the Civil War. The Court declared that the Civil War amendments had only a limited purpose, the "freedom of the slave race." The justices warned that shifting the power to protect citizens' rights from the states to the federal government threatened to bring "the entire domain of civil rights" into the federal courts.[9] This the Supreme Court refused to do. A decade later the Court remained steadfast in its determination to protect the powers of the states over their citizens. In the *Civil Rights Cases*, the Supreme Court declared portions of the 1875 equal rights law unconstitutional. There came a time, the Court declared in one callous passage, when former slaves had to join the ranks of mere citizens "and cease to be the special favorites of the law."[10]

Even with no federal help forthcoming, Tennessee state law looked promising. Wells's lawyer must have advised her that in 1881 the Tennessee legislature had charged that railroad companies habitually collected first-class fares from blacks and then relegated them to second-class smoking cars. The legislature required railroad companies to furnish truly first-class accommodations for African American purchasers of first-class tickets. The next year the legislature amended the 1881 law, toughening its provisions. The new law declared that all purchasers of first-class railway tickets "shall be entitled to enter and occupy first-class passenger cars."[11]

Wells testified at the trial on her suit, describing her aborted attempt to ride ten miles from Memphis to Woodstock station. Her attorney called four black men as witnesses on her behalf. Three identified themselves as passengers in the integrated passenger car, and two reported they had themselves smoked in this car. G. H. Clowers and Silas Kerney both agreed that this car, where they had seen others also smoking and some people drunk, was not a "fit place for a Lady."[12]

The railroad also produced four witnesses. Conductor William Murry said the two cars offered truly equal accommodations. The railroad had made a rule, Murry explained to the court, that only "white Ladies and Gentlemen" could ride in the rear car on the train. This rule pleased most passengers, Murry claimed, and avoided "unpleasant associations and antagonism of race." Murry described Wells's resistance much as she did, admitting he "got the worst of it," bleeding freely where Wells had bitten him. Contrary to Wells's witnesses, Murry insisted that no one had smoked in the first, integrated passenger car. If anyone had done so, Murry claimed, he would have stopped it. Nor had he seen any rowdy or drunken behavior in that car. The only two drunken men on the train had been in the rear car. The other three witnesses uniformly agreed that Murry strictly enforced the rule against smoking in the integrated car. But these witnesses for the railroad supported Wells's claim in critical ways. Dr. J. E. Blades, a regular rider of the train to Memphis, agreed that Murry did not allow smoking in the forward car, but he conceded that smoking nonetheless occurred. Dick Moody, a porter on the train, further undermined the railroad's case by describing the forward coach as the "second class car" and not equal to the whites' "first class car." With its own witnesses conceding pivotal points to Wells, the railroad, not surprisingly, lost its case, and the judge awarded Wells $200.

When the railroad company appealed to the state supreme court, Wells's lawyer used soaring rhetoric to insist that law should be above racist appeals. Her chief attorney, a white Shelby County judge originally from Holly Springs, Mississippi, named James Greer, insisted the railroad had failed to offer equal accommodations. Even the conductor's testimony indicated passengers in the forward car smoked, he reasoned, since the conductor said he repeatedly enforced the no-smoking rule. Greer reminded the justices that the railroad's own witnesses had described the forward passenger car as "second class." Greer described Wells as "decent, well educated" and called the act of throwing her off the train "monstrous." He denounced racial prejudice: "Waves of passion break against the doors of the temple of justice," he orated. He called race prejudice enforced by law "a startling proposition" and urged the court away from such a course.[13]

Wells and her attorneys faced a phalanx of former Confederates on the high court. Chief Justice Peter Turney had so enthusiastically supported secession that he raised the first Confederate regiment in Tennessee, acting even before his state had seceded. The rest of the judges had similar backgrounds. Horace Harmon Lurton served in Morgan's Cavalry, riding with the famed raider into Ohio. He was an uninspired thinker known chiefly for his hostility to foreign immigrants and any threat to states' rights. (Lurton nonetheless befriended William Howard Taft, and in 1909, Taft appointed Lurton to the U.S. Supreme Court.) William C. Folkes had been seriously wounded at the first battle at Manassas but had returned to the Confederate army anyway, losing a foot in a later battle. Even without his foot, Folkes continued his service in the army throughout the war. David Lafayette Snodgrass and Waller Cochran Caldwell had missed Confederate service only because they were children when the Civil War started.

The Tennessee supreme court found against Wells. Ignoring the conductor's testimony that his fight with Wells left him scratched, bitten, and bloody, Tennessee's highest court insisted Wells had been "politely assisted from the car by a colored porter." The court further ignored the rough behavior of passengers in the forward car, writing that the front car differed not at all from the rear car, as the railroad had furnished and equipped the cars identically. Ignoring the railroad's own witnesses, the court said Wells's testimony of having seen a person smoking in the front car had been contradicted by another witness. "We know of no rule," the justices concluded, "that requires railroad companies to yield to the disposition of passengers to arbitrarily determine as to the coach in which they take passage."

This defeat challenged Wells's hopes for a truly pluralistic society. Passion had overwhelmed the temples of justice. Wells wrote in her diary that she felt "sorely, bitterly disappointed." She had put her faith in the law, she wrote, and felt "utterly discouraged" and shorn of her confidence in justice through law. The words that follow are telling. Wells wrote that "if it were possible [I] would gather my race in my arms and fly far away with them."[14] Truly higher law independent of political manipulation promised a biracial society; law manipulated by former Confederates meant a racist society dominated by the color line. Wells's train trip to Memphis had turned into a journey that took her away from her faith that white lawyers could be bound by higher law. And Wells understood that without the myth of a higher law in place, a genuinely pluralistic society was not possible. The moment she lost confidence in truly neutral law marks the instant she hardened herself anew to life in a hopelessly segregated society.

Wells did not wait long to act on her new conviction. Seven days after learning of her defeat in court, Wells attended a meeting of the Negro Mutual Protective Association. The idea of a self-help organization came to Wells at a propitious time, just as she reeled from her loss of faith in the law. Organizers urged African Americans to find strength in their own people. Racial unity offered the only protection. The energy of the speakers impressed Wells, and she came away from the meeting "very much enthused."

The Tennessee Supreme Court had thwarted Wells's effort to impose broader-than-local standards on Tennessee railroads, but the case ultimately allowed her to personally transcend locality in new ways. Wells's account of the lawsuit appeared in the religious weekly *Living Way*, and Wells soon purchased a third interest in the Memphis *Free Speech and Headlight*. The railroads gave free passes to journalists, and Wells traveled up and down the Mississippi valley, selling subscriptions. She was determined to make a living from her new occupation. Her travels paid off. Subscriptions to *Free Speech* increased all along the spur of the Illinois Central Railroad in the Mississippi River Delta. For a woman to work as a correspondent and an editor was, Wells wrote later, a "novelty," but she had found her calling.

In the 1880s Wells became a writer. In 1892, Memphis whites directed the focus of her writing by lynching grocers Thomas Moss, Calvin McDowell, and Henry Stewart. Ultimately, the murders of Moss, McDowell, and Stewart changed Wells's identity from journalist to crusader against lynching. Before the lynching, Wells had accepted the idea that although lynching violated law and order, "unreasoning anger over the terrible crime of rape" prompted lynching violence.[15] She probably accepted Victorian stereotypes of gender in which male sexuality had a brutish side. Whereas women lacked passion, men struggled to keep their animal passions under control

and did so only imperfectly. "Perhaps," Wells wrote of male lynching victims, "the brute deserved death anyhow and the mob was justified in taking
his life."[16] But these three grocers had committed no crime against white
women; rather they had been economically successful, Moss owning his
own home. Their deaths challenged Victorian conventions. Rather than a response to male brutishness, their murders seemed a calculated conspiracy to
eliminate economically successful African Americans. Race rather than gender had motivated the lynchers.

Black residents of Memphis responded as a cornered people. Many fled to
Oklahoma. Wells herself advised black Memphis residents to leave Tennessee for the West, quoting Moss as urging his fellow blacks to move west
just before lynchers murdered him. African Americans not leaving Memphis
lashed out at whites with an unprecedented unity. They boycotted the streetcars. The superintendent and treasurer of the City Railway Company came
to Wells's office in hopes she would call on blacks to patronize the streetcars
once again. "The streetcar company had nothing to do with the lynching,"
one of the white men protested. Wells answered, "We have learned that
every white man of any standing in town knew of the plan and consented to
the lynching of our boys. . . . The colored people feel that every white man
in Memphis who consented to his death is as guilty as those who fired the
guns."[17]

Wells responded to the lynching of her friends the grocers by trying to
prove black males no more capable of rape than whites. In May 1892, she
wrote, "Nobody in this section believes the old thread-bare lie that Negro
men assault white women."[18] Wells investigated a series of cases where
whites alleged rape, finding every time that the supposed white female victim had willingly agreed to the liaison. Alice Walker, author of *The Color Pur-
ple*, brilliantly captured Wells's determination to circle the wagons of her
race: Walker imagines Wells urging her to "Deny! Deny! Deny!" that black
men ever raped white women. "It will be used against black men and therefore against us all."[19]

Wells's denials prompted such an angry white reaction that the antilynching crusader considered a move to Oklahoma herself. She clearly could not
go back to Memphis; the Memphis *Commercial Appeal* reprinted her editorial
and called for its author to be lynched. Her friend and fellow journalist
T. Thomas Fortune offered a more appealing option, calling on Wells to
move east instead, and she agreed to at least visit New York. A mob destroyed the Memphis offices of the *Free Speech* on May 27, 1892, while Wells
was en route to New York. She took a position on the *New York Age*.

Wells's work for the *New York Age* taught her that merely putting her story
in print could not sway the communities and neighborhoods where white
lynch mobs found sustenance. Wells published a detailed analysis of lynching in the *New York Age*, documenting instances of white women fabricating
rape charges that led to lynching. In some cases these women felt enough re-

morse to confess what they had done. Wells quoted one woman as admitting "a strange fascination" for her black lover. When neighbors saw him going to her house, "I hoped to save my reputation by telling . . . a deliberate lie."[20] Wells mounted an assault on the myth of white feminine purity, and her publisher was determined to put her words in the face of white America. The *New York Age* printed ten thousand copies of that issue to be distributed across the United States, one thousand copies on the streets of Memphis. The reaction of the Northern press to her explosive revelations disappointed Wells. She had assumed it had remained silent only because it did not have the facts. But after a year of printing her shocking stories in the *New York Age,* Wells could see that whites had given her only "a meager hearing, and the press was dumb."[21]

The key to the door in the wall of white indifference lay not just outside the local white communities supportive of lynchers but outside the United States. The Scottish author Isabelle Fyvie Mayo, outraged by a terrible Texas lynching, offered to pay Wells's passage to England. In some ways Mayo's life paralleled Wells's. Wells had become a writer while teaching; Mayo had become a writer while pursuing secretarial work. Wells broke barriers to become a journalist. Mayo wrote that she had to break through "unnecessary limitations" to escape the "straight groove in which I had been reared." In fact, though, the similarities were mostly superficial. Mayo's parents did not work as servants; they employed them. The "groove" she had escaped was her own bourgeois upbringing. Mayo recalled that the escaped slave her father had employed as a handyman was driven to suicide by the horrors he had experienced. Her memory of the old man who called her "Missie" might have made her more sympathetic to the plight of lynching victims, but there were limits to her sensitivities. She warned her readers against toleration of "female 'easiness of virtue.'" Mothers of illegitimate children, she lectured, must be consigned to the factory or put to work washing clothes. Decent folk should not be exposed to someone "a-wrestling with unruly passions."[22]

Mayo thought that an American denouncing lynching in England would arouse public sentiment in America against extralegal violence. White Americans might ignore Wells's writings in America, but they would find it harder to resist an aroused English public. Americans looked to the English as particularly cultured. If the civilized British denounced lynchers as uncivilized, white Southerners would be embarrassed. For Wells, arousing English indignation must have seemed an opportunity to set a higher legal standard against mob violence. If white judges could not be made to hew to the line of incorruptible law, perhaps a kind of higher law could be established in the popular culture—with the help of the English news media.

Wells sailed for England on April 5, 1893. In England and Scotland she gave lectures and received good notices in the press. When one English citizen asked why British citizens should take an interest in "the local police arrangements" in American towns, Wells penned a reply. "The pulpit and press of our own country remains silent," she wrote. "It is to the religious and moral sentiment of Great Britain we now turn. . . . Americans cannot and will not ignore the voice of a nation that is her superior in civilization."[23]

Wells's visit to England had resulted from an alliance between Mayo and Catherine Impey, an opponent of the caste system in India. It was Impey who had suggested Wells's name to Mayo. The alliance between Wells, Mayo, and Impey ended after Impey wrote a letter declaring her love for a member of a "darker race." In fact, the object of her desire felt no love for Impey and turned her letter over to a very shocked Mayo. When Wells would not join Mayo in repudiating Impey, Mayo withdrew her support. Wells went home.

This reversal did not end Wells's effort to enlist the British in her fight against lynching. In 1894 she returned to England. Whereas her first tour had aroused little press coverage in America, the second attracted all the attention she could have hoped for. By June 23, Wells could report that her lecturing and writing had aroused the South. Georgia's governor had denounced Wells, urging the English to get their facts from a more reputable source. The Memphis *Daily Commercial* attacked Wells's character. "From one end of the United States to the other," Wells wrote, "press and pulpit were stung by the criticism of press and pulpit abroad."[24] Her campaign in England convinced at least some Americans to distance themselves from their earlier toleration of lynching. In her autobiography, Wells would credit English denunciations of American extralegal violence with also shaming American leaders into distancing themselves from lynching.

When whites counterattacked, they charged that Wells had not actually breached the walls that confined African Americans. Temperance leaders such as Frances Willard sought white Southerners' votes to achieve a constitutional amendment prohibiting alcohol, which was allowed in some Southern communities. Her need for white votes may have influenced her position, which like lynching itself remained stubbornly provincial. Willard announced she favored literacy tests to prevent illiterate foreigners and blacks from voting. The ideas of the plantation Negro, Willard declared, "are bounded by the fence of his own field and the price of his own mule."[25] Willard even complained that the presence of blacks trapped white women and children. Menaced by brutal black men, Willard insisted, white women dared not go beyond sight of their own rooflines.

Some feminists feared that Wells's marriage to F. L. Barnett in 1895 would confine her to the sight of her own roofline. Though Wells carried her babies with her when making speeches and lobbying Congress for a federal antilynching law, she did believe she had to put her family ahead of public works. Newspapers criticized her for deserting the cause, and Susan B. Anthony rebuked her for becoming a mother and housewife. At the same time, Wells helped found the Afro-American Council only to be maneuvered out of a leadership role in that organization.

Despite her family obligations, Wells continued her efforts against white racism. In this campaign, she confronted not just white opposition but black provincialism as well. On the Sunday after the 1908 Springfield, Illinois, race riot, she called on her Sunday school class to organize, passionately denouncing blacks' apathy. At first just three members of her church class responded, but Wells pushed ahead, organizing the Negro Fellowship League. In 1909, she again confronted local blacks' indifference after Cairo, Illinois, whites lynched Will "Frog" James for the murder of a white woman. In 1905 the Illinois legislature had enacted a strong law stipulating that when lynchers murdered a prisoner under a sheriff's care, the governor was required to remove that sheriff from office. After the James lynching, the governor of Illinois dutifully removed Sheriff Frank Davis from office. The law also allowed the ousted sheriff to make his case for reinstatement in a hearing before the governor. In Cairo, Wells found that many blacks had written letters to the governor asking that the sheriff be returned to office. Narrow political concerns controlled the thinking of local blacks. As one local African American explained to Wells, the ousted sheriff had been a friend to Cairo blacks and had hired black deputies. His replacement, a Democrat, had turned out all the black deputies. Wells argued that Cairo blacks endangered the lives of blacks all over Illinois by permitting such local concerns to determine their course. She declared that blacks must unite against lynchings in Illinois by repudiating the sheriff, and she succeeded in persuading some Cairo blacks to sign a petition. Traveling to Springfield, she made a powerful speech against the sheriff and countered the petitions he produced with her own resolutions. In the end, the governor agreed with her that Davis could not be reinstated because he had not properly protected his prisoner. Wells had once again triumphed over localism.

The Springfield riot also prompted formation of the National Association for the Advancement of Colored People (NAACP). With some reluctance, organizers called on Wells to lend her support to the association, although her fundamental approach to racial problems differed from its guiding principles. In a 1909 article that articulated the founders' ideas, W. E. B. Du Bois urged that the Negro "problem" not be segregated from other reform movements. Poverty and ignorance represented a "human problem," not a black problem, Du Bois declared. The solution lay in "human methods."[26] Years earlier Wells had been frustrated in her own attempts to surmount race. In her autobiography, she judged the NAACP harshly. It lasted longer than other such movements, she wrote, but fell short of its founders' expectations. Wells blamed the NAACP's troubles on the chair of its executive committee, a white woman named Mary White Ovington. Wells complained that Ovington had experience only in New York City and Brooklyn and lacked the ability to seize situations in a "truly big way."[27] Wells's daughter explained that her mother thought the leadership of the NAACP should be entirely black.

Ida B. Wells lived until 1936. She had broken through gender barriers to make herself an international spokesperson for her race and broken into a career not previously open to women. She defined her life by her ability to transcend geographic boundaries. The end of slavery allowed her to leave her plantation, but she escaped Memphis and the South through her own efforts. Her scheme to attack lynching in America by going to England represented a masterstroke, one that might not have appealed so strongly to someone who did not associate freedom with physical mobility. In England, Wells was able to speak to American whites in a way that she could not in the United States. But for all her work, she never breached the boundary of race. The anguish she expressed after her defeat before the Tennessee Supreme Court shows that she understood the tragic significance of the failure of incorruptible law. Without truly impartial law to referee relations between the races, all she could do was "gather my race in my arms and fly far away with them." Wells abandoned faith both in law and in a truly pluralistic United States, instead concentrating on survival strategies in a hopelessly brutal, segregated society.

NOTES

Thanks to Lynne Curry and Ballard Campbell for their comments on an earlier version of this chapter.

1. *State v. Caesar*, 31 NC 414 (1849).
2. Hubert Howe Bancroft, *Popular Tribunals*, 2 vols. (San Francisco: History Company, 1887), 1:9.
3. Miriam DeCosta-Willis, ed., *The Memphis Diary of Ida B. Wells* (Boston: Beacon Press, 1995), 42.
4. DeCosta-Willis, *Memphis Diary*, 183–87.
5. DeCosta-Willis, *Memphis Diary*, 141; Mildred I. Thompson, *Ida B. Wells-Barnett: An Exploratory Study of an American Black Woman, 1893–1930* (Brooklyn: Carlson Press, 1990), 15.
6. *An Act to Protect All Citizens in Their Constitutional and Legal Rights, U.S. Statutes at Large* 18 (1875): 336.
7. Joseph H. Cartwright, *The Triumph of Jim Crow: Tennessee Race Relations in the 1880s* (Knoxville: University of Tennessee Press, 1976), 104–5.
8. *West Chester and Philadelphia Railroad Company v. Miles*, 55 PA 309 (1867).
9. *Slaughter-House Cases*, 83 US 71, 77 (1873).
10. *Civil Rights Cases*, 109 US 25 (1883).
11. 1881 Tennessee Acts 211; 1882 Tennessee Acts 12.
12. *Chesapeake, Ohio, and Southwestern Railroad Co. v. Ida B. Wells*, West Tennessee 312, 319 (Tennessee State Library and Archives, Nashville). Further quotes from the trial are from this court transcript.
13. *Chesapeake, Ohio, and Southwestern Railroad Company v. Wells*, 85 Tennessee 613 (1887). All further quotations regarding the railroad's appeal are from this source.

14. DeCosta-Willis, *Memphis Diary*, 141.

15. Elizabeth Pleck, *Domestic Tyranny: The Making of Social Policy against Family Violence from Colonial Times to the Present* (New York: Oxford University Press, 1987), 53–54.

16. Ida B. Wells, *Crusade for Justice: The Autobiography of Ida B. Wells*, ed. Alfreda M. Duster (Chicago: University of Chicago Press, 1970), 64.

17. Wells, *Crusade for Justice*, 54–55.

18. Wells's article appeared in pamphlet form as *Southern Horrors: Lynch Law in All Its Phases*. See Trudier Harris, comp., *Selected Works of Ida B. Wells-Barnett* (New York: Oxford University Press, 1991), 17.

19. Alice Walker, "Advancing Luna—and Ida B. Wells," in *You Can't Keep a Good Woman Down* (San Diego: Harcourt Brace Jovanovich, 1981), 94.

20. Ida B. Wells, *Southern Horrors: Lynch Law in All Its Phases*, in Harris, *Selected Works of Ida B. Wells-Barnett*, 20–21.

21. Wells, *Crusade for Justice*, 86.

22. Isabelle Fyvie Mayo, *Recollections: Of What I Saw, What I Lived Through, and What I Learned, during More than Fifty Years of Social and Literary Experience* (London: J. Murray, 1910), 18, 71–115, 271–349.

23. Wells, *Crusade for Justice*, 100–101.

24. Wells, *Crusade for Justice*, 189.

25. Wells, *Crusade for Justice*, 207.

26. Charles Flint Kellogg, *NAACP: A History of the National Association for the Advancement of Colored People* (Baltimore: Johns Hopkins University Press, 1967), 25.

27. Dorothy Sterling, afterword in DeCosta-Willis, *Memphis Diary*, 197; Wells, *Crusade for Justice*, 321–33.

SUGGESTED READING

Ida B. Wells wrote an autobiography that is in print and is the most important source for her life: *Crusade for Justice: The Autobiography of Ida B. Wells*, ed. Alfreda M. Duster (Chicago: University of Chicago Press, 1970). Wells's extant diaries have also been published: Miriam DeCosta-Willis, *The Memphis Diary of Ida B. Wells* (Boston: Beacon Press, 1995). For Wells's writings, see Trudier Harris, comp., *Selected Works of Ida B. Wells-Barnett* (New York: Oxford University Press, 1991), 20–21. In addition, see Mildred I. Thompson, *Ida B. Wells-Barnett: An Exploratory Study of an American Black Woman, 1893–1930* (Brooklyn: Carlson Press, 1990). Linda O. Murry has written Wells's biography: *To Keep Waters Troubled: The Life of Ida B. Wells* (New York: Oxford University Press, 1998). Gail Bederman has analyzed Wells's life in "'Civilization,' the Decline of Middle-Class Manliness, and Ida B. Wells's Antilynching Campaign (1892–94)," *Radical History Review* 52 (1992): 5–24; and also in *Manliness and Civilization: A Cultural History of Gender and Race in the United States, 1880–1917* (Chicago: University of Chicago Press, 1995). For Tennessee race relations generally for the 1880s, see Joseph H. Cartwright, *The Triumph of Jim Crow: Tennessee Race Relations in the 1880s* (Knoxville: University of Tennessee Press, 1976).

5

❧

A. Philip Randolph: Labor and the New Black Politics

Eric Arnesen

Over the course of his long life, black activist A. Philip Randolph participated in and decisively influenced numerous movements for social change in twentieth-century America. A committed socialist and antiwar activist during World War I, he coedited the fiery Messenger *magazine, advancing a radical alternative both to the leading civil rights organization—the National Association for the Advancement of Colored People—and to Marcus Garvey's nationalist Universal Negro Improvement Association. During the 1920s and 1930s he headed the Brotherhood of Sleeping Car Porters and helped it to win both a union representation election and the first contract between a national black union and a major U.S. corporation. As the Brotherhood's president, Randolph contributed to black workers' growing acceptance of unionization in the 1930s and 1940s; by his advocacy of militant protest, he also pushed established black civil rights groups in a more activist direction. He crusaded relentlessly against discrimination in the labor movement and in the labor market. In many ways, Randolph's contributions to twentieth-century black political and social movements constitute a crucial link between an earlier civil rights tradition based in black unions and the broader civil rights tradition of the 1960s.*

Roughly 250,000 Americans gathered on the mall before the Lincoln Memorial in Washington, D.C., on August 28, 1963, in a protest calling for "jobs and freedom." The largest demonstration in American history to that date, the 1963 March on Washington attracted African Americans and whites, civil rights activists, trade unionists, and liberal supporters of black equality. The March subsequently became enshrined in Americans' historical consciousness, and understandably so. After all, Martin Luther King Jr. delivered his memorable "I Have a Dream" speech there, and John Lewis, the impatient young Southern activist, stirred controversy with his "We Are in a Serious Revolution" speech, which presaged the impending splits in the civil rights coalition. Since the 1960s, however, historical memory has only partially preserved the message of the March in the sweeping term "freedom," which embraced the demands for an end to segregation and all forms of Jim Crow, on the one hand, and for genuine equality before the law, on the other. The other half of the March's slogan, "jobs," has been conveniently forgotten.

For some of the organizers, "jobs" and "freedom" were inextricably linked. Also on the stage on that hot August day was the dean of black activism, A. Philip Randolph, for whom the March was the culmination of almost a half century of personal struggle for black equality. In 1961, Randolph had proposed a "Job Rights March and Mobilization" to focus on black unemployment (especially for teenagers), inferior education, and the need for federal solutions to black economic inequality. In 1963, combining the forces of King, the National Association for the Advancement of Colored People (NAACP), the National Urban League, and other civil rights groups, the March organizers broadened the focus to "jobs and freedom." "We are the advance guard of a massive moral revolution," Randolph declared before the assembled crowd. This "civil rights revolution is not confined to the Negro, nor is it confined to civil rights. . . . We know we have no future in a society in which six million black and white people are unemployed and millions live in poverty. . . . We want a free democratic society dedicated to the political, economic and social advancement. . . . It falls to us to demand full employment and to put automation at the service of human needs, not at the service of profits." Ultimately, Randolph's agenda would be only partially realized: the laws against legalized segregation would soon fall, but the broader social democratic vision of economic equality for all Americans would not come to pass.[1]

Asa Philip Randolph was born in Crescent City, Florida, in 1889, almost a quarter century after the nation's Civil War had dealt chattel slavery its death blow. His father, James Randolph, was a minister in the African Methodist Episcopal (AME) church. Unable to support his family on his salary from the New Hope AME Chapel in Jacksonville, which he built himself, James Randolph, together with his wife, Elizabeth Robinson Randolph, cleaned and repaired clothes out of their home and operated a wood-selling business. Young Asa and his older brother, James William Jr., grew up in a household that was short on material possessions but placed great importance on matters educational and spiritual. James and Elizabeth encouraged their boys to read, exposing them to classical literature and the African American religious press. Asa later recalled that his father "drilled into us

A. Philip Randolph (Image courtesy of the Library of Congress Prints and Photographs Division.)

the idea that there was nothing beyond you if you studied to equip yourself for it." His parents also nurtured a firm belief in equality and the possibilities of individual achievement despite racial oppression. By one account, James Randolph did not permit his sons to ride on the city's segregated streetcars or read in the segregated public library. The elder Randolph was "highly racially conscious," teaching his children that "there isn't a single Negro in Jacksonville who has any immunity from persecution by whites," his younger son recollected.[2]

James Randolph was merely teaching his sons the stark realities of life in the American South at the turn of the century and at the same time inculcating a sense of dignity and racial pride. In the late nineteenth and early twentieth centuries, Florida's state legislature and local governments passed innumerable Jim Crow laws mandating the segregation of the races in education, transportation, parks, and other public facilities. "Separate but equal" may have been the claim, but in practice it inevitably meant "separate and unequal" for African Americans. Racial violence also escalated toward the century's end, and changes in Florida's election laws (particularly the cumulative poll tax) effectively disfranchised its black male citizens in 1889. The world Asa grew up in held out few opportunities to African Americans who aspired to more than manual labor. In 1911, several years after graduating from Jacksonville's Cookman Institute, Randolph resolved to leave the South and headed for New York, ostensibly to take a summer job. Two years later, at age twenty-four, he married Lucille Campbell Greene, whose beauty shop business helped support her husband's activities over future years. Randolph made his permanent home in the North, returning to the South only on political organizing and speaking trips.[3]

New York in the 1910s was a dynamic and challenging city that captured Randolph's imagination and allowed him to pursue his intellectual and political interests. While working odd jobs, he took acting and elocution lessons, gave public dramatic readings, and performed in a number of Shakespearean theatrical productions. He also immersed himself in evening courses and lectures at New York's City College, the socialist-leaning Rand School of Social Science, and the New York Public Library, studying economics, sociology, and history. His growing political radicalism was fueled by his classes and reading, the stream of socialists and labor leaders and black activists whose lectures he attended, and his participation in the world of soapbox oratory on the street corners of Harlem. In 1916, Randolph joined the Socialist Party and was ready to step out into the political spotlight as an independent figure in his own right.[4]

In 1917, joining forces with Chandler Owen, Randolph launched the *Messenger*, a monthly journal promoting black equality, labor radicalism, and socialism. In its pages he eloquently and passionately castigated white America for lynchings, peonage, race riots, segregation, the activities of the Ku Klux Klan, and the denial of basic rights to blacks. African American leaders, too, received relentless verbal drubbings as the editors took to task black Republicans for their conservatism and timidity, black civil rights activists such as W. E. B. Du Bois for their moderation, and black racial radicals such as Marcus Garvey for their narrow nationalism. But the *Messenger* did not stop with analyzing the shortcomings of America's racial politics; its pages offered an extended critique of the failings of capitalism. Unemployment, low wages and poverty, corporate antiunionism, workers' lack of basic rights, and the suppression of radical trade unionists by the government received scathing coverage. Accordingly, Randolph urged black workers to unionize, advocated the cooperation of white and black labor, supported the syndicalist (and interracial) Industrial Workers of the World (IWW), and promoted a broader struggle against the nation's political and economic system, which he believed rested upon the subordination of both African Americans and the nation's working class. For his opposition to U.S. involvement in World War I—he and Owen called on blacks to avoid conscription and instead fight to "make America unsafe for hypocrisy"—he was arrested (but not convicted) under the Espionage Act, and the *Messenger* was temporarily banned from the mails. To Justice Department officials, Randolph had become the "most dangerous Negro in America."[5]

However great his passion and eloquence, Randolph still had little to show for his efforts by the early 1920s. Race relations in the United States went from bad to worse following the signing of the armistice ending the war in late 1918; by the summer of 1919 the number of lynchings of blacks had increased, and savage race riots had broken out across the country. The American socialist movement was in sharp retreat, having suffered from substantial governmental repression during the war and from its own internal splits and defections. The American Federation of Labor (AFL) lost most of the new members it had gained during the war and went down to defeat in a series of strikes, large and small, between 1919 and 1923. The radical IWW, which had advocated interracial industrial unionism, lay in shambles, and the AFL's door remained as tightly shut as ever against black members, rendering Randolph's hope of an interracial working-class alliance nothing more than a chimera. Large numbers of black Americans found the message of Garvey's nationalist Universal Negro Improvement Association or the civil rights program of the NAACP more attractive than Randolph's message of socialism, working-class unity, and black equality. The *Messenger* survived but remained plagued by financial problems into the 1920s. Its editor's palpable impatience with the racial status quo and his aggressive pursuit of change reflected and influenced the emergence of a new mood among growing numbers of black Americans, symbolized by the visibility of the so-called New Negro of the World War I years and the 1920s. Yet Randolph remained a public figure without a movement, an exhorter with few followers.

That changed dramatically in 1925, when a small group of veteran Pullman porters approached Randolph about assuming the leadership of a new union, the Brotherhood of Sleeping Car Porters (BSCP). Since 1867 the Pullman Company had provided the long-distance traveling public with railway "palace cars" and luxury service through the employment of a small army of porters, black men whose job it was to keep Pullman sleeping cars clean and well stocked with necessities, lower and raise sleeping berths, shine riders' shoes, and otherwise cater to passengers' every whim. The Pullman Company capitalized on popular white associations of race and servility, for only blacks would be hired as porters (Pullman conductors were another matter: only whites were hired for those supervisory positions). With much of the skilled job market closed to blacks because of their race, portering was for many an attractive alternative. In their communities, porters were often seen as civic pillars and as labor aristocrats. Yet relatively low wages—roughly $27.50 per month for most porters in the early twentieth century—compelled them to work hard for tips. The work was also exhausting: porters had to report to work hours before a train's departure to set up (with no pay); their hours for sleep were few and their sleeping accommodations nonexistent. Whatever the drawbacks, however, black men sought out portering jobs, which held out the opportunity for stable employment and the chance to see much of the country.[6]

Those seeking to unionize Pullman porters in the 1920s had an uphill fight ahead of them. With roughly twelve thousand blacks on its payroll by World War I, the Pullman Company was the single largest employer of black labor in the United States, a fact that neither the company nor its black supporters failed to point out on every occasion. Generous financial donations to black hospitals, YMCAs, churches, and social clubs ensured that many local black leaders would repay Pullman's paternalism by coming to the company's defense and denouncing any challenges to its authority or reputation. The Pullman Employee Representation Plan—a company union—provided a formal mechanism for communicating with or manipulating employees, while a network of spies reported back to company officials any evidence of union sympathy. The porters themselves were in a poor bargaining position: the withdrawal of their services would inconvenience passengers but would in no way stop rail transportation. The question of how to compel the Pullman Company to recognize and bargain with a bona fide union perplexed the newly formed BSCP from its inception until well into the 1930s.[7]

Randolph's reputation as a powerful street speaker, a passionate journalist, and a committed activist made him an attractive choice to the handful of men seeking to build the BSCP. So, too, did his status as an outsider to the Pullman Company; because he was not an employee, managers could not threaten his dismissal as a means of silencing him. Once committed to the cause, Randolph placed the *Messenger* at the porters' disposal, using its pages to criticize the Pullman Company and to make the case for needing a union. Ignoring the porters' high standing in their own communities, Randolph and BSCP organizers portrayed them as virtual slaves forced by low wages to engage in obsequious behavior to solicit tips from whites. The company had deprived the porters of their manhood, they charged; the company union was a farce offering no protections to its workers; the company's sponsorship of performing porters' quartets made porters the "monkeys of the service." The BSCP's goals included union recognition, a "living wage" and shorter hours, compensation for all time actually worked (to eliminate the extensive but unpaid preparatory time), respect for seniority, a legitimate grievance procedure that ensured fairness, and the rehiring of all porters fired for their union activity.[8]

Above all, the quest for racial dignity lay at the heart of the BSCP's campaign for the porters' allegiance. The "old" Pullman porter, Randolph declared, was often an Uncle Tom suffering from a "slave psychology." He would "bow and lick the boots of the company officials"; he was characterized by "fear, fear to think, to speak or to act."[9] The BSCP championed a "new" porter who would stand tall and proud. Porters and maids "have changed," Randolph insisted, just as the "entire Negro race has changed." The new porter's creed was "independence without insolence; courtesy without fawning; service without servility . . . opportunity without alms." Only through organization—and joining the Brotherhood—could Pullman employees put to rest the old porter and ensure the creation of the new.[10]

That proved to be no simple matter. From 1925 to 1935, Randolph and his colleagues fought a difficult battle against the powerful company. Pullman unleashed a barrage of hostile attacks against the fledgling union, relying heavily upon the black ministers, politicians, journalists, and civic leaders it had cultivated over the years to condemn the BSCP for its denunciation of the benevolent Pullman Company. Equally damaging was the company's own crackdown, through the use of spies and informants, involving the harassment and dismissal of declared union supporters. Randolph's efforts to provoke federal intervention on the BSCP's behalf also failed. Under the 1926 Watson-Park Act a presidential emergency board could be created if a railroad union threatened to disrupt interstate commerce. To create such a realistic threat, BSCP members voted to strike, but government officials rightly concluded that a porters' strike would do little to obstruct interstate commerce. Facing an indifferent government, a company prepared to do battle to the end, and a membership that in all likelihood would fail in its challenge, Randolph canceled the threatened strike. The BSCP encountered harsh criticism in the black press, its membership dropped drastically, its financial crisis deepened, and the union was evicted from its New York office in 1933. To many outside observers the Brotherhood appeared essentially dead.[11]

Such travails notwithstanding, the Brotherhood survived. Over the course of the late 1920s and early 1930s it reached out to white liberals and black community and religious leaders, slowly spreading the gospel of black trade unionism. When the BSCP launched its crusade for recognition and dignity in 1925, it had confronted a black elite that was largely, if not entirely, indifferent or hostile to unions. The track record of the AFL and its constituent unions was terrible: they not only refused most black workers membership but effectively kept them out of numerous sectors of the economy as well. Employers, however much they may have discriminated against blacks, nonetheless had one thing to offer that black workers were desperate for—jobs. Black leaders' pro-employer and antiunion tendencies had a long history, predating by several decades Booker T. Washington's turn-of-the-century advice to black workers to eschew unions and ally with

capital. Although working-class African Americans often ignored that advice in practice, elite blacks' coolness to organized labor represented a real
obstacle to union advocates such as Randolph. Nevertheless, the BSCP
leader cultivated NAACP officials, clergymen, and members of the Chicago
Woman's Forum, the Ida B. Wells Club, and other black women's clubs, en-
listing their support in his organizing drive. More than any other single individual, Randolph contributed to the historic shift in opinion of the black
middle class from anti- to pro-union.[12]

It took more than supportive community leaders and activists, however,
to revive the Brotherhood's fortunes. New Deal–era changes in labor law
transformed the playing field and allowed Randolph and the BSCP to compete more effectively against their far more powerful corporate opponent.
The 1934 amendments to the Railway Labor Act cleared the way: railway
workers, Pullman porters included, gained the "right to organize and bargain collectively through representatives of their own choosing . . . free from
the interference, restraint, or coercion of employers of labor, or their agents."
Toward that end, the new National Mediation Board would oversee fair and
free union elections. In June 1935 the BSCP squared off against the Pullman
Porters and Maids Protective Association—ostensibly an independent body
that was in reality the renamed Pullman Employee Representation Plan, the
company union—which attracted some support from older porters opposed
to the Brotherhood. In an election administered by the National Mediation
Board, the BSCP won 5,931 votes to the association's 1,422.[13] Winning legal
union recognition and winning a contract, however, were two different matters. For the next two years the Pullman Company dragged its heels until, in
1937, it finally relented. The unprecedented contract hardly revolutionized
the porters' working lives, but it did ensure basic improvements and constituted, in Randolph's words, "a foundation on which the future of the
porters' well being and a constructive and powerful Brotherhood" could be
built.[14]

The porters' victory, Randolph believed, would reverberate far beyond the
ranks of Pullman employees. "It should serve as one great stimulant to the
organization of Race workers in all industries throughout the country. . . .
The Race has the courage, the spirit and the will to fight for economic freedom and justice like all other workers."[15] Randolph's high profile and the
BSCP's success did, in fact, inspire numerous other black workers to organize. In the railroad industry, two groups of service workers—dining car waiters and station redcaps—unionized in 1936–1937, often with the organizational support of the BSCP. But although Randolph inspired and contributed
to the unionization of many black workers during the Great Depression,
other powerful forces were at work. The rise of the Congress of Industrial
Organizations (CIO) in 1936 profoundly altered the dynamics between black
labor and the union movement. Organized along broad industrial, as opposed to craft, lines—that is, all workers in a given workplace would belong

to the same union—and committed to recruiting with no regard to race or gender, the CIO offered an attractive alternative to the conservative, racist AFL. "Seldom in the world's history has a social movement achieved such speedy and spectacular success" as the CIO, concluded four black railroad union officials in Los Angeles in 1937. Through its "amazing series of organizing successes," the CIO "changed the psychology of the American Labor movement from one of discrimination, segregation and defeatism to a movement of liberality, swayed by [the] principle of democracy giving assurance and victory to all workers irrespective of color, class, or creed." An exaggerated assessment, to be sure, but the statement accurately reflected a new and positive mood on the part of one segment of organized labor, a mood that contributed to the unionization of hundreds of thousands of African American workers in basic industry.[16]

Randolph did what he could to foster the pro-union mood among African American workers. He also aspired to expand the BSCP's jurisdictional scope to make it a union of more than just Pullman porters. With redcaps and dining car workers well ensconced in their own associations and loath to relinquish organizational autonomy, Randolph sought to help several other groups of beleaguered black railroaders, particularly locomotive firemen and porter-brakemen/train porters, who were under siege by influential, all-white railroad unions. But he quickly discovered that he could not duplicate the success of the BSCP. For one thing, many Southern firemen and brakemen remained aloof from his Provisional Committee to Organize Colored Locomotive Firemen, formed in 1941, on account of loyalty to their local organizations and their distrust of both outsiders such as Randolph and the racist AFL with which Randolph's BSCP (though not his Provisional Committee) was affiliated. (It is likely that Randolph's decision against affiliating with the CIO and to keep the BSCP in the AFL—where it hoped to fight the federation's racial policies from within—hurt the porters' organizing prospects.) Randolph also confronted a much stronger set of white foes determined to resist any and all efforts on the part of black workers in the railroad operating trades. With his leadership challenged from many quarters, the BSCP leader expended tremendous organizational energy in sharp but largely fruitless jurisdictional battles that pitted him not only against the independent associations but also against the redcaps' and dining car waiters' unions. His dream of unifying the disparate railroad unions came to naught.[17]

Nevertheless, Randolph did more than inspire and assist black unionists in the 1930s and 1940s; he helped to forge a new kind of labor organization that fused traditional workplace concerns with a civil rights agenda. From its inception the BSCP had insisted that the struggle for a porters' union involved the dignity and manhood of its members.[18] The union also turned outward to community and political affairs, engaging in a wide range of civil rights issues in the 1930s and beyond. When President Herbert Hoover

nominated Judge John J. Parker to the U.S. Supreme Court, the BSCP joined
a coalition of civil rights and labor groups opposed to Parker's confirmation. Their grassroots campaign, stressing Parker's hostility to both African
Americans and organized labor, was successful; Parker was not confirmed.
Members also participated in a wide range of organizations that opposed
Southern poll taxes and supported antilynching legislation; they advocated
laws mandating fair employment and promoted consumer cooperatives;
they sponsored black history week celebrations and labor history classes.
Randolph joined with disaffected NAACP members and other black radicals to establish the National Negro Congress in 1936, bringing together religious, civic, and trade union groups to promote militant grassroots activism. (Randolph served as its president through 1940, when he resigned
over the increasingly dominant role played by Communist Party members;
for much of his life, he was a staunch anticommunist.) By the late 1930s and
early 1940s, Randolph and other BSCP leaders, working in concert with an
emerging "New Crowd" network of black activists, effectively challenged
the older black politics based on patronage and civility and thereby decisively shifted the tone and substance of black protest.[19]

Who is the foremost leader of black Americans? one African American
journalist asked in 1943. "Up to now the name of A. Philip Randolph looms
higher than anyone because of the national fight he is making for the Negroes in time of need."[20] This was no exaggeration. Events during the early
1940s cemented Randolph's position among the nation's most prominent
and important black leaders, one whom government officials had to take
into account when framing their policies toward blacks. A hero to growing
numbers of black Americans and white liberals, Randolph increasingly became a thorn in the side of political leaders who sought to balance blacks' demands for racial equality with white conservatives' demands for the maintenance of the racial status quo. During the tumultuous years of World War
II, maintaining that balance proved increasingly difficult. Ultimately, Randolph found his broader goals sacrificed on the altar of wartime efficiency.

By the early 1940s, the American economy had largely recovered from the
hardships of the Great Depression. The nation's industrial sector geared up
for war production. The new prosperity, however, was not equally enjoyed
by all Americans. Unemployment rates dropped steadily for white workers,
but blacks' access to new jobs lagged far behind. Large numbers of employers refused to hire blacks for anything but menial or unskilled work; few
risked promoting them to skilled positions, even when the supply of labor
was tight; and numerous trade unions remained reluctant to admit blacks or
represent their interests. If employment discrimination was wrong under
normal circumstances, it appeared absurd to many in the context of growing
labor shortages.[21]

Randolph placed the issue squarely and prominently on the national
agenda in January 1941, when he publicly announced the creation of a March

on Washington Movement (MOWM), aimed at ending discrimination both in wartime production and in the armed forces: "If the Negro is shut out of these extensive and intensive changes in industry, labor and business [prompted by the war], the race will be set back over fifty years." His MOWM declaration insisted, "We Loyal Negro American Citizens Demand the Right to Work and Fight for Our Country." To accomplish these ends, Randolph proposed a march of 10,000 African Americans—a number that was shortly inflated to 100,000—on Washington to force the hand of the administration of President Franklin Delano Roosevelt. Thousands would descend on the capital, one black paper predicted. "They will come from the voteless South and the job-less North, united in protest over a way of life which offers neither freedom nor opportunity. They will make articulate the demands of the oppressed people who have been caught in the vise of racial intolerance and economic slavery." If African Americans could not stop discrimination outright, they could, nonetheless, "tear the mask of hypocrisy from America's democracy."[22]

Fearing political embarrassment and potential disorder and violence in the nation's capital, the Roosevelt administration did everything it could to persuade Randolph to cancel the march—to no avail. Finally, determined to stop the march, Roosevelt issued Executive Order 8802 on June 25, 1941, declaring that "there shall be no discrimination in the employment of workers in defense industries or government because of race, creed, color, or national origin." To ensure compliance, he established the Fair Employment Practice Committee (FEPC) to investigate complaints of discrimination. Randolph declared victory and called off the march, promising to use the MOWM as a watchdog and pressure group to make sure the government lived up to its promise.

In the ensuing four years, Randolph and the MOWM had their work cut out for them. Indeed, some march supporters, angered by the decision to cancel the demonstration, believed that Randolph had settled for too little and had squandered an opportunity to press for even greater change. The Roosevelt administration had completely ignored Randolph's demand to end discrimination in the military, and its newly created FEPC possessed few resources and even less real power to compel compliance with Executive Order 8802. Black grassroots activists in and out of the MOWM rallied behind the beleaguered federal agency, expending considerable energy in new battles to preserve its autonomy and to prevent its dismemberment by conservative politicians and government administrators who sharply disagreed with the FEPC's mission. Conferences, pickets, marches, and mass demonstrations in support of civil rights and the FEPC's campaign against employment and union discrimination were regular occurrences in churches, auditoriums, parks, union halls, and streets around the nation during the war. Randolph remained in the headlines, constantly berating the administration for allowing discrimination in defense industries to persist.[23]

Contemporaries and subsequent historians have disagreed as to the effectiveness of the FEPC, but there is general agreement that certain sectors of the economy remained unaffected by its efforts. Investigations and hearings notwithstanding, few unions and employers in the railroad industry or the West Coast shipbuilding industry made more than cosmetic changes, retaining their discriminatory barriers largely intact. After the war, congressional opponents of the beleaguered federal agency cut off its funding. Randolph's new National Council for a Permanent FEPC held rallies and marches and lobbied Congress but failed to accomplish the goal of extending the FEPC's life. Although individual states passed weak fair employment acts, the federal government did not. Under federal law, employment discrimination would, in effect, remain legal until the 1964 Civil Rights Act finally outlawed it.[24]

Randolph, of course, could not be held responsible for the political and moral failures of the Roosevelt administration or congressional opponents of fair employment. It was widely understood that the FEPC was held hostage by much larger and powerful political forces. During and after the war, Randolph maintained a feverish pace in his crusade against discrimination in the military, defense production, government, and any other area of American society where it existed. The U.S. Navy's maintenance of a color line and policy of segregating blacks was an "insult to the race," he declared in 1942. In response to persistent Jim Crowism in the U.S. Treasury Department's office in Chicago's Merchandise Mart, Randolph and the local MOWM picketed the vast building; in 1944 he mobilized an MOWM picket around the Metropolitan Insurance Company's Harlem office over its refusal to employ black insurance agents. Speaking to a Toledo, Ohio, YMCA conference in 1943, Randolph called upon the Christian organization to face racism "courageously" and abolish its segregated YMCA branches for African Americans, for such segregation was "wholly untenable and indefensible." Before a crowd of twelve thousand in Chicago, the BSCP president "hailed Roosevelt as a champion of democracy" but found "democracy in the United States" to be a "miserable failure." Democracy, he declared, cannot continue "with a first-class and a second-class citizenship with one section of the country free to vote and another section disfranchised by the poll tax and white primaries." In Jacksonville, Florida, he denounced police brutality and terrorism in 1944, calling on blacks to "get the fear out of your hearts and protest."[25] For his efforts on so many fronts, Randolph received the NAACP's prestigious Spingarn Medal for the "greatest achievement by a Negro" in 1942 and the Clendenin Award of the Workers Defense League in 1944.[26]

In 1948, as Congress debated the Universal Military Training (UMT) bill, which called for an unprecedented peacetime draft, Randolph raised once again the problem of segregation in the armed forces. Testifying before the Senate Armed Services Committee in March, the BSCP leader pledged himself "to openly counsel, aid and abet, both white and Negro, to quarantine any Jim Crow compulsory system. . . . I personally will advise Negroes to refuse to fight as slaves for a democracy they cannot possess and cannot enjoy."[27] Several months later he explained that the "peacetime draft law," with "no provisions against the elimination of Jim Crowism in it, will set back the cause of civil rights 100 years." The previous year, he had helped found the Committee against Jim Crow in Military Service and Training; when no congressional action against military segregation materialized and the UMT act was passed in May 1948, he cofounded the League for Nonviolent Civil Disobedience Against Military Segregation, which launched pickets in front of the White House and at both the Democratic and Republican party conventions and prepared a campaign to encourage noncompliance with the law.

Many American whites opposed Randolph's campaign—protesting employment discrimination was one thing, but interfering with national security was another—and black Americans were divided, appreciating the goal but uncertain as to the means. A group of black Georgia clergymen accepted Randolph's purpose but denounced his advocacy of civil disobedience. "The Negro has never been guilty of treason," they explained, "and we believe that the Negro race will not give their assent to such an act now." But even many of those who were reluctant to endorse civil disobedience found Randolph's denunciation of military segregation the "most fateful ever uttered by a recognized Negro leader." "I believe that there is unanimous agreement among this group," declared the Urban League's Lester Granger to a delegation of sixteen civilian black spokespersons meeting with Secretary of Defense James Forrestal and military leaders, "that there is no section of opinion among American Negroes that does not share the intense resentment and moral indignation which prompted" Randolph's statement before the Senate.[28]

Needing black support for his election campaign in 1948, President Harry S Truman issued two executive orders in late July that mandated "equality of treatment and opportunity for all persons in the armed services without regard to race, color, religion, or national origin." Yet "equality" implied an end to segregation, not just discrimination. The term therefore represented a "misleading move," Randolph announced, for the executive orders appeared to continue the "destructive separate but equal pattern which has kept the American Negro in semi-slavery since the end of the Civil War." Assured by Truman's representatives that the executive order did cover discrimination, Randolph called off the campaign of the League for Non-Violent Civil Disobedience, although some members, skeptical of the president's promise, continued their protests. Randolph was by no means alone in pressing for the desegregation of the armed forces, but his widely publicized advocacy of noncompliance with the selective service law kept the issue in the spotlight and exerted political pressure on the White House.[29]

From his early editorship of the *Messenger* in 1917 until his death in 1979, Randolph consistently preached the gospel of an interracial labor movement in which exclusionary barriers and discriminatory treatment had no place. It was a battle he never fully won. The AFL, with which the BSCP had affiliated, tolerated a wide range of racial policies among its constituent unions: some accepted black members and accorded them a modicum of respect and equality, but many did not. One black weekly paper's assessment in 1943 was undoubtedly a unanimously held view among African Americans: the AFL was "more anxious to maintain its lily-white policy than to serve as a constructive, progressive organization for working men."[30] Again and again, Randolph called upon the AFL to ban discrimination in its ranks, end all racial restrictions on union membership, and abolish inferior, segregated "auxiliary" unions. The AFL "cannot say it is democratic unless it cleans its house and says that, regardless of race, color and creed, any worker can join any AF of L union—and that any union which does not have this spirit of democracy will be expelled from the federation," the BSCP president declared before delegates to the federation's 1942 convention.[31]

Many white trade union officials, however, either ignored or denounced Randolph's continual charges of racism. In twenty years of "pounding away against discrimination in the federation," one black journalist concluded in 1943, Randolph "has not been able to win one major concession. Year after year, he has made his eloquent plea and year after year, the convention and the offending internationals have ignored him." Or worse, another paper believed. "Each year Mr. Randolph addresses the annual AFL convention in behalf of Negro workers who are being discriminated against by several of the most powerful AFL unions," the *Michigan Chronicle* observed. "Just as regularly the same AFL bosses take the offensive and accuse the Negro labor leader of insolence and arrogance."[32] With the merger of the AFL and the CIO in 1955, Randolph became, along with CIO leader Willard S. Townsend, one of two black vice presidents of the new AFL-CIO. From that position he persisted in his Sisyphean task, founding and leading the Negro American Labor Council—composed of black AFL leaders frustrated with the slow pace of change—and hammering away at the federation's racist practices. Again the AFL struck back. "Who the hell appointed you as the guardian of all the Negroes in America?" an angry George Meany, the AFL-CIO president, shouted at Randolph in 1959; two years later, the AFL-CIO executive council voted to censure the BSCP president for what it claimed were "baseless charges" against the federation.

Not until its 1961 convention, with black disaffection growing and the struggle for civil rights expanding across the South, did the AFL-CIO adopt a civil rights program that broke with past practice. "While the resolution on civil rights did not have as strong sanctions against unions that practice discrimination" as the BSCP delegates wanted, it was "nevertheless the most comprehensive and soundest civil rights resolution" ever passed by the AFL-CIO, the *Black Worker* concluded. As he had done since the 1920s, Randolph continued to use his position of leadership in the House of Labor to call attention to its racial problems and to insist upon their elimination.[33]

Until the end of his life, Randolph maintained that equality for black Americans required both civil and economic rights, that progress for black Americans required not only the passage and enforcement of civil rights and antidiscrimination laws but also economic policies designed to ensure the economic health of black Americans. Working with the new civil rights movement based in the Southern black churches, Randolph made sure that the 1963 March on Washington raised fundamental economic issues. Among the March's demands were calls not only for desegregation but also for passage of a federal fair employment practices act, a higher minimum wage, and a serious public works program designed to help the unemployed. In 1965 he went further, proposing a federal "Freedom Budget" of $180 billion to end poverty in the United States through full employment, higher incomes, medical care, and education.[34]

By the middle and late 1960s, however, the civil rights coalition had fractured, and liberalism was increasingly divided over the war in Vietnam. The elderly Randolph found himself criticized as too conservative by younger militants, whose turn to Black Power Randolph himself had sharply denounced. His social democratic proposals received scant attention from more conventional civil rights organizations. And the labor movement to which he had dedicated roughly half a century of his life only gradually became more receptive to the needs of African Americans and other minority workers, often under pressure from those groups themselves. In some ways, Randolph's decades-long efforts fell substantially short of their goals. Yet much had changed. In a lifetime of activism on behalf of civil rights, black equality, and the emancipation of labor, Randolph had witnessed—indeed, he had contributed centrally to—nothing less than a revolution in labor and race relations in America.

NOTES

1. On Randolph's role in organizing the 1963 March on Washington, see Paula F. Pfeffer, *A. Philip Randolph: Pioneer of the Civil Rights Movement* (Baton Rouge: Louisiana State University Press, 1990), 240–67.

2. See Jervis Anderson, *A. Philip Randolph: A Biographical Portrait* (New York: Harcourt Brace Jovanovich, 1972), 42. The quotations are from Beth Tomkins Bates, *Pullman Porters and the Rise of Protest Politics in Black America, 1925–1945* (Chapel Hill: University of North Carolina Press, 2001), 33–34.

3. On Randolph's early years, see Eric Arnesen, *Brotherhoods of Color: Black Railroad Workers and the Struggle for Equality* (Cambridge, Mass.: Harvard University Press, 2001), 88–89; and Anderson, *A. Philip Randolph*, 23–52.

4. *Seattle Northwest Enterprise*, July 2, 1947; Anderson, *A. Philip Randolph*, 76–77.

5. Bates, *Pullman Porters*, 34–39; Anderson, *A. Philip Randolph*, 108–9.

6. Arnesen, *Brotherhoods of Color*, 16–23.

7. William H. Harris, *Keeping the Faith: A. Philip Randolph, Milton P. Webster, and the Brotherhood of Sleeping Car Porters, 1925–37* (Urbana: University of Illinois Press, 1977), 16–20; Bates, *Pullman Porters*, 40–48.

8. A. Philip Randolph and Milton P. Webster, "Sixth Annual Statement of Achievements and Hopes of the Porters' Union," *American Federationist* 39, no. 3 (March 1932): 301. On the rise of the BSCP, see Arnesen, *Brotherhoods of Color*, 84–115.

9. *New York World*, August 20, 1925; A. Philip Randolph, "The New Pullman Porter," *Messenger* 8 (April 1926): 109; "The Slacker-Porter," *Messenger* 8 (June 1926): 176; George S. Schuyler, "Blessed Are the Organized," *Messenger* 8 (November 1926): 347.

10. A. Philip Randolph, "To the Brotherhood Men," *Messenger* 8 (November 1926): 235.

11. Arnesen, *Brotherhoods of Color*, 90–94.

12. Bates, *Pullman Porters*, 81–86.

13. T. Arnold Hill, "Labor: The Pullman Porter—The Big Boss," *Opportunity* 13, no. 6 (June 1935): 186; *New York Age*, July 6, 1935.

14. A. Philip Randolph, "Brotherhood and Pullman Company Sign Agreement," *Black Worker* 3, no. 7 (October 1937): 1.

15. *Minneapolis Spokesman*, July 5, 1935.

16. *Oklahoma Black Dispatch*, March 25, 1937.

17. A. Philip Randolph, "The Crisis of the Negro Railroad Workers," *American Federationist* 46, no. 8 (August 1939): 815; Arnesen, *Brotherhoods of Color*, 146–50, 206–20.

18. A. Philip Randolph, "Pullman Porters Need Own Union," *Messenger* 7 (August 1925): 289; Randolph, "The Pullman Company and the Pullman Porter," *Messenger* 6 (September 1925): 312–14, 355–56; R. W. Dunn, "Company Unions à la Pullman," *Messenger* 7 (December 1925): 394–95; *New York World*, October 11, 1925, in Tuskegee Institute News Clippings File, 1976, reel 23, Division of Behavioral Science Research, Carver Research Foundation, Tuskegee Institute, Tuskegee, Alabama.

19. Bates, *Pullman Porters*.

20. *Northwest Enterprise*, September 29, 1943.

21. "Negro Workers and the National Defense," in *The Negro Handbook*, ed. Florence Murray (New York: Wendell Malliet and Company, 1942), 86–87; *Northwest Enterprise*, March 21, 1941.

22. Anderson, *A. Philip Randolph*, 248–49; *Michigan Chronicle*, June 28, 1941; *Northwest Enterprise*, March 21, 1941.

23. Arnesen, *Brotherhoods of Color*, 181–202.

24. A. Philip Randolph, "We Need a New FEPC," *New Leader*, July 9, 1951.

25. *Northwest Enterprise*, April 24, 1942; *Chicago Defender*, July 4 and August 15, 1942; *Seattle Northwest Herald*, October 18, 1944; *Michigan Chronicle*, April 24, 1943; *Sunday Chicago Bee*, April 2, 1944.

26. *Chicago Defender*, July 25, 1942; *Sunday Chicago Bee*, April 30, 1944.

27. *Chicago Defender*, April 3, 1948.

28. *Norfolk Journal and Guide*, April 10 and May 8, 1948; *Chicago Defender*, May 1, 1948.

29. *Northwest Enterprise*, May 12, July 7, and August 4, 1948; Pfeffer, *A. Philip Randolph*, 133–68; Mary L. Dudziak, *Cold War Civil Rights: Race and the Image of American Democracy* (Princeton, N.J.: Princeton University Press, 2000), 84–88.

30. *Minneapolis Spokesman*, November 5, 1943.

31. *Baltimore Afro-American*, October 24, 1942, and October 23, 1943; *Michigan Chronicle*, December 9, 1944.

32. *Pittsburgh Courier*, October 30, 1943; *Michigan Chronicle*, December 9, 1944.

33. "The AFL-CIO Convention and Civil Rights," *Black Worker* 32 (December 1961): 4–5.

34. Pfeffer, *A. Philip Randolph*, 286–90.

SUGGESTED READING

Since 1980 there has been a small explosion in studies of African American workers and working-class and union race relations. Two overviews of recent developments in the field are Rick Halpern, "Organized Labor, Black Workers, and the Twentieth-Century South: The Emerging Revision," in *Race and Class in the American South since 1890*, ed. Melvyn Stokes and Rick Halpern (Oxford, England; Providence, R.I.: Berg, 1994), 43–76; and Eric Arnesen, "Up from Exclusion: Black and White Workers, Race, and the State of Labor History," *Reviews in American History* 26, no. 1 (March 1998): 146–74.

A. Philip Randolph's life and politics are treated in Jervis Anderson, *A. Philip Randolph: A Biographical Portrait* (1972; reprint ed., Berkeley: University of California Press, 1986); and Paula F. Pfeffer, *A. Philip Randolph: Pioneer of the Civil Rights Movement* (Baton Rouge: Louisiana State University Press, 1990). Pullman porters have received significant attention from historians of black labor. Beth Tomkins Bates, *Pullman Porters and the Rise of Protest Politics in Black America, 1925–1945* (Chapel Hill: University of North Carolina Press, 2001), is the best single study of the BSCP and its broader agenda. Other important works include William H. Harris, *Keeping the Faith: A. Philip Randolph, Milton P. Webster, and the Brotherhood of Sleeping Car Porters, 1925–37* (Urbana: University of Illinois Press, 1977); Jack Santino, *Miles of Smiles, Years of Struggle: Stories of Black Pullman Porters* (Urbana: University of Illinois Press, 1991); David D. Perata, *Those Pullman Blues: An Oral History of the African American Railroad Attendant* (New York: Twayne, 1996); and Melinda Chateauvert, *Marching Together: The Women of the Brotherhood of Sleeping Car Porters* (Urbana: University of Illinois Press, 1997). Eric Arnesen, *Brotherhoods of Color: Black Railroad Workers and the Struggle for Equality* (Cambridge, Mass.: Harvard University Press, 2001), explores the worlds of porters, redcaps, dining car waiters, locomotive firemen, and brakemen.

On Randolph's involvement with the MOWM and the FEPC, see Arnesen, *Brotherhoods of Color*, 181–202; Herbert Garfinkel, *When Negroes March: The March on Washington Movement in the Organizational Politics for FEPC* (1959; reprint ed., New York: Atheneum, 1969); and Merl E. Reed, *Seedtime for the Modern Civil Rights Movement: The President's Committee on Fair Employment Practice, 1941–1946* (Baton Rouge: Louisiana State University Press, 1991).

Other studies of black workers in the twentieth century include Michael Honey, *Southern Labor and Black Civil Rights: Organizing Memphis Workers* (Urbana: University of Illinois Press, 1993); Roger Horowitz, *"Negro and White, Unite and Fight!": A Social History of Industrial Unionism in Meatpacking, 1930–90* (Urbana: University of Illinois Press, 1997); and Rick Halpern, *Down on the Killing Floor: Black and White Workers in Chicago's Packinghouses, 1904–54* (Urbana: University of Illinois Press, 1997).

6

Lucy Randolph Mason:
"The Rest of Us"

Susan M. Glisson

Lucy Randolph Mason was the first Southern organizer for the Congress of In-dustrial Organizations (CIO). Race was the fulcrum upon which the Southern labor drama turned. Mason's appointment as a Southern ambassador for the CIO was meant to mitigate the ire of factory owners, ministers, and editors, who used race-baiting, charges of Communism, and the specter of outside agi-tators to control cheap labor. Mason's job was to organize among elite white people like herself to accept labor unionism and interracialism in order to smooth the CIO's way in the South. Mason was almost alone as a female or-ganizer in a male arena. Yet she was highly effective. As with her work for the National Consumers League, Mason used her identity, her status as a "South-ern lady," to camouflage her radical actions; in short, she used her image self-consciously to accomplish her goals. In many instances of potential violence, the presence of a soft-spoken, white-haired, elderly lady from Virginia calmed tensions. Certainly, the fact that a person like Mason would attach herself to such a suspect cause defused its threat for many Southern officials. More im-portantly, Mason's status paved the way for many Southern editors to listen to labor's demands and to consider union organizing because it seemed less dan-gerous when supported by Mason. Thus, Mason lent legitimacy to the labor movement.

Given the even greater obstacles to unionization in the postwar period, Lucy Mason's ability to appeal to owners, government officials, police, ministers, ed-itors, and other opinion makers was especially important and offered the great-est potential to Southern labor organizing in the postwar period. Ultimately, however, few resources, pervasive racism, and antiunion fervor overwhelmed her contributions and the CIO's Operation Dixie. Labor unions backed away from civil rights activity and interracial work in response to their Southern members, who increasingly joined newly forming White Citizens' Councils. However, as the CIO relaxed its commitment to racial equality, Mason redoubled hers. Race relations captured her attention most fully at the end of her life. Through moral suasion and an active campaign of publicity that used her access to an elite white base of power, Lucy Mason was able, for a time, to help aid the cause of labor and racial justice in the South. But it would fall to a new generation to enforce the truth of Mason's prediction that whites and blacks could work together.

In the spring of 1948, the Tifton, Georgia, chapter of the United Packing House Workers of America enlisted the aid of the Congress of Industrial Organizations (CIO), an industrial federation of unions formed in 1935, to assist them in their strike against local packing companies. On the evening before the arrival of the CIO representative, guards hired by the companies seized a striking African American worker, beat him repeatedly, and threatened to burn his home if he did not go back to work and convince others to do the same. The next morning the CIO intermediary arrived in Tifton. The organizer met with the man who had been beaten and then proceeded directly to the sheriff's office to register a complaint. Finding the sheriff unavailable, the CIO emissary visited the local judge and requested assistance. Later in the afternoon, a meeting between the sheriff, his deputies, the local union organizers, and the CIO representative escalated into a shouting match and threats of violence. When a physical assault seemed imminent, the CIO organizer stepped between the men, calming them and ushering the labor leaders out of the building, promising a full investigation by the U.S. district attorney's office into violations of civil rights. The Federal Bureau of Investigation began the promised investigation, and the packing companies and workers negotiated to settle the strike successfully. A newly elected sheriff replaced the sheriff who had condoned violence against the union workers and proved more amenable to labor activity.[1]

While this scene is a frightening and stirring example of union organizing in the American South, a surprising element of the story is the identity of the fearless CIO organizer who faced down the sheriff and helped bring an effective resolution to the strike. The courageous union representative was a petite, sixty-year-old, white-haired, blue-blooded member of the "First Families of Virginia" named Lucy Randolph Mason. Although her immediate family was not wealthy, Mason's aristocratic lineage offered her connections to a world of privilege. Forgoing the potential security offered by that heritage, Mason devoted her life to a variety of liberal causes, with workers' rights, women's suffrage, and justice for African Americans among them. Mason represents a small but significant population of Southern whites who

Lucy Randolph Mason (Image courtesy of the Library of Congress Prints and Photographs Division.)

are what historian Morton Sosna defines as "Southern liberals," those who loved their region but dissented from its cultural restrictions in matters of race and class.[2] Amid a predominantly male presence, the women of this group were even more remarkable because their activism challenged not only white supremacy and class hierarchy but also the patriarchal system that undergirded Southern society.

Like Jessie Daniel Ames, who lobbied against lynching, Mason used her persona as a white woman of the Southern elite to effect change. She was cognizant of the acceptable role allotted to her and used that role to challenge the foundations of her society. She did so by manipulating elite, Northern women's networks of reform and by very deliberately inserting herself into a predominantly male world—constructed by ministers, newspaper editors, politicians, and factory owners in the South—and interrupting it. She appealed to her connections with George Mason and Robert E. Lee, her most well-known male relatives, when attempting to sway men of importance. Her organizing strategies were reformist; she did not seek to change the political and economic systems of the country. Rather, she used the ideals of these systems to argue that their benefits should apply equally to everyone.

Mason's strategies for challenging the political and economic practices of her time grew out of her experience in a variety of social movements—from early support of industrial workers through the YWCA to the battle for suffrage to the interracial conference movement of the 1930s and 1940s and finally to working in the labor movement. Her efforts, along with others, bore fruit, for a time, as manifested in more equitable wage laws for working women and interracial unions throughout the historically antiunion South. Despite this success, she unstintingly gave credit for these reforms to the men with whom she worked. Mason's life offers broader understanding of Southern race relations, community organizing, and labor activity.

Three fundamental beliefs were central to Mason's worldview: the importance of education, the responsibility of government and members of the middle class to work against oppressive social conditions, and the crucial participation of those oppressed in shaping responses to their own conditions.[3] Mason's implicit belief in the rights and strengths of the working class initially seemed at odds with her reliance upon governmental action and her belief in the necessity of middle-class involvement in social change. But Mason believed that democratic principles, undergirded by Christianity, united all segments of society, and she worked to strengthen these connections in her attempts to bring economic and racial justice to the South.

A SWEETER, KINDER WORLD

The daughter of an Episcopal minister, Lucy Randolph Mason was born in northern Virginia on July 26, 1882, at a tumultuous time in the South.[4] By the year of her birth, the Civil War had been over for almost twenty years. By the 1880s, white Southerners were moving with increasing vehemence to wrest from black Southerners the rights that they had won over the previous two decades. During the early years of Mason's life, the South was becoming increasingly segregated, changing patterns of biracial living that had existed even under slavery.[5] In 1890, when Mason was eight, the state of Mississippi passed the first state constitution since Reconstruction. It instituted segregation, which created a system of legal separation between blacks and whites. The rest of the South quickly followed suit, making segregation or "Jim Crow" legal.[6]

Into this changing, often confusing, and sometimes even violent environment, the Masons gave birth to Lucy, who took her place among a family of famed lineage in a state that prized its esteemed names. To be born a Mason in the Commonwealth of Virginia was no minor matter. The first Mason to arrive in the new colony in 1651 prospered, became a member of the House of Burgesses, and established a reputation as a protector of the rights of the underprivileged.[7] The practice of aiding those perceived as less fortunate became a paternalistic pattern in the Mason family, one repeated by Mason's parents.[8]

Despite her pedigree, Mason was not wealthy. Mason's family relied on her father's small church salary, "paid mostly in black-eyed peas and bacon."[9] Mason attended the exclusive Powell's School for Girls in Richmond, but she did not finish high school because her parents could not afford it.[10] While Mason's parents did not leave her a legacy of wealth, they bestowed upon her a commitment to community service, having, as Mason described, "a strong sense of social responsibility [growing] out of religious conviction."[11] It was easy to find people who needed help in Richmond, Virginia, during Mason's adolescence and young adult life. From the end of Reconstruction and into the early part of the twentieth century, the city, like the larger South, struggled to define itself. Visions of the Lost Cause of the Confederacy warred with a growing industrial economic base made up of quarries, flour and paper mills, and new tobacco- and iron-processing factories. But these industries were on the decline as Birmingham and Atlanta outpaced Richmond in iron and the North Carolina Piedmont began to monopolize the new cigarette industry.[12] As a result, workers in Richmond struggled to make a living as wages decreased and competition increased for jobs. And Mason wanted to assist in their plight. In 1903, in an early example of her commitment to the rights of labor, she refused to ride Richmond's trolley cars, in support of a strike by streetcar operators, despite the deep divisions caused by the protest.[13]

When she was eighteen, Mason taught a Sunday school class in a mission church in one of Richmond's working-class districts. The bleakness of her students' lives struck Mason and piqued her social conscience.[14] She began a period of self-education, including reading the work of Walter Rauschenbusch, who advocated the idea of Christian social action that became the ideological basis of the Social Gospel movement. The philosophy of the Social Gospel inspired Mason to depart decisively from the religious understandings of her region. Social Gospel theology advocated a systemic rather than an individual approach to helping others. In its approach on changing the system in order to affect the individual, Social Gospel theology reversed the focus of evangelical Protestant Christianity in the South. Southern evangelicals focused on the individual and individual sin in a sort of macabre compromise with slavery; whereas religion had traditionally been used to critique society, Southern evangelicals subsumed that element of Christianity in their culture dominated by slave labor.

In Social Gospel theology, Mason saw the beginnings of an organized response to the ills around her.[15] The Social Gospel differed from the tenets of evangelicalism in its understanding of the relationship between the individual and society. Where evangelicalism placed the responsibility for morality or the lack thereof squarely on the shoulders of the individual, the Social Gospel stressed the negative effects of an exploitive socioeconomic system on the moral lives of individuals, thus blaming society rather than what it saw as society's victims for their failures.[16] Lucy Mason believed in the ultimate potential of that system to be redeemed and became a steadfast adherent, despite larger denominational resistance to the Social Gospel theology in the South.[17]

Mason's experiences in her first occupation reinforced her understanding of the need for an organized response to inequities in the workplace. Instead of a life of economic ease, Mason worked most of her life, chiefly from necessity resulting from her family's lack of wealth.[18] In doing so, she began to encounter others whose lives differed drastically from her own. At the age of twenty-two, Mason taught herself stenography and, through a family connection, found a job with a Richmond law firm, which often handled large insurance casualty cases that stemmed from industrial injuries. As an employee there for eight years, Mason witnessed how little protection employers afforded workers injured on the job. She toured factories and saw firsthand the poor working conditions. She was particularly struck by the effects of these conditions on female workers.[19] "I saw girls of 14 working 10 hours a day for less than a living wage as a matter of course," she said later. "I saw women who had worked under those conditions from 14 to 25. They looked like women of 50."[20] In one instance, a seventeen-year-old woman lost part of her hand on the job. A lawyer who employed Mason convinced the woman to accept a seventy-five-dollar settlement. Mason "was appalled." "That is what I mean when I talk about the indifference of most of us to what happens to the rest of us," she recalled later. "How could that young lawyer have stood by and seen a girl of 17 get $75 for her right hand? The loss of her right hand meant that she was unfit for work in a factory and that was all she knew how to do," Mason remembered. She professed, "I can never forget her. All my life, she has followed me."[21]

The frequency of injury and the inability of workers to protect themselves or receive compensation disturbed Mason, leading her to consider solutions to the problems faced by the working class. Mason's practical response was to include an economic analysis in her critique of society. Mason began to fashion a more sophisticated appraisal of the dangers of an unregulated marketplace in her justifications for aiding others; in short, she began to respond to specific injustices around her, to identify solutions based on particular conditions, and to incorporate critiques of structural inequities created by a capitalist economic system. Low wages, poor working conditions, and the lack of insurance combined with the indifference of most employers led Mason to begin to lobby for labor reform.

Mason became convinced of the need for labor unions to assist working people. She would later say that she did not know when she became "union conscious." Rather she seemed to express particular concern for those who suffered from industrial accidents and in the process noticed that "the best paid workers were union and [they] had an eight-hour day and a half a day off on Saturday."[22] Two years into her employment at the law firm, in 1906, she became a member of the Union Labor League of Richmond and began lobbying for an eight-hour working day for women, and she also worked for the Equal Suffrage League and the League of Women Voters because, she said, "both were interested in labor and social legislation."[23] Mason gravitated toward protective legislation for women, a position that would later divide suffragists but that reflected Mason's belief at the time that white, middle-class women must protect women less fortunate than themselves.

In 1914, Mason was forced to leave her law firm to stay home and care for her ailing father. His death in June 1923 allowed her to accept a full-time position as general secretary of the Richmond Young Women's Christian Association (YWCA). Her growing interest in interracial activities led Mason to her position in the YWCA. Early in the twentieth century, evangelical Christianity heavily influenced the YWCA in the South, as its members focused on personal morality and individual salvation.[24] But by the time Mason served as industrial secretary of the YWCA's Richmond branch, the Social Gospel had made inroads in the organization, and the YWCA began to develop a larger, sociological critique of the conditions of working women as well as the solutions to their problems.[25] It began to focus more overtly on race relations, in addition to its work with working-class women, their employment conditions, and their lives outside the factory.

In its efforts to support working women, the national YWCA supported labor unions. Even in the South, where state and local governments and factory owners largely condemned union activity, local YWCA officers held very progressive positions on labor issues. Mason proved no exception. Her work with the YWCA cemented her concern for the working class and her belief that labor unions were a way of alleviating some of the problems among working people. In addition, a growing interest in securing aid for all of Richmond's citizens, both black and white, led in 1929 to Mason's public disavowal of segregation. A courageous stand in the former capital of the Confederacy, Mason's opposition to segregation and her public statements on matters of race indicate a growing commitment to working with and on behalf of blacks.[26] While religion certainly played a major role in Mason's thinking, it seems likely that her experience with the YWCA contributed much to her radical thinking on race.

During her tenure as an industrial secretary for the YWCA, Mason became a member of the Virginia Commission on Interracial Cooperation, and in 1928 she cochaired a subcommittee of the Richmond Council of Social Agencies, which examined the economic status of Richmond's black community.[27] The conditions she found horrified her; the subcommittee concluded that the "inferior economic status" of Richmond's black community "constituted its most fundamental and pressing problem."[28] That problem caused Mason's outspoken support of improvements for Richmond's black citizens, including the reorganization of Richmond's Urban League.[29] Her support endeared her to Richmond's black community, which honored her just before she left Richmond a few years later. And a growing number of Richmond's white community members supported Mason's beliefs, although perhaps not as stridently. As one of those friends wrote of Mason in this period, "I admire her for her many splendid qualities, but most of all for the fact that she is not afraid of tomorrow."[30]

Having labored to secure legislation that insured fair employment practices for women on a small scale in Richmond, Mason went to work full-time for an organization devoted primarily to labor rights for women. And she did so in 1932, at a time when the direct influence of women in government was perhaps the highest it had ever been. Heretofore, in organizing on behalf of working-class women, Mason had started from the proposition that political access and appeals to democratic processes would create and maintain a fair market; hence her efforts to secure the vote for women. But in the years after the passage of the Nineteenth Amendment, as Mason worked for the National Consumers League, she began to realize that a political voice did not necessarily guarantee equitable conditions for women in industry or fair employment practices for anyone. Political democracy did not beget economic parity between industry and its workers; rather, economic and political justice reinforced and created each other. In short, economic power undergirded political freedom, and the latter could not be achieved without redress of the former. As she said, "Reverse [the] old slogan that political democracy [must precede] industrial democracy. Political democracy is dependent on industrial democracy."[31]

Mason's understanding of the interaction between the market and government became clear to her during her work with the National Consumers League. Primarily middle-class, Northern white women formed the League in 1891 to respond to deplorable employment conditions for working women.

Mason's predecessor, Florence Kelley, had propelled the League to new heights during the twenties; it grew tremendously under Kelley's direction and added many new chapters.[32] The League produced several well-trained women, including Frances Perkins. With the demise in the 1920s of the notion of women's lives as primarily private and separate from the public culture of men, some women's groups began to coalesce, asserting their influence on society based on an understanding that women represented the embodiment of virtue within civil society.[33]

White women, especially middle-class white women, had some access to the resources of the state. In particular, a growing network of these women attained unprecedented influence within Roosevelt's administration. Through the League, Mason used that accessibility to win concessions for working-class women in a variety of forums, especially in matters of employment in industry. Prior to Mason's appointment, the League advocated primarily for white, immigrant, working-class women, creating a pattern of interclass cooperation with middle-class activists acting as liaisons between the working class and the government. During Kelley's tenure, this cooperation was chiefly between whites: there were few African Americans in the North in the early part of the twentieth century, and the League focused on that region. In part, Kelley designated Mason her successor to redirect the League's focus to the newly industrializing South. The announcement of Mason's hiring called her "a Southerner by ancestry. Her great grandfather was a friend of Thomas Jefferson and wrote the Bill of Rights. She has been active in many community and inter-racial projects although the industrial worker has been her chief interest."[34] Historians of the League in its Progressive-era heyday differ over whether it was an elite association of experts or a grassroots movement of activists; in fact, its strength lay in its combination of the two.[35] And Mason brought the strengths of both to her position.

Lucy Mason attempted to create a new pattern in the League. She asserted that women should have the right to work, whether single or married. But Mason also maintained that women "should not be driven to work by poverty when home and children need care."[36] Although she shared some of her colleagues' beliefs that men would not assist in the care of children, unlike them, Mason did not believe mothers, single or otherwise, should be penalized for having children. Rather, she wanted them to have good jobs with fair wages. "The work of women in industry," she insisted, "must be made truly an opportunity to develop to the fullest their powers as workers, both for their own happiness and for the service of society. To this end," she asserted, "they must have adequate schooling before entrance into industry, and be free to choose their occupations, to secure training for them, to enlarge their opportunities as their experience grows, to receive fair compensation, and to work under safe and wholesome conditions."[37] Mason believed in a fair distribution of opportunities, training, and wages for women, not because of their sex but because of the resulting discrimination experienced by them because of their sex. Mason dubbed the League simply "the consumer's conscience."[38]

Mason continued this emphasis as secretary of the League, but she knew she had been chosen for the position because of her connections in the South. An address delivered in 1936 affirmed Mason's commitment to working in the industrial South. "The Southeastern region of the United States can become one of the richest domestic markets of the nation or its economic swamp," she wrote. The South could only improve "with cooperation from the federal government and an increasing interest in the importance of high standards in public service and government administration."[39] She addressed the need for both outside federal support, a concept typically resisted in the South, and an invigorated and active citizenry working toward alleviating the South's ills. She did her part to create this civic culture by devoting most of her efforts with the League to conditions in the industrializing South, often receiving criticism from other members of the League who felt she neglected the rest of the country.

As part of her Southern strategy, Mason traveled throughout the region in the 1930s, establishing local League branches of middle-class women and women workers. "Owing to the difficulty of making an outside organization effective in the South," she reported, "we asked nearly two hundred leading Southern people from ten states to serve on a Southern committee of the League."[40] She knew the provincialism of Southerners that led them to mistrust "outsiders" and organized around this suspicion. She believed that the crucial work of obtaining fair treatment for workers would come in the cooperation between classes and races, between liaisons with the highest seats of government and local people working on a community and state level to win protections for labor. Unlike the National Woman's Party, which was often criticized for abandoning its chapters, the National Consumers League under Mason's direction maintained a close alliance between the national and local branches. The information collected by each group reinforced the whole effort and gave each local tools to attack their particular conditions.[41]

Mason worked especially to develop either interracial branches or white and black branches that would work together. Such a task was, not surprisingly, very difficult in the South. Interracial branches working for fair employment practices not only challenged industrialists' ability to gain access to cheap, unorganized labor but also assailed the notion of white supremacy that undergirded that system. Southern manufacturers typically opposed the League's efforts, and such controversy made the organization of local branches almost impossible for Mason. Thus, while she could win converts on issues like protective legislation, she was not able to change many minds on the issue of race.

Despite her energetic direction of the League and a growing friendship with Eleanor Roosevelt, Mason seemed unable to pull the organization out of the doldrums. The national Depression was an obvious concern for an organization that relied primarily on fund-raising for income, and Mason seemed unable to muster the financial support needed to keep the League functioning. The tension within the League finally came to a head in 1937, and Mason resigned. She left the League that year to return south.

Mason's desire to work in her home region in support of organized labor directed her next profession. She had mentioned to her brother-in-law, Taylor Burke, that she would like to go to the South, "where I could work with organized labor and interracial groups. I was particularly concerned with the status of Negroes in the new unions."[42] Her sister-in-law arranged a meeting with John L. Lewis, a friend of her husband's and a leader of the newly created federation of industrial unions, the CIO. Impressed with Mason, Lewis saw the advantages of having a Virginia aristocrat organizing in the South. He appointed her to the position of public relations representative for the CIO in the South. As she explained, she wanted to work in the South, "because it is the most backward section."[43] A new chapter in her life began.

In the mid–1930s, some union workers began a new organizing strategy, shifting from craft-oriented unions to those organized by industry. In addition, they explored the possibilities of working in the South. Simultaneously, Lucy Mason began to look for a way to return home. In 1937, when the CIO's John Lewis tapped Sidney Hillman to direct the energies of the newly formed Textile Workers Organizing Committee (TWOC) to create a Southern campaign, he sent Mason to Hillman to assist in the work. As the head of an organization with purported ties to communism, Lewis immediately saw the advantages of having a public relations representative with "blood in her veins bluer than indigo."[44] Virginia Durr, a friend of Mason's, also known for her progressive work against racism, asserted, "As his public relations person Miss Lucy would be very disarming." She continued, "All the fierce police chiefs and sheriffs and newspaper editors would be looking for some big gorilla to come in, and Miss Lucy would appear. She was the kind of perfect Southern lady for whom men would instinctively rise to offer a seat."[45] Hillman quickly assigned her to his Atlanta office, where she remained the rest of her working life.

Mason arrived in Atlanta as the CIO made its first forays into the region. It was a young organization and represented an attempt by some union organizers to find new ways to cope with the country's economic crisis. In the midst of the Depression, Americans had sought a variety of remedies to their economic woes. The 1930s had seen a rise in labor organizing as workers attempted to bargain for better pay and improved working conditions. Before 1935, the largest labor alliance in the country was the American Federation of Labor (AFL). The AFL represented a coalition of mostly skilled workers' unions organized primarily in industrial areas of the North. And yet, despite the craft workers who represented the core of AFL strength, there were some attempts to organize industrial unions.[46] But many in the

AFL resisted organizing unskilled workers because it considered them more risky than highly skilled craftsmen who could not be easily replaced. Racism and sexism undergirded this resistance to unskilled workers. So unskilled workers, especially women and blacks, faced falling wages and faster production lines without assistance from AFL organizers.

In 1935, some members of the AFL began to lobby from within for internationals organized by industry rather than by craft, in order to make inroads into the large mass-production industries like rubber and auto manufacturing in which there were few skilled workers and therefore initially no unions. Led in part by John L. Lewis of the United Mine Workers, these industrial unionists formed a coalition within the AFL, the Committee of Industrial Organizations, to help spark this new mass labor movement. A series of successful campaigns in 1936, highlighted by victory at a Flint, Michigan, General Motors plant, offered a new union tactic, the sit-in, and cemented the CIO's reputation as a bold, new alternative to the stodgy and exclusive AFL. Prior to the development of the sit-in, workers had staged walkouts, which left them vulnerable to antiunion police as well as hired company thugs. It also allowed companies to hire other workers to break the strike. The sit-in forced the company to deal with strikers who were, in effect, holding the company's equipment and workplace hostage. That the new stage of the civil rights movement also began with sit-ins in 1960 is an interesting historical complement.[47]

While the focus of much of the CIO organizing in the 1930s and early 1940s was in Northern industries, union activists knew that a Southern strategy was necessary to the strength of unions as a whole. The growing textile industry in the South, the largest industrial group in the region in 1934, represented more than 200,000 virtually unorganized workers.[48] And, as organizers in other unions had learned, the lack of organization in the South forced down wages, with repercussions in the North, undermining collective bargaining everywhere because Northern industrialists would threaten to relocate to the nonunion South. In fact, many of them did.[49] But the South presented its own organizing challenges. Race was the fulcrum upon which the Southern labor drama turned. Southern capital was notoriously antiunion, and a confederation of politicians, ministers, and newspaper editors reinforced that fervor with allegations of interracialism and communism against the CIO, though Lewis himself was fiercely anticommunist. He did, however, tolerate communist organizers for a time, lending credence to those charges against the organization.

Mason's appointment as a Southern ambassador for the CIO was meant to mitigate the ire of factory owners, ministers, and editors. Employers hoped to maintain their control of unorganized and cheap labor, using race-baiting and charges of Communism to do so.[50] In addition, the favorite specter of "outside agitators" circumscribed union activity as well, playing on white Southerners' mistrust of people from outside the region. Because the organization's greatest challenge lay in the South, Lewis and Hillman realized the potential in Mason's assistance. Mason's job was to organize among elite white people like herself to accept labor unionism and interracialism in order to smooth the CIO's way in the South.

While it is not certain that the CIO intended a specific biracial strategy in the region, factory owners and local government leaders often used the threat of race to raise antiunion sentiment among workers. Thus race was always an issue, whether the CIO prompted it or not. In any case, when a local encountered tension or harassment because of interracial activity, Mason went in to provide assistance. Mason's ability to call on the president as well as to mention her famous Southern kin often helped calm such incidents. Mason's status paved the way for many Southern editors to listen to labor's demands and to consider union organizing because it seemed less dangerous when supported by Mason. In other words, Mason lent legitimacy to the labor movement. One man who knew her emphasized her charm, stating that "she used her sweetness and Southern manners and blue blood to persuade people."[51]

Still, Mason doubted her effectiveness. Two months into the job, in a meeting with her supervisor Steve Nance, Mason said, "My conscience is hurting me. I ought to get off this staff. I ought to make way for a man." Working in an arena dominated by male organizers, Mason believed she had reason to question the value of her assistance to the cause. She had previously worked in organizations composed predominantly of women and had directed her efforts at primarily protective legislation for female workers. Now she advocated for men as well, and the newness of her position must have been intimidating. However, Nance knew her value to the CIO and reassured her, "Lady, you are doing a real job and don't forget it. You go places and do things the men can't do."[52]

Not all of her colleagues were so immediately supportive. One director, Van A. Bittner, suggested in a meeting that the best "way to take care of civil rights is to have more men with you than against you and to strike before you are struck when the blow threatens." Mason responded that "a safer and surer way is to follow a procedure some of us have been using—to visit the local authorities and point out the rights guaranteed by federal law in a firm but friendly discussion." Mason expected to be fired, but in a supreme test, Bittner gave her three civil rights cases in South Carolina to handle. They included "two civil rights cases involving the police and a third case involving a minister who demanded that the textile workers choose between God and the CIO." Mason does not report how she dealt with these cases; she relates only that she "reported the success of the mission in some detail to Mr. Bittner."[53] After these achievements, Bittner asked her to take on all of their civil rights cases. In time, these cases constituted the bulk of Mason's work for the CIO. While her focus was on persuading elite whites either to aid labor or, at least, to step aside, she also responded to the concerns of workers whose rights had been violated as they tried to organize. She visited their homes and helped with leaflet distribution to protest their cases. She related that "some were jailed for no offence except attending a gathering where a few Negroes and many white people were holding a union meeting. More of my time has been spent trying to maintain the civil rights of our people than in any other phase of my manifold job."[54]

Memphis, Tennessee, lies at the northern edge of the Mississippi-Yazoo Delta on the banks of the Mississippi River.[55] Highway 61 connects Memphis to the rich agricultural land of the Mississippi Delta to the south and to the industrial mecca of Chicago to the north. It was a road of promised but too-often-illusive deliverance for African Americans and whites caught in the backbreaking sharecropping system of the deep South in the early decades of the twentieth century. Farther north up Highway 61, Memphis seemed to offer more opportunity, and in some ways it delivered. Blacks and whites found jobs on the docks or in factories that supplied parts to Ford Motor Company or other industries. While blacks did not receive the same wages nor the same jobs as whites, whites did not fare much better. Memphis had been sold to Northern industrial owners by E. H. Crump, a mayor so ruthless and controlling that he had been labeled "the Führer in Memphis."[56] The advances and retreats of organized labor in Memphis reflect the promise and the failures of the labor movement in the South, and Mason's experiences mirrored that ebb and flow.

Mason traveled to Memphis many times to aid in union organizing there. She noted that "unions grew rapidly in Memphis in the years between 1937 and 1940," especially in small plants.[57] In one example, a union steward told Mason, "The bosses asked us what we wanted so they could keep us from organizing, but they were too late. We had already organized."[58] "[In] Memphis," she asserted, "it was easier than usual to get both whites and Negroes into the unions right from the beginning, because the white workers realized that without the colored they could not represent the majority needed to build a union."[59] Mason visited the city often to help in the organizing process because she had heard of the vicious attacks on union organizers, especially against blacks. She remembered as she walked along the river to one meeting, "Because of the stories I had heard about unwanted Negroes being shackled and dumped into the Mississippi, the dark water with its broken reflections of lights had a sinister look."[60] In contrast, the meeting she attended, like others in Memphis, was very powerful and uplifting. Mason noted the spiritually driven services: "I think I never heard people pray more sincerely than did those humble union folk."[61] She noted that while "whites organized the CIO meetings, black dominated their spirit and content."[62] Historian Michael Honey argues that such instances of black union fervor convinced Mason and others of "the extraordinary power of black unionism and the radical change it might potentially bring to social and class relations across the South."[63]

Their spirit, unfortunately, would not protect blacks from growing resentment against unions and, eventually, aggravated the racial divide that ultimately prevented biracial unions in Memphis. Memphis, like the rest of the United States, began to increase its defense industry production, and factory owners manipulated the issue of patriotism to elicit any antiunion sentiment. Sixteen states in the South and Southwest passed sabotage and sedition laws to prevent union organizing, and this restrictive atmosphere circumscribed union activity until the country entered the war in 1941.[64] Mason described the laws as a "skillful admixture of patriotic sentiments and invitation to institute labor baiting and witch hunts."[65] Public suspicions of labor in this period were particularly volatile in the South because of the fear of organized black labor. Mason's work garnered much suspicion. She wrote to Eleanor Roosevelt that "a friend heard I am a dangerous person, that I am down here to incite the Negroes to an uprising as part of the CIO program."[66] And she was.

In addition to its campaign in Memphis, the CIO sought to organize the textile industry. Textiles presented unique challenges. There were more than six thousand textile plants in twenty-nine states, employing more than one million workers. Each plant represented an array of economic situations and organizing challenges. Although the South represented one of TWOC's greatest challenges, owing to its antiunion sentiment, Hillman and his colleagues appointed only one hundred fifty of the five hundred organizers TWOC employed to work in the Southern textile organizing drive.[67] Thus, in what would prove later to be a serious underestimation of the need there as well as a harbinger of the CIO's postwar defeat, Hillman allocated only 30 percent of the organizers assigned to the textile campaign to the South. Lucy Mason was one of them. She cautioned Hillman that "moderate statements gain more friends than militant ones" and set off on a letter-writing effort to win support for TWOC's efforts.[68] Hillman appeared to listen to Mason and "preached the virtues of moderation" to his Southern TWOC representatives.[69] Mason's knowledge of the South was exactly the advantage the CIO would need. "It is my hope to contribute a little towards understanding of the aims and methods of the Textile Workers Organizing Committee campaign," Lucy Mason wrote to President Roosevelt, shortly after coming south for TWOC. She went on to elaborate that "my contacts will be chiefly with editors, ministers, educators, and others who help to make public opinion."[70]

Mason knew that she would have admittance to these seats of power; her conscious use of that access to organize elite whites informed her organizing strategy. It is not coincidental that Mason informed Roosevelt of her plans. She would call for his intervention in the years to come, when resistance to a particular strike became violent or a union organizer disappeared; more importantly, in some instances, she would receive his help. In 1940, for example, the president responded to Mason's request for assistance in a situation in Gadsden, Alabama. Roosevelt had someone investigate a local plant owner's adherence to Defense Commission labor policies, "in order to protect labor's rights," and secured a promise from the owner that the policies would be followed.[71] At other times, Mason wrote Roosevelt regarding a particular situation but received no detectable reply from the president.[72] She did, however, use that relationship to pressure local authorities. She also used the contacts she had made through the National Consumers League to aid in the labor struggle in the South, writing to Molly Dewson, among others.[73]

Mason felt an affinity for the people in the region, from factory workers to mill owners, and she used her knowledge of the South and its people to part the veil between the section and the rest of country. She knew that the Southern labor movement "was being built from the bottom up, by and for Southern folk," but she believed that the movement would be meaningless without the "corresponding national movement."[74] Thus, Mason would have parallel conversations, assessing needs in the labor movement, imploring business and civic groups to support the movement, and translating the needs of both and the tensions between the two to national listeners, who could then intervene. She began these conversations immediately; during the summer of 1937, she visited local organizing centers, acquainting herself with the people in the field and issues they confronted. She quickly followed this tour with a circular letter to four hundred twenty-five Southern ministers, in which she introduced herself as a Southerner, a child and grandchild of Episcopal ministers, and "an interpreter of the organized labor movement."[75] Those first letters had the "desired effect," according to her biographer. Several ministers responded, some simply to agree to meet with her, but others offering support.[76] She had hoped to just "get her foot in the door" in order to lobby for the importance of the CIO's role in the South.[77] That role of translation and advocacy would be continually tested.

Early in her work for the CIO, a kidnapping of a union organizer measured Mason's ability to negotiate between local, state, and federal spheres of influence. In April 1938, anti-CIO garment workers kidnapped Jimmie Cox, a union representative working in Tupelo, Mississippi. A colleague notified Mason, and after requesting more information, she began to contact a variety of officials, including those in the White House and at the FBI, "appeal[ing] for immediate action in behalf of Cox."[78] His kidnappers returned him, beaten but alive; Mason and the CIO feared continued problems in Tupelo and urged Cox to file statements against those who had held him. Mason continued to monitor the case in July, urging the FBI to protect the organizers in Mississippi.[79] Working with local union supporters, she "arranged a short-term scholarship to the Highlander Folk School for him, and had helped support his family while he was away."[80]

Officials in Mississippi then took notice of Mason. One sheriff in Jackson attempted to track Mason down, implying to a YWCA representative that she was "a subversive character." Mason later noted that the representative refused to take the bait and "the baffled sheriff gave up hope of discovering a dangerous character in the shape of an elderly white-haired woman." Concluding, "I have not heard from him since," Mason downplayed the danger of the event.[81] Yet she challenged local authorities when necessary, camouflaging her actions.

In addition to intervening in particular crises, she began to suggest new tactics to her CIO superiors. Mason wrote to Sidney Hillman early in her TWOC tenure that the CIO could aid its cause by developing other community organizing campaigns, to take some of the pressure off of the beleaguered TWOC.[82] She noted that TWOC organizers were already assisting other unions in organizing; consolidating these under a CIO umbrella would help each union present a stronger, united front. She also became a savvy manipulator of the press; in particular, she "urged the people to keep in touch with the newspapers and to lose no chance to bring about friendly public opinion."[83] She continued to assist in these attempts to sway public opinion with a series of circular letters to ministers and newspaper editors.

Letter campaigns helped Mason develop working relationships with an important contingent of liberal newspaper editors. She corresponded regularly with Ralph McGill of the *Atlanta Journal-Constitution*; Hodding Carter of the *Delta Democrat-Times* in Greenville, Mississippi; and Virginius Dabney of the *Richmond Times-Dispatch* in Virginia. She grew especially close to Jonathan Daniels of the Raleigh *News and Observer*; Daniels would write Mason often for clarification of labor issues, and he attempted to introduce her to other editors, although he admitted that "I wish I could provide you safe conduct to more of my editorial colleagues but I am afraid the number of them that would trust even George Mason's descendent in connection with labor unions in the modern South is strictly limited."[84] Mason also maintained a close friendship with the journalist and essayist Lillian Smith. It was, in fact, Mason who introduced Smith and her *North Georgia Review* partner Paula Snelling to the Roosevelts, in a typical attempt to connect liberals together who might be able to help each other. As she wrote, "[She] share[s] with me a great and warm admiration for you and what you have contributed to progressive causes in this country. It will be an inspiration to [her] to have a chance to talk with you. So when [she] call[s] Miss Thompson by phone, I trust she can say that you will see [her]."[85]

The rapport she developed with these journalists aided her work; as journalist John Egerton relates, "her name got her in the door but once she was there no man could resist her charm. She reminded them of the white-haired little lady who sat in the pew in front of them in church."[86] "Be a good girl now," Grover Hall, the editor of the Montgomery *Advertiser*, warned Mason facetiously, "and do not stab any textile executives."[87] Hall's ability to joke with Mason on such a personal level implied his great feeling for her and their closeness. Clearly, he knew Mason was far more than a "little old lady."

But it was not enough for Mason to simply plead labor's case with these friendly newspaper colleagues. She was careful to investigate the conditions of workers and the responses to their attempts to organize, so that accurate information appeared in the press. This penchant for accuracy and avoidance of slick propaganda won Mason many admirers, among them McGill, Carter, Dabney, and Daniels, the four best-known moderate newspaper editors. A favorite forum for Mason's articulation of these labor "facts" was the college campus. In 1939 at a forum at the University of Kentucky, Mason contended that "students had a responsibility to understand the situation."[88] She believed that labor and the higher education community must collaborate to support the union cause.[89] She carried the same message to the University of North Carolina campus the next week; the student newspaper, while skeptical of labor's cause, believed Mason to be a persuasive spokesperson:

> Miss Lucy Mason, a charming lady from Virginia who had devoted her life to the American labor movement, spoke Friday night to an audience of students and townsfolk who had crowded into the small lounge of Graham Memorial to hear her. As a representative of the Textile Workers Organizing Committee of the CIO, Miss Mason spoke enthusiastically of the great work which the CIO was doing, slowly but surely, in giving labor strength and bargaining power.[90]

The editorial went on to argue that, while the CIO might be securing that bargaining power, it often did so with violence, and hence the paper called for caution. Mason reflected that the paper's editor was not alone in his suspicion of labor. Local union people introduced her to a resident who objected to her presence on campus. He believed Mason's appearance would tinge "the public image of [the university] in the state." As a union supporter and employee of the CIO, Mason represented his worst fears of Communism and organized labor. Rather than avoid him, Mason arranged to sit next to the man at a luncheon and "did all [she] could to educate him on the labor movement," though she does not record the results of efforts to convert him to her cause.[91]

A colleague noted later that Mason was "a good advocate for the CIO." "Feeling a bit flattered," Mason asked why. "You look mild," he said.[92] The visit to the University of Kentucky did inspire union supporters on that campus to continue their efforts. A student wrote to Mason after her talk there, "We become discouraged at times when there is such complacent indifference in the face of such grave problems. Your visit gave us new inspiration to keep 'plugging away' at the job."[93] In addition to the renewed vigor of these students, Mason reported that her contacts from the tour "were well worthwhile for the CIO and TWOC."[94]

While she would continue this speaking tour to college campuses, Mason increasingly involved herself in national events, as a voice from the South, and became involved in a variety of progressive efforts in addition to her work with labor. In June 1938, President Franklin Roosevelt wrote to Mason with a request. The president was convening a "group of distinguished Southerners having special knowledge of and interest in the needs of their region" under the auspices of the National Emergency Council in order to "bring together certain information relating to economic conditions in the South." He wanted Mason among them.[95] Roosevelt's request reflected years of both deliberation and missteps by the federal government.[96] Earlier in Roosevelt's administration, Francis Pickens Miller had assembled the Southern Policy Committee in April 1935 to address "agrarian policy, democratic institutions, social objectives, and economic planning."[97] To the otherwise all-white, male group, Pickens added sociologist Charles S. Johnson and Lucy Mason. Several members promptly resigned. Eventually the group folded amid intraregional bickering, but it managed one positive result. The committee had suggested in 1935 that Roosevelt document the South's economic problems in order to bring the nation's attention to the region's plight. The group suggested that Southerners do the work, anticipating the typical suspicion by white Southerners of so-called outsiders. It was not until 1938 that the president acted upon the Southern Policy Committee's suggestion. The Committee on Economic Conditions in the South convened in 1938, and in the summer of that year the president issued a fifteen-chapter report that the committee had drafted. Its most well-known assertion was that "the South was the nation's number one economic problem."[98] Lucy Mason compiled much of the information in the report, and she was the committee's only female member.

Shortly before the release of the report, Mason met Joseph Gelders, a young, Jewish, Southern, middle-class progressive, at a strike in Tupelo, Mississippi. After discovering their shared interests in eradicating poverty and racism, Mason introduced Gelders to the Roosevelts. The informal summit resulted in the idea of a Southern conference that would draw a "broad panoply of Southern progressives to the cause of civil liberties."[99] FDR, in a deft political move, suggested that the conference respond to the report from the Committee on Economic Conditions in the South, and before the meeting adjourned, Eleanor Roosevelt had encouraged the involvement of the Highlander Folk School and promised that she would attend as well. The newly formed Southern Conference for Human Welfare (SCHW) met in Birmingham, Alabama, in November 1938 and was the largest assemblage of Southern progressives since Reconstruction. John Egerton relates that the SCHW gently but insistently shook the South to consciousness from decades of slumber and was far and away the most significant attempt by Southerners, up to that time, to introduce a far-reaching agenda of change. "It would be remembered," Egerton insists, "not for what it achieved but for what it aspired to and what it attempted."[100]

The threat of an impending war, beginning in 1940, brought increased charges of communism and treason. Business owners, selfishly, and a growing number of citizens believed strikes during a time of crisis were unpatriotic and dangerous. The contested nature of labor activity in this period called on all of Mason's strengths as an organizer. Her chief contribution during this period was in reporting acts of brutality against union organizers that would have gone unreported. In Memphis, Mason documented at least one murder of a black longshoreman in 1940, presumably a victim of the company he sued for back wages. His employers summoned him for a "conference," and he was never seen again. Another Memphis organizer, who had won a dispute with his company over union activities, was picked up by the police and ordered to leave the state. In hiding, the worker "made his account available to Mason, but ceased his agitation."[101]

Because of the heightened sensitivity to her work in this period, Mason was careful to mask her subversive behavior even more. She continued her letter-writing campaign, maintained contacts with the press, and informed the White House and other officials when she needed their help. But she was cautious about how openly she carried out these activities. Specifically she told union representatives, "I never want any publicity. It will ruin my usefulness if my letters or actions are put in print."[102] In other words, she manipulated her visibility as a "Southern lady," using it to gain her entry to people who were antiunion and to attempt to gain protections for organizers through her ties to federal power. She downplayed the latter part of that work when it was convenient to avoid frightening opinion makers in the South whose support the union needed. Mason withdrew from the limelight at times, not so much from modesty but because exposure would defeat her purpose. Mason's goal was to persuade authorities by "playing the lady," which she could not do if her name were splashed across papers as a CIO rabble-rouser. The result, however, is that Mason is only faintly remembered by historians, especially those who rely on newspapers as their principal sources of information.

In 1942, Mason turned sixty, and years of traveling and intervening in stressful civil liberties cases began to take its toll. Illness limited the last ten years of her work for the CIO. She focused on encouraging interracialism. In her official capacity as public relations representative for the CIO, Mason turned her attention to the election of officials who were sympathetic to labor. This political advocacy was, of course, not a new concern for Mason. By the end of World War II, the number of Southern industrial workers had jumped from 1.6 million to 2.4 million. War labor boards had ensured higher wages, union membership provisions, and other benefits in many places. Nationally, union membership was at the highest in its history with 10 million AFL members and 4.5 million CIO members. Even in the South, the CIO claimed 400,000 members and the AFL, 1.8 million members. These factors combined to produce a "degree of respect" for unionists.[103] The war effort had strengthened industrial labor's position due to governmental intervention in labor-management disputes to keep the war machine operating. Mason, too, was caught up in that optimism. She noted that "six years ago it was practically impossible for a CIO representative to appear on a college campus, before a civic association, or a ministerial forum," but those times had changed.[104] Thus, as the CIO came out of the war with increased numbers and a heretofore unknown "cultural credibility," it seemed poised to obtain even greater concessions from business. Mason was particularly optimistic about the possibilities for interracial organizing. Indeed, Michael Honey suggests that "by the middle forties, many black workers had experienced unionization, increased wages, and improved conditions. Now they expected the CIO to begin to deliver on its larger promises of support for equal rights, promises that most whites opposed."[105]

The AFL and the arrival of Northern industries to the nonunion South aided red-baiting and race-baiting companies. In the postwar period, the continuing strength of industrial unionism nationally depended in large measure on a Southern strategy because of the number of industries moving to the region.[106] Mason could not predict, however, the virulent renewal of hostilities between the United States and the Soviet Union nor the impact the Cold War would have on the American labor movement. Southern employers had long employed the rhetoric of anticommunism to discredit trade union organizers in the South, but that strategy became especially bitter and effective in the context of the Cold War. However tentative the CIO's commitment to interracialism may have been, the CIO's small steps across the racial divide made it vulnerable to charges of radicalism, where in the context of the Jim Crow South, it surely was. In mobilizing against union organizing in the postwar period, therefore, employers were able to marry interracialism and anticommunism by literally conflating unionism and miscegenation.

Given the even greater obstacles to unionization in the postwar period, Lucy Mason's ability to appeal to owners, government officials, police, ministers, editors, and other opinion makers was especially important and offered the greatest potential to Southern labor organizing in the postwar period. Ultimately, however, few resources, pervasive racism, and antiunion fervor would overwhelm her contributions. Those deterrents would also defeat the CIO's Operation Dixie. The change was reflected in labor unions' backing away from civil rights activity and interracial work in response to their Southern members, who increasingly joined newly forming White Citizens' Councils.

Historian Alan Draper describes the dilemma of labor activists in the post-*Brown* South. He asserts that a racist backlash in response to court-ordered integration impelled union organizers to eschew working for black civil rights, as they had in the past, and instead focus on economic issues in the workplace. They discovered, Draper insists, that combining civil rights activity with labor's goals alienated many white union members, some of whom participated in the White Citizens' Councils; however, if organizers downplayed or distanced themselves from support of civil rights movement activity, blacks still joined. Draper concludes that, while labor leaders rooted for civil rights advances from a distant sideline and believed those changes would aid their own movement, union organizers chose to leave black civil rights to blacks, a decision that "new Southern labor historians" have castigated, yet one that Draper insists reflected the political realities of the time. Draper's assertions suggest that despite contemporary judgments of the choices labor made during the civil rights movement, nevertheless union leaders made those choices based on their perceptions of political realities. The circumstances were such that a concerted white supremacist resistance to integrated unions, while not absent in the pre-*Brown* era, seemed muted or mitigated by growing industrialization and greater opportunity, as well as by the effects of the New Deal and World War II. The *Brown* decision exacerbated what many believe to be the most sensitive fear of whites regarding integration. School integration, with its inherent specter of interracial sex, inspired a backlash against the nascent movement that effectively obliterated most previous ambivalence.[107]

The CIO stopped short of pushing for racial equality because such methods alienated its white constituency. However, as the CIO relaxed its commitment to racial equality, Mason redoubled hers. Unable, perhaps, to achieve these ends through the labor movement, she supplemented her work with the CIO by participating in three other organizations that were directly engaged in efforts to change white opinion in the South. Race relations captured Mason's attention most fully in this period. She participated in a variety of initiatives dedicated to eradicating racism and increasing interracial cooperation. She seemed to understand that education and intervention by whites were crucial to improved racial interactions. To that end she worked with the National Council of Churches on race issues as well as with the Southern Regional Council.[108] Of the latter, she said, "I regard the SRC as the most important organization dealing with the whole matter of promoting justice, understanding, and opportunity for the Negro people in our region."[109]

Mason spent the last active years of her life writing a book that documented her experiences with the CIO. She reacquainted herself with old friends through the process, in an attempt to include others' thoughts in the work. In particular, she worked with Eleanor Roosevelt, who wrote a foreword to the book. The process of writing the book was valuable but ultimately debilitating. With the book published in 1952, Mason was too tired to continue working. She retired from the CIO in 1953 and died in 1959.

Through moral suasion and an active campaign of publicity that used her access to an elite white base of power, Lucy Mason was able, for a time, to aid the cause of labor and racial reconciliation in the South. While she was able to sway the opinions of some, much work remained in the South. On the day that Mason passed away, the *Atlanta Journal-Constitution* published the report of a black man's lynching in Poplarville, Mississippi.[110] The coincidence is striking. Mason had written once that "a Mississippian said to me many years ago, 'The CIO will never organize the South; Negroes just won't join unions; and the white people won't work in the same unions with Negroes.'" Mason labeled him "a false prophet," and yet the accusation inherent in a tragic episode of racial violence in the "middle of the iceberg" made the Mississippian's charge ring true.[111] It would fall to a new generation to enforce the truth of Mason's prediction that whites and blacks could work together.

NOTES

1. Lucy Randolph Mason, *To Win These Rights: A Personal Story of the CIO in the South* (New York: Harper, 1952), 114–17.

2. Morton Sosna, *In Search of the Silent South: Southern Liberals and the Race Issue* (New York: Columbia University Press, 1971), viii–ix. Sosna uses a framework provided by Gunnar Myrdal's *An American Dilemma* to define a southern liberal as "those white Southerners who perceived that there was a serious maladjustment of race relations in the South, who recognized that the existing system resulted in grave injustices for blacks, and who actively endorsed or engaged in programs to aid Southern blacks in their fight against lynching, disfranchisement, and blatant discrimination in such areas as education, employment, and law enforcement. The ultimate test of the white Southern liberal was his willingness or unwillingness to criticize [the South's] racial mores" (viii).

3. See Lucy Randolph Mason, "I Turned to Social Action Right at Home," in Liston Pope, ed., *Labor's Relation to Church and Community* (New York: Harper & Brothers, 1947), 145–55.

4. John A. Salmond, *Miss Lucy of the CIO: The Life and Times of Lucy Randolph Mason, 1882–1959* (Athens: University of Georgia Press, 1988), 1–14. Salmond's work is invaluable for biographical information on Mason. However, as he admits, he is unable to determine the sources for her views on race, nor does he attempt to conjecture. This work will attempt to provide more information on Mason's views on race.

5. See C. Vann Woodward's *The Strange Career of Jim Crow* (New York: Oxford University Press, 1974) for more on the creation of slavery. Howard Rabinowitz differs slightly from Woodward's widely accepted thesis. He suggests that segregation had been a pattern in the urban South prior to Reconstruction. See Howard N. Rabinowitz, *Race Relations in the Urban South, 1865–1890* (New York: Oxford University Press, 1978).

6. The state of Virginia did not institute legal segregation until 1902. See Peter J. Rachleff, *Black Labor in Richmond, 1865–1890* (Urbana: University of Illinois Press, 1989). See also Neil R. McMillen, *Dark Journey: Black Mississippians in the Age of Jim Crow* (Urbana: University of Illinois Press, 1989), 38–43.

7. Salmond, *Miss Lucy*, 1–14; Lucy Randolph Mason, *To Win These Rights*. In speeches later in her CIO work, Mason often touted the actions of her dissenting grandfather. In actuality, George Mason failed to free his own slaves when the opportunity became available. Christopher and James Collier suggest that, instead, Mason refused to sign the Constitution because he had not written its Bill of Rights. See Christopher Collier and James Collier, *Decision in Philadelphia* (New York: Ballantine Books, 1986), 332–50. In addition, see Landon R. Y. Storrs, "Civilizing Capitalism: The National Consumers' League and the Politics of 'Fair' Labor Standards in the New

Deal Era" (PhD diss., University of Wisconsin–Madison, 1994), 74. Historians disagree on Mason's reasons for refusing to sign the Constitution. Several attribute Mason's refusal to the document's failure to include a Bill of Rights similar to the one Mason had written for Virginia's Constitution. See Collier and Collier, *Decision in Philadelphia*, 332–50. Michael Kammen, ed., *The Origins of the American Constitution: A Documentary History* (New York: Penguin, 1986), 255–58, reproduces a November 1787 statement by Mason as to his objections to the Constitution. His first line is "There is no Declaration of Rights. . . ." Others tie Mason's objections to the Constitution's failure to abolish the slave trade. Jack N. Rakove notes Mason's disquiet that the Constitution did not immediately end the slave trade, a position not unusual for Virginians who had abolished their own trade in 1778. See Jack N. Rakove, *Original Meanings: Politics and Ideas in the Making of the Constitution* (New York: Alfred A. Knopf, 1996), 138. Rakove notes that Oliver Ellsworth ridiculed Mason's opposition by noting he had three hundred slaves, and an end to the slave trade would have benefited Mason. Lucy Mason preferred to believe Mason's refusal grew from more altruistic motives (305).

8. See Salmond, *Miss Lucy*; and Mason, *To Win These Rights*.

9. Mason, *To Win These Rights*, 1.

10. Salmond, *Miss Lucy*, 6.

11. Mason, *To Win These Rights*, 22.

12. Marie Tyler-McGraw, *At the Falls: Richmond, Virginia, and Its People* (Chapel Hill: University of North Carolina Press, 1994), 184–214.

13. Salmond, *Miss Lucy*, 10. The governor called in the state militia to quell the strike.

14. Salmond, *Miss Lucy*, 8. Salmond quotes early drafts of Mason's *To Win These Rights*.

15. Mason, "I Turned to Social Action," 146–47.

16. Ronald C. White Jr. and C. Howard Hopkins, *The Social Gospel: Religion and Reform in Changing America* (Philadelphia: Temple University Press, 1976), 5–35.

17. Mason, "I Turned to Social Action," 146–47. There is some historical debate about the presence and pervasiveness of the Social Gospel movement in the South. Samuel Hill has argued that the Social Gospel did not make a significant impact in the region. But others, namely John Lee Eighmy and Wayne Flint, have dissented from that opinion. See John Lee Eighmy, *Churches in Cultural Captivity* (Knoxville: University of Tennessee Press, 1987); J. Wayne Flynt, *Poor But Proud: Alabama's Poor Whites* (Tuscaloosa: University of Alabama Press, 1989). For further discussion, see my thesis, "'Life in Scorn of the Consequences': Clarence Jordan and the Roots of Radicalism in the Southern Baptist Convention" (master's thesis, University of Mississippi, May 1994). Suffice it to say that for Lucy Mason, who was a Southerner and who worked primarily in the South, the Social Gospel was of significant influence.

18. See Mason, *To Win These Rights*, 1–18; Salmond, *Miss Lucy*, 8–14.

19. Salmond, *Miss Lucy*, 9–18.

20. Salmond, *Miss Lucy*, 9–18.

21. Salmond, *Miss Lucy*, 9–18.

22. Mason, *To Win These Rights*, 5.

23. Mason, *To Win These Rights*, 4.

24. According to one of its historians, the YWCA was founded in 1866 in Boston for the temporal, moral, and religious welfare of young women who were dependent

on their own exertion for support. Its founders patterned the organization on similar workers' relief efforts in London. Developed out of a desire to address the religious training needs of working women and the more predominant effort to support working women, the organization held its first national convention on December 5, 1906, successfully merging the two efforts. Grace H. Wilson, *The Religious and Educational Philosophy of the Young Women's Christian Association* (New York: Bureau of Publications, Teachers College, Columbia University, 1933), 6.

25. Wilson, *Religious and Educational Philosophy*, 14–28.

26. Another Richmond woman who worked tirelessly for suffrage and for black causes was Maggie Lena Walker. A contemporary of Mason, Walker, an African American women, was the first woman bank president in the United States. Walker was particularly active in the Independent Order of Saint Luke, an mutual benefit society that "combined insurance functions with economic development and social and political activities. As such they were important loci of community self-help and racial solidarity." Thus, while Mason's work on behalf of the black community is significant, there were successful parallel efforts among the black community to address its own challenges. It seems likely that Mason and Walker would have known each other, but there is no evidence of that relationship at this time. See Elsa Barkley Brown's "Womanist Consciousness: Maggie Lena Walker and the Independent Order of Saint Luke," in Vicki L. Ruiz and Ellen Carol DuBois, eds., *Unequal Sisters: A Multicultural Reader in U.S. Women's History* (New York: Routledge, 1994), 268–83.

27. Margaret Lee Neustadt, "Miss Lucy of the CIO: Lucy Randolph Mason, 1882–1959" (master's thesis, University of North Carolina at Chapel Hill, 1969), 8. The committee investigated three questions. The questions were: 1. Why does the Richmond Negro live on the average almost fifteen years less than the white man of Richmond? 2. Why is the Richmond Negro arrested so much more often than the white man of Richmond? 3. Eliminating from consideration all biological and anthropological factors, are the medical, educational, recreational, economic, and social opportunities of the Richmond Negro adequate to his needs? Negro Welfare Survey Committee, *The Negro in Richmond, Virginia* (Richmond, Va.: Richmond Council of Social Agencies, 1929), foreword by June Purcell Guild, director of the survey, November 20, 1929, 1, quoted in Neustadt, "Miss Lucy," 8.

28. Neustadt, "Miss Lucy," 8.

29. Neustadt, "Miss Lucy," 8.

30. Neustadt, "Miss Lucy," 12.

31. Mason quoted in Storrs, "Civilizing Capitalism," 102.

32. See Kathryn Kish Sklar, *Florence Kelley and the Nation's Work: The Rise of Women's Political Culture, 1830–1900* (New Haven, Conn.: Yale University Press, 1995), for the first in a two-volume series on Kelley's biography and her role in the transformation of women's public culture.

33. Sklar, *Florence Kelley*, xiii.

34. Announcement to members, National Consumers League, Lucy Randolph Mason Papers, Operation Dixie Collection, Duke University Library, reel 62, June 1, 1932.

35. Storrs, "Civilizing Capitalism," 104.

36. Mason quoted in Storrs, "Civilizing Capitalism," 101.

37. Mason quoted in Storrs, "Civilizing Capitalism," 101–2.

38. Mason, *To Win These Rights*, 12.

39. Lucy Randolph Mason, "The Industrial South," Lucy Randolph Mason Papers, Operation Dixie Collection, Duke University Library, reel 62, June 4, 1936.

40. Mason, "The Industrial South."

41. Storrs, "Civilizing Capitalism," 105–6.

42. Mason, *To Win These Rights*, 16.

43. Letter to Robert Rivers Lamonte from Lucy Randolph Mason, National Consumers League Papers, Library of Congress, reel 29, June 23, 1936.

44. Ralph McGill, "Miss Lucy of the CIO," *Atlanta Constitution*, May 9, 1959, quoted in Neustadt, "Miss Lucy," 22. The article appeared as a eulogy for Mason.

45. Hollinger F. Barnard, ed., *Outside the Magic Circle: The Autobiography of Virginia Foster Durr* (Tuscaloosa: University of Alabama Press, 1990), 118.

46. Robert H. Zieger, *The CIO, 1935–1955* (Chapel Hill: University of North Carolina Press, 1995), 14.

47. See Zieger, *The CIO*, 22–65; and Barbara S. Griffith, *The Crisis of American Labor: Operation Dixie and the Defeat of the CIO* (Philadelphia: Temple University Press, 1988), 3–11.

48. Zieger, *The CIO*, 74.

49. Zieger, *The CIO*, 74.

50. See Zieger, *The CIO*, 66–89; Steve Rosswurm, ed., *The CIO's Left-Led Unions* (New Brunswick, N.J.: Rutgers University Press, 1992); and Michael Kazin, *The Populist Persuasion: An American History* (New York: Basic Books, 1995).

51. G. MacLeod Bryan, interview by the author, notes in author's possession, Winston-Salem, N.C., November 4, 1994.

52. Mason, *To Win These Rights*, 24, 26, 29–30.

53. Mason, *To Win These Rights*, 26.

54. Mason, *To Win These Rights*.

55. See James C. Cobb, *The Most Southern Place on Earth: The Mississippi Delta and the Roots of Regional Identity* (New York: Oxford University Press, 1992), for more on the Mississippi Delta.

56. Michael Honey, *Southern Labor and Black Civil Rights: Organizing Memphis Workers* (Urbana: University of Illinois Press, 1993), 52. See this work for a complete description of the history of Memphis and labor organizing there.

57. Mason, *To Win These Rights*, 106.

58. A union steward in Memphis, Tennessee, quoted in Mason, *To Win These Rights*, 109.

59. Mason, *To Win These Rights*, 107.

60. Mason, *To Win These Rights*, 107.

61. Mason, *To Win These Rights*, 108.

62. Mason quoted in Honey, *Southern Labor*, 138.

63. Honey, *Southern Labor*, 138.

64. Honey, *Southern Labor*, 145–46.

65. Mason quoted in Honey, *Southern Labor*, 146.

66. Letter to Eleanor Roosevelt from Lucy Randolph Mason, Lucy Randolph Mason Papers, Operation Dixie Collection, Duke University Library, reel 62, May 28, 1940.

67. Zieger, *The CIO*, 75–76.

68. Mason, *To Win These Rights*, 77.

69. Mason, *To Win These Rights*, 77.

70. Letter to Franklin Delano Roosevelt from Lucy Randolph Mason, Lucy Randolph Mason Papers, Operation Dixie Collection, Duke University Library, reel 62, August 12, 1937.

71. Letter to Lucy Mason from Franklin D. Roosevelt, Lucy Randolph Mason Papers, Operation Dixie Collection, Duke University Library, reel 62, October 7, 1940.

72. See letters to Roosevelt from Mason, August 12, 1937; March 25, 1938; April 19, 1938. Lucy Randolph Mason Papers, Operation Dixie Collection, Duke University Library, reel 62.

73. See letter to Molly Dewson from Lucy Mason, Lucy Randolph Mason Papers, Operation Dixie Collection, Duke University Library, reel 62, September 6, 1937.

74. Lucy Randolph Mason, Circular Letter, February 24, 1938, quoted in Neustadt, "Miss Lucy," 34.

75. Lucy Randolph Mason, Circular Letter to Ministers for Labor Day, Lucy Randolph Mason Papers, Operation Dixie Collection, Duke University Library, reel 62, August 25, 1937.

76. Salmond, *Miss Lucy*, 82–83.

77. Salmond, *Miss Lucy*, 82–83.

78. See Mason correspondence to Eleanor and Franklin Roosevelt, John E. Rankin, and the FBI of April 15, 1938, Lucy Randolph Mason Papers, Operation Dixie Collection, Duke University Library, reel 62. See also Mason, *To Win These Rights*, 50–53; Neustadt, "Miss Lucy," 38–41; Salmond, *Miss Lucy*, 82–83.

79. See letter to Lucy Randolph Mason from J. Edgar Hoover regarding his assignment of the case to "Joseph B. Keenan, The Assistant to the Attorney General, U.S. Department of Justice, Washington, D.C. for such attention as he may deem appropriate," Lucy Randolph Mason Papers, Operation Dixie Collection, Duke University Library, reel 62, July 16, 1938.

80. Salmond, *Miss Lucy*, 82–83.

81. Mason, *To Win These Rights*, 75.

82. Neustadt, "Miss Lucy," 31.

83. Mason, *To Win These Rights*, 54–55.

84. Letter to Lucy Mason from Jonathan Daniels. Lucy Randolph Mason Papers, Operation Dixie Collection, Duke University Library, reel 62, September 9, 1937.

85. See letter to Eleanor Roosevelt from Lucy Mason, Lucy Randolph Mason Papers, Operation Dixie Collection, Duke University Library, reel 62, March 20, 1942.

86. John Egerton, phone interview by author, notes in author's possession, July 29, 1999.

87. Letter to Lucy Mason from Grover C. Hall, Lucy Randolph Mason Papers, Operation Dixie Collection, Duke University Library, reel 65, January 18, 1938.

88. Address by Lucy Randolph Mason, Lucy Randolph Mason Papers, Operation Dixie Collection, Duke University Library, reel 65, May 8–12, 1939.

89. Neustadt, "Miss Lucy," 50.

90. *Daily Tar Heel*, "The Necessity of Skepticism," March 24, 1939, quoted in Neustadt, "Miss Lucy," 50.

91. Letter to Mary Jane Willett from Lucy Randolph Mason, Lucy Randolph Mason Papers, Operation Dixie Collection, Duke University Library, reel 62, March 31, 1939.

92. Mason, *To Win These Rights*, 39–40.

93. Letter to Lucy Mason from Elizabeth Cowan, Lucy Randolph Mason Papers, Operation Dixie Collection, Duke University Library, reel 62, March 27, 1939.

94. Neustadt, "Miss Lucy," 52.

95. Letter to Lucy Mason from Lowell Mellett, Executive Director, the National Emergency Council, Lucy Randolph Mason Papers, Operation Dixie Collection, Duke University Library, reel 62, June 25, 1938.

96. FDR had spent part of the 1937–1938 election year campaigning against anti–New Deal Southern representatives, like Georgia's Walter George. His attempts to prevent their reelections began to backfire, and his reputation in those areas suffered. He saw in the *Report on the Economic Conditions of the South* an opportunity to challenge any anti–New Deal sentiment. If the report failed, the Southerners who had helped write it would shoulder some of that burden and he could continue to work with the representatives against whom he had campaigned. See John Egerton, *Speak Now Against the Day: The Generation Before the Civil Rights Movement in the South* (New York: Knopf, 1994), 177–81.

97. Egerton, *Speak Now*, 175. Egerton does not indicate if the white male members resigned in protest against Johnson, Mason, or both.

98. Egerton, *Speak Now*, 174–80. See also Linda Reed, *Simple Decency and Common Sense: The Southern Conference Movement, 1938–1963* (Bloomington: Indiana University Press, 1991).

99. Egerton, *Speak Now*, 174; Reed, *Simple Decency*, 9–19, especially on Mason's role in the creation of the Southern Conference for Human Welfare.

100. Egerton, *Speak Now*, 181–87, 197.

101. Honey, *Southern Labor*, 115.

102. Neustadt, "Miss Lucy," 81.

103. Honey, *Southern Labor*, 214.

104. Honey, *Southern Labor*, 214–15.

105. Honey, *Southern Labor*, 219–20.

106. Griffith, *The Crisis of American Labor*, 16–21.

107. Alan Draper, *Conflict of Interests: Organized Labor and the Civil Rights Movement in the South, 1954–1968* (Ithaca, N.Y.: ILR Press, 1994), 3–14, 17–27. See Glisson, "'Life in Scorn of the Consequences.'" See Lillian Smith, *Killers of the Dream* (New York: Norton, 1961); and John Miller Spivey, "Agnes Pryor: An Oral History," unpublished interview transcript, December 8, 1993.

108. See Neustadt, "Miss Lucy," 117, 126.

109. Letter to William R. Moody from Lucy Randolph Mason, Lucy Randolph Mason Papers, Operation Dixie Collection, Duke University Library, reel 62, October, 25, 1951.

110. Neustadt, "Miss Lucy," 131. Mason had been involved in Jessie Daniel Ames's Southern Women for the Prevention of Lynching.

111. Address by Mason, Lucy Randolph Mason Papers, Operation Dixie Collection, Duke University Library, reel 65, circa 1951.

SUGGESTED READING

Draper, Alan. *Conflict of Interests: Organized Labor and the Civil Rights Movement in the South, 1954–1968*. Ithaca, N.Y.: ILR Press, 1994.

Egerton, John. *Speak Now Against the Day: The Generation Before the Civil Rights Movement in the South*. New York: Knopf, 1994.

Honey, Michael. *Southern Labor and Black Civil Rights: Organizing Memphis Workers*. Urbana: University of Illinois Press, 1993.

Mason, Lucy Randolph. *To Win These Rights: A Personal Story of the CIO in the South*. New York: Harper, 1952.

Salmond, John A. *Miss Lucy of the CIO: The Life and Times of Lucy Randolph Mason, 1882–1959*. Athens: University of Georgia Press, 1988.

Sullivan, Patricia. *Days of Hope: Race and Democracy in the New Deal Era*. Chapel Hill: University of North Carolina Press, 1996.

III

&

AWAKENINGS

7

ॐ

Amzie Moore:
The Biographical Roots of
the Civil Rights Movement
in Mississippi

Jay Driskell

Amzie Moore was one of the key leaders of the black freedom struggle in Mississippi in the years prior to what we understand as the civil rights movement. It was Moore who would identify an illiterate sharecropper named Fannie Lou Hamer and see in her the potential to lead the entire movement. Moore would also meet Bob Moses, the first field secretary that the Student Nonviolent Coordinating Committee (SNCC) sent into the Magnolia State. With decades of organizing experience under his belt, Moore would introduce the young activists from SNCC to an older generation of black freedom fighters in the Delta. According to SNCC veteran Sam Block, "Amzie Moore was really the father of the movement" in Mississippi. However, before he could do this, Moore first had to understand himself as a leader.

A deeply religious man, Moore did not initially believe that civil rights were in God's plan for African Americans. However, his experiences as a soldier in Burma and India during World War II transformed his religious beliefs. He could no longer believe he was a simple subject of God's will. Moore returned from the war on a religious mission to continue the fight he had begun against race supremacy abroad.

Most importantly, he kept the fight for civil rights alive in the wake of the repression that followed the Supreme Court's 1954 decision in Brown v. Board of Education. *At a time when every other local leader had fallen to an assassin's bullet or fled the state, Moore stood his ground—even though it cost him his marriage, his business ventures, and probably his health. His experiences during these years radicalized Moore, led to his break with the National Association for the Advancement of Colored People (NAACP), and transformed his notion of who was capable of leadership. The leadership of the movement in Mississippi would no longer reflect just the black middle class, but rather the full range of black experience in the state.*

"God must love white people; they must be His choice . . . His special people," he thought.[1] Each time the young Amzie Moore entered a white household he invariably compared it with his own. What especially struck him was that all the white people he knew growing up in Mississippi had indoor plumbing, while many of his black friends and family still lived in shacks without electricity, let alone bath fixtures. He recalled walking "three to five miles to church, and [having] . . . to get out of the road when somebody [white] passe[d] in a car," but he did not feel "bitter or frustrated because here I thought that God had so designed for a specific reason."[2] The material evidence overwhelmingly seemed to prove that white people were indeed God's chosen.

The future black freedom fighter did not inherit the family traditions of pride and resistance that had marked the childhoods of other civil rights veterans. Instead, like many others in his position, Moore embraced a brand of religious fatalism that helped him explain the subjugation of African Americans he had witnessed since childhood. If it was God's plan to put white people in charge, then the lot of black Southerners was not due to any inherent racial flaw. When white Southerners sought to control every meaning black people sought to give their lives, Moore's religious beliefs enabled him to redeem a sense of meaning, determined not by the prerogatives of white supremacy but rather by the inscrutable design of God. Such beliefs were necessary for simple survival in Jim Crow Mississippi. Prior to World War II, the anger of individual African Americans at white dominion was often futile and self-destructive and, if carried into action, nearly always fatal. As Ralph Ellison observed, during Jim Crow the urge to revolt had to be suppressed in black children. For a boy like the young Amzie Moore, this was necessary "to protect him from those unknown forces *within himself* which might urge him to reach out for that . . . equality which the white South says he can not have. Rather than throw himself against the charged wires of his prison he annihilates the impulses within him."[3]

Amzie Moore went on to become one of a handful of local black leaders courageous enough to keep the light of freedom shining throughout the long dark night of Jim Crow. The influence of these leaders is evidenced in the strategy and tactics of the Student Nonviolent Coordinating Committee (SNCC), a civil rights organization that came to the Delta in the 1960s. Moore's guidance is responsible for SNCC's emphasis on voter registration as well as the idea for Freedom Summer, in which hundreds of white college students risked their lives to help register black voters in the Delta. In 1960, Moore would introduce Bob Moses, SNCC's first Mississippi field secretary,

to the extensive network of activists that he himself helped to build. In so doing, he would pass the torch on to the next generation of freedom fighters.
Before he would be able to do so, he would first have to kindle that flame
within himself. Moore's story is not only that of the development of a grassroots political leader struggling to overcome white supremacy; it is also the
story of his liberation from that electrified cage into which he was born.

Born in 1912, Moore grew up on the Wilkin Plantation in Grenada County,
Mississippi. Though the separation of his parents and the death of his
mother left Moore impoverished, his parents may not have started out poor.
In the late nineteenth century, Moore claimed, his grandfather owned about
640 acres of land and had saved somewhere in the neighborhood of twenty
thousand dollars by the time he died. Nonetheless, Moore's family, like
many others, went bankrupt during the agricultural recession that swept the
South just prior to the Great Depression of the 1930s. Despite these setbacks,
Moore managed to achieve a tenth-grade education at Stone Street High
School in Cleveland, Mississippi—the highest grade the school offered. It
was a remarkable feat when one considers that in 1920 roughly one in three
black Mississippians was illiterate and in the years 1930–1931, only slightly
more than one in every hundred black teenagers was able to finish the tenth
grade.[4] Ironically, it was the death of his mother and his abandonment by his
father that freed Moore from sharecropping to attain an education. During
this time, Moore stayed with a number of relatives in the area, did odd jobs,
and was often able to eat only because he was able to convince other kids at
school to buy him food. Moore recalled in 1977: "Had [my mother] lived, I
would have had the responsibility of being there with her, and helping her.
Until I had grown to be a man and I would probably just marry somebody
and we would work together for the rest of my life." Having attained such
an education at a time when many black parents found it impossible to dis-
pense with the labor of their school-age children allowed Moore, though impoverished, to aspire to the ranks of Mississippi's black middle class.[5]

Republican national committee member E. P. Booze understood these aspirations in Moore and invited the twenty-year-old Moore to join the Black and
Tans, the African American wing of the party of Lincoln. Though conservative, the political philosophy of the Black and Tan leadership was fundamentally different from that of the political leadership of the white South.
Whereas the latter concerned itself primarily with the defense of white property interests, the former took upon itself the uplift of the black South. Furthermore, considering the ability of the self-proclaimed "party of white supremacy" to mobilize retaliatory violence, Republican Party activists like
Charles Banks of Mound Bayou believed that participating in any organization that could align black citizens against the all-white Democratic Party was
"fraught with dangers and altogether unwise."[6] Consequently, the primary
purpose of the organization was neither to elect black candidates nor to develop black electoral influence, but rather to distribute political spoils to local

Amzie Moore (Image courtesy of the Wisconsin Historical Society.)

party members, sustaining a local black leadership class that would otherwise have had no other means of support. In addition, Black and Tan party leaders managed to win offices for sympathetic whites and occasionally were able to block the appointment of the most virulent white supremacists.

There were, of course, other political traditions manifest in the history of the local freedom struggle, but the political realities of Jim Crow Mississippi severely limited their viability. The poverty of most black Mississippians and the tenuous position of the black bourgeoisie made independent political action all but impossible. Black resistance to white supremacy through the labor movement was not an option either. Black labor organizers in the Magnolia State met violence and insurmountable racism from within the rank and file of the white union movement as well as from its opponents. Furthermore, the daily forms of covert resistance every black American practiced did not, in pre–World War II Mississippi, coalesce into an organization capable of openly challenging the white power structure. Though these other strategies would be important for later manifestations of the black freedom struggle, the leadership of Mississippi had no other politically viable choice but to position itself as a mediator between the needs of black citizens and the economic power of white elites to fulfill those needs. Despite their tenuous position, Mississippi's black leadership was not always unified behind such an accommodationist strategy, nor were they always popular with the black Mississippians they claimed to be leading.

The most prominent of these mediator/enforcers was the Committee of 100. Founded in 1923 by conservative black Republicans, the Committee aspired to become a statewide conference of leading race men and women. Their lack of any real political power compelled the Committee to rely upon moral suasion and negotiation with white political, religious, and business leaders. At the beginning of the 1930s, when Moore became active among this group, the Committee's program called for protection from white vigilante violence, called for higher living standards, and pressured Mississippi's segregationists to uphold the *equal* in "separate but equal." In exchange, they would encourage obedience to the law, good citizenship, and racial progress through separate economic development. An early editorial by Committee founder Isaiah T. Montgomery claimed that black Southerners "are gaining a respectable hold upon the business interests of the country" and expressed the hope that "as they adapt themselves to sound business principles, more and more will come to them the recognition that is due to every useful and upright citizen."[7] Though Moore did not embrace the philosophy of his early mentors, he did cut his political teeth among this group of race leaders who, shut out from the political sphere, learned to define race uplift through entrepreneurial success. Later generations of civil rights activists dismissed the Committee as ultraconservative. In response, the son of Committee founder J. E. Johnson asserted that "had blacks pushed in the 1920s like they did in the 1960s, they would have been slaughtered."[8] Even though their efforts were constrained by the limits of Jim Crow, the decades of persistent, low-key pressure on the part of the Committee of 100 and similar organizations sustained a tradition of resistance to white supremacy in Mississippi—a tradition that established the networks upon which the activists of the 1960s would build.

While it would take Moore almost two decades to abandon this vision of black bourgeois leadership, his days with the Republican Party were numbered. Unwilling to toe the party line in 1936 and support Alf Landon for president against Roosevelt, he quit the Black and Tans. Like many other black Americans during the Depression, he "turned Lincoln's picture to the wall" and registered to vote as a Democrat. Even though the civil rights record of the Roosevelt administration was not the greatest, FDR's New Deal dramatically improved the economic circumstances of most black Americans. Moore recalled the 1930s: "So many banks [were] closing and jobs were so few. And the Red Cross was issuing a small piece of meat with some brown flour. That was the extent of what we had. . . . it was really tough."[9] Additionally, since the 1920 election, the Republican Party had been attempting to purge African Americans from the party in order to better compete against the Democrats in the South. While these were the two biggest reasons Moore abandoned the party of Lincoln, the twenty-year Democratic ascendancy that FDR's 1932 election ushered in certainly played a role. The Republican loss of the White House signaled the collapse of the patronage networks that had sustained the Black and Tans for the last half century.

The pressures generated by the Depression marked the beginning of the end for the Black and Tan Republicans but not the end of Moore's political career. In 1940, Moore took part in a mass meeting of some ten thousand African Americans held at Delta State College in Cleveland, Mississippi. The meeting was organized under the auspices of the Delta Council, an organization founded by white planters to promote economic development, secure federal funding for highway and levee construction, and, most importantly, reform the plantation system in an effort to retain workers and combat labor unions and civil rights advocates. Though Moore dubbed the meeting the "first awakening," he also explained that the black political leadership of the day was still "talking about 'separate but equal.'"[10] The agenda of the Delta Council gathering included rural electrification and the accreditation of church schools. The organizers of these campaigns hoped that if black Mississippians had their own accredited schools based in black churches, they would prove less receptive to overtures from the NAACP and their expanding school desegregation campaign. Moore described the consolidated school system of the Delta as "the world's largest," but black students were not allowed to attend. Instead, there were "about 105 church schools that the blacks went to." He was willing to go along with the Delta Council in the preservation of Jim Crow in exchange for what he hoped would be a fairer distribution of resources; however, he had his doubts. "We could always see the separation, but in nowhere did we see the equality. . . . We, at that time, were perfectly willing to try to do that [though] our experience had taught us [otherwise]."[11] Such skepticism was well founded. In the same year of the Delta Council meeting, the state of Mississippi spent $38.96 per white pupil and only $4.97 per black pupil—even though black taxpayers contributed as much if not more than did white taxpayers. Ten years later, annual state expenditures on black education increased six-fold to $32.55 per pupil. Regardless, inequality proceeded apace—Mississippi then spent $122.93 per white pupil over the same period of time.[12]

In 1942, Amzie Moore entered the army, which then shipped him from one segregated army base to another for two and a half years. Though he grew up in the Delta, Moore "didn't know what segregation was like" until he entered the army. In El Paso, Texas, the separate-but-equal barracks were built in the middle of the desert far from town. Moore and his fellow black enlisted men were forbidden from both the main PX and the recreational facilities. To go into town, PFC Moore was forced to ride in the back of a Jim Crow bus. The same pattern repeated at every domestic base at which he was stationed: "Everywhere we went, we were faced with this evil thing—segregation." When Moore's unit went to Calcutta, he discovered that the enlisted men's club was segregated. The irony reverberated in Moore's mind: "Why were we fighting? Why were we there? If we were fighting for the four freedoms that Roosevelt and Churchill had talked about, then . . . we felt that the American soldier should be free first." Sergeant Jim Crow hounded him all the way over the Himalayas into Burma, where Japanese propaganda broadcast "day and night" reminded black soldiers "about segregation in America . . . that there would be no freedom, even after the war was over." Ironically, on orders from U.S. Army Intelligence, Moore lectured black troops on their stake in the war, "that after the war, things would be different, that men would have a chance to be free." Somehow, Moore recalled dryly, "some of us didn't believe it."[13]

On leave in Calcutta, Corporal Moore experienced an epiphany that would mark his life forever. Weary and glad to be away from the Pacific theater, he stood before the remains of a beautiful Hindu temple, admired the elegance of its arches, and rested in the coolness of its shadows. From its vistas, he gazed upon the remarkable symmetry of the roads, the magnificent extent of the city. His own experiences as a black American, however, also led him to see alongside those avenues people naked, hungry, dying in the doorways of the ancient buildings. Later, reflecting upon that experience, he thought, "there's always something that destroyed a civilization . . . and it had to be wrong or it wouldn't have destroyed it. . . . The conditions that I saw in India . . . People dying in the streets and people walking by them like they aren't even there; kids being born in the streets . . . you look at their buildings . . . some of the finest architects the world has ever seen. I tell you when you look at the folks whose ancestors did it, you wonder 'what in the world happened?'"[14]

Moore came to understand that unless there could be freedom and justice within the United States, it too would suffer the same fate. "We have to win the confidence and the hearts of the people by showing some degree of freedom. You can't set up an aristocracy and expect to stay afloat. . . . I'm thoroughly convinced that there's a coming down, and like the great wheel of time, every spoke comes on over and then it goes in the dirt."[15] To Moore, like other black soldiers, a U.S.-issue uniform cut to fit was a symbol of power independent of and greater than the white supremacist South. Not only did the sight of black men in uniform unnerve the defenders of white supremacy, this symbol also had great appeal for those black Mississippians, especially men, still dressed in the baggy trousers of the sharecropper. When black veterans like Moore returned home, their experiences overseas enabled them to penetrate the veil of postwar patriotism and persist in their fight for democracy. With both hands, they would grab the spokes of that mighty wheel and turn the South upside down.

Amzie Moore overcame his fatalistic deference to white people when he went overseas and "saw the world first hand. . . . People are just people: some good, some bad. Some rich, some poor."[16] After visiting other corners of creation, Moore concluded that "God is no respecter of person. People all over the world, where I've seen, they live and die; they survive and perish," regardless of color. In the wake of this revelation, Moore concluded that "there is no justification . . . to assume that God wanted . . . to make [slaves]. . . . People did it."[17] The experience of seeing different races in positions of both power and subjugation helped him to realize that the racial order in Mississippi was not ordained by God, but rather by human beings themselves.

Rather than consolation for the realities of white domination, religious faith became the rock upon which Moore built his struggle for justice and freedom. He no longer believed it was the will of God to elevate the white race and keep blacks in their place. Reflecting on his experiences in India, Moore later wrote a "Prophetic Outline of World History," based upon the story of the destruction of Babylon, "the mightiest of them all, the mightiest of the world," as told in the book of Isaiah 13:17–22.[18] As Babylon, the glory of all man's kingdoms, fell; as India fell, so shall Mississippi fall, "as when God overthrew Sodom and Gomorrah."[19] The God in which Moore came to believe sided with the righteous and punished the wicked. Not only do empires fall, but this God also hastens their destruction. Moore found the strength to become the agent of God's will on earth in his belief that "God will take care of his out casts [*sic*] who for his sake are driven from among men."[20] This was no small thing considering how many activists were exiled from Mississippi through economic pressure and violence. Given the odds that black civil rights activists were up against in Mississippi, it certainly helped to believe the Lord was on their side. As profoundly religious as Moore was, he had to explain his commitment in terms of his faith. The fatalism of Moore's Christianity had to change before he was able to hope for a world without white supremacy. It allowed him to rebel against Babylon without also rebelling against the will of God.

Just before entering the army, Amzie Moore married Ruth Carey and purchased a house in Cleveland, Mississippi. He was eager to return both to raise a family and to continue the struggle against white supremacy he had begun overseas. Following his demobilization in January of 1946, Moore arrived in Mississippi, only to discover that local whites had organized a "home guard" to protect their families from returning black soldiers. The response of white Southerners to returning black GIs strained the credibility of U.S. wartime propaganda, and Moore later estimated that, for most of that year, at least one black Deltan was killed each week. Undaunted, he pursued the black American dream. Following a fire that claimed their first home, Ruth and Amzie Moore built themselves another in July of 1953 "and planned to settle down to the job of living." Amzie Moore's canceled checks from this period reflect his ascendancy to the black middle class. In January 1953, he spent nearly $450 on clothes, furniture, and "auto body finishing." At the end of June, he spent $608.45 on a "washing machine and [a] range." The next month, he wrote a check to the Jordan Furniture Company for a "15% down payment" on furniture. By the end of the year, he bought a television set and five suits, and paid off the furniture. In February 1954, he bought a TV antenna from Wolfe's TV Company for $96. Moore and his wife also supported other black business ventures.[21] In 1951, they invested $1,000 in the Magnolia Mutual Life Insurance Company, founded by Dr. Theodore R. Mason Howard, a black entrepreneur and civil rights leader from Mound Bayou, Mississippi.[22] By February of the following year, Mr. and Mrs. Moore joined the company's board of directors along with the future president of the state NAACP, Aaron Henry. Three months later, a Magnolia Mutual Life letterhead listed Henry and Moore as secretary and assistant secretary respectively, with Dr. T. R. M. Howard as president.[23] By the early 1950s, Moore had situated himself solidly in the ranks of Mississippi's black bourgeoisie.[24]

As a black entrepreneur, Moore felt it was both his prerogative and his responsibility to step forward as a local political leader. On December 28, 1951, Dr. Howard, Moore, Henry, and others founded the Delta Council of Negro Leadership, later renamed the Regional Council of Negro Leadership (RCNL). It remains unclear why the founders of the RCNL felt the need to establish an alternate civil rights group from the NAACP, to which most if not all RCNL officers also belonged. The organizers may have found the program of the NAACP wanting in several respects. Perhaps most critically, the RCNL addressed economic issues, an area the NAACP did not emphasize during this period. Furthermore, due to the sheer physical danger of belonging to the NAACP in Mississippi, the nation's most prominent civil rights organization kept quiet in the state throughout the immediate postwar years. The NAACP's strategy was to give low priority to work in Mississippi itself, focusing instead on change in the surrounding states. In the words of 1960s civil rights veteran Charles Cobb, the NAACP "surrounded

Mississippi and . . . squeezed it with breakthroughs in Tennessee and Kentucky and Georgia and Arkansas."[25] The RCNL may have provided, for Mississippi's activists, the organizational vehicle to do the local civil rights work the NAACP could not do.

The NAACP's strategy toward Mississippi proved especially frustrating for Amzie Moore. Like other local organizers, he felt constrained by the NAACP's nationally focused legal strategy. Rather than using its resources to sustain local leadership, the best the NAACP could typically offer was legal representation to black Deltans with civil rights grievances. Furthermore, the NAACP was constantly on the verge of bankruptcy throughout the 1950s, and any case they spent money on had to be winnable and had to advance the organization's national agenda. This litigious strategy placed a premium on the highly specialized skills of lawyers and lobbyists and left little room for the active participation of middle-class leaders lacking them, including Moore or even Dr. T. R. M. Howard. Since the NAACP focused on a strategy of national legislation and litigation, many members of the association had little to offer the organization aside from moral and financial support. While the legal and legislative successes of the civil rights movement would have been unthinkable without the NAACP, the strategy the organization's leaders chose to pursue could never have produced the mass democratic movement the Delta witnessed in the 1960s. Without an alternate organization such as the RCNL in the 1950s or SNCC in the following decade, civil rights activists such as Amzie Moore would never have had a chance to develop their leadership. Moore himself realized he was largely ignorant of legal "methods and procedures" and had little to offer someone primarily interested in being a defendant in an NAACP-sponsored lawsuit. Amzie Moore recognized the limits of legal strategies for change and felt they didn't go far enough. As he suggested, "always it was the legality of what's done, [but] how are you going to fight it with lawyers and judges?"[26]

The major purposes of the RCNL were to encourage the economic development of the black community as well as to teach first-class citizenship, to assist in the paying of poll taxes, and eventually to elect black Mississippians to public office. At its height, the RCNL claimed the area on both sides of the Mississippi River from Memphis, Tennessee, in the north to Greenville, Mississippi, in the south. Thousands of people attended the organization's first mass meeting in May of 1952 to hear Chicago's black congressman, William Dawson, speak, and two years later, 13,000 people showed up for NAACP attorney Thurgood Marshall's speech. *Ebony* magazine covered this meeting and included a photo of Amzie Moore handing out pamphlets on voter registration. The caption beneath the photo states that Moore started a "near-riot" as people scrambled to get a copy of the pamphlet. The organization was composed mainly of the traditional black leadership of the Delta, whom Moore called the "professional people—principals of schools . . . teachers. All that crowd was more or less involved."[27] Though the membership was never that large—one estimate places it at 500 spread over twenty-nine counties—the RCNL, for a time, wielded a great deal of influence in the region, even threatening to displace the NAACP.

Ostensibly operating within the confines of Jim Crow, the first major project of the RCNL appeared not to call for an end to segregation, but only to call for its reform. Targeting black gas station owners as well as white, the "No Rest Room, No Gas" campaign attempted to force gas station operators to provide segregated restrooms for black patrons, boycotting those who did not. While in the eyes of the NAACP this amounted to acceptance of the doctrine of separate but equal, RCNL organizers maintained they were trying to bankrupt Jim Crow—adding an extra bathroom to each gas station would certainly be pricey. Also, in a state whose white supremacy was far more virulent than any other in the nation, a frontal assault on segregation in the early 1950s was far too risky. Even a well-funded and nationally connected organization like the NAACP could not afford to do so.

Significantly, the restroom campaign allowed the RCNL to mobilize the Delta's black working class. Before the *Brown v. Board of Education* decision in 1954 and the Montgomery bus boycott two years later, most other desegregation efforts primarily benefited the black bourgeoisie; for instance, opening up formerly all-white restaurants and theaters for black people primarily benefited those with the money to afford them. Given the concentration of black wealth in cities, these sorts of campaigns were probably effective challenges to Jim Crow in urban areas such as Atlanta. However, in the primarily rural Delta, the black middle class was relatively small and politically weak. Many black farmers and agricultural laborers owned farm vehicles and everyone, of course, had a bladder. Conceivably, the restroom campaign could benefit all black Deltans. As Moore recalled years later, "At one time, [black] people driving from Chicago, south to Vicksburg, to New Orleans, their families could never use the rest room. You could buy your gas, but you couldn't use the rest room. . . . You had to get off the highway and out of sight of your family—the physiology of [black] bodies is just like anybody else you know."[28] By the end of the campaign, an RCNL press release claimed that many filling stations had provided segregated rest rooms and posted signs reading "Clean Rest Room for Colored."[29] Given the indignities that black travelers endured before the campaign, the boycott must be considered a success, even if bounded by the language of Jim Crow.

The restroom campaign was a success in other ways. It garnered the support of hundreds of black Mississippians, each of whom proudly displayed the bumper stickers provided by the RCNL that admonished other black drivers: "Don't Buy Gas Where You Can't Use the Rest Room."[30] In her memoirs, Myrlie Evers, the widow of slain civil rights leader Medgar Evers, recalls seeing the bumper stickers on the "usually beat-up automobiles of Delta Negroes" throughout the region. "It may sound silly," she recalled, "but even that sort of protest required a considerable amount of courage."[31]

Those who did participate may have found the will to do so because, rhetorically, the campaign did not contradict the language of segregation. Though everyone who took part knew otherwise, they could disguise their protest in the clothing of Jim Crow, avoiding the retaliation that would have followed had they openly called for desegregation. That the RCNL was successful and did not betray these little sacrifices made by countless black Deltans won them influence in the black community far beyond their numbers. Capitalizing on this newly established authority, they won further concessions from the white power structure. Dr. T. R. M. Howard and other RCNL leaders met with the state police commissioner to air grievances against the Mississippi State Highway Patrol. They were also able to persuade county registrars to allow potential black voters to pay their poll tax in several Delta counties.

Though important blows to the legitimacy of Jim Crow, none of these early victories required a direct frontal challenge to the white power structure that kept Jim Crow in place. Civil rights activists could not by themselves mobilize financial or political resources even remotely approaching those controlled by the white supremacist South. Therefore, instead of directly pursuing real political, economic, and military power, they chose to accommodate to (and hopefully influence the exercise of) white power. The reason accommodation endures as such a compelling strategy comes from a true appreciation for the balance of power between those with it and those without it. Black Southerners sought federal intervention so earnestly because the U.S. government—evidenced by the experience of both the Civil War and Reconstruction—controlled the only heap of guns and money sufficient to challenge the local white power structure, a fact that Southern defenders of white supremacy tacitly acknowledged every time they stumped for "state's rights." Until the black freedom fighters of the early twentieth century had the power and resources of the federal government behind them, they were forced to fight within the limits set by segregation. Though the restroom campaign formally accepted the premises of "separate but equal," the RCNL's position was more strategic than anything else. To transgress these bounds would require the power to stop domination and oppression, not merely to change its expression. By 1953, the RCNL would openly agitate for desegregation and unqualified black voting rights. In so doing, it would voice a fundamentally democratic stance against Jim Crow, assuming the radical competence of all people to govern themselves, a move that would be too much for Mississippi's segregationists. Within two years, they would crush the RCNL and drive most of its leaders into exile.

Inspired by his work in the "No Rest Room, No Gas" campaign, Moore decided to open his own business. He had become restless and dissatisfied with his job at the local post office, which he had held since 1935. After finding a well-situated lot, Moore undertook construction of a gas station and beauty parlor. He had a difficult time at first finding a business loan—Mississippi's white-owned banks were unwilling to take a risk on black business ventures. There were no black lenders in the state to whom Moore could turn since the few black-owned banks in Mississippi that had existed perished during the Great Depression. He even wrote President Eisenhower: "Since we are giving away billions to other Countries will it be possible for one G. I. to borrow $10,000 from his Government to build a business . . . ? Please don't say no, I have tried so hard to get a loan, don't you turn me down."[32] Eventually, with the help of the Veterans Administration, Moore was able to scrape together approximately $37,000 in loans—enough capital to open a gas station on Highway 61. And then, Amzie Moore's troubles began in earnest.

Within thirty days of Amzie's opening his shop in September of 1953, a Cleveland city councilman accompanied by two state troopers paid Moore a visit. They requested he either put a sign reading "Colored Only" over the grill window or post a sign over the door—"All Colored," suggesting this would protect him from "poor whites" and keep them from bombing his place. Moore retorted that he would be happy to comply, but "[he] would feel kind of bad, washing your car, and you do nine or ten dollars worth of business, then I have to send you around to the back window to get a hamburger . . . that's just not human." He asked them, "Would you want to go around?"[33] Moore refused to segregate his gas station. To reward his intransigence, local white authorities encouraged white drivers to boycott his station, coercing those who did not voluntarily go along. When his income dried up, he found it impossible to get a loan to sustain his business. Though it would ultimately ruin him, Amzie Moore had no choice but to refuse. He could not serve only black patrons, since he relied on white commuters and travelers for the bulk of his business. And he could not decide to serve his black customers through the back door or the side window and retain his position within the black community. Indeed, Moore claimed that his major motivation to open a gas station was to fight the daily indignities black Southerners had to endure under Jim Crow. He managed to keep his business open to the end of the decade; however, Moore's decision to place principle before profit and keep his business desegregated ruined him as a businessman: his filling station would have to fold before he would segregate it.

If Moore's refusal to operate a Jim Crow gas station did not make him a marked man in the eyes of the Delta's white power elite, his unexpected election to the presidency of the Bolivar County NAACP did. Moore had joined the NAACP while in the service, but he never had any intention of becoming an officer—a position for which he surely felt qualified but that would certainly interfere with his business aspirations. The local chapter was first organized in November of 1954, with Charles P. Hey as president. The position soon proved too hot to handle, and Hey quickly stepped down.

As a result, in the midst of the backlash against the *Brown* decision, the Bolivar County branch of the NAACP elected Moore its president in absentia on January 3, 1955. Feeling that they were merely "passing the buck, getting rid of it as a hot potato," he was initially reluctant to serve and even resentful at his nomination. Amzie Moore felt that "the individuals who met and had [him] elected were people who really didn't want to fool with it, 'cause they weren't going to fall out with their white friends."[34] Considering the pressure that NAACP leaders in the South had to endure during the post-*Brown* backlash, no black person with any business aspirations desired any official position in the NAACP. According to Moore, it was a job few people wanted. However, once he took the position, he "didn't run from it."[35]

By the middle of the 1950s, membership in the RCNL became just as risky as membership in the NAACP. In the year after the 1954 *Brown* decision, several sensational killings and a campaign of economic sabotage decimated the rising leadership cadre. The Reverend George Lee, an RCNL officer, was shot dead. His friend, Gus Courts, was also shot. He survived but soon left the state for Chicago. Dr. C. C. Battle, an important figure in both the RCNL and the NAACP, also fled the state. After discovering his name on a Klan death list, even Dr. T. R. M. Howard, affluent enough to afford armed guards, also fled for Chicago. By the end of 1955, only three men of the original eight RCNL leaders on the list remained. Moore had invested too much in his business and decided not to flee. And if he was going to stay, it did not make sense to him to quit the RCNL or the NAACP: "When I found myself already caught up, there wasn't nowhere for me to go because if I decided I was going to get out I could have been killed. Either way . . . it seemed to me I was doing the wrong thing."[36]

The White Citizens' Council (WCC) targeted Moore as an "undesirable" to be driven from the state. Founded in response to *Brown v. Board of Education*, the WCC was a region-wide organization dedicated to the preservation of segregation and white supremacy. Wishing to distance itself from the Ku Klux Klan, the WCC publicly eschewed violence. Instead, it employed economic pressure to silence black political leaders. Dissident farmers and entrepreneurs could not get the bank credit they needed, and immediate payment in full was demanded on home loans and mortgages. Dr. T. R. M. Howard, negotiating a complex real estate deal, found himself nearly bankrupted when a White Citizens' Council member bought the negotiable papers and demanded immediate payment. Boycotts also devastated the business of entrepreneurs like Amzie Moore. In 1955, the year when WCC pressure began in earnest, the gross income of Moore's gas station totaled $39,856. Two years later, that figure had dropped to $24,991, a business loss of nearly 40 percent. The balance remaining in his checking account at the end of each month declined from an average of $1,000.93 for 1954 to an average of $18.50 for 1955. In addition, the bank that held the mortgage on his home and service station called his debts immediately due, leaving Moore with a liability in excess of $6,000. As if that were not enough, in 1956, the Mississippi State Tax Commission threatened to seize and sell Amzie's station for a mere $60.81 in past-due taxes. In an appeal for funds, he wrote to the National Sharecroppers Fund in New York City that the tax collector told him "this would just about close this negro up." Moore felt "they would love that more than they would collecting the taxes."[37]

In response to these tactics, the NAACP executive secretary Roy Wilkins wired the White House, requesting an immediate audience with President Eisenhower.[38] In addition, the chairman of the NAACP's board of directors, Channing Tobias, informed Eisenhower that the WCC was subjecting "Negro leadership in Mississippi . . . to undisguised economic intimidation," but to no avail.[39] Dr. Howard suggested that the NAACP establish a loan fund at the Tri-State Bank of Memphis, Tennessee, to assist victims of the White Citizens' Council's campaign of economic terrorism. He envisioned the fund beginning with $100,000 in deposits "to pay off the accounts of Negroes being pressed by the whites" throughout the region.[40] The organization took Dr. Howard's suggestion and, by mid-1955, the NAACP mobilized deposits totaling $280,000 to be dispersed in $12,000 monthly allocations. This amount, however, was far from enough.

In the wake of white backlash to the *Brown* decision, the NAACP's ability to operate in the South was tenuous at best, and this forced the organization to use its scarce resources both sparingly and strategically in order to help those facing economic sanctions. To establish some means of deciding whom to fund, the Tri-State fund stipulated that "applicants will have to satisfy the usual requirements of the bank" and that "no money is to be ladled out on the mere assertion of prosecution."[41] Predictably, these conditions severely undermined the fund's utility. Out of thirty-one loan applications received by June of 1955, the Tri-State Bank had only approved eight loans totaling $41,849.66. Tri-State rejected fourteen, or nearly half of the applicants, due to inadequate security or credit references.[42] Underlying the NAACP's efforts was the assumption that the only black leaders worth saving were those who were not just middle class, but solvent as well. Not only did the NAACP relief program omit the vast majority of poor and working-class black Mississippians, but it also omitted those middle-class leaders who, like Moore, were judged to be poor entrepreneurs. Moore's failure to live up to these standards led not only to his falling out with both the leadership of the RCNL and the NAACP, but also to a reevaluation of his own standards for political leadership.

In early January of 1955, Moore applied for a loan in the amount of $7,500 from the Tri-State Bank, an amount in itself not enough to cover his need. However, the bank would only agree to a loan of $1,600, and only if he could secure the backing of one of Tri-State's other depositors. Moore appealed the decision to NAACP executive secretary Roy Wilkins, explaining that, upon hearing about the loan fund, several people had approached him, as the local chapter president, for assistance in obtaining a loan. "I don't know what to tell them, I only know that I was turned down by the Tri-State Bank. I don't think it would be wise to tell them that."[43] Locally, the legitimacy of both Moore and the NAACP was inextricably connected to the ability of Moore to mediate between the need for relief of local activists feeling the pinch and the resources that the NAACP had supposedly made available for that purpose. Further exacerbating the problem, an article printed in the *Chicago Defender* exaggerated that a million dollars was available for emergency loans, which generated a response the Tri-State fund could never have handled. Moore nonetheless felt that his ability to sustain his business in the face of this economic pressure would be the extent to which he would retain his legitimacy as a local leader. As he wrote in one of his many appeals for help during this era: "I can't do any better unless I am helped from the outside. This thing has been a struggle with me for years. . . . I don't want any free gifts, but . . . my business is tied up with my leadership."[44]

Moore's attempt to sustain both his business and his local position in the NAACP was made even more difficult by Dr. T. R. M. Howard's lack of sympathy for his situation. Wilkins relied upon Dr. Howard, a member of the bank's board of directors and one of the wealthiest black men in the state, to determine the need and worthiness of potential applicants. Even though Moore, during these dangerous times, managed to increase the local membership of the NAACP from sixty-nine to more than four hundred, neither Dr. Howard nor Wilkins felt that Moore deserved emergency relief, believing that his financial woes were not "because of his activity on behalf of civil rights," but rather due to "the financial position in which he had placed himself."[45] Both Wilkins and Dr. Howard failed to recognize that the importance of Moore to the civil rights movement was not his success as a businessman, but rather his success as an organizer. Moore's inability to uphold his business disqualified him as a leader deserving of support, and his sacrifices on behalf of the black freedom struggle were irrelevant to the Tri-State Bank. What preceded Moore's political leadership in the eyes of both Wilkins and his trusted adviser was Moore's business acumen.

Due to the white supremacist repression of black self-assertion, Moore found few sources of help in the state. During this period, most of his black neighbors kept a fearful distance. He managed to squeak by for a few years, relying on loans from friends in Mississippi, but few of them had much to spare. Moore launched a letter-writing campaign to raise more funds but was only able to drum up another $1,000 from the National Christian Protective Association based in Chicago. In one appeal for funds he wrote: "As president of the Cleveland Branch NAACP all my credit has been cut off and the whites are suing me for accounts unpaid—I cannot stock my place [and] therefore I have nothing to sell. . . . I shall have to close up because I cannot operate without capital. . . . With the whites in Mississippi controlling 90% of the wealth they control the Land + Banks and they can say if the people of the Colored Race eat or not."[46] He requested a direct loan of $4,500 from Congressman Charles Diggs Jr. of Michigan, explaining that "the local white citizens who control the banks will not make a loan to me unless I make a public statement that I am against the Supreme Court's Dicisions [*sic*] and tell the Colored people not to press their claim for freedom."[47]

Having failed thus far in his attempts to secure outside assistance, Moore appealed to the NAACP one last time. In a courteous letter dated October 11, 1955, he attempted to persuade Wilkins to assist him. He wrote, "Much as I dislike the idea of asking anyone to be inconvenienced by my circumstances, I am obliged to borrow Fifty-Five Hundred Dollars until January 1, 1960, and I take the liberty, knowing your confidence in me and your generosity to ask you (that is, the NAACP) to accommodate me with a loan."[48] His mounting desperation and sense of frustration is evident in the contrast between the tone of this letter and the one he sent the very next day, dated only "Wednesday Morning—10 O'Clock." One can easily imagine that Moore slept fitfully, if at all, the night before penning this second missive. The difference in tone is especially striking—whereas the former letter was polite, even deferential, the fury of the second letter could barely be contained by the words on the page.

In a significant turning point in Moore's political thought, in his second letter he distanced himself from both his former allies among the black bourgeoisie and their political strategies. Moore criticized the futility of the loan fund and voiced the frustration of the local NAACP membership at the obstacles they faced in obtaining assistance from an organization that claimed to represent their interests. Moore also chastised Wilkins for his high-handed manner: "The day you talked to me at Belzoni . . . you gave the impression that you knew very little about our problems and cared less. We are not beggars, every man hopes to pay his debts, but if we have no help from outside then we shall have to leave the State." He accused the national leadership of the NAACP of being out of touch with the membership: "We are losing too many good people because their future is uncertain. . . . You don't know what it's like to have to sleep with your gun in your hand, where every passing car might mean Death! We are not crying but we do think that a few dollars to help these hard pressed people to live would give them the courage to carry on."[49] Prior to this point, Moore framed his politics in the first person. "*My* leadership is tied up with *my* business." Now, saying "we" instead of "I," he begins to define racial uplift as something that cannot be reduced merely to the advancement of certain people. His later experiences with SNCC would underscore this new commitment to the belief that leadership is not the monopoly of a certain class, but rather that it inheres in everybody.

To his credit, Wilkins responded positively. In an exchange of letters over the following weeks, he admitted that the policies of the Tri-State Bank prevented the NAACP from helping the "small farmer who needs a loan and who already has a long-term mortgage on his property," effectively excluding most NAACP members in the Delta from consideration. He even indicated that the NAACP was "giving [crop loans] . . . a great deal of thought," and requested Moore's assistance, explaining that "we are city people accustomed to urban ways of handling financial matters. . . . No one has ever taken the trouble to explain to us in detail just how . . . small farmers proceed financially."[50] Given both the urban and middle-class emphasis of the NAACP, this ignorance is not at all surprising. Even though he promised Moore that he was doing all he could to help, Wilkins seemed less interested in assisting local leaders suffering for their involvement in the NAACP than in reassuring "the people who put up the money that everything would be handled on a business-like basis."[51] Bound by the perilous state of NAACP finances as well as his own business sense, there was no way for the executive secretary of the NAACP to even conceive that money should just be given, not loaned, to local organizers to mitigate the reaction they endured. Ultimately Wilkins, at the urging of NAACP field secretary Medgar Evers, personally approved the $1,192 Moore needed to prevent foreclosure on his home and business. In exchange, Moore drew up a mortgage on his home for the full amount and offered it as security.

Even though he was finally able to find some relief, this failure of political solidarity among middle-class civil rights leadership (to which Moore assumed he had to this point belonged) embittered Moore greatly. His surviving correspondence during this period is punctuated with acrimonious denunciations of the black bourgeoisie. See, for example, this letter to a friend in New York City: "The professional Negros and Negros [sic] with money in the State have no interest in the race. They have their own home . . . and money and they are not concern[ed] with the welfare of the poor Negroes of Miss."[52] Moore's anger at Wilkins, Tri-State, and the NAACP easily translated into anger at the black middle class in general. In tones of bitter reproach, Moore castigated the class to which he so recently had aspired:

> The Negroes with money are in a world of their own here in Mississippi. They live to themselves and they don't want things to change, they are happy, as you know they don't support our Organization, they are not interested in the freedom of the common Negro of Miss., they have enough money in the white banks to help all the Negroes of Mississippi, but they buy their fine cars, furs, homes, and stay very much to themselves. That's funny isn't it? But that's how it is down here.[53]

Prior to his confrontation with Wilkins, Moore had still aspired to get rich. "I thought this was the answer. I built a brick house, and I built a service station, and I had a store, and I worked from early morning to late afternoon. I was buying [land] . . . and trying to get ahead."[54] At around this time, somebody asked him to travel east of Mound Bayou to visit a sharecropper and her family. Moore met a woman living in a tar-paper shack and taking care of fourteen children, most naked from the waist down. In an attempt to heat the flimsy dwelling, they burned cotton stalks in an old metal barrel, and the entire family slept on the floor, as there was "not a single bed" in the whole house. Only "a few old raggedy quilts" kept the children warm, and there was no food. He could tell how hungry these children felt because he too had felt that way throughout much of his youth. "Just looking at that . . . really changed my whole outlook on life. I figured it was a sin to think in terms of trying to get rich in view of what I'd seen, and it wasn't over seventeen miles from me. I guess I could have seen it before then."[55] Given the economic realities of black life in the Delta, it would have been impossible for Moore not to see it. Indeed, he had *seen* it before then; but did not *know* it. And this knowledge would profoundly transform Moore's conception of the efficacy of black middle-class leadership.

In the middle of the 1950s, two-thirds of the people in Bolivar County were African American, and they lived mostly in rented dilapidated housing with neither running water nor heat. The neighborhoods of most black Deltans were without street lights, paved roads, or even garbage collection. According to Moore's own research, the per capita annual income of black Deltans in 1954 ranged from $399 in Shelby to a high of $741 in Coahoma County, while the per capita income for the entire state was $844. Some 70 percent of the "sharecroppers, tenant farmers, and day laborers" in Mississippi were African American. Sharecroppers in the Delta spent an average of thirty-seven cents a day on food. Moore described "[t]he homes of the Negro rural masses" as "usually no more than Hovels, not far removed [from] the [former slave] Cabins 75 years ago."[56] Moore realized that it mattered little whether Dr. T. R. M. Howard was the wealthiest black man in the Delta or if another black entrepreneur joined the ranks of the bourgeoisie if the majority of black Mississippians were still living in abject poverty. By 1955, he could no longer assume that the economic success of the black middle class translated into success for the race as a whole.

Despite this, he did not abandon the ideal of the "group economy." Given this name by W. E. B. Du Bois, the group economy is based on the understanding that political gains for African Americans cannot be secured without a solid black economic base. It is a strategy that calls for the economic development of black communities, not as a replacement for (or even a precursor to) political agitation, but as a necessary component of black liberation. As the mechanization of Southern agriculture displaced thousands of black agricultural laborers, Moore began to develop plans for a new group economy. In an appeal to the National Sharecroppers Fund, he outlined a plan to purchase and develop some 10,000 acres of land in the Mississippi Delta, which would then be cooperatively worked by 400 of these displaced black farmers. He requested from $800 to $2,000 for each farm to get started. Moore added that "for the Big Farms of the Negro race it would take 30,000 for one farm—but we are interested in the small farmers."[57] Moore endeavored to undertake wide-scale economic development within the black community that would ideally lead to the development of a large and economically secure black yeomanry.

Moore acted within a local tradition that stretched back to the late nineteenth century. In 1887, Isaiah T. Montgomery, who also founded the Committee of 100, founded the all-black town of Mound Bayou as an attempt "to realize the promise of racial uplift through industry, thrift, self-help and economic solidarity." Unfortunately, Mound Bayou was an island of black economic power in a sea of white cotton, and the prosperity of the town became dependent upon the favor of Northern philanthropy and local white benevolence, both of which were as unpredictable as the volatile cotton market that regulated the wealth of the early-twentieth-century Delta. This vision of an all-black separatist utopia would continue to animate the partisans of the black freedom struggle. Indeed, one of the main reasons for the establishment of the RCNL was "to pursue economic development . . . to [re]build Mound Bayou and let it become one town in the United States owned and operated by blacks, that could project something."[58]

The RCNL ultimately failed to build a black-owned economic base in Mound Bayou, but this did not dissuade Moore. In March of 1956, he drafted another plan to purchase four thousand acres of Delta land for black farmers thrown out of work by the mechanical cotton harvester. Moore believed "farm ownership [to be] the only definite source of relief for the farm Laborer." Foreshadowing the exhortations of Malcolm X, Moore's vision of separate economic development put human needs first and put black people in a position of power. "When Negroes control millions of Dollars of Cattle, hogs, poultry, dairy products, cotton, corn, wheat and other necessities of life . . . and are able to market these products cooperatively and intelligently, we will not only find for ourselves a larger and more important place in the life of the South + Nation, but we shall be the [model] . . . for Negroes who live in our cities."[59]

Moore's 1956 scheme did not place the established black bourgeoisie in the vanguard, but rather aimed itself at "the unskilled Negro farm Laborer, share-cropper, and tenant farmer." For those who could not be included in the farm development program and remained dependent upon the Delta planters for their livelihood, "vocational rehabilitation" would be made available in order to get them out from under their white employers.[60] Moore's plan placed the black rural working class in the center of his story as the inheritors of the struggle and ultimately the ones who should hold the power. He would pursue this vision of a black land of plenty until he died. As late as 1969, Moore had been in contact with the Foundation for Cooperative Living, which had been advising Black Power advocate Floyd McKissick on his variant of the "Mound Bayou proposition," and Moore had among his papers a copy of McKissick's plan for Soul City, North Carolina. Only illness and old age could prevent him from trying once again to build his all-black city on a hill.

Amzie Moore's protracted efforts to obtain assistance from the Tri-State loan fund attracted the attention of *Jet* magazine and the *Pittsburgh Courier*, both of which ran stories soliciting aid for him. This prompted a flurry of letters from angry NAACP members to the national office, several of which reflected the enduring class tension that underlay any calls for racial solidarity. Richard J. Henry of Detroit wrote to Roy Wilkins: "I am only a $3.50 a year member of the NAACP and maybe my opinion won't count for much but I would rather see my money going to help in cases like Mr. Moore . . . than to read in the papers that the NAACP has won another round and now I can sit in a beer garden beside a white man and drink beer." Henry exhorted Wilkins to understand the value of grassroots organizers to the NAACP: "The best way to destroy any cause . . . is to destroy the *Leaders*. Leaderless we will . . . disintegrate. It seems to me that the Southern White-man knows that better than you. You never read where they shot a rank and file member of the NAACP. All of the reprisals are at Ministers—Teachers—Organizers—Businessmen. . . ." With a keen understanding of the tactics of the White Citizens' Councils, Henry rebuked Wilkins:

> What better club do the White man need . . . than to be able to cast into [our] face that Our Greatest Organization will abandon [us] when we are in trouble. . . . We do not expect the NAACP to come to our rescue when ever a note on our home is past due but when a man is willing to give up his life, his business— everything for an ideal and that Organization lets him down, I think it is a mighty poor organization.[61]

Predictably, the $2,000 received from the Tri-State fund was insufficient to secure both Moore's livelihood and his ability to organize. To make matters worse, the White Citizens' Council stepped up its campaign of intimidation. Following several months of threats from local white supremacists, the New Hope Baptist Church in Cleveland, Mississippi, where the local branch of the NAACP had been meeting burned before dawn on May 10, 1957. On April 11, 1958, in conjunction with the Mississippi State Sovereignty Commission, the post office where Moore had worked for more than twenty-three years decided to cut his hours down to sixteen hours a week from full time. By November, they tried to fire him altogether. Unwilling to be driven from the state, Moore turned down both better pay and working conditions as a postal carrier in both Washington, D.C., and Memphis. Topping it all off, the Tri-State Bank threatened to bring suit against Moore for the nonpayment of his loan. At this point, Roy Wilkins intervened, and with a stern admonition, Wilkins agreed that the NAACP would assume responsibility for the debt but assured Moore that no more assistance would be forthcoming.[62]

Though the NAACP's national office felt incapable of assisting Moore, other allies would soon step forward. In addition to the help he received from the American Friends Service Committee, the exiled Dr. T. R. M. Howard, and the National Sharecroppers Fund, Moore came to the attention of former

NAACP staffer Ella Baker and her organization, In Friendship. Organized earlier in the decade, In Friendship offered assistance to black activists facing economic reprisals in both Mississippi and South Carolina after *Brown*. In Friendship endeavored to preserve local grassroots leaders and support their efforts, regardless of their credit rating. In February of 1957, Ella Baker contacted Moore and informed him, "it seems highly important to keep you where you are rather than have you leave," and asked only that Moore continue his civil rights activities.[63] He was also to advise them of other local people who had been suffering at the hands of the White Citizens' Councils and other white supremacist groups, and to become the conduit for aid from outside the state.

Unfortunately, In Friendship lacked the resources necessary to pull Moore out of the very deep hole into which the WCC had pushed him. In the middle of 1958, Moore sent out another batch of fund-raising letters. One of these letters landed in the mailbox of Anne and Carl Braden, Southern white integrationists who had just recently joined the Southern Conference Educational Fund (SCEF). With its roots in the Southern Conference for Human Welfare and the Popular Front of the 1930s, SCEF was unswervingly committed to the overthrow of white supremacy. The Bradens forwarded Moore's letter to the desk of SCEF director James Dombrowski, who in turn wrote Moore. Dombrowski promised his assistance in exchange for Moore's "work in connection with achieving a greater measure of democracy" in the Delta and "the contribution [he was] . . . making . . . to the South and the nation."[64] Using SCEF's extensive fund-raising network in Northern cities, SCEF found sixteen people each willing to contribute $1,000, including former first lady Eleanor Roosevelt. This money would then be loaned to Moore, repayable at a rate he could afford.

It took Dombrowski nearly two years to raise the money, during which Moore almost lost his home. On November 28, 1960, Moore received a notice from the U.S. attorney in Oxford, Mississippi, demanding payment in full of his Veterans Administration home loan or face foreclosure. Two days later, at the end of his rope, Moore received a letter from Dombrowski stating that all the money had been collected and would be available as early as December 16, 1960. Rescued from the jaws of debt, Moore was able to maintain and strengthen his political leadership in the Delta. Ultimately, access to such resources allowed Moore to position himself as a mediator between the needs of impoverished Mississippi activists and the resources of the American left. Though the White Citizens' Council would continue to harass Moore, he would remain in the state to mentor the youthful SNCC volunteers in the ways of Mississippi politics.

While the NAACP approached Moore's situation with suspicion and distrust, both SCEF and In Friendship believed Moore when he said that his financial problems were due to economic reprisals. Even though in Dombrowski's eyes Moore's business judgment was questionable, he felt that this was because he spent too much time "helping people to get registered [to vote] and on civil rights business." He wrote to SCEF board member Aubrey Williams that if Moore "were just another business man, playing it safe and protecting his . . . investment," SCEF "would not [have been] interested in this project in the first place."[65] Moore was worth helping, not because he was creditworthy, but because he was an effective grassroots political leader, daring to risk his life, family, home, and business for the sake of democracy. Anne Braden echoed this sentiment years later, saying, "if you help the people that are out in front, the courageous people[, to] survive, . . . that helps build a movement." Moore never repaid the SCEF loan, but few of the contributors ever expected to profit on their investment. Right before Carl Braden died, he wrote to each of the sixteen investors and asked them to cancel Amzie Moore's debt, explaining that it "never was a good business investment, but it was a good political investment."[66] The faith SCEF placed in Moore's political abilities, in their mind, was separable from their doubts over his business acumen, which stands in marked contrast to the class and cultural assumptions manifested in Roy Wilkins's response to Moore's plight.

Before the arrival of SNCC in the 1960s, the resources that SCEF provided gave Moore the power to identify local leaders and see to it that the sacrifices they made were recognized. In addition, allies such as SCEF and In Friendship are to be praised for what they did not do. While they were mediators between the money of white liberals and local people such as Amzie Moore, they did not try to "enforce" a certain set of class or cultural values upon which their aid was contingent. They trusted Moore to build the local movement by dispensing the resources these groups made available to him. This trust, in turn, rested in a notion of radical competence, which allows the oppressed not only to define their own freedom but, more importantly, to chart their own course to that freedom. Moore's resulting independence from both the local white power structure and the NAACP enabled him to identify as legitimate leaders people such as Mrs. Fannie Lou Hamer. Illiterate and the youngest of twenty children, she became one of the most prominent figures in the civil rights movement. Incidentally, Mrs. Hamer would become one of the first people to receive a grant from Operation Freedom, SCEF's successor in the Delta.

As the movement picked up steam in Mississippi during the early 1960s, Moore would encourage the next generation of activists to continue the fight he had begun in the preceding decade. According to SNCC activists, it was Moore's idea to recruit white college students to come into the Delta and help register black voters, which later became known as "Freedom Summer." Since white lives were worth more to the white power structure than black lives, he thought that the presence of these volunteers would help to deter the violence directed at the activists. Furthermore, Moore also understood that the national and international attention that the presence of the children of

America's liberal elite would bring to the Delta could mobilize resources that were far beyond the reach of black activists at the time. Additionally, once black voter registration began in earnest in the Delta, Moore went on to help organize Mississippians United to Elect Black Candidates, which sought to translate the promise of the vote into political reality. Today, largely due to the efforts of Moore and those he mentored, Mississippi has the highest proportion of black elected officials in the United States.

Amzie Moore was one of few courageous local leaders, a list of whom could be numbered in the single digits. He sustained the struggle for freedom in Mississippi for nearly thirty years during a time that many consider to be completely absent of activism. When Bob Moses, SNCC's first field secretary, came to the state in 1960, Moore was waiting to introduce him to the next generation of local black militants. Moore and local people like him transformed what SNCC was, but SNCC also showed these veterans what they themselves were capable of. As a result, Moore said his farewell to the NAACP when SNCC came to town. Explaining his decision to interviewer Howell Raines, Moore described the inner transformation that his experiences with SNCC brought him:

> When [I] . . . stood at a courthouse like the courthouse in Greenwood . . . and watched tiny figures [of the SNCC workers] standing against a huge column . . . [of white] triggermen and drivers and lookout men riding in automobiles with automatic guns . . . *how they stood* . . . how gladly they got in front of that line, those leaders, and went to jail! It didn't seem to bother 'em. It was an awakening for me.[67]

The radically democratic transformation of political thought and practice that undergirded SNCC's success in the Delta is to be found in precisely this relationship. It was neither essential and pre-existent, nor did the SNCC import it wholesale into the Delta. In a 1996 interview, when asked about SNCC's organizing philosophy, Charles Cobb commented:

> Being young, we were . . . not set in our ways, but were open, willing to experiment and . . . take risks. [W]e found in places like Mississippi . . . all these people waiting for something like that to come at them that way—there were the Amzie Moores and the E. W. Steptoes, the Hartman Turnbows and the Henry Siases. They were waiting. It's not like SNCC came in a vacuum; there had been decades of work going on in these places. These . . . people . . . structured the way we functioned in those places, the way we were present, . . . the way we thought.[68]

And when Bob Moses got off the bus in the Delta, Amzie Moore was waiting for him. As he drove the young Moses to his home in Cleveland, Mississippi, Moore introduced him to a social and political landscape both disfigured by white supremacy and studded with the monuments of black resistance. According to organizer Sam Block: "Amzie served as a teacher to

Bob. . . . He knew people in areas and could get Bob into doors that Bob could not have gotten into himself. Anytime he had a question that he couldn't deal with, he would call Amzie. Amzie Moore was really the father of the movement."[69]

NOTES

1. Amzie Moore, interview by Michael Garvey, Mississippi Oral History Program, University of Southern Mississippi, March 29, 1977 (hereafter, "Garvey Interview"), 28.

2. "Garvey Interview," 9.

3. Ralph Ellison, *Shadow and Act* (New York: Quality Paperback Book Club, 1953), 90.

4. Neil R. McMillen, *Dark Journey: Black Mississippians in the Age of Jim Crow* (Urbana: University of Illinois Press, 1990), 88–89.

5. "Garvey Interview," 10–13.

6. McMillen, *Dark Journey*, 57.

7. McMillen, *Dark Journey*, 154.

8. McMillen, *Dark Journey*, 310.

9. "Garvey Interview," 3.

10. "Garvey Interview," 29.

11. "Garvey Interview," 29.

12. McMillen, *Dark Journey*, 72–73.

13. James Forman, *The Making of Black Revolutionaries* (Seattle, Wash.: Open Hand Publishing, 1985), 278–79.

14. "Garvey Interview," 47, 78–79.

15. "Garvey Interview," 79.

16. "Garvey Interview," 9.

17. "Garvey Interview," 30.

18. "Prophetic Outline of the World's History," in Amzie Moore, "Papers, 1941–1970," Box 7, Folder 6, State Historical Society of Wisconsin (hereafter, SHSW).

19. Isaiah 13:17–22, King James Version.

20. Handwritten notes, Amzie Moore, "Papers, 1941–1970," Box 7, Folder 6, SHSW.

21. Canceled checks, January 1953–April 1954, Amzie Moore Papers, Box 9, Folder 3, SHSW.

22. Moore to Tri-State Bank, January 3, 1955, Amzie Moore Papers, Box 10, Folder 6, SHSW.

23. Magnolia Mutual Life Insurance Company Letterheads, February and May 10, 1952, Amzie Moore Papers, Box 1, Folder 2, SHSW.

24. Amzie Moore to Fay Bennett, n.d., Amzie Moore Papers, Box 2, Folder 2, SHSW.

25. Charles Cobb interviewed by John Rachal, University of Southern Mississippi Oral History Program, October 21, 1996, 8–9.

26. Howell Raines, *My Soul Is Rested: Movement Days in the Deep South Remembered* (New York: Viking Penguin, 1983), 234; "Garvey Interview," 25.

27. "Garvey Interview," 19.

28. "Garvey Interview," 24.

29. "Accomplishments and Objectives of the RCNL," RCNL Press Release, n.d., Amzie Moore Papers, Box 7, Folder 2, SHSW.

30. "No Rest Room, No Gas," RCNL Press Release, n.d., Box A466, group 2, NAACP Papers, Library of Congress, Washington, D.C.

31. Myrlie Evers, *For Us, the Living* (Jackson: University Press of Mississippi, 1967), 87–88.

32. Amzie Moore to President Eisenhower, February 8, 1954, Amzie Moore Papers, Box 1, Folder 2, SHSW.

33. "Garvey Interview," 24.

34. Raines, *My Soul Is Rested*, 233–34.

35. "Garvey Interview," 26–27.

36. Amzie Moore, interview by John Dittmer, April 22, 1981, OHP 382, Mississippi Department of Archives and History, 43.

37. Moore to Fay Bennett (New York City), August 9, 1956, Amzie Moore Papers, Box 1, Folder 2, SHSW.

38. Minutes of the Board of Directors, January 3, 1955, Group 1, Series A, Box 6, NAACP Papers [NAACP microfilm: Part 1, supp. 1, reel 1].

39. John Dittmer, *Local People: The Struggle for Civil Rights in Mississippi* (Urbana: University of Illinois Press, 1994), 48.

40. Roy Wilkins to T. R. M. Howard, February 11, 1955, Box A466, group 2, NAACP Papers.

41. Roy Wilkins to T. R. M. Howard, February 11, 1955, Box A466, group 2, NAACP Papers.

42. Minutes of the Board of Directors, June 13, 1955, Group 1, Series A, Box 6, NAACP Papers [NAACP microfilm: Part 1, supp. 1, reel 1].

43. Moore to Roy Wilkins, January 17, 1955, Box A422, group 2, NAACP Papers.

44. Moore to Fay Bennett, n.d., Amzie Moore Papers, Box 2, Folder 2, SHSW.

45. Roy Wilkins to T. R. M. Howard, February 11, 1955, Box A466, group 2, NAACP Papers.

46. Moore to Lucille Jackson, n.d., Amzie Moore Papers, Box 2, Folder 2, SHSW.

47. Moore to Congressman Charles Diggs Jr., July 28, 1955, Amzie Moore Papers, Box 1, Folder 2, SHSW.

48. Moore to Roy Wilkins, October 11, 1955, Box A422, group 2, NAACP Papers.

49. Moore to Roy Wilkins, "Wednesday Morning—10 O'Clock," Box A422, group 2, NAACP Papers.

50. Roy Wilkins to Moore, October 20, 1955, Box A422, group 2, NAACP Papers; Roy Wilkins to Moore, December 2, 1955, Box A422, group 2, NAACP Papers.

51. Roy Wilkins to Moore, October 20, 1955, Box A422, group 2, NAACP Papers.

52. Moore to Lucille Jackson, n.d., Amzie Moore Papers, Box 2, Folder 2, SHSW.

53. Moore to Roy Wilkins, "Wednesday Morning—10 O'Clock," Box A422, group 2, NAACP Papers.

54. Raines, *My Soul Is Rested*, 233–34.

55. Raines, *My Soul Is Rested*, 233–34.

56. Notes, March 1956, Amzie Moore Papers, Box 2, Folder 4, SHSW.

57. Amzie Moore to Lucille Jackson (New York City), n.d., Amzie Moore Papers, Box 2, Folder 2, SHSW.

58. "Garvey Interview," 16, 19.

59. Untitled proposal, March 1956, draft copy in Amzie Moore Papers, Box 7, Folder 11, SHSW.

60. Untitled proposal, March 1956, draft copy in Amzie Moore Papers, Box 7, Folder 11, SHSW.

61. Richard J. Henry (Detroit, Mich.) to Roy Wilkins, December 14, 1955, Box A422, group 2, NAACP Papers, emphasis in original.

62. Affidavit of Rev. E. C. Smith, n.d., Amzie Moore Papers, Box 6, Folder 3, SHSW; "Garvey Interview," 25; Postmaster Josephine Webb to Moore, April 11, 1958, Amzie Moore Papers, Box 1, Folder 3, SHSW; Agent Van Landingham to Director, Sovereignty Commission, January 12, 1959, Sovereignty Commission Papers, Mississippi Department of Archives and History; Moore to James Dombrowski, November 10, 1958, Amzie Moore Papers, Box 1, Folder 3, SHSW; Moore to T. R. M. Howard, May 24, 1958, Amzie Moore Papers, Box 1, Folder 3, SHSW; "Book" to Moore, n.d., Amzie Moore Papers, Box 2, Folder 2, SHSW; Moore to Jessie Turner (Tri-State Bank), November 19, 1956, Amzie Moore Papers, Box 1, Folder 2, SHSW; Roy Wilkins to Moore (unopened), April 30, 1957, Amzie Moore Papers, Box 1, Folder 3, SHSW.

63. Ella Baker to Moore, February 5, 1957, Amzie Moore Papers, Box 1, Folder 3, SHSW.

64. James Dombrowski to Moore, July 25, 1958, Amzie Moore Papers, Box 1, Folder 3, SHSW.

65. Dombrowski to Aubrey Williams, August 21, 1959, Sovereignty Commission Papers, Mississippi Department of Archives and History.

66. Reminiscences of Anne Braden (June 11, 1980), 155–59, in the Columbia University Oral History Research Office Collection.

67. Raines, *My Soul Is Rested*, 236–37.

68. Charles Cobb, interviewed by John Rachal, University of Southern Mississippi Oral History Program, October 21, 1996, www.lib.USM.edu/%7ESpcol/crda/oh/cobb.htm.

69. Charles Payne, *I've Got the Light of Freedom: The Organizing Tradition and the Mississippi Freedom Struggle* (Berkeley: University of California Press, 1995), 63.

SUGGESTED READING

Dittmer, John. *Local People: The Struggle for Civil Rights in Mississippi*. Urbana: University of Illinois Press, 1994.

Ellison, Ralph. *Shadow and Act*. New York: Quality Paperback Book Club, 1953.

Evers, Myrlie. *For Us, the Living*. Jackson: University Press of Mississippi, 1967.

Forman, James. *The Making of Black Revolutionaries*. Seattle, Wash.: Open Hand Publishing, 1985.

McMillen, Neil R. *Dark Journey: Black Mississippians in the Age of Jim Crow*. Urbana: University of Illinois Press, 1990.

Payne, Charles. *I've Got the Light of Freedom: The Organizing Tradition and the Mississippi Freedom Struggle*. Berkeley: University of California Press, 1995.

Raines, Howell. *My Soul Is Rested: Movement Days in the Deep South Remembered*. New York: Viking Penguin, 1983

8

James Lawson: The Nashville Civil Rights Movement

Ernest M. Limbo

Civil rights activists of the 1960s widely used the techniques of nonviolent direct action or nonviolent protest in their demonstrations. Most of these activists first learned of the potential efficacy of these techniques in reports of India's overthrow of British rule. Thousands of unarmed Indians eventually overthrew one of the world's greatest colonial powers using nonviolent tactics developed by Gandhi. With the example of India fresh in their minds, a number of African American leaders began thinking about the possibility of nonviolent protest against segregation and racism in the United States.

One of the most significant of these persons was James Lawson Jr. Lawson was a minister and a son of a minister in Ohio. In college, he joined the Fellowship of Reconciliation (FOR) and became a pacifist and a conscientious objector to war. When drafted for service in the army during the Korean War, he refused induction and was sentenced to three years in prison. After eleven months, he was paroled, and he quickly traveled to India to continue his study of nonviolence with former students of Gandhi.

In 1957, soon after his return to the United States, he met Martin Luther King Jr., who, upon hearing of Lawson's training in nonviolent protest, implored Lawson to come to the South immediately to train civil rights activists. With the assistance of FOR, Lawson moved to Nashville, Tennessee, enrolled in the Vanderbilt Divinity School, where he was one of its first black students, and in 1958 began holding workshops in the techniques of nonviolent protest. The students trained by Lawson launched protests in Nashville that ended segregation at the downtown lunch counters by May of 1960.

> *This group was among the core leaders of the student activists who founded the Student Nonviolent Coordinating Committee (SNCC). These students spread out across the South, and to many seemed the activists most willing to risk their lives to end segregation. They rescued and continued the Freedom Rides in Birmingham after the Klan had attacked both of the initial buses and beaten many of the Freedom Riders. The president of SNCC, John Lewis, was the youngest person to deliver an address at the March on Washington in 1963. Though he kept a low profile, Lawson and the students he inspired were invaluable assets to the civil rights movement because of their dedication and their intensive training in nonviolent protest.*

When the civil rights movement is mentioned, the names of certain Southern cities almost immediately come to mind—Birmingham, Selma, Jackson, Albany, Atlanta, and Greensboro. What about Nashville? Some history books state that James M. Lawson Jr., a Vanderbilt divinity student, held some workshops in nonviolent protest for area students and organized some lunch counter sit-ins. What these books often fail to say is that among this group of students were Diane Nash, Bernard Lafayette, Marion Barry, John Lewis, and James Bevel. For several years after the Nashville protests, these five students were among the most influential students in America's civil rights movement. When the first Freedom Ride was on the brink of failure in Birmingham, the Nashville students salvaged it and saw to its success. At the founding convention of the Student Nonviolent Coordinating Committee (SNCC), James Lawson delivered the keynote address; Barry was elected president; Nash served as the first field representative; and Lewis later served as president.

No single factor can be called the catalyst for the success of the Nashville civil rights movement, for an almost perfect combination of several factors was at work. The first factor was the presence of James Lawson, who was more highly trained in nonviolent protest than anyone in the civil rights movement. The nonviolent workshops he organized provided the philosophical grounding and discipline that aided the formation of dedicated student leaders. The second factor that contributed to the success of the Nashville civil rights movement was the students. As the home of four black colleges, Nashville had no shortage of African American students, but the students attracted to Lawson's workshops were exceptional. They were dedicated, intelligent, and brave beyond their years. They had no single charismatic leader; through consensus the Nashville protesters reached decisions about where and when to demonstrate. Moreover, the Nashville students were largely free from the political maneuvering and control of large organizations such as the Southern Christian Leadership Conference (SCLC), the Congress of Racial Equality (CORE), the National Association for the Advancement of Colored People (NAACP), or even their sponsor, the Nashville Christian Leadership Council (NCLC). The third factor was the presence of local African American preachers who supported the civil rights movement. The two most important were C. T. Vivian and Kelly Miller Smith. Vivian, a Northerner from Illinois, attended Nashville's American Baptist Theological Seminary and served as pastor of the First Community Church. Smith, a graduate of Morehouse and Howard, was pastor of Nashville's most prominent African American church, the First Baptist Church, Capitol Hill. Both worked tirelessly for civil rights, but they did so in different ways. Vivian confronted, Smith negotiated. Vivian challenged, and Smith secured the gains achieved from those challenges. A fourth factor, whose importance cannot be overstated, is the support that Nashville's adult black community gave the students. The black community supplied money, demonstrators, and moral support to the student protesters. In few cities during the civil rights movement was the community support for the protesters as strong as it was in Nashville.

In January of 1957, the Reverend Kelly Miller Smith, president of the Nashville chapter of the NAACP and pastor of First Baptist Church, Capitol Hill, attended the organizing meeting of the Southern Christian Leadership Conference in Atlanta's Ebenezer Baptist Church. At first Smith wondered why a representative from Nashville had even been invited; after all, Nashville had desegregated its buses with no violence. It had black councilmen and black policemen. There were also many interracial organizations, including the Tennessee Council on Human Relations and the NAACP. Surely, Nashville was mature enough to accept social change.

In September 1957, Smith learned that he was mistaken concerning Nashville's level of maturity when the Hattie Cotton Elementary School was bombed in protest of the desegregation of the city's public schools. As Smith further examined the racial situation in his home city, he became convinced that Nashville indeed belonged in the category with Birmingham, Jackson, and Montgomery. While blacks could attend Scarritt College as freely as they could attend Boston University, the Tennessee Preparatory School was as segregated as the public schools of Birmingham. Nashville had its interracial organizations as well as its segregated country clubs. Blacks could rides buses with whites but could not eat with them at restaurants or lunch counters. Nashville was far from being an integrated city.

By the end of 1957, Smith began organizing an affiliate of Dr. Martin Luther King Jr.'s SCLC in Nashville. While the NAACP was largely responsible for the desegregation of Nashville's schools and was fully capable of fighting legal battles on behalf of the black community, Smith believed that a complementary organization should be formed to attack racial injustice more directly. He sent out letters to all black ministers, inviting them to a meeting with Dr. King. On January 18, 1958, a meeting held at Capers Memorial Colored Methodist Episcopal (CME) Church led to the formation of the Nashville Christian Leadership Council. NCLC, as an affiliate of Martin Luther King Jr.'s Southern Christian Leadership Conference, sought to unite clergy and laypersons into an organization that attempted to establish justice in American society through Christian love and nonviolent protest.

In the first week of March 1958, two representatives of the Fellowship of Reconciliation, Glen Smiley and James Lawson, attended a regular meeting of NCLC and offered to hold a workshop in nonviolent protest. NCLC accepted this offer and decided that a workshop would be held March 26–28 at the Bethel African Methodist Episcopal (AME) Church. Lawson, Smiley, and Rev. Ralph Abernathy of the SCLC conducted the workshop. The purpose of the workshop was to explain the philosophy of Christian nonviolence and to demonstrate how Christian nonviolent protest could be used to challenge racial discrimination. Attending this workshop were several persons who would later become prominent in the movement, including Nash, Bevel, Lewis, and Barry. At this workshop NCLC members learned that Lawson would enter the divinity school of Vanderbilt in the fall.

Lawson was a native of Massillon, Ohio. His father, James M. Lawson Sr., was a minister in the African American Episcopal Church, Zion (AME Zion). From his father, Lawson learned that in addition to saving souls for the afterlife, the church must also seek justice in this life. The senior Lawson was not only a minister but also an activist who organized NAACP and Urban League chapters in several cities where he had lived. However, Lawson's father was no proponent of nonviolence. He taught his son the importance of defending himself against white children intent on roughing up the child of a local black minister.

If Lawson came to appreciate the importance of the church from his father, it was his mother, Philane Cover Lawson, who initiated Lawson's dedication to nonviolence. Lawson's mother objected to his fighting, even in self-defense. One day when he was about ten, his mother sent Lawson to the store on an errand. On his way home, he walked past a parked car with the windows rolled down. From inside the car a young boy of five or six yelled, "Hey, nigger!" Without hesitation, Lawson walked to the car, reached inside, and, as hard as he could, slapped the young boy. Returning home, he sat down in the kitchen where his mother was cooking and proudly recounted the story of his retaliation against this young racist to his mother as she attended to dinner on the stove. Without turning around, his mother asked a simple question that would change Lawson's life: "What good did that do, Jimmy?" Philane then turned and explained that both she and his father loved him and that his sisters and brothers loved him and that most importantly God loved him. Because of all that love, she said that their family had a good life and that he was going to continue to have a good life. She continued,

> With all that love, what harm does that stupid insult do? It's nothing, Jimmy, it's empty. Just ignorant words from an ignorant child who is gone from your life the moment it was said. That child is gone. You will never see him again. You do not even know his name.[1]

Rev. James Lawson (Image courtesy of The Tennessean.*)*

Lawson was stunned and disarmed. He later recalled this was the moment that set the course for his life. From that point he vowed never to strike anyone again.

Several years later when he entered Baldwin-Wallace College in the early years of the Cold War, Lawson's pacifism and his opposition to injustice caused him to question American foreign and domestic policy. For Lawson, there was more to understand about the world than what persons and nations were and were not Communist. From reading accounts in the black press, Lawson came to see Mohandas Gandhi as a symbol of the victory of nonwhite peoples who fought to rid themselves of white colonial oppressors. He viewed the conflict between the nonwhite oppressed peoples and white oppressors as a global injustice. Lawson came to understand the plight of blacks in America as but one example of the global oppression of nonwhite peoples.

During his first year at Baldwin-Wallace, Lawson joined the local chapter of the Fellowship of Reconciliation, an interfaith organization dedicated to peace and nonviolence, and was introduced to A. J. Muste. It was Muste more than anyone else who introduced and steeped Lawson in the intellectual traditions of the nonviolent Christian left, providing an intellectual foundation for Lawson's pacifism. Through Muste's influence, Lawson began to ask a simple, yet profound question. If Jesus were alive today, how would he respond to American foreign and domestic policy? Lawson concluded that Jesus would be on the side of the oppressed. He would not serve in the military, nor would he engage in any violent act. Though he had registered for the draft when he was eighteen, in 1949, when he was a sophomore, he received a second classification notice from his local draft board and refused to fill out the form because to do so would be to cooperate with a violent system. His local draft board declared that he was in violation of the national draft laws and had a warrant issued for his arrest. Lawson learned of the warrant and turned himself in. He was fingerprinted, charged, and released on bail. At his trial several months later in the spring of 1951, a federal judge decided to make an example of Lawson. He sentenced Lawson to three years in federal prison despite the testimony of several ministers and professors who cited Lawson's exemplary character.

Lawson entered a minimum-security federal prison at Mill Point, West Virginia, in April 1951. Before entering prison he talked with several other conscientious objectors who had been incarcerated. When he entered prison, he felt mentally prepared for the challenge. Indeed, during much of the time that he spent at Mill Point, he found conditions tolerable if not often intellectually stimulating because of the presence of several other conscientious objectors. This changed, however, when President Harry Truman ordered the integration of the federal prison system. As a member of FOR, Lawson was identified by pro-segregationist inmates and administrators as a racial agitator. In late December, prison officials transferred Lawson and some of the white integrationists to another federal prison in Ashland, Kentucky, where he was placed in solitary confinement. Lawson's only real scare in prison came when a number of the larger and more muscular inmates threaten to gang-rape him. Lawson struggled with how to respond to this threat. Would he or should he remain nonviolent if attacked? Fortunately, the would-be rapists never carried through on their threats.

In May 1952, after only eleven months of incarceration, he was paroled and was offered an opportunity to work with the Methodist Board of Missions in India. There he studied the teachings of Gandhi, which reinforced his pacifism and gave him greater insights into civil disobedience and passive resistance. In Gandhi, Lawson found a person who he believed was closer to being Jesus Christ in modern dress than anyone he had known.

After returning to the United States, Lawson enrolled in the Oberlin School of Theology. Just months after he arrived at Oberlin, Martin Luther King Jr. delivered a series of talks at the invitation of a young Oberlin professor and chaplain, the soon-to-be-famous theologian Harvey Cox. Cox had taken an immediate liking to Lawson and invited him to an informal luncheon with King. The men—both twenty-eight, both ministers and sons of ministers, both intellectuals—felt an immediate kinship. Lawson admired King's speaking ability and his use of nonviolence in the Montgomery bus boycott. As the men talked, King expressed his interest in studying with Gandhians, and Lawson described his interest in working in the South. Lawson further described his time in prison as a conscientious objector to the Korean War. King quickly realized that he was speaking with someone who had more training and was likely more dedicated to nonviolent protest than anyone in America. Lawson laid out his career plans to King—after finishing Oberlin, he would attend Yale to complete a Doctor of Divinity degree and then move south to work for civil rights. King interrupted, "Don't wait! Come now! We don't have anyone like you down there. We need you right now. Please don't delay. Come as quickly as you can. We really need you." In seconds, and without reflection or planning, Lawson declared, "Yes, I understand. I'll arrange my affairs, and I'll come as quickly as I can."[2]

Lawson contacted A. J. Muste and told him of his decision to move south. Muste created a position in FOR for Lawson. He would become FOR's first Southern field secretary. Lawson would be a roaming troubleshooter in the South as the civil rights movement was gaining momentum faster than the activists could keep up. With Lawson's position within FOR settled, the next question was also important. Lawson and FOR had to decide what city would be Lawson's base of operations. Lawson had initially thought of Atlanta, but Muste urged him to first talk with Glenn Smiley, FOR's national field director, who knew much about the South.

Smiley encouraged Lawson to consider Nashville over Atlanta. Though Atlanta was wealthier than Nashville, it was still the capital of an anything-but-reconstructed Southern state as far as the issue of race was concerned.

Georgia's senators had signed the Southern Manifesto declaring their opposition to the Supreme Court's 1954 decision in *Brown v. Board of Education*, which ordered the desegregation of public schools. White supremacist groups including the Ku Klux Klan were plentiful in Georgia. Moreover, while Atlanta wore a progressive veneer with skyscrapers, ambitious businessmen, and an upbeat mayor, there were few whites who could be called moderates on the issue of race. Smiley thought Lawson needed a base where his life would not be threatened. Smiley recommended Nashville.

As the home of four black institutions of higher learning—Fisk University, Meharry Medical College, Tennessee Agricultural and Industrial College (now Tennessee State University), and American Baptist Theological Seminary—a great number of young, well-educated African American students lived in Nashville. Many of these students were in high school when the Supreme Court issued the *Brown* decision and when Martin Luther King Jr. led the Montgomery bus boycott. Their expectations of freedom and full citizenship for African Americans were rising, and many were looking for ways to accelerate the fulfillment of these expectations.

Nashville was also largely free from hard-line segregationist organizations such as the White Citizens' Council and the Ku Klux Klan. Tennessee's politicians were more moderate than Georgia's. Neither Tennessee senator had signed the Southern Manifesto, and Nashville's mayor Ben West was at least moderate, if not outright liberal concerning race. Among its white elites, Nashville had faculty members from Vanderbilt University, and while Vanderbilt was no hotbed of radicalism, it was generally tolerant of those who questioned the status quo—so long as they did not directly challenge it.

Finally, the composition of Nashville's elite black community was also important to the success of the civil rights movement. In many Southern cities the elite black community consisted of businessmen who had made their fortunes through an explicit or at least implicit acceptance or toleration of segregation. In many Southern cities, civil rights activists would find wealthy blacks to be obstacles to civil rights organizing. In contrast, many of Nashville's black elite were faculty members at Nashville's black colleges or physicians at Meharry Hospital and had no economic or social interest in the continuation of segregation. Indeed, Nashville's black community supplied much financial support to the demonstrators. Lawson decided that he would make his home in Nashville and enter the Vanderbilt Divinity School—arguably the finest and most liberal divinity school in the South.

Although the first NCLC-sponsored workshop on nonviolence took place in March of 1958, it was not until Lawson moved to Nashville to attend divinity school that they were held with any regularity. In the fall of 1958, the workshops became much larger and more organized. Lawson gave the participants detailed outlines of the technique of nonviolence and suggested reading lists, which included Eastern philosophy, writings on Christian pacifism, "Civil Disobedience" by Thoreau, and several books by Leo Tolstoy.

After several months of preparation, the participants and NCLC decided to attempt the desegregation of the lunch counters in the downtown department stores and drugstores because these businesses received much patronage from blacks, yet would not serve blacks at their lunch counters. Since it was estimated that the black community contributed from 10 to 15 percent of total sales to each of the major department stores and these stores refused to serve blacks at their lunch counters, this seemed a logical place to begin, particularly to men.

The decision to attempt to desegregate these businesses was more than a logical place to begin for middle-class black women. Several middle-class women, often with children and usually members of Kelly Miller Smith's First Baptist Church, had begun attending Lawson's workshops and finally opened up and declared to the men in the group that the men knew nothing about downtown since they did not shop there. One after another, women told stories concerning the indignities they suffered while shopping downtown. The department stores would gladly take their money, but would not allow the women to try on clothes. Several stores had no restroom facilities for African Americans whatsoever, and those that did had facilities that were inconveniently located and dirty. Women shopping with children faced additional humiliation. DeLois Wilkinson recounted her visits to Harveys, which along with Cain-Sloan was one of Nashville's two main department stores. Harveys had designed a small lunchroom for children called the Monkey Bar. It featured live, caged monkeys. Wilkinson's son always wanted to eat at the Monkey Bar and was too young to understand why the color of his skin should prevent him from doing so. Wilkinson described her pain and humiliation as she lied to her son about being in too big a hurry to eat in the Monkey Bar each time they visited Harveys. Other women described how their children had wet themselves because no restroom facilities were available in many stores. Another woman explained what happened when her exuberant son went into a small juice bar and climbed onto a stool. The man behind the counter exclaimed, "Get that nigger kid off that stool!"[3] The downtown stores were not only logical targets economically, but they could also unite the entire black community and garner the sympathy of many whites, who could understand the injustice of stores' taking African Americans' money on an equal basis with whites but refusing, in every other way, to treat them equally.

After deciding to desegregate the downtown lunch counters, NCLC's projects committee, chaired by James Lawson, contacted Fred Harvey of Harveys department store and John Sloan of the Cain-Sloan department store and tried to persuade them to open their lunch counters voluntarily on the grounds that it would be better for the stores to make the change in a calm atmosphere than in a situation of nonviolent protest. Harvey received the representatives cordially and apologetically, while Sloan was condescending and adamant in his stand against integration. In the end both gentlemen argued that by integrating their lunch counters they would lose more business than they would gain. They did express their willingness to open to blacks if the rest of the city also made the same move, but they refused to make the first move toward desegregation.

Although assured that these department stores would enforce segregation and not allow blacks to eat at their lunch counters, NCLC's projects committee decided that they should take some action to demonstrate that this tradition was still being enforced. On November 28, 1959, the first test sit-in was held at the downtown location of Harveys, and on December 5, the second was held at Cain-Sloan. Both resulted in the refusal of service; however, at Cain-Sloan a waitress took the orders of the participants before a store official came over to the lunch counter, questioned the persons, and established that they were in fact Negroes and not Filipinos or Indians. This questioning occurred because, as the home of several Protestant denominations' national headquarters, Nashville had long been open to Crusade Scholars[4] but not to African Americans. It was said at this time that a black couple could eat anywhere in the city if the man wore a turban, the woman wore a sari, and both effectively imitated a foreign accent.

At the next regular meeting of NCLC on January 3, 1960, Lawson reported the results of the test sit-ins at Harveys and Cain-Sloan and made several suggestions for further action that were approved by NCLC. First, Lawson suggested that the nonviolent workshops be expanded to include more volunteers. Second, a letter was to be sent to both Harveys and Cain-Sloan requesting that a group of blacks be permitted to eat at one of the lunch counters to test the reaction of whites eating at the counter. Third, it was decided that if these stores did not voluntarily change their policies, NCLC and the students would launch a full-scale nonviolent protest on the stores during the month of February.

After Harveys and Cain-Sloan affirmed their policy of segregation, NCLC's projects committee continued preparing for sit-ins at the downtown lunch counters. The workshops held in preparation for the demonstrations had a strong theme of redemptive suffering in them. There was little regard for what would happen to the individual, for any suffering that might be encountered would be a small price to pay for the redemption of the larger society. The participants wanted to create "a beloved community," so the technique used would be Christian nonviolence. From Lawson, the demonstrators learned that the concept of "a beloved community" required that the demonstrators refrain from violence and show only love toward all persons, particularly those who opposed their efforts. Like Jesus Christ, who accepted suffering to redeem the world, the demonstrators would accept abuse and even violent attacks from members of a mob in order to create a more just society. The students identified strongly with this technique and even used Christian themes for the freedom songs that they sang throughout the movement, whether they were protesting or sitting in jail. The black church had often compared the plight of black people with the persecution of the children of Israel. Those involved identified with this symbolism and saw the sit-ins as a holy crusade that would benefit the whole nation.

To insure that the demonstrators would remain nonviolent in the actual demonstration, mock sit-ins were held, complete with "store employees" and "hecklers." Demonstrators would seat themselves facing the walls, and the "manager" would sternly explain that the establishment did not serve African Americans. After the protesters were denied service, "hecklers" would assault the demonstrators. They would blow cigarette smoke into the faces of the students, pull their hair, and insult them in imitation of the real hecklers that they would encounter at the actual sit-ins. If a person became violent or insulting during a mock sit-in, he or she would not be allowed to participate in the actual sit-in. A person who could not adhere to the strict rules proposed by the students would be assigned a task that did not involve actual demonstrations, such as running the mimeograph machine.

On February 1, 1960, the Nashville students received word that there had been a sit-in in Greensboro, North Carolina. And several days later, amid much talk on the Fisk and Tennessee State campuses of possible protests, Lawson received a phone call from Douglas Moore, a personal friend and fellow Methodist minister, in Durham, North Carolina, who asked if the Nashville students could do anything to demonstrate sympathy for the North Carolina sit-ins. Lawson discussed this request with Rev. Kelly Miller Smith, president of NCLC, and they decided to contact some Fisk and Tennessee State students to see if they would want to take immediate action and carry out the protests for which they had long been preparing. Indeed they did. The next night about fifty students met in the science building at Fisk and discussed exactly what they wanted to do. It was a group decision that led the students to decide where and when to sit in. The stores at which the students chose to demonstrate were chosen largely because they were the same type of stores where protests were being held in North Carolina.

On February 6, 1960, the first sit-ins were staged in Nashville. Despite four inches of snow (enough to all but close this mid-Southern city), approximately 124 students from American Baptist Theological Seminary, Fisk University, and Tennessee State University sat in at three downtown lunch counters—Kress, Woolworth's, and McClellen's. Five days later, 200 students sat in at the three original lunch counters and also at Grant's department store. Two days later, 340 students demonstrated again at five lunch counters. Thanks to the presence of the police and the discipline of the demonstrators, all of these sit-ins were nonviolent, but things were going to change.

Nashville's business leaders convinced Mayor Ben West to make the demonstrations more costly for NCLC. The mayor ordered Chief of Police Douglas Hosse to meet with Lawson and inform him of a law that stated, among other things, that it was illegal for any person to engage in an activity that was calculated to incite others to violence. A violation of this law could result in a person being fined up to $500.

This threat created new problems for NCLC. If mass arrests did occur, what could NCLC do? At the time the organization had only $87.50 to its name. It could not pay the students' bonds—much less their fines if convicted. NCLC had not even retained an attorney in the event of legal problems related to the sit-ins. Could NCLC ask the student protesters to risk spending a considerable amount of time in jail during the middle of an academic semester? Additionally, word of the planned events had been passed around town, so the thugs who might commit acts of violence at such a protest would have ample time to prepare. Would the students remain loyal to their nonviolent training? Could an athletic young man simply sit by and watch his girlfriend be beaten? If any of the demonstrators fought back, it was possible that a full-scale race riot could occur. If it did, the cause of civil rights in Nashville could be set back drastically.

On the morning of February 27, the executive committee of NCLC met at the First Baptist Church and discussed the protests scheduled for later in the day. Lawson reported on his meeting with Nashville's chief of police the day before. Soon the students began arriving at the church, and the executive committee felt obligated to tell the students of the potential problems that could be encountered. Several officers of NCLC and the student leaders met and discussed NCLC's lack of funds, the high probability that violence would occur if sit-ins were held that day, and the intention of the police to make arrests. The NCLC officers, including Kelly Miller Smith and James Lawson, had doubts about whether the protest should be held, especially considering the organization's lack of money. These officers suggested that the sit-ins be postponed until the next week so that NCLC's ministers would have time to take up a special offering to support these protests. They felt that a few days would make no difference. Paul LePrad, an exchange student at Fisk and the only white student participating in this important meeting, was inclined to agree with the adults of NCLC but stated that he would abide by the decision of the students. Jim Bevel, a bright and mature seminary student at American Baptist, spoke up and emotionally declared, "If we wait until next week, we may be asked to wait until next month and on and on. Personally, I'm tired of this business of waiting." Diane Nash and Angeline Butler, both of Fisk University, emphatically agreed with Bevel. The officers of NCLC realized that these students had learned well the lessons of Christian nonviolence in Lawson's workshops and were ready to accept the consequences of their fight for freedom. In the face of the strong faith and courage of the students, Smith began to see the words of NCLC's "adult wisdom" as sounding more like the "whimpering of kindergarten children." Smith then told the students, "We are all in this together—when you go down to the stores, you will go with our full support."[5]

Somewhat annoyed by the delay this unplanned meeting had caused, the students walked into the sanctuary, where the other students were waiting to begin the march toward downtown. John Lewis, an Alabama native and a student at American Baptist Seminary, had recently read Martin Luther King's *Stride Toward Freedom* and was responsible for writing a set of rules that was duplicated and distributed to the waiting students:

DO NOT:

1. Strike back or curse if abused.
2. Laugh out.
3. Hold conversations with floor walker.
4. Leave your seat until your leader has given you permission to do so.
5. Block entrances to stores outside nor the aisles inside.

DO:

1. Show yourself friendly and courteous at all times.
2. Sit straight; always face the counter.
3. Report all serious incidents to your leader.
4. Refer information seekers to your leader in a polite manner.
5. Remember the teachings of Jesus Christ, Mahatma Gandhi, and Martin Luther King. Love and non-violence is the way.

MAY GOD BLESS EACH OF YOU[6]

Lawson instructed the students to follow the instructions to the letter and to not even think of striking back.

Approximately four hundred students participated in the fourth series of sit-ins in ten different stores. There were several outbreaks of violence against the demonstrators that day. White hecklers crushed their lighted cigarettes against the backs of girls sitting at the counter and poured ketchup in the demonstrators' hair. The hecklers pushed, pulled, and assaulted the students in a variety of ways, but no demonstrator struck back or even insulted a heckler. Ironically, Paul LePrad, who had tended to side with the adult NCLC members in the meeting earlier that day, was the first victim of the leather-jacketed white teenagers who were obviously organized to confront the students. The teenagers jerked him from the counter and soundly beat him. As his assailants left, he stood up, brushed himself off, and returned to his seat. When asked by a reporter if he thought that all of this was accomplishing anything, he replied, ". . . only time will tell."[7]

When police finally moved in to stop the violence and break up the sit-ins, it was necessary for them to stop traffic for one block downtown. At Woolworth's a crowd of three hundred fifty onlookers had gathered to antagonize the protesters, who remained outwardly calm. "Hey, boy, why don't you go back to your own restaurants? You don't see us coming in your restaurants, do you?" yelled someone from the crowd. "They'd know what to do with you in

Mississippi," yelled another. Then a teenager known to persons in the crowd as "Green Hat" marched up to the counter and jerked Maurice Davis, an eighteen-year-old Tennessee State student, from his stool and beat him mercilessly; many in the crowd helped with Davis's beating, but fortunately he was not seriously injured. The police then entered the store and told everyone to leave; those who refused were arrested, but they made no attempt to arrest any of the white teenagers who had beaten the students. The remaining crowd cheered loudly as the students were loaded into paddy wagons. But to the dismay of the crowd, new demonstrators immediately assumed the positions of those arrested. Rev. Smith heard an elderly white man say, "'I've never seen the like of it in all my life; just as soon as they arrest one bunch of them, here comes another bunch.'"[8]

At the fourth series of sit-ins the police were conspicuously absent when the violence started. When the police did arrive, they immediately arrested the civil rights activists as ordered by the chief of police and the mayor. In a speech Lawson made at SNCC's founding convention in April 1960, he blamed the police for allowing the violence to occur in hopes that further sit-ins would be discouraged.

> Only police permissiveness invited young white men to take over store after store in an effort to further intimidate or crush the sit-in. Law enforcement agents accustomed to viewing crime were able to mark the well-dressed students waiting to make purchases as loitering on the lunch-counter stools, but they were unable even to suspect and certainly not to see assault and battery. Thus potential customers, quietly asking for service, are disorderly, breaching the peace, inciting riots, while swaggering, vilifying, violent, defiant white young teenagers are law abiding.[9]

The students arrested were charged with trespassing and disorderly conduct. Early in the afternoon, black attorneys Avon Williams and Z. Alexander Looby went to the metropolitan jail to offer their services to the students. Looby, who was still recovering from a serious automobile accident, and Williams were so impressed that they remained with the students all afternoon and part of the night. By late afternoon fourteen black lawyers had offered their services to the students free of charge. Though the students had told the lawyers that they did not want to post bond, the deans of the students' colleges had arranged for the students' release, citing the schools' responsibility to the students' parents as the reason for arranging their release. Later that day all of the seventy-five protesters arrested were released into the custody of their deans.

On February 29, 1960, amid many rumors of probable further violence, the mayor of Nashville, Ben West, returned from a trip to attempt to mediate a solution. That evening he met with about seventy-five black ministers and activists at Kelly Miller Smith's First Baptist Church, Capitol Hill. Both

Nashville newspapers had identified Lawson as the leader behind the sit-ins; therefore, Lawson was active in discussions with Mayor West. West conceded that the students had the legal right to sit in while the lunch counters remained open, but he stressed that when they remained at a lunch counter after its closing was announced, they violated state law. He wanted assurances that the students would comply with the law. He felt that this would relieve tensions and allow him time to negotiate.

Unlike most of his colleagues at this meeting, Lawson was unwilling to submit to Mayor West's request. He felt that since the arbitrary closings of lunch counters were obvious attempts to inhibit the student protests, the law referred to by Mayor West was simply an excuse to prevent blacks from exercising their rights. Therefore, Lawson felt that the students should continue their sit-ins. In an editorial appearing the morning after the meeting, "publisher James Stahlman of the *Nashville Banner* concluded that there was 'no place in Nashville for flannel-mouth agitators, white or colored—under whatever sponsorship, imported for preachments of mass disorder, self-supported, vagrants, or the paid agents of strife breeding organizations.'"[10]

The stand that Lawson took against Mayor West led to his expulsion from Vanderbilt. Regardless of what Lawson actually said, Mayor West, both newspapers, Chancellor Harvie Branscomb of Vanderbilt University, and the general populace of Nashville interpreted his comments as encouraging the students to violate the law. Many in the white community thought Lawson was unwilling to work with the mayor, who claimed to be on the side of civil rights. For many whites, West had taken on the role of an executive who looked to the good of the community as a whole. He wanted to prevent violence from reoccurring, and to preserve order. He claimed to believe in the goals of the students, but he felt that these goals should be achieved through the courts. West could not understand why the protests could not wait until victory had been won through the legal system.

Because of all of the newspaper publicity concerning Lawson, Vanderbilt chancellor Branscomb felt forced to act (though he gave no specific reason why he felt he had to act immediately). Significant factors contributing to Branscomb's haste were publisher Stahlman's suggestions in his editorials that Vanderbilt's board of trustees might act if Branscomb failed to do so. Stahlman's suggestions or threats were not without merit since he served on the executive committee of the board. On the morning of March 1, just a few hours after Mayor West had met with Lawson and the other ministers, Branscomb called J. Robert Nelson, dean of the Divinity School, who was home with the flu, and ordered him to talk with Lawson about the meeting the previous evening. That afternoon, Dean Nelson and Robert McGaw, an assistant to the chancellor, met with Lawson. They were instructed to ask Lawson whether he had been quoted accurately concerning his defiance of the mayor and to request that Lawson prepare a statement that would reverse his reported stand against the mayor. Lawson was dismayed that the chancellor had made such a request of Nelson. He did not accept the exact words that the media had quoted him as having said, but he would not retract his position against the mayor. He would also not agree to ask the students to end the sit-ins. That afternoon Nelson and McGaw told Branscomb of Lawson's refusal to retract his position.

After his first attempt failed, Branscomb again used Nelson as an errand boy. Nelson was to make Lawson aware of a regulation in the student handbook that prohibited students from participating in "disorderly assemblies," or assemblies likely to lead to disorder. This regulation had been created to control panty raids; therefore, it had never been applied to anyone except undergraduates. No graduate or professional student had ever had any reason to be aware of this regulation; it was highly debated whether this rule even applied to Lawson. Branscomb blamed Lawson not for participating in any "disorderly assembly," since he had not yet participated in a sit-in, but for failing to pledge to obey this misapplied regulation. Branscomb had never begun the long process that would normally precede the expulsion of a graduate student. He had committed himself to the possibility of immediate expulsion if Lawson failed to accept this regulation because to cooperate with the long process that would normally be the prologue to expulsion would show a weakness in his determination.

The faculty of the Divinity School was already becoming disturbed by the chancellor's actions regarding Lawson and had drafted a statement, which was given to Nelson on Wednesday, March 3, before he met with the executive committee of the board of trustees at their regular meeting at noon that day. The statement supported Lawson and his activities and condemned the way he was being portrayed in the press. It also asserted that if Lawson were expelled, they would consider resigning; nine of the Divinity School's sixteen faculty members had signed this statement.

At the meeting of the executive committee, Branscomb brought before the committee a proposal to dismiss Lawson. Dean Nelson read a statement Lawson wrote explaining his perception of the situation. In his statement, Lawson flattered the university. He expressed regret that such an episode had ever occurred and denied claims that he was the leader of the sit-ins. "He condoned civil disobedience only when a law or law enforcement agency had, in reality, 'ceased to be the law,' and then he chose it only in 'fear and trembling before God.'"[11] After reading Lawson's statement, Nelson requested that the committee postpone making a decision until the entire Divinity School faculty could be included. The committee denied Nelson's request. After the presentations and some discussion, the committee (Harold S. Vanderbilt [chairman], James Stahlman, Harvie Branscomb, Sam M. Flemming, Cecil Sims, John Sloan, William Walker, and Jesse Wille) voted unanimously to expel Lawson. Stahlman, publisher of the *Nashville Banner*, and Sloan, owner of Cain-Sloan, were influential members of the committee, so there had been little doubt about the outcome of the vote. It was hardly an impartial jury. Lawson was given a choice: he could withdraw by 9 a.m. the next day, or he could be expelled.

Later that same afternoon, Branscomb met with the faculty of the Divinity School and informed them of the executive committee's ruling. Most of the faculty exploded at this announcement. Dr. Langdon Gilkey declared that everything that Hitler did in Germany was legal. In a statement of foreshadowing, Dr. Gordon Kaufman exclaimed that Mr. Lawson was simply putting the teachings of his professors into action, and if he was being asked to withdraw then maybe all Divinity School faculty should withdraw. The faculty was infuriated both by the executive committee's action and at its disregard of the faculty's demand for a delay for further consideration in this action.

On Thursday morning, March 4, Chancellor Branscomb spoke to a closed meeting of the faculty and students of the Divinity School. The chancellor explained the executive committee's reasons for dismissing Lawson as well as the terms of the resolution adopted by the executive committee. Since Lawson had not visited the registrar's office and withdrawn by 9 a.m. that morning, Branscomb declared that Lawson was expelled. Lawson's tragic flaw, in Branscomb's mind, was that he had reserved the right to say that certain laws are unjust and should not be obeyed. For Branscomb, this was unpardonable. He voiced his agreement with the end at which the sit-ins aimed, but he could not accept their method. He felt that the protesters had made their point, and it was now time for the courts to resolve this issue. Branscomb said that the conspicuous nature of Lawson's activities had forced the university into a position from which it had to act.

After the chancellor left, Lawson addressed the faculty and students of the Divinity School. Lawson claimed to have received no written request to refrain from participating in the sit-ins or any written notification of the board's decision that he must withdraw by 9 a.m. that morning or be expelled. Lawson explained his role in the sit-ins as having taught the students the techniques of nonviolence without which the sit-ins could have been blood baths. After the previous Saturday's violence, Lawson urged the leaders of NCLC and the students to accept the mayor's call for a cooling-off period, but the students and leaders were not willing to wait any longer for segregation to come to an end.

That same day, on the coldest March 4 in Nashville's history, around twenty students picketed in protest of Lawson's expulsion. Most were divinity students who marched in shifts for approximately five hours beneath Chancellor Branscomb's office. A large crowd of students was on hand to watch the pickets. Some of the students threw snowballs at the marchers, and one even tried to join the demonstration holding a sign that supported Lawson's expulsion.

Later at the First Baptist Church, Capitol Hill, before he could participate in the scheduled sit-in, Lawson was arrested along with seventy-five students, and was charged with conspiring to break a state law that required demonstrators to leave when the owner announces the closing of the counter. The faculty of Vanderbilt's Divinity School raised the $500 necessary to bail Lawson out of jail. They also started a fund to use in Lawson's defense.

Any Nashvillian who believed that the African American residents of Nashville were happy with segregation and that the sit-ins were the result of outside agitation was gravely surprised when the black community raised approximately $45,000 in three days to cover the bonds of the demonstrators. Many suspicions were aroused in the white community about the source of this money. Central in these suspicions was the Citizens Bank of Nashville, a black-owned and black-managed bank. Early in the week after the $45,000 was raised to post bond for the demonstrators, Will D. Campbell, a white Baptist preacher who worked with the National Council of Churches and supported the sit-in movement, came into the Citizens Bank, where he had long done business, and noticed white men behind the counter and in the vault apparently examining the bank's records. He asked a bank officer why these men were there. The officer replied that in all of his years of association with the bank this was the first time he had ever known of both federal and state auditors coming unannounced on the same day. He said that while they would find some overdrawn checking accounts and late loan payments, they would not find the $45,000 in fraudulent loans used to bail the students out of prison for which they were looking because no such loans had been made. The $45,000 had come from the entire black community—Nashville was dealing with a wholly dissatisfied black community, and not the stirrings of a few outside agitators.

March 4 marked the end of the lunch counter sit-ins for about a month. After this series of sit-ins, the demonstrators accepted a tentative settlement that called for the formation of a biracial committee appointed by Mayor Ben West to negotiate an end to the crisis. During this month there were no formal protests, but a new tactic emerged to fight segregation.

This tactic was the economic boycott and was reportedly envisioned by four women during a bridge party. These four women thought that if segregation is evil, then they should not patronize businesses that enforced segregation. Thus the economic boycott of downtown Nashville began. Each of these four women agreed to call ten other people and to ask them to call ten others. Word of the boycott was also spread at the mass meetings that were being held weekly. The leaders of the Nashville movement saw the boycott as a great success and boasted that for seven weeks 98 percent of the African American business that would have normally been done downtown was done elsewhere or not at all. This was one point on which the business leaders and Nashville's black community agreed, for every downtown business felt the effects of the boycott.

The boycott signaled the fall of segregation at downtown lunch counters, for not only did virtually all blacks refuse to shop downtown, many white customers who lived outside Nashville would not shop there because of the tense atmosphere that existed downtown. The merchants had long argued that if they opened their lunch counters to blacks, they would lose a significant percentage of their white customers, but they were beginning to change their minds. Increasingly merchants had to measure a known economic loss as a result of the sit-ins and boycott against an unknown and indefinable loss if they accepted integration. The known loss soon became more significant than any potential loss. Economic pressure forced the merchants to change whether they wanted to or not.

The biracial committee studied the situation of both the merchants and the demonstrators and made a recommendation to both parties. It called for the merchants to separate their lunch counter into two sections, one for whites only and another for both races. This was to be done on a trial basis for ninety days. Also, if no further demonstrations occurred during this ninety-day period, all of the charges against the students would be dropped. NCLC and the student movement denounced this plan, charging that it ignored the moral issues involved and created another system of segregation. Also, the merchants privately disapproved of this plan. They felt alone in this confrontation, for neither the newspapers, the Chamber of Commerce, or the city government took a strong position for or against the integration of lunch counters. In Nashville there were no laws enforcing segregation in public places, only tradition. The merchants were hesitant to break the tradition until they knew how the white community would respond.

Sensing the hesitation of the merchants to act in good faith, the demonstrators decided to begin the sit-ins again. This time the students adopted a hit-and-run tactic in which they would sit down at a lunch counter and wait until the manager closed the lunch counter and asked them to leave. Then they would leave and do the same thing at another lunch counter, and then go back to the first lunch counter, which by this time had reopened. This tactic led to few arrests and still kept the lunch counters closed. Also, the students would only fill two-thirds of the seats at a lunch counter, thereby giving any sympathetic whites the opportunity to eat along with the students. Often whites would attempt to order, but their sympathetic gesture was only that, for during a sit-in, the counter was closed to all.

On April 19, 1960, at 5:30 a.m., dynamite thrown from a car destroyed the home of Z. Alexander Looby. One of Nashville's two black councilmen, Looby headed the defense for the students in court. The explosion was so powerful that it shattered 147 windows at Meharry Medical College across the street. Looby and his wife were asleep in a back bedroom when the blast occurred and were not seriously injured. Despite the bombing, Looby vowed to continue defending the students. NCLC quickly raised more than $4,000 to aid in the rebuilding of Looby's home.

In response to the bombing, approximately 4,000 students and citizens of Nashville marched to the courthouse to confront Mayor Ben West. On the steps of the courthouse, Rev. C. T. Vivian charged that West had not addressed the moral implications in this struggle and must share in the responsibility for the bombing of Looby's home. Vivian challenged the mayor to use all of the moral power of his office to force the city's lunch counters to integrate. West sharply refuted Vivian's charges and declared his horror at this bombing, and he pointed to his political record as evidence of his longstanding support for civil rights. However, West stated that he could not force the city's lunch counters to desegregate because they were owned by private citizens who had the right to choose who they wanted to serve. Diane Nash, in what she would later describe as a divine inspiration, suddenly saw the mayor in a different light. He was no longer the powerful, white politician she feared; he was a mayor with limited powers being pressed by many factions. Remembering Lawson's teachings in the workshops—that all people should see one another as fellow human beings rather than enemies—she asked the mayor if he personally believed that segregation was wrong and if he would use his prestige as mayor to end segregation. West did. "'I appeal to all citizens to end discrimination, to have no bias, no hatred,' he said." Nash continued, "Then Mayor, do you recommend that the lunch counters be desegregated?" "'Yes,' he found himself saying."[12] Three weeks after West voiced his support for integration, lunch counters began serving blacks on an equal basis with whites.

The following day Martin Luther King Jr. visited Nashville and spoke to thousands of persons in and around Fisk's gymnasium. King called the Nashville movement "the best organized and the most disciplined in the Southland." He declared, "I did not come to Nashville to bring inspiration but to gain inspiration from the great movement that has taken place in this community. . . . [S]egregation is on its deathbed now, and the only uncertain thing about it is the day it will be buried." King recognized greatness in the students who had taken the tactic of nonviolence even further than had King himself.[13]

The lunch counter sit-ins in Nashville had been a tremendous success. They had not only opened downtown lunch counters to blacks; they had united the black students and adult community behind a common cause. They aided the development of some of the South's finest civil rights workers. Through the stress placed upon the moral correctness of the demonstrations, they established a sense of pride in being black that many had never had. However, much still remained to be done. Few restaurants served blacks, and most major hotels remained segregated. Two of Nashville's largest hospitals still did not accept black patients, and few blacks had been hired to fill non-menial positions. Though these demonstrations had not completely eliminated segregation, they had paved the way for many more nonviolent protests in the months and years to follow.

One institution that would never be the same after the Nashville civil rights movement was the Vanderbilt Divinity School. Though many had initially congratulated Vanderbilt after Lawson's expulsion on March 3, many faculty members protested that decision and sought some way to reinstate Lawson. Throughout the spring semester, the divinity faculty continued to negotiate with Branscomb and other administrators, but all faculty proposals were rejected. Many of the faculty in the university and most faculty in the divinity school also began to consider resigning in protest of Lawson's expulsion.

On May 10, when downtown merchants agreed to desegregate the downtown lunch counters, the faculty began to change its view about the Lawson affair. A few days after this announcement, the city announced that it would drop all charges against those arrested in the sit-ins. The faculty reached the conclusion that Vanderbilt should be no less generous than the city and therefore should reinstate Lawson to rectify the injustice that had been done to him. The divinity faculty decided to make one final attempt to readmit Lawson. The faculty noted that the chancellor had stated on March 15 in the University Senate that Lawson might be readmitted to the university through normal channels. The faculty agreed to attempt to have Lawson admitted to the summer session. The faculty prepared several additions to Lawson's dossier, and Lawson himself wrote a fourteen-page clarification of his role in the sit-ins and his views on civil disobedience. He stated that he had resigned his position as a field representative with the Fellowship of Reconciliation and that he intended to devote his summer to his pastoral duties at Scott Memorial Methodist Church in Shelbyville, Tennessee, and to personal reflection and writing. In addition to Lawson's statement, there were letters of reference from Rev. Kelly Miller Smith and Dr. John Oliver Nelson of Yale University.

Ultimately, Chancellor Branscomb and the Vanderbilt board of trustees denied Lawson's readmittance to the Divinity School, prompting eleven of the sixteen divinity faculty to resign. These resignations made news all over the country, and several respected seminaries offered to hire the professors who had resigned. The president of the Chicago Theological Seminary offered to hire all divinity faculty who resigned. With only a fraction of the faculty left, the Divinity School had little chance of attracting any professor of national status; therefore, Branscomb was faced with a choice—he could give up on the Divinity School, which had been emerging as one of the finest in the nation, or he could attempt to reach some sort of compromise.

Branscomb decided to attempt to compromise. In the end, the chancellor issued a statement that allowed both sides some sense of victory. His statement allowed Lawson to receive his degree either by transfer of credits from another institution or by written examination—he could not be readmitted; gave the Divinity School faculty ten days to withdraw their resignations; and announced that the Lawson affair was now closed.

Branscomb's statement convinced all but one of the divinity faculty to withdraw their resignations. Nevertheless, the faculty was demoralized.

Most sought other employment within a few years. Years would pass before the Divinity School would be able to again recruit nationally known religious scholars. Although Lawson could have elected to receive his degree from Vanderbilt, after several discussions with the divinity faculty, Lawson decided to complete his degree during summer school at Boston University. He did return at the end of the summer to resume his participation in the nonviolent demonstrations and to continue his ministry in Shelbyville, Tennessee, at Scott Memorial Methodist Church.

The legacy of James Lawson's instruction in nonviolence lived on in the students who participated in the civil rights movement. Student leaders from Nashville either led or were involved with most every civil rights campaign in the South until 1965. After 1965, the rise of the Black Power movement (particularly within the Student Nonviolent Coordinating Committee) reduced the influence of the Nashville activists on the civil rights movement. Despite the setbacks of the nonviolent forces in SNCC, many of the Nashville students remained active in the movement. Nash, who remained in Nashville for several years, later became involved in the antiwar movement and traveled to North Vietnam. John Lewis delivered a controversial speech at the 1963 March on Washington as president of SNCC, but soon thereafter was ousted from office in a dispute over SNCC's commitment to nonviolence and white involvement in the organization. Lewis is now a U.S. representative from Georgia. James Bevel left SNCC, joined the SCLC, and worked closely with King in several projects, including those in Chicago and Alabama. In August 1962, James Lawson was appointed minister at Centenary Methodist Church in Memphis, then the largest black Methodist church in the South, and participated in protests there. Lawson initiated King's involvement in the sanitation workers' strike in Memphis, where King was assassinated in April 1968. In 1974, Lawson became pastor of Holman United Methodist Church in Los Angeles. Holman was a large, middle-class congregation, and Lawson served there until his retirement. Lawson also served as president of the Los Angeles chapter of the SCLC. Bernard Lafayette organized SNCC's Alabama project in February 1963 and then returned to college. In 1965 the Alabama project became SNCC's major focus. Later Lafayette received a PhD from the Harvard Divinity School. He later returned to Nashville to serve as president of the American Baptist Theological Seminary, the institution that trained John Lewis, Jim Bevel, himself, and many other activists. These are but a few examples of individuals from Nashville who contributed greatly to the civil rights movement.

By comparison with other events and persons of the civil rights movement, neither the American public nor historians have paid much attention to James Lawson and the students he inspired. Hollywood has not produced a movie about the struggle. Cities across America have not named streets after James Lawson. Nevertheless, the theory and practice of nonviolent protest—taught by Lawson and spread throughout the South by the young women and men he inspired—was integral to the civil rights movement. Nonviolent protest, as inspired by Lawson, remains the element for which the American civil rights movement is known and admired throughout the world.

NOTES

1. Quotations from David Haberstam, *The Children* (New York: Ballantine, 1998), 31.
2. Halberstam, *The Children*, 16.
3. Halberstam, *The Children*, 91.
4. Crusade Scholars were students from the native churches of Third World nations who were sponsored by mission boards to attend college in Nashville. These students often had dark skin.
5. Kelly Miller Smith, *Pursuit of a Dream*, Chapter 6, "Day of Crisis," 9–11. This is an unpublished book manuscript found in the Kelly Miller Smith papers in Special Collections of the Vanderbilt University Library.
6. From the Kelly Miller Smith papers. A loose copy of the rules that were given to the waiting students was included in these papers.
7. Smith, *Pursuit of a Dream*, Chapter 6, "Day of Crisis," 14.
8. Smith, *Pursuit of a Dream*, Chapter 6, "Day of Crisis," 15–16.
9. August Meier, *Black Protest in the Twentieth Century* (Indianapolis: Bobbs-Merrill, 1965), 310.
10. Foster Document, 5–6. This is a document located in the Lawson Affair Collection in Special Collections at the Vanderbilt University Library. Dr. Andrew Foster was a professor in the Divinity School during the controversy.
11. Foster Document, 7–8.
12. Halberstam, *The Children*, 234.
13. Milton Viorst, *Fire in the Streets* (New York: Simon & Schuster, 1979), 117.

SUGGESTED READING

Branscomb, Harvie. *Purely Academic*. Nashville, TN: Vanderbilt University Press, 1978.
Campbell, Will D. *Forty Acres and a Goat*. Atlanta: Peachtree, 1986.
Conkin, Paul Keith. *Gone with the Ivy: A Biography of Vanderbilt University*. Knoxville, TN: University of Tennessee Press, 1985.
Halberstam, David. *The Children*. New York: Ballantine, 1998.
Lewis, John. *Walking with the Wind: A Memoir of the Movement*. Orlando, FL: Harcourt Brace, 1998.

9

ॐ

Charles Sherrod and Martin Luther King Jr.: Mass Action and Nonviolence in Albany

Robert E. Luckett Jr.

From the fall of 1961 to the summer of 1962, the civil rights movement hit high gear in Albany, Georgia. Led by Charles Sherrod and the Student Nonviolent Coordinating Committee (SNCC), the Albany Movement became a grassroots effort to overthrow all aspects of Jim Crow in that southwest Georgia city. With the arrival of Martin Luther King Jr. and his organization, the Southern Christian Leadership Conference (SCLC), Albany gained much-needed recognition and financial support. Yet King's presence also fueled bitter infighting, especially between SNCC and the SCLC, over who was in control and who would receive the credit for any gains made. This internal confusion, coupled with the baffling strategy of police chief Laurie Pritchett, who trained his forces to respond to the nonviolence of activists with nonviolent tactics, crippled the movement and its immediate effects. In the long run, however, the Albany Movement laid the foundations to undermine Jim Crow there and provided important lessons for the rest of the civil rights movement.

In 1961, factions within the Student Nonviolent Coordinating Committee (SNCC) were immersed in an intense debate. The question facing the civil rights organization, known for its youth and vitality, was one of methods. The more traditional activists leaned toward a conservative program of voter registration, which had been a staple of the civil rights movement from the beginning. For this older contingent of SNCC, the disenfranchisement of African Americans in the South was still the defining characteristic of Jim

Crow—the segregationist political system—and they believed it could be toppled only through nonviolent, black political participation.

Another segment of SNCC proposed a new course of direct action protests, made famous by the Freedom Rides and the sit-ins of 1960 and early 1961. Militant yet still nonviolent, these SNCC activists saw mass protests as the best way to force the federal government into taking a stand on behalf of civil rights for African Americans. A founder of SNCC, Ella Baker, came forward with a commonsense solution to the debate. SNCC should form two branches: one to focus on voter registration and the other on direct action. Baker believed time would prove that both forms of activism were one and the same, and SNCC accepted her proposal to break into two wings. In the fall of 1961, Charles Sherrod and Cordell Reagon moved to Albany, Georgia, in the southwest corner of the state to start a SNCC-led voter registration drive.

At the age of twenty-two, Sherrod was four years older than Reagon and was hired as SNCC's first paid field secretary in charge of the voter registration program. Both were experienced civil rights workers. Each had been a Freedom Rider hardly a year earlier, and Reagon had been involved in the Nashville student movement while Sherrod had led sit-ins in Richmond, Virginia. Sherrod's impoverished upbringing in Petersburg, Virginia, also informed his civil rights activism.

Sherrod was born to a teenage mother who had left school in the eighth grade and raised six children alone. Forced to work at an early age to support the family, Sherrod soon found a way out of the slums through education and the Baptist Church, graduating from Virginia Union University with a degree in religion and becoming a preacher. His background and his religious training drew him toward the nonviolent, liberal Christian theory of the civil rights movement that advocated equality and salvation for all people regardless of race and class. He believed in "the recognition of human dignity in all human beings" and in the uplift of entire communities so that the people may have "power in the system and over how the system is styled."[1] Sherrod stepped naturally into the sit-ins and the Freedom Rides and became inextricably tied to the movement.

His life experience and his ministry also taught him that most poor blacks in the South were skeptical of voter registration drives and of strangers who promised to deliver uplift through the civil rights movement. For poor Southern blacks, the threat of violent white repercussions and the task of staying alive outweighed the importance of voting. "When we first came to Albany, the people were afraid, really afraid . . . ," Sherrod noted. "People walking in the same direction would go across the street from us, because they were afraid; they didn't want to be connected to us in any way."[2] For those few African Americans who were middle class in the context of Albany, their horizons, as Sherrod saw it, hardly rose "further than a new car, a bulging refrigerator, and an insatiable lust for more than enough of everything we call leisure."[3] For them, the civil rights movement threatened what

Charles Sherrod with Carl Braden (Image courtesy of the Wisconsin Historical Society.)

little stability they had created. Reagon rationalized the fear: "They were extremely afraid of us, because we represented something that had never been done before."[4] Sherrod and Reagon thus spent their first several months attempting to fit into a reluctant community that had been known for its fairly peaceful race relations.

With a population of sixty thousand that was 40 percent black, Albany sat in Dougherty County in southwest Georgia, where African Americans had been able on occasion to register and vote, while a somewhat benign white police force had combated Ku Klux Klan violence. Segregationists nonetheless denied African Americans any position of real power and any true hope of rising above the poverty that defined most black lives. When the black community finally began to move, Sherrod and Reagon were ecstatic. Sherrod exulted: "The people are thinking. They are becoming. In a deep southwest Georgia area, where it is generally conceded that the Negro has no rights that a white man is bound to respect, *at last*, they sing, 'We Shall Overcome.'"[5] After months of concerted efforts to prove their sincerity, the two activists found themselves leading a movement that would go far beyond any initial thoughts of a voter registration campaign.

African Americans in Albany were the first to willingly engage in mass action protests and to seize their freedom through actual militancy. In the well-known style of SNCC, Sherrod and Reagon first looked to the young people of Albany for support—a tactic opposed by the more traditional Southern Christian Leadership Conference (SCLC) led by Martin Luther King Jr. The SCLC believed that it made more sense first to organize adults and ministers in particular, who could then convince congregations to follow their leads. On the other hand, SNCC felt that the SCLC's attempt to organize an ambivalent black middle class was futile. Instead, SNCC and Sherrod knew that young people "were searching for a meaning in life,"[6] and their less-conservative nature and presence in the movement had the potential to shock and cajole adults into similar efforts. Sherrod's status as a minister appealed to both young and old, SNCC and SCLC alike.

Before long, the Baptist Ministerial Alliance and the Interdenominational Alliance were supporting SNCC's efforts in Albany, and night schools began in churches, where the nonviolent tactics and the spiritual songs of the civil rights movement were taught and became identified with Albany. High school and college students, especially from the historically black Albany State College, filed into these classes, and soon another SNCC worker, Charles Jones, came to reinforce Sherrod and Reagon. The three activists began to organize students in order to test public accommodations in Albany, which the Interstate Commerce Commission (ICC) had recently ordered desegregated.

On November 1, 1961, the required day of compliance for the ICC's mandate, Albany's first sit-in took place at the Trailways Bus Station. African Americans from the entire community gathered to watch the spectacle, but so had the Albany police. Upon Chief Laurie Pritchett's order to disband, the group of students peacefully left the station as planned and prepared to file a petition of grievance with the ICC. A persistent and unique foe of the movement, Pritchett had prepared his men to begin working double shifts on October 30 as the rumor of the sit-in spread across town. Pritchett would never be caught off guard.

The sit-in created a stir of controversy among both whites and African Americans in Albany. SNCC had drawn black adults into the movement through the organization of students and prompted the black community to create a coalition of activist organizations. Established on November 17, 1961, the Albany Movement, as it was officially known, comprised the Ministerial Alliance, the Federation of Women's Clubs, SNCC, the Negro Voters' League, the Criterion Club, and the NAACP Youth Council. The NAACP and its Georgia field secretary, Vernon Jordan, hoped to control the Albany Movement and to limit any future direct action efforts, but the NAACP was in decline in Albany and had little hope of supplanting the leadership of SNCC.

The once-powerful Albany NAACP was founded in 1919 and had more than one thousand members by 1946, but its power began to wane after the Supreme Court's *Brown v. Board of Education* decision in 1954. The Albany NAACP Youth Council, in contrast, was thriving after its inception in May of 1961, and its positions resembled the principles of SNCC. The rift between SNCC and the original NAACP organization prefigured a division over similar issues between SNCC and the SCLC that would become a major dilemma of the Albany Movement. For the time being, SNCC accepted its anointed leadership role and pushed the movement in a more freethinking direction.

The Albany Movement made ambitious plans, which may have been a cause of early ineffectiveness. It hoped to end all public and private disparities between blacks and whites in the city by using mass arrests and demonstrations as its primary tools of influence. Its stated goals included fair employment for all, an end to any police brutality, the desegregation of all transportation and city facilities, and the creation of a biracial committee to negotiate with the city over civil rights issues—a sticking point throughout the Albany Movement. At the time, just two African Americans worked for the city, both of whom were relegated to the study of minority group housing on the twenty-six-member Citizens' Advisory Committee on Urban Renewal.

The leaders of the Albany Movement elected William G. Anderson, a black osteopath, as president and named a black real estate agent, Slater King, as vice president. Although a relative newcomer to Albany, having arrived in 1957, Anderson was an influential man who had befriended Ralph Abernathy in college at Alabama State and Martin Luther King Jr. in Atlanta. Recognizing the momentum of the movement, Anderson remarked: "This thing was evolving to the extent that it was going to become community-wide, and we said, 'Well, we better get together and do something.'"[7] As the nominal heads of the Albany Movement, Anderson and Slater King were respected, but their leadership would prove tenuous and never unifying. Still, in just a few short days after its inception, the movement was in high gear.

On November 22, 1961, Chief Pritchett and the Albany police arrested three NAACP Youth Council members for attempting to eat at the Trailways Bus Station and arrested two students from Albany State for entering the whites-only waiting room at the same station. Pritchett was well prepared

for the students' direct action efforts. Using black informants and police sur-
veillance to learn where and how the Albany Movement would strike, he
prepared his police forces four to five months in advance with new and in-
ventive strategies.

Pritchett studied the civil rights movement and the Gandhian tactics espoused by Martin Luther King Jr. Pritchett recognized that the most significant
gains for activists had come when whites responded to the movement with violence. Part of the nonviolent strategy of the civil rights movement was to invite violence from white supremacists and thereby focus national and worldwide media attention and criticism on the South, which in turn would bring
federal intervention. Pritchett, hoping to turn the tables on the movement, instructed his police forces to use nonviolence themselves when making arrests.
"I realize I'm living in a changing world," Pritchett commented. "You've got
to adapt yourself to the situation. We are not living in the old school."[8] Pritchett's methods and the restraint of the Albany police garnered commendations
from people as prominent as U.S. Attorney General Robert Kennedy.

In another calculated turn, Pritchett charged the activists in Albany with
nonracial offenses such as disturbing the peace and marching without a permit, as opposed to the violation of segregationist laws. In that manner,
Pritchett was able to maintain the pretense that he was doing his job instead
of having to stand by racist laws that were themselves subject to criticism
and threatened by judicial decisions. Pritchett even "had planned for mass
arrests"[9] and prepared to spread the prisoners across jails throughout southwest Georgia so that his own prisons would never be overflowing.

Knowing that his limited jail space in Albany would be no match for the
twenty-four thousand black residents of the city and their outside supporters, Pritchett made arrangements to ship prisoners as far as one hundred
miles away. Then he allowed their bonds to be paid only in cash, forcing
many people to stay in jail for much longer than anticipated and sapping
much of the energy of the movement. His strategy worked and would become a pivotal factor in the outcome of the Albany Movement. Later, Pritchett took the lessons of nonviolent police action to law enforcement officers in
Birmingham, where his advice fell on the deaf ears of Public Safety Commissioner Bull Connor and where the civil rights movement garnered significant sympathy.

The arrests of the five students on November 22 led to the first mass meeting of the movement at the Mount Zion Baptist Church three days later.
Preparing for a demonstration on the trial date of November 27, the packed
church sang "We Shall Overcome" and listened to the students recount their
experiences in the Albany jail. When it was announced that two Albany State
students, Bertha Gober and Blanton Hall, had been expelled by the school's
conservative president, Charles Jones led four hundred marchers from the
trial in order to sign a petition demanding that Gober and Hall be reinstated.
The white-owned *Albany Herald* decried the march, which only led to a black

boycott of *Herald* advertisers. Reeling and searching for a quick resolution to the controversy, the city agreed to negotiate with the Albany Movement, but two weeks later events would take a different turn.

Although close to a deal with Mayor Asa Kelley and the city, ten civil rights activists who were participating in a Freedom Ride on the Georgia Central Railroad arrived from Atlanta. Once in Albany, James Forman, Bob Zellner, and Norma Collins of SNCC launched an integrated sit-in at the train station and began a new wave of protests on Sunday, December 10. Forman was impressed by the newfound unity of the black community, which "had developed an awareness of social justice to the point that young people, old people, rich people, and poor were able to unite to protest injustice, an awareness that made the community feel what affected one affected all."[10] Some community members, both white and black, denounced the new activists as agitators who would hurt the negotiation process. Pritchett announced: "We will not stand for these troublemakers coming into our city for the sole purpose of disturbing the peace and quiet of the city of Albany,"[11] and he proceeded to arrest the Freedom Riders while hundreds looked on. The infusion and arrests of the activists started a week of mass protests that forever changed the Albany Movement.

While some African Americans disapproved of the resurgence of mass demonstrations, Mayor Kelley saw the arrests of Forman, Zellner, and Collins as one of the few mistakes by the white power structure, especially with a negotiated settlement close at hand. The arrests spurred black community members and activists in Albany to continue to take a more militant path filled with demands that would seem to dash any hopes for a truce over the next few days.

On Monday, December 11, Forman addressed a mass meeting and formulated plans for a demonstration on the following day at the trial of the train station protesters. The 267 black high school and college students who marched to the trial were all arrested for their failure to disperse. Most of the students decided not to post bond and remained in jail. On Wednesday morning, the vice president of the Albany Movement, Slater King, was arrested for leading a prayer service at the courthouse, while 200 more demonstrators were imprisoned for parading without a permit at city hall.

Almost 500 protesters sat in jail by Thursday, and the threat of more demonstrations forced the governor of Georgia, Ernest Vandiver, to order 150 National Guardsmen into Albany. The governor's action prompted white city officials to renew their efforts to address the demands of the Albany Movement, including the release of all prisoners and the immediate integration of transportation facilities. Seizing his new bargaining power and acting independently as president of the Albany Movement, William Anderson heightened the pressure on the city and called in his old friends, Ralph Abernathy and Martin Luther King Jr. Anderson hoped that the prestige and presence of King and Abernathy would encourage white officials to negotiate a settlement favorable to the Albany Movement. In the end, Anderson got much more than he asked for.

When King and Abernathy agreed to appear at the Shiloh Baptist Church on Friday, December 15, a crowd of more than a thousand people swayed to spirituals and freedom songs and cheered King's speech, as he implored: "Don't stop now. Keep moving. Don't get weary. We will wear them down with our capacity to suffer."[12] Moved by the crowd's response and by the exhortations of Anderson, King yielded to requests that he lead a prayer march to city hall on the following morning. An emboldened Anderson then issued an ultimatum to the city: if the demands of the Albany Movement were not met in full by the next day, then mass demonstrations and boycotts would continue indefinitely.

Anderson's announcement backfired. An angry and offended City Commission announced that all talks would end immediately, and Chief Pritchett arrested King and 250 others at the scheduled prayer march. King issued a surprising response: "I will not accept bond. If convicted, I will refuse to pay the fine. I expect to spend Christmas in jail. I hope thousands will join me."[13] King's impulse decision to stay in jail through the holidays prompted the SCLC to dedicate its full resources to the Albany Movement. As executive director of the SCLC and with Anderson's blessing, Wyatt Walker came to Albany to direct the logistics of the movement. Walker meant to take control and put the SCLC at the forefront of all activities. In what many civil rights workers saw as an arrogant style of leadership, he worked doggedly to accomplish that task and ignored sensitive relationships, especially with SNCC.

Charles Sherrod, Cordell Reagon, Charles Jones, Ella Baker, and all of the SNCC rank and file criticized the SCLC for its opportunism. They saw no reason for the SCLC to be in Albany and referred derisively to King as "De Lawd."[14] SNCC felt threatened by the SCLC because it feared that King's presence would leave SNCC without any credit. Leadership in the civil rights movement as a whole was up for grabs. Sherrod and Jones felt slighted because their efforts from the beginning had fueled the fires of change in the black community. They had risked their lives to organize black support during the dangerous initial stages; to them, Albany was a SNCC movement. The SCLC had not done any of the dirty work but was taking advantage of the publicity.

After King's arrest and announcement, Sherrod, Reagon, and Jones were ready to leave Albany to the SCLC. They aimed sharp criticism at the SCLC and accused it of leaving them out of meetings and press conferences. In return, the SCLC labeled SNCC as a group of young firebrands and charged it with factionalism. In truth, the three SNCC activists did not recognize that most of the black community in Albany wanted King and the SCLC to be there. Anderson, however, realized that Albany blacks believed in King and would follow his leadership. Moreover, King's presence produced much-needed money for the Albany Movement, as his access to coffers and fund-raisers outside of Georgia was vast. King also brought media attention to Albany. In the end, the SNCC veterans decided not to abandon all the work they had started but to try internal measures to persuade King and the SCLC to leave.

The dissatisfaction of SNCC with the SCLC was coupled with the desire of the segregationist leadership in Albany to rid itself of King. King's arrest and decision to stay in jail had commanded the first national media coverage of the civil rights movement since the Freedom Rides. With seven hundred people in jail, Albany stood out as a national disgrace. The City Commission found its chance to reverse the situation when Charles Jones and SNCC convinced Anderson's assistant, Marion Page, to hold a press conference on December 17. While Anderson, King, and Abernathy were in jail, a nervous Page discredited the leadership of Wyatt Walker and announced that the SCLC was not in charge in Albany and any such insinuations were "an unfortunate misrepresentation of fact. . . . We welcome any help from the outside . . . but as of now we need no help."[15] In this confused atmosphere, the city again agreed to negotiations.

With the movement in disarray from its internal strife, Page felt pressured to reach a settlement with the city and secure the release of the seven hundred prisoners. Many of those in jail were respected community members, facing unknown conditions in prison as well as job layoffs once out of it. Page feared that the movement was on the brink of total failure and agreed to a truce with the City Commission on December 18, 1961. The oral agreement included five conditions: the return of all bond money paid by prisoners, their release and an indefinite postponement of their trials, the desegregation of buses, and the creation of a biracial committee to address all civil rights issues. Learning about the truce and hearing that Anderson was on the verge of a mental collapse in jail, King and Abernathy agreed to be released and left Albany on the following day.

For their part, the leaders of the Albany Movement accepted a thirty-day hiatus in activities, but it soon became clear that the city simply wanted to get Albany out of the world spotlight. On January 23, 1962, Anderson and Page asked the city to fulfill its promises, but a newly installed and more conservative City Commission responded a week later and refused to recognize any part of the truce. Anderson recognized his mistake: "I should never have come out of jail until there was a written agreement. We were guilty of being inexperienced."[16] The City Commission then proclaimed a victory over the forces of the civil rights movement and rebuked African Americans in Albany for their lack of morality.

From the start, many activists expressed their skepticism over the oral nature of the December accord and were vindicated when the City Commission broke its end of the deal. Led by C. B. Pritchett, the police chief's brother, the Commission was able to ignore the Albany Movement as well as

Mayor Kelley's voice of relative moderation and compromise. After such a tremendous blow, the movement almost died during the winter and spring of 1962.

SNCC's continued efforts to combat segregation had limited effects. In April, Jones and Reagon went to jail for a lunch counter sit-in, and each received sixty days. That same month, Albany police arrested twenty-nine SNCC demonstrators at city hall for protesting the police shooting of a black man who was allegedly resisting arrest. Along with some picketing and a sit-in at the Carnegie Library in Albany, these actions did little good, and the movement trudged forward hoping for a better day to come. By June, the Albany Movement had dropped its basic demand for a biracial committee to work out civil rights issues. The lone success during the winter and spring was a continued black boycott of white businesses and buses.

Although white businessmen in Albany petitioned the City Commission to rethink its decision to renege on the December agreements, the city allowed the bus company to go out of business instead of underwriting it with a subsidy or integrating the buses as the company was prepared to do. The Commission also noted that it would no longer work with the Albany Movement. From then on, movement leaders would have to communicate their wishes to an unyielding Chief Pritchett. During those winter and spring months, Pritchett himself helped to cripple the Albany Movement when he refused to allow the people waiting for their trials to redeem their cash-only bonds, which totaled $400,000. Albany's segregationists had found renewed strength in their racist stance.

The initial stage of the Albany Movement was coming to a close and appeared to be a failure. After the bus company went out of business, black community interest in SNCC and the Albany Movement rapidly declined. Martin Luther King Jr. even doubted his effectiveness in the civil rights movement as his presence had proved to be a double-edged sword, cutting the Albany Movement much deeper than it had the white supremacist power structure. Although he boosted the visibility of the movement, King had heightened tensions between SNCC and the SCLC. Both organizations blamed each other for their failure in Albany. Nevertheless, the Albany Movement revived during the summer when King and Abernathy were forced to return to face trial for their December arrests.

On July 10, a judge and jury convicted King and Abernathy and sentenced them either to forty-five days in jail or to a $178 fine. Both again chose to serve out their jail time, and, on July 11, another mass meeting was held at the Mount Zion Baptist Church. Beforehand, a march to city hall had ended in thirty-two more arrests and in a violent standoff between police and brick-wielding black students. For the first time, the riot undermined the Albany Movement's claim to nonviolence. The tension was obvious but eased on the following day when an anonymous man, whom Pritchett described as a "well-dressed Negro male,"[17] entered the police station and paid both King's and Abernathy's fines. Abernathy smirked: "I've been thrown out of lots of places in my day, but never before have I been thrown out of jail."[18] With King and Abernathy reluctant but forced to be released, the Albany Movement lost steam once again.

The identity of the unidentified black man who bailed out King and Abernathy remains a mystery. One civil rights activist indicated that a rich, white lawyer had bailed out King and Abernathy after pressure from J. Edgar Hoover and Robert Kennedy. The SCLC, SNCC, and Albany Movement leaders pointed to the City Commission and Chief Pritchett. Years later, Pritchett suggested that at a meeting between conservative blacks and segregationist whites, a black man was hired to pay the bail so as to curtail further activism in Albany. No matter who paid the fines, King and Abernathy were out of jail and were faced with the delicate question of how to proceed.

Disavowing their earlier criticisms and recognizing the benefits of having King in jail, SNCC pushed for King to continue demonstrations and to be arrested again. To the disappointment of both the SCLC and SNCC, King refused due to a lack of time and resources, but he hoped that negotiations could resume with Mayor Kelley. Instead, the City Commission declined to talk and threatened to press charges on the other seven hundred demonstrators who had been arrested in December. The threat induced King to continue demonstrations, but another roadblock appeared when federal district judge Robert Elliot issued an injunction on July 20 against further marches by the Albany Movement.

To the astonishment and dismay of SNCC, the conservative side of King led him to abide by the federal injunction. In showing deference to the courts, King acknowledged that the civil rights movement had won its few victories in the judicial system. To disregard a court order now would undermine civil rights positions in the future. On July 22, SNCC leaders met with King to express their disapproval and to note that King's faith in the judicial system was misguided. Jones pointed out that the community was prepared to disobey the order from the segregationist Georgia judge who was a part of the problem. Appeasing the NAACP, which did not want to break the court order, King accepted the criticism with quiet deference and stood by his conviction that the injunction had to be overturned through the legal system. To many observers, King had given in to white supremacy when he could have taken the lead and unified the incoherent Albany Movement, but he believed that the leadership of the SCLC was rightfully more conservative than that of the significant but youthful and rash SNCC organization. Ultimately, his resistance to continued demonstrations did increase the internal strife of the Albany Movement and decreased the motivation of the masses to participate in a stalled nonviolent direct action campaign.

Some demonstrations did continue during the injunction. On July 23, the Reverend Sam Wells led 150 marchers from Shiloh Baptist Church, where King had to hide in the pastor's study. By the next day, though, Court of Appeals

Judge Elbert Tuttle reversed the Elliot injunction, vindicating King in his belief in the courts. King had no time for celebration, as another group of demonstrators on the same day, marching to city hall from the Mount Zion Baptist Church, turned into a stone-throwing mob. The renewed violence brought more National Guardsmen to Albany and prompted King to declare a "day of penance." On July 25, King, Abernathy, Anderson, Sherrod, and Jones toured the black district known as Harlem in Albany and pleaded for local blacks to remain nonviolent.

Two days later, King prepared for another prayer march and to return to jail. Arrested again along with Abernathy and Anderson, King looked to remain in jail as long as necessary to mobilize enough pressure on the City Commission to force its acquiescence. When Chief Pritchett summoned King to his office, King refused to go because he did not want to be tricked out of jail again. Pritchett's control of the situation was waning. Some well-publicized police violence and the sheer number of prisoners began to strain even his forward-thinking plans, but without pressure from the federal government, Pritchett and the City Commission were not backing down.

While visiting prisoners, Slater King's pregnant wife was knocked unconscious by a deputy sheriff, and his brother, attorney C. B. King, was caned by the sheriff of Dougherty County, who remarked: "Yeah, I knocked the hell out of the son-of-a-bitch, and I'll do it again. I wanted to let him know . . . I'm a white man and he's a damn nigger."[19] These incidents put pressure on the federal government to intervene. William Taylor of the Civil Rights Commission asked President Kennedy to nominate a negotiator to settle the conflict in Albany and to set a precedent for future civil rights crises, but to no avail. At best, the president was willing to urge that a settlement be reached between the city and the Albany Movement. Chief Pritchett would later claim that Kennedy's reluctance was due to a desire to elect Carl Sanders as a more moderate governor of Georgia in 1962. No matter the reason, the federal government refused to intervene in Albany, and the city had no rationale for agreeing to a compromise with the Albany Movement.

Just two weeks after being arrested, King, Abernathy, and Anderson were convicted, given suspended sentences, and released from jail. The next day King and Abernathy left Albany for good, and Wyatt Walker grumbled that the SCLC had been "dragged" into Albany to begin with.[20] A frustrated Albany Movement faced another looming defeat. By the end of August, a few picket lines were left, and the City Commission took the time to ridicule continued protests and to declare victory.

The SCLC tried one last prayer march on August 28, where seventy ministers, priests, and rabbis were arrested. Pritchett met the group and chided them: "You apparently came here as law violators, and my advice is to go back to your various cities, clean your various cities of the evils of segregation before you come down and throw rocks at us."[21] The city would not budge on its views and rejected another proposal in February of 1963 for a biracial committee. Even when the state of Georgia announced that desegregation was inevitable, the obstinate City Commission repealed its segregationist codes so that private businesses could claim compliance with the law while blacks would be arrested for trespassing if they entered those businesses. The Commission closed what other public facilities it could, but the bus and train stations did desegregate, as did the library, which then had all of its tables and chairs removed.

Although it never regained the same energy and emotion, the Albany Movement was not a complete failure. It survived until the late 1960s with Slater King as president after 1963, and SNCC continued its work in Albany with some limited success. There were also important lessons to be learned from the Albany Movement. Before the annual SCLC conference in September of 1962, Martin Luther King Jr. called for a meeting to discuss what went wrong in order to make adjustments before the SCLC tackled its next target in Birmingham. The SCLC as well as SNCC and the rest of the Albany Movement had made some mistakes that were correctable and others that would plague them for years to come.

The first and most obvious lesson was that African Americans were willing to engage in mass protests and that young people could lead the way in that effort. At the fore of the Albany Movement, SNCC proved that an entire black community could be mobilized without threatening local black leadership and that the community would even embrace the once-notorious stigma of going to prison. In addition, spirituals and other freedom songs could harness powerful emotions and motivate black people to act. In this sense, Albany served as a model for the organization of black communities as well as a training ground for mass militancy. Led by Charles Sherrod, SNCC in particular, whose spark and vigor made up in large part for its lack of financial resources, gained the needed confidence to take a leadership role throughout the rest of the civil rights movement.

On a more strategic level, poor planning was a major problem of the Albany Movement. The infighting between SNCC and the SCLC meant that meetings were dominated by arguments rather than tactical planning, and the efforts of the City Commission in Albany revealed that strong segregationist leadership could exploit that division. White leaders could take advantage of the conservatism of Martin Luther King Jr., the SCLC, and the NAACP as well as the vast ambitions of the Albany Movement to end all forms of discrimination. Rather than attack segregation in general, they needed to focus on specific manifestations of Jim Crow. Economic boycotts seemed to be the most promising endeavors. When the movement confronted politicians, it made little progress, but when their profits took a downturn, white businessmen could apply significant pressure on those politicians. At the very least, future movements needed clear, concise goals as well as contingency plans to deal with factors like having seven hundred people in jail at once.

More importantly, the success of nonviolent direct action depended upon maintaining nonviolence—an endeavor that would prove difficult with the advent of Black Power in the late 1960s—and upon provoking violent responses from white supremacists. Filling up the jails with civil rights protesters would not be enough. White violence prompted the necessary media coverage and worldwide sympathy to force the federal government into a position of intervention and to mobilize support for sweeping civil rights legislation. Chief Pritchett proved that mass arrests without violence could prevent federal interference. As much as anything, the brutality of Bull Connor and the Birmingham police led to the success of the civil rights movement there.

Although lessons were learned, the disappointment of a mobilized black community in Albany was palpable. The limits of nonviolent, Christian ideals became obvious, and some, like Charles Sherrod, began to question the willingness of African Americans to suffer abuses without resorting to violence. Ever the minister, Sherrod held on to a firm belief in nonviolence. Changes would come to the South slowly but surely. Although they had ulterior motives, white leaders in Albany created their own demise by abolishing their segregationist codes, and, by the 1980s, Sherrod was elected as a member of the Albany City Commission. The Albany Movement had complicated and complemented the civil rights movement, and its immediate failure foreshadowed future problems as well as future successes.

NOTES

1. Charles Sherrod, quoted in Richard H. King, *Civil Rights and the Idea of Freedom* (Athens: University of Georgia Press, 1996), 144.

2. Sherrod, quoted in Howard Zinn, *SNCC: The New Abolitionists* (Boston: Beacon, 1965), 125.

3. Sherrod, quoted in Zinn, *SNCC*, 126.

4. Cordell Reagon, quoted in David J. Garrow, *Bearing the Cross: Martin Luther King, Jr., and the Southern Christian Leadership Conference* (New York: William Morrow, 1986), 174.

5. Sherrod, quoted in Zinn, *SNCC*, 131.

6. Sherrod, quoted in Zinn, *SNCC*, 126.

7. William G. Anderson, interview with John Ricks, Detroit, August 1981, quoted in Garrow, *Bearing the Cross*, 176.

8. Laurie Pritchett, quoted in "Determined Police Chief," *New York Times*, July 23, 1962, 13.

9. Pritchett, quoted in Howell Raines, *My Soul Is Rested: Movement Days in the Deep South Remembered* (New York: Penguin, 1983), 361.

10. James Forman, *The Making of Black Revolutionaries* (Washington, D.C.: Open Hand Publishing, 1985), 253.

11. Pritchett, quoted in Forman, *Black Revolutionaries*, 253.

12. Martin Luther King Jr., quoted in Zinn, *SNCC*, 131.

13. Martin Luther King Jr., quoted in Vic Smith, "Trials Delayed; City Confers with Negroes," *Albany Herald*, December 18, 1961, 5.

14. David L. Lewis, *King: A Biography* (Urbana: University of Illinois Press, 1979), 152.

15. Marion Page, quoted in John Pennington, "60-Day Truce Debated in Albany Race Issue," *Atlanta Journal*, December 18, 1961, 10.

16. Anderson, interview by Ricks, quoted in Garrow, *Bearing the Cross*, 190.

17. Pritchett, quoted in Vic Smith, "'Somebody' Pays King Out of Jail; Mayor Stays Mum," *Albany Herald*, July 12, 1962, 1.

18. Ralph Abernathy, quoted in Zinn, *SNCC*, 134.

19. Cull Campbell, quoted in Zinn, *SNCC*, 135.

20. Wyatt Walker, quoted in Garrow, *Bearing the Cross*, 218.

21. Pritchett, quoted in Raines, *My Soul Is Rested*, 364.

SUGGESTED READING

Carson, Clayborne. *In Struggle: SNCC and the Black Awakening of the 1960s.* Cambridge, Mass.: Harvard University Press, 1995.

Fairclough, Adam. *To Redeem the Soul of America: The Southern Christian Leadership Conference and Martin Luther King, Jr.* Athens: University of Georgia Press, 2001.

Forman, James. *The Making of Black Revolutionaries.* Washington, D.C.: Open Hand Publishing, 1985.

Garrow, David J. *Bearing the Cross: Martin Luther King, Jr., and the Southern Christian Leadership Conference.* New York: William Morrow, 1986.

King, Richard H. *Civil Rights and the Idea of Freedom.* Athens: University of Georgia Press, 1996.

Lewis, David L. *King: A Biography.* Urbana: University of Illinois Press, 1979.

Raines, Howell. *My Soul Is Rested: Movement Days in the Deep South Remembered.* New York: Penguin, 1983.

Watters, Pat. *Down to Now: Reflections on the Southern Civil Rights Movement.* New York: Pantheon, 1971.

Watters, Pat, and Reese Cleghorn. *Climbing Jacob's Ladder: The Arrival of Negroes in Southern Politics.* New York: Harcourt, Brace and World, 1967.

Zinn, Howard. *Albany: A Study in National Responsibility.* Atlanta: Southern Regional Council, 1962.

Zinn, Howard. *SNCC: The New Abolitionists.* Boston: Beacon, 1965.

IV

꧁

FREEDOM IS A CONSTANT STRUGGLE

10

ç

Diane Nash: "Courage Displaces Fear, Love Transforms Hate": Civil Rights Activism and the Commitment to Nonviolence

Jennifer A. Stollman

This chapter explores civil rights activist Diane Nash's background and the events that encouraged her induction into civil rights activism and traces her monumental contributions as a leader, teacher, organizer, and activist in the push for black equality. While her middle-class Catholic upbringing and notions of female respectability and racial uplift influenced Diane Nash's decision to become involved in the civil rights movement, she later employed both Christian principles of love and the Gandhian principle of nonviolence or Satayagraha *to end racism and segregation and promote African American equality and political activism.*

> This will be a black baby born in Mississippi, and thus where ever he is born he will be in prison. . . . If I go to jail now it may help hasten that day when my child and all children will be free.

In 1962 a pregnant Diane Nash calmly but forcefully uttered these words to the judge sentencing her to two years in prison for civil disobedience. Never before in her life did she imagine herself to be this bold. In later interviews detailing this event, Nash revealed that she was terrified and continuously sublimated her fear for much more important aims—to end segregation and the subordination of African Americans. In most volumes on civil rights, Diane Nash is presented as a minor figure, yet to many movement historians and participants, Nash was in fact a formidable individual in the desegregation and voter registration movements of the early 1960s. Nash was both an unlikely and an exemplary figure in the civil rights movement. Influenced by her religious upbringing, a family philosophy that emphasized personal and collective advancement, and the Reverend James Lawson's workshops on Christian and Gandhian strategies of nonviolent *Satayagraha*, and empowered by the actions of other movement activists, Diane Nash would become a pivotal force in ending segregation in the South and encouraging African American voting.

Nash's early childhood and adolescence both prepared her to fight and yet shielded her from many forms of racial discrimination. Born in 1938 and reared in a middle-class Catholic household on the south side of Chicago, Diane Judith Nash attended private elementary schools and public high schools. A devout Catholic, at a young age Nash thought about becoming a nun. Her father, Leon Nash, grew up in Canton, Mississippi, and moved to Chicago during the turn-of-the-century African American migration. During World War II, he served as a clerical worker in the armed forces and later studied dentistry. Dorothy Bolton Nash, Diane's mother, worked as a keypunch operator in a factory during the war. Because of her parents' absence during much of the war, their subsequent divorce, and her mother's remarriage, Diane Nash spent much of her early childhood with her grandmother. A strong woman, Carrie Bolton profoundly shaped Nash's identity as an empowered religious African American activist woman.[1]

In many ways, Bolton's own history contributed to Nash's self-conceptualization and her legacy as a civil rights leader. Bolton was born and grew up in an era that encouraged "racial uplift" and understood black women's pivotal roles in such projects. Racial uplift consisted of a series of individual and communal efforts designed to improve the economic, social, and political status of blacks. Often supported by local communities, African Americans expected the women in their community to dedicate their lives to advancing the social, political, and economic goals of African Americans. Though she was raised in an era that underscored black pride, Bolton's own material circumstances regularly forced her to confront whites' prevailing racist assumptions about themselves and African Americans. Raised in Memphis, Tennessee, at the age of nine Bolton went to work for a wealthy white physician's family. Her experience in that household was transformative. The family's possessions, mannerisms, and etiquette enchanted Bolton. Bolton's favored status in the home made quite an impression on her. The physician took a special interest in her and schooled her on her abilities in opposition to other African Americans. The doctor impressed upon Carrie that she was different, better than other blacks, and that to ensure her own success, she should learn and assimilate white cultural customs. The doctor attempted to reinforce his opinions by continuously indoctrinating her about black inferiority and white superiority. This left a considerable impression on Bolton.[2] In raising Diane, Bolton rejected whites' notions of black inferiority and instead emphasized Diane's responsibility to improve her world.

Despite the fact that she lived in a rather protected environment and did not have much experience challenging white society as a child, Nash's own experiences within the turbulent era of the 1940s and 1950s influenced her later philosophies on racism as well her civil rights activism.[3] Nash's family provided her with models that emphasized personal and collective advancement. Such models attempted to overlook race and instead conform to white standards of respectability. Nevertheless, Nash understood the institutional racism that was pervasive throughout the country. She recognized the hypocrisy of World War II—fighting German racism while an American infrastructure systematically encouraged racism against blacks and reinforced African Americans' second-class citizenship status. She understood that her race marked her as different and somehow unequal.

In many ways, her adolescent experiences enabled her to develop the necessary skill of self-confidence and prepared her for her leadership role in the movement. She was a beauty pageant contestant and in fact enjoyed some success as the runner-up in Chicago's Miss America trials.[4] Aside from pageant competitions, Nash focused on academics. After graduating high school in 1956, Nash first attended Howard University as an English major with hopes to study law. She transferred to Fisk University in 1959. The protected environment of historically black universities shielded Nash from the growing white supremacist backlash after the *Brown* court decision. This buffer from overt racism further advanced Nash's sense of African American community and a recognition that blacks deserved civil rights. Because this was the 1950s, Nash's education was prescribed by gender. She, as an educated black woman, was expected to carry on the project of "racial uplift" through those activities that were acceptable for women. For Nash and other women, this project would take place in the home and in the community. Nash was expected to be a model wife and mother. Seemingly her life would play out like thousands of other black and white middle-class women. They would be expected to marry and have children, all the while subordinating their interests for the good of family and community.[5] Nash, however, would be different. She would employ models other than motherhood and traditional notions of community to gain African American civil rights.

Nash's initiation into the civil rights movement was similar to that of the hundreds of other young black men and women who would find themselves risking their lives in the civil rights movement—an incident of racial discrimination. While a student at Fisk University in 1959, Nash experienced racism on a more personal scale at the Tennessee State Fair. Going to the ladies' room, Nash was confronted by the Jim Crow laws of the South and the separate facilities for blacks and whites. Signs marked "colored women" reinforced to Nash that, despite her middle-class upbringing and her family's concerted efforts at respectability, white Southern society viewed her

Diane Nash with unidentified man (Image courtesy of The Tennessean.*)*

and other blacks as inferior. This event was life-changing and politicized Nash. She remembered:

> [It] was the first time that I had encountered the blatant segregation that exists in the South. I came then to see the community in sin. Seeing signs designating "white" or "colored," and being told "Go around to the back door where you belong," had a tremendous psychological impact on me. To begin with, I didn't agree with the premise that I was inferior, and I had a difficult time complying with it.[6]

From that moment on, Nash was painfully aware of the rigid and offensive segregation present in public facilities in the South. Her middle-class respectability had served as a buffer to racist insults. Humiliated and shocked, Nash was moved by the fair's signs and was driven to fight racism. Additionally, she was stunned to see the seeming complacency of Southern blacks who, according to Nash, blindly followed Jim Crow laws. Disturbed that her friends were not similarly affected, Nash actively sought compatriots who refused to accept blacks as inferior and refused to allow the Jim Crow system to continue.

In February of 1960, Nash met the individual who, in part, shaped her spiritually and politically as well as provided her with effective tools to fight racial discrimination.[7] Nash related to the Reverend James Lawson because the methods that he employed to end segregation and fight racism resonated with Nash's own sensibilities. Lawson was not a stranger to resisting government imperatives in his personal life. In his early college years Lawson became politicized and deeply influenced by Christian teachings. Strongly impressed and guided by the teachings of Jesus Christ, Lawson employed Christian notions of love as a foundational political, social, and legal strategy by which to effect change. Practicing his beliefs of nonviolence and love, while studying for the ministry Lawson spent almost a year in prison as a conscientious objector during the Korean War. After being released from prison, Lawson, still moved by strategies of love, traveled to India as a missionary. Though he was a deeply Christian man, India and its religious philosophies made a profound impression on Lawson.

Exposed to Gandhian philosophies as a university student, Lawson more comprehensively studied these principles during his three-year sojourn in India. Mohandas Gandhi had envisioned a peaceful world that could be achieved through a strategy of nonviolence or *Satayagraha*. The philosophy of *Satayagraha* encompasses three basic philosophies. *Sat*, or truth, instructs that each person's opinions and beliefs represent part of the truth and that individuals must share their truths cooperatively. In order to do so, individuals must advance their communication skills and resist the impulse to categorize individuals.[8] *Ahimsa*, or the refusal to inflict injury on another, is dedicated to the notion that communication is tantamount and that violence inhibits communication. *Ahimsa* recognizes that individual and collective humanity must be respected and as such one must learn to understand and love one's adversaries.[9] *Tapasya*, or self-sacrifice, the third philosophy, asserts that one must bear the burden of any struggle that he or she initiates rather than foist it on his or her enemies, because of a fear that their different but individual truths would be lost. It also proposes that an exit strategy must be provided so as not to alienate the enemy and thus lose his or her contributory truth.[10] The philosophy of *Satayagraha* emphasizes individual improvement, creating a new social order, and forceful campaigns of resistance against inequality and injustice. *Satayagraha* demands from its followers a refusal to engage in psychological or physical violence, active interest and care toward one's enemies, and a concerted effort to convert others to strategies of nonviolence.[11] Followers of *Satayagraha* were unconditionally committed to nonviolence and employed this strategy specifically to address humanitarian concerns.[12]

Once stateside and confronted again with the racial division and discrimination, Lawson believed that he could successfully employ *Satayagraha* principles to end segregation in the South. It was a philosophy that had yet to be tested in this country and particularly in a region that had been familiar with racial violence for more than two hundred years. Impressed by the Reverend Martin Luther King Jr. and thousands of African Americans' efforts to end desegregation of Montgomery's bus lines through the famous bus boycott, Lawson worked to encourage other activists to use strategies that emphasized love and reason and resisted all forms of violence to underscore that African Americans were entitled to equal rights and political, social, and economic equality. As a minister, Lawson believed not only that combining Gandhian and Protestant principles would aid in ending segregation, but also that nonviolence could successfully be used to completely transform society by transcending hate and violence and emphasizing love and forgiveness.[13] Lawson helped pioneer this movement in America, and from different parts of the country and different classes, hundreds of American youth joined a movement that would change the social, economic, and political tenor of the United States.

Lawson, along with other movement leaders, was successful in encouraging others to adapt the Christian principle of love and the Indian philosophy of *Satayagraha* to suit the American context. Such strategies of nonviolence proved to be an effective tool in social struggles. In the American South, nonviolence did not specifically depend on the third aspect of *Satayahgraha*— that of converting its opponents to using nonviolence—but instead emphasized a forceful opposition to physical and psychological violence. Therefore, in the United States civil rights movement, the strategy of love and *Satayagraha* was not just about being nonviolent. It meant employing traditional political strategies associated with a democratic republic like protest and demanding government protection for all citizens.[14] Likewise, nonviolence did not avoid conflict in the United States because it causes conflict in an alternative manner. Lawson's initial aim was to employ this strategy of nonviolence to expose and end the inequality of segregation laws. Lawson's first test case would be Nashville's segregated lunch counters. Diane Nash would play a pivotal leadership role in the desegregation process.

In the fall of 1959, dozens of students from Fisk University, Meharry Medical College, Tennessee State University, and American Baptist Theological Seminary, including Nash, and several civil rights community activists gathered to hear Lawson's strategy of nonviolence. From September through November, Reverend Lawson held a series of weekly workshops at Highlander Folk School in Monteagle, Tennessee. Focusing on specific ways to bring about social change. Lawson trained university students in both *Satayagraha* and Christian philosophies, specifically techniques of nonviolence, potential real-life scenarios, and nonviolent self-protection to challenge Jim Crow laws. In those workshops, Lawson put forth several maxims. True faith relied on an adherence to nonviolence and underscored the strategy of employing love and reason and not hate and violence to overcome difference and understand others' different points of view. Those who resorted to violence—be it members of their own group or their adversaries—demonstrated intellectual and spiritual weakness. Rage and violence emerged out of fear or ignorance, and despite the historical precedents that "might makes right," Lawson challenged the students to embark on a different spiritual and political path. Lawson advised that most assuredly the students would encounter violence and that they needed not only to learn to control their rage and anger against their perceived enemies but also to learn to process their own anger that was sure to follow in contentious situations.[15] To drive home his point, Lawson emphasized scriptural passages in which Jesus and his disciples resisted violence and had succeeded. Through Lawson's efforts, Nash learned that employing Christian and Gandhian principles of nonviolence meant facing your enemies with respect but letting them know peacefully that their actions are unacceptable. As Diane Nash would later comment in a speech in front of a Penn State audience, "The problem with using violence to solve problems is that you physically kill the other individual but leave the real problem 'unattacked.'"[16]

It was during these workshops that Nash finally found the political and spiritual community that she sought after experiencing that racist day at the Tennessee fair. Initially, Nash believed that such a strategy would be futile against an angry and violent South, yet again and again she returned to Lawson's seminars. Eventually, in addition to using such strategies to fight social injustice, like Lawson, Nash used these ideals to fashion a spiritual framework. For the rest of her life, these principles shaped not just her political agenda but also her daily experiences.

Diane Nash's poise, perhaps learned in part from her grandmother or from beauty pageants, impacted those around her. The students in Lawson's seminars were so impressed with Nash's calm attitude, ideas, and fortitude that when they formed a central committee to act as the decision-making body for the group, they looked to her as one of their dependable and main leaders.[17] She initially balked at becoming the group's head, insisting instead that she never wanted to be a leader, but rather a part of the solution. While she never officially accepted a leadership position, student activists routinely looked to Nash for leadership. More comfortable with an ensemble position, Nash preferred to work in an auxiliary position to implement the Christian and Gandhian principles in the group's political activities. Using nonviolence as a framework, the students drew up a code of conduct to follow during violent encounters:

> Don't strike back or curse if abused. Don't laugh out loud. Don't hold conversations with floor walkers. Don't block aisles or entrances to the store. Show yourself courteous and friendly at all times. Sit straight and always face the counter. Remember love and nonviolence. May God bless each of you.[18]

Empowered by their knowledge and drive to end segregation, Nash and the other students were eager to test the strategy of nonviolence. After the successful February 1, 1960, Greensboro sit-in effected by four North Carolina A&T students, Nash and others hoped to carry out their own political displays against segregation. Nash and her fellow students acted out scenarios to prepare themselves for the adverse reactions they would receive at the lunch counters and restaurants.[19]

The Nashville sit-in movement quickly followed Greensboro on Saturday, February 6, 1960, when 124 students began sit-ins in Nashville's busy department store lunch counters. The students implemented their strategy of nonviolence—they were well-dressed, respectful, courteous, and brave.[20] The fearful yet stoic students sat for hours and did not encounter violence—nor did Nashville police arrest them.[21] In later interviews, Nash noted that she was stunned by the success of the strategy of nonviolence. Eschewing any previous doubts, she was convinced that it would be an effective method to end segregation and discrimination. Electric with their success, Lawson's students planned a second sit-in for the following week.[22]

Nash's informal yet strong leadership during the first sit-in underscored initial opinions about her leadership capabilities. The Nashville movement members decided that she was the most logical leader for the central committee—a position vested with making decisions for the Nashville sit-in movement. According to historian Lynne Olson, Nash "was hardworking and outwardly fearless, and she did not seem to have the ego problems that a lot of the men had."[23] Flattered and yet uneasy by this vote of confidence, Nash decided through a conversation with her fellow member and later husband James Bevel and others never to assume a leadership position. They concluded that the leader should avoid arrest. Nash knew then that she did not want to be a leader. She joined the movement to become an active participant, not solely one who would be in charge of recruiting or arranging bail for those arrested. Members eventually acquiesced to Nash's decision.

Avoiding violence did not mean that Nash and the other student activists immediately enjoyed success in their desegregation efforts. Uneasy city officials began negotiations with black clergy to arrive at an agreement that would both avoid violence and, more importantly, divert media attention. Hoping to avoid a violent confrontation, African American church leaders asked the Nashville students to hold off on further sit-ins until some sort of agreement could be achieved. Driven by the initial responses of previous sit-ins, such pleas fell upon deaf ears, and in fact, the Nashville movement gained momentum as well as population strength. More than three hundred students carried out another sit-in at the Woolworth's counter on Saturday, February 27. For the first time, the Nashville students encountered violence from angry whites. Hostile protesters "yanked them from their stools and threw them to the floor, beat them with fists and clubs, kicked them, spat on them, extinguished lighted cigarettes on their backs and in their hair."[24] When the police arrived, they did not focus on the violent protests but instead arrested the young black students. After police escorted the first group of students out of the restaurant to jail, per Lawson's instructions, another group of students practicing nonviolence moved in to take their place.[25] This confrontation marked the first test of the students' philosophy of nonviolence, which was truly put to the test. All in all, police arrested eighty-one students and released them on bail.[26] As news traveled of the students' courage to sacrifice, twenty-five hundred of Nashville's African Americans demonstrated in front of the courthouse.[27] Two days later, a judge tried and convicted the students of disorderly conduct and fined each of them fifty dollars.[28]

As Nash would make others understand, Christian and Gandhian principles of nonviolence did not end at the lunch counter. Many of the students were willing to pay the fine and continue planning another sit-in. Nash believed, however, that paying the fines "would be contributing to and supporting injustice and immoral practices that have been performed in the arrest and conviction of defendants."[29] Others followed Nash's example and refused to pay their fines. Sixteen students were jailed. Nash's strategy worked, and the "jail, no bail" policy became standard in the movement.[30]

This event successfully galvanized Nashville's African American population. The mayor of Nashville, Ben West, wanted to avoid city unrest or national media attention and strived to negotiate with the students. To stave off potential violence from both whites and African Americans, the mayor agreed to release the students and to appoint a biracial commission to examine the desegregation of Nashville if the students agreed to end the sit-in protests. Nash and others had forced a major segregated Southern city to reexamine its racist laws, statutes, and policies of segregation.

In March, the Nashville sit-in movement was suspended, and a truce was declared. Several black clergymen formed a local biracial citizens' committee to more closely examine the city's segregationist policies. Much to Nash's and the other students' dismay, the commission was largely ceremonial and made no real recommendations. Not content with political appeasement, she and several students resumed their political strategies and held another sit-in at the Greyhound bus terminal lunch counter. To their disbelief, they were served without a problem. Once again, Christian and Gandhian principles of nonviolence had enabled Nash and her fellow students to score a major victory against segregation. The Nashville students felt energized by their success and thus expanded their nonviolent activities. They began a boycott of downtown stores and picketed the town's public buildings.[31] Nash continued her forceful yet respectful approach to desegregation. She believed:

> Our struggle does not end here. Rather we shall continue to insist in a non-violent Christian, loving fashion that the inequalities of segregation be recognized and dealt with in such a manner that true brotherhood within the democratic society can be achieved.[32]

Continued violence against the region's African American population hardened Nash's resolve. When segregationists bombed Z. Alexander Looby's house and other homes near Meharry, Nash once again assumed a public stance. Nash felt that the city commission investigating desegregation was ineffective and stalled. The only recommendation the commission had made was that all city dining areas should have a segregated and a desegregated dining section. For Nash and the other student activists this was hardly achieving the goals of the movement. After the bombing, Nash and three thousand of Nashville's white and African American protesters marched to city hall and demanded Mayor West's attention. Sensing that chaos was about to erupt, the mayor meekly responded that he would work to arrest the bombers but that desegregation was another matter to be dealt with by the biracial commission. West, in a halfhearted attempt to control the swelling ire of the crowd, argued that he had denounced segregation when he entered office seven years earlier, and instead of offering concrete plans to end desegregation, he asked that everyone pray together. Not content with being patronized by another politician, Nash, as the unofficial leader of the student movement, decided to press the issue. Remembering the philosophies of nonviolence, Nash navigated her strategy so as not to incite violence. She also understood, however, that nonviolence did not mean being nonconfrontational. Nash moved to the front of the crowd in order to be within earshot and sight of the mayor. West continued patronizing the protesters by promising to further investigate the bombing. Clearly he was stalling so that he could avoid mob violence and having to take a stand on the issue. Fearful yet driven by her mission, Nash called for the mayor to put some action behind his words. Pointedly and forcefully, she asked the mayor whether he believed that it was wrong to discriminate based on race. The style and wording of the question left West with no other choice but to finally state his position. He responded "yes." Nash responded and asked if the mayor would consider eating with them. When West answered "yes," Nash pressed the mayor on his views regarding the segregation of the city's lunch counters. West responded that he was in favor of desegregating the city's lunch counters. Through a nonviolent confrontation Nash forced the mayor to make a final decision, and amid a media barrage, the city's lunch counters were integrated three weeks later. Nash understood that she had successfully employed nonviolence against a major city political figure to get him to voice his opinions against segregation. In his position as mayor, he could potentially begin the process of ending discrimination against African Americans.

Though fearful, Nash "had been transformed by her experiences, and now she was a true believer, surrendering her heart and soul . . . to nonviolence and the fight for freedom."[33] Despite her bravery and boldness, Nash recalled that at the start of every protest, in front of every judge, or in the public, she trembled with fear. She was terrified of confrontation but understood that her responsibility was to advance the cause of desegregation. Nash's image was splashed across the country's newspapers and televisions. Consequently, her fame as one of the "agitators" placed her in greater danger as opponents of desegregation came to recognize her and train their hostility onto her. Frequently, Nash found herself the target of white mob violence. An oft-published quote by several racist whites speaks to the violence directed at Nash while she engaged in a sit-in: "That's Diane Nash. She was in the paper. She's the one to get."[34] But Nash understood that her mission was greater than her fear. She commented:

> I'd take five minutes during which I'd make a decision that I was going to either put the fear out of my mind and do what I had to do, or I was going to call off the sit in and resign. I really just couldn't function effectively, as afraid as I was. And I found the courage to put the fear out of my mind and keep functioning.[35]

In later interviews, Nash remarked that she was constantly faced with fear but overcame her anxiety in pursuit of her mission.

After her repeated success in Nashville, Nash sought out other activists who were working toward black equality. In April 1961, under the encouragement of civil rights activist Ella Baker, students strove to expand their political activities to end segregation and fight racial discrimination. Baker convened a conference of the student sit-in leaders. She encouraged them to form an organization. The Student Nonviolent Coordinating Committee (SNCC) and its nonviolent principles attracted Nash. Originally tapped as chair, Nash avoided election by arriving to the vote late. This new organization employed the nonviolent principles of Christianity and *Satayagraha* derived from the early sit-in movements. Their mission statement included:

> We affirm the philosophical or religious ideal of non-violence as the foundation of our purpose, the presupposition of our faith, and the manner of our action.

Non-violence as it grows from the Judaic-Christian tradition seeks a social order of justice permeated by love. Integration of human endeavor represents the crucial first step towards such a society. Through non-violence, courage displaces fear; love transforms hate. Acceptance dissipates prejudice; hope ends despair. Peace dominates war; faith reconciles doubt. Mutual regard cancels enmity. Justice for all overthrows injustice. The redemptive community supersedes systems of gross social immorality. Love is the central motif of non-violence. Love is the force by which God binds man to Himself and man to man. Such love goes to the extreme; it remains loving and forgiving even in the midst of hostility. It matches the capacity of evil to inflict suffering with an even more enduring capacity to absorb evil, and all the while persisting in love. By appealing to conscience and standing on the moral nature of human existence, nonviolence nurtures the atmosphere in which reconciliation and justice become actual possibilities.[36]

Through Nash's and other students' efforts, SNCC grew into a strong and long-standing civil rights organization. Beginning in early 1961, Nash wholeheartedly involved herself in SNCC and led several workshops teaching other students about nonviolent strategies.

As national violence increased, so did SNCC's involvement. In addition to nonviolent protests and sit-ins, another civil rights group, Congress of Racial Equality (CORE), wanted to challenge segregation by testing a new Supreme Court decision on interstate travel. To register voters, CORE and later SNCC activists set out on a series of Freedom Rides into the Deep South states. The Freedom Ride buses were routinely met with violence and arrest. Time and time again, Nash's leadership and activism proved essential to the movement. In late spring 1961, Freedom Riders left Washington, D.C., and traveled through Virginia and North Carolina, headed toward New Orleans. A mob stopped, attacked, and firebombed them outside Anniston, Alabama. Beaten riders received treatment and moved to the airport to leave, but mobs prevented them from doing so. The Kennedy administration worked doggedly to persuade the riders to stop and order an airline to fly them to Louisiana. Many in CORE were intent on ending the rides. John Lewis, one of the Nashville students, had participated in the initial ride. He called Nash to alert her that the rides might end. The continuation of the Freedom Rides was a point of contention for many student activists. Nash and other Nashville activists feared that if they stopped, violence would win, and the credibility of their mission would be undermined. Still others in the movement believed the Freedom Rides were too risky and put students in danger. Nash wholeheartedly disagreed and publicly indicted those who would stop or interfere with the Freedom Rides. She busied herself recruiting riders.

Nash was not content to just enlist fellow riders—she often sought out the support of the movement's leaders. At one point, she solicited the efforts of Dr. Martin Luther King Jr. Nash knew that his very public and respected face added visibility to the rides. She hoped it might increase credibility and create a measure of protection for the riders. When his advisers warned him that he might become an assassination target if he supported the rides, King balked. Nash also solicited the advice of other prominent civil rights leaders but was again rejected because of the program's riskiness. Undeterred, Nash believed that with or without the assistance of the movement's elder leaders, students could and would carry on the Freedom Rides and that they would fulfill its mission of ending racial discrimination. While she failed to recruit the movement's leaders, she successfully enlisted the efforts of hundreds of students. Once again Nash had proven that nonviolence worked. Because of her dedication and successful recruiting tactics, Nash was the undisputed Nashville coordinator, and she planned the Freedom Ride campaign.[37]

Despite requests from Attorney General Robert F. Kennedy, Nash, Ella Baker, and other members of SNCC continued to send Freedom Riders from Washington, Atlanta, Nashville, and Montgomery. Subsequent Freedom Rides were met with continuous violence. In one instance, the riders from Nashville headed for Birmingham on May 16, and Nash was in charge of co-ordinating the efforts of the riders as well as monitoring the situation in Birmingham. In addition to her coordinating duties, she also kept in close contact with the Justice Department. Nash and government officials watched the riders' movement with bated breath. Nash was charged with tracking potential violence and doing her best to apprise the riders of po-tential encounters as well as to strategize with them to keep the students safe. The infamous Birmingham, Alabama, sheriff, Bull Connor, greeted the riders and proceeded to segregate the Freedom Riders from other passen-gers. After Connor escorted them to jail, the students spent two days in jail, and in the early hours on Thursday night, Connor escorted the riders to the Alabama-Tennessee border. Connor dropped them off in a potentially dan-gerous and unsheltered area, and the riders made their way to the homes of sympathetic African Americans. The riders ate and contacted Nash, and cars were sent to drive them back to Alabama. In Birmingham, other students ar-rived to protest, and thus with increased numbers the riders proceeded with their mission. Despite repeated requests from the Justice Department, Nash refused to advise the students to abandon their mission. Overriding Nash's and the other students' wishes, the Justice Department and Alabama's gov-ernor arranged to safely move the riders through the state. Later that morn-ing on Saturday, May 20, students and the press were attacked by a Mont-gomery mob. Due to violence and chaos the riders became separated. Antimovement protesters used lead pipes, knives, and guns to beat and bloody the students. Images of the violence streamed over televisions, glared from newspapers' front pages, and blared from car and home radios. Nash tried desperately to account for all of the students. While tracking her stu-dents, Nash also had to decide what the students should do next. Such fo-cused public attention could make or break the campaign's efforts. Birming-ham was coming apart at the seams.

Nash and the students knew that they had to act fast. After being released from the hospital, the students met with Martin Luther King Jr., C. T. Vivian, Ralph Abernathy, and Nash at Montgomery's First Baptist Church on Sunday evening. Anti-SNCC protesters surrounded the church and threatened violence. Understanding that violence was inevitable, the Alabama National Guard dispersed the mob. Sure that violence would greet the Freedom Riders at every turn, Dr. King implored Nash and the students to halt the rides. Once again Nash and the esteemed civil rights leader disagreed. She and her students were committed to the strategies of nonviolence and seeing the end of segregation through their efforts. Tensions rose between the student-run Freedom Ride movement and the King-led Southern Christian Leadership Conference (SCLC).

Shirking the advice of King and the Kennedy administration, the riders set off on May 24, 1961, and headed for Jackson, Mississippi. The riders were promptly arrested in Jackson for disturbing the peace. Nash raced to Jackson to seek help from local civil rights advocates. Meanwhile, the riders, observing Nash's "jail, no bail" policy, opted not to pay their bail and served their jail sentences. Fearing more violence, the U.S. attorney general, Robert Kennedy, stepped in and called a meeting with civil rights activists and offered to release money for voter registration drives if the activists ceased their grassroots campaigns. Nash rejected the offer and instead believed this to be a dangerous pact.

When Nash participated in one of the Freedom Rides in Rock Hill, South Carolina, a mob attacked her and other riders. The police promptly jailed the riders. Sentenced to jail for thirty days, Nash underwent still another life-changing experience as she sat with African American women who had also been arrested. For Nash, this was an intense learning event. Listening intently, she learned about regional, class, and race issues that impacted these women's everyday lives. Raised in the North and in a middle-class home and trained among middle-class student activists, Nash found herself for the first time really understanding the issues that working-class Southern black women faced. Now, for her, the movement went beyond lunch counters and bus stations. Energized by her experiences with these women, Nash used her month in prison to further study regional race and class issues and *Satayagraha* and Christian philosophies of nonviolence. Her experience in jail taught Nash that violence and discrimination against blacks was due not to black apathy or laziness, but rather to an insidious and institutional racism that threatened to remain static without the political activities and strategies of nonviolence effected by Nash and others. Her jail stay convinced Nash that she should not remain a student and instead should devote her energies to the movement. Nash dropped out of college, rented a room at the YWCA, and scouted more activist opportunities. For Nash and thousands of student activists, solving the nation's racial struggles seemed more important than achieving a college degree. Experiences over the previous years solidified

Nash's decision to become a full-time activist. Over the next few years she would work as a field worker for SNCC and the SCLC. She never regretted her decision. The Freedom Rides proved essential to the movement. In the words of historian Lynne Olson, the Freedom Rides reinvigorated the movement.

With tensions escalating, SNCC used the summer to plot its strategy. There was great debate, but Nash supported continued direct action. Under the advisement of Ella Baker, two student groups were formed. Initially Nash's group concentrated on direct action, and the other group centered its efforts on voter registration.

Nash recognized that the only way to effect change was to continue to spread the message of nonviolent political action throughout the Deep South. Thus, she embarked on a crusade to recruit more students to the philosophy and strategies of nonviolence. Relocating to the state of Mississippi in 1962, she and her husband, Jim Bevel, began to lead hundreds of students in workshops housed in churches, schools, and private locations. Recognizing the specific needs of the state, Nash directed her workshop and organizational efforts on securing a voter rights act and encouraging black voter registration. Nash witnessed some of the worst acts of violence during her time in the state. Angry whites routinely threatened the activists, and mobs appeared at meeting sites with weapons. Despite threats of violence, Nash and Bevel continued their work. In Mississippi, Nash encountered the famous black activist Fannie Lou Hamer from Ruleville. A grassroots organizer, Hamer was moved to action by the couple's suggestion that blacks organize, register to vote, and use their vote to oust racist white leaders. The three worked together along with other activists to form the Freedom Democratic Party. A crucial political organization, the party endeavored to highlight the fact that the state's existing Democratic Party catered to racist whites. In creating this second party, they hoped to register black voters, hold legitimate elections, and showcase the existence of thousands of disenfranchised blacks. This party had a profound impact on the state's politics and jump-started black political activism. The tremendous demand for political representation encouraged Nash and Bevel and other student activists to travel extensively throughout the state campaigning for black political representation. Their message reached thousands.

While in Mississippi, Nash became pregnant. In addition to facilitating classes on nonviolence and voter registration, Nash insisted that an important component in securing freedom for all blacks involved educating the next generation. She regularly instructed children on Gandhian and Christian principles. Viewing her as dangerous, local authorities in Jackson, Mississippi, arrested a pregnant Nash for teaching nonviolent strategies to children, and the judge gave her a two-year jail sentence for contributing to the delinquency of minors. Despite her pregnancy, Nash again followed her "jail, no bail" policy and opted to serve out the jail term. While enduring the discomforts of a

Southern jail, Nash penned a letter to students clarifying why the "jail, no bail" policy was crucial to achieving the aims of the movement:

> I believe the time has come, and is indeed long past, when each of us must make up his mind, when arrested on unjust charges, to serve his sentence and stop posting bonds. I believe that unless we do this our movement loses its power and will never succeed.[38]

Speaking to the students, Nash issued this challenge:

> We in the non-violent movement have been talking about jail without bail for two years or more. It is time for us to mean what we say. We sit in, demonstrate and get beaten up. Yet when we are arrested we immediately post bond and put the matter entirely into the hands of the courts even though we know we won't get justice in these courts.[39]

Next, Nash indicted the courts and explained how the "jail, no bail" policy destabilized the corrupt judicial system:

> Southern courts in which we are being tried are completely corrupt. We say this is a moral battle, but then we surrender the fight into the legal hands of corrupt courts. . . . When we leave the jails under bond we lose our opportunity to witness—to prick the conscience of the oppressing group and to appeal to the imagination of the oppressed group and inspire them. We stifle any effort to use what we in the nonviolent movement see as truth force and soul force.[40]

Contemplative yet full of conviction, Nash understood her activities and those of her fellow protesters to be nothing less than transformative on a monumental scale. She believed the continued efforts would crush the nation's immoral racist system and replace it with a system based on justice, equality, and humanity.

> We renounce the concept of redemption through suffering. Gandhi said the difference between people who are recklessly breaking the law and those who are standing on a moral principle is that those who stand on principle are willing to take the consequences of their action. When they do this a whole community, indeed a whole nation and the world may be awakened, and the sights of all society are raised to a new level. . . . History also shows—both recent history and down through the ages—that a few people, even one person, can move mountains. And even if we cannot honestly foresee great effects from our stand, it is my belief that each of us must act on our conscience—do the thing we know in our hearts is right.[41]

Recognizing the potential for negative publicity in having a child born in jail, the Mississippi judicial system released Nash, and she delivered her daughter on August 5, 1962.

Over the next year Nash and her husband worked on desegregation efforts and voter registration drives in Mississippi, Atlanta, and North Carolina. In September of 1963, Nash was deeply shaken by news of the Alabama Sixteenth Street Baptist Church bombing, in which four young girls were murdered. Consequently, Nash stepped up her efforts at getting African Americans to register and vote. Gradually, Nash shied away from the public view. She preferred to be less visible in the movement but continued her efforts begun in Lawson's nonviolent workshops a few long years before. In all of her civil rights activities, Nash stressed the importance of nonviolence as a particularly efficient political strategy as evidenced by the low numbers of individuals injured or killed.[42] Employing such strategies and working with Deep South communities and local and state women's groups, Nash aided in the all-important passage of the 1964 Civil Rights Act and the Voting Rights Act of 1965.

Nash did not limit her nonviolent activities to SNCC. When she returned to her home in Chicago and divorced Bevel, Nash continued her activist efforts in various businesses and nonprofit organizations. She applied the same commitment to social change in her involvement in protesting the Vietnam War.

In later interviews and in public speaking engagements, Nash continued to stress that nonviolence in both its Christian and Gandhian permutations exists not merely as political strategy but as a lifelong philosophy. For Lawson, Nash, and other subscribers, nonviolence served as a spiritual position to be employed by individuals in their daily thought processes and experiences. She stated in the student newspaper *Earlham Word*,

> I got a very good grounding in the philosophy and strategy. It has made just a major difference in my life because I also use the principles that I learned in those workshops in many areas of my life. You can use nonviolence as a tactic or as a way of life. I was using it as a tactic first but I came to understand it more and more deeply through action and through seeing how successful and powerful it is and I use it as a way of life.[43]

Several decades later, Diane Nash continues her project of social and political activism. In interviews, articles, and public speaking events, Nash stresses the importance of nonviolence in confronting societal inequality. In recent years she has focused her attention on education and establishing mentor programs for youths across the nation. Nash has also broadened her spiritual and political focus to encompass a new philosophy—Agapic energy. Agapic energy, or "love of mankind[,] is similar to Christian and Gandhian ideals of non-violence and love."[44] Agapic energy represents a new methodology used to resist inequality and injustice and to build community. This contemporary nonviolent philosophy imagines a world filled with peace, social justice, economic well-being, and political participation. For more than four decades, Diane Nash has successfully employed strategies of nonviolence to end segregation and racial discrimination.

Inspired by success and Gandhian philosophies, Nash found her participation in the movement politically and spiritually transformative. She transcended her sheltered childhood, her Catholic upbringing, and her beauty-pageant days and became a full-fledged politicized being. Through her experiences in Lawson's classroom, at the sit-in counters, and in jail, Nash had moved beyond the oft-taught black middle-class philosophies that hard work would ultimately result in equality for blacks. She sidestepped the prevalent notion that African American women could only assist members of their race through their connections within their families and communities. Christian ideals of love and Gandhian philosophies of *Satayagraha* inspired Nash to carry on her protests against racial discrimination. She met violence with nonviolence. She knew that violence and attempts to consign blacks to political, social, and economic equality must be challenged.

NOTES

1. Rosetta E. Ross, *Witnessing & Testifying: Black Women, Religion, and Civil Rights* (Minneapolis: Fortress, 2003).

2. Ross, *Witnessing & Testifying.*

3. Lynne Olson, *Freedom's Daughters: The Unsung Heroines of the Civil Rights Movement from 1830 to 1870* (New York: Scribner, 2001), 153.

4. Olson, *Freedom's Daughters*, 14.

5. Olson, *Freedom's Daughters*, 154.

6. Ross, *Witnessing & Testifying*, 168.

7. Olson, *Freedom's Daughters*, 154.

8. dfong.com/nonviol/basicsat.html.

9. dfong.com/nonviol/basicsat.html.

10. dfong.com/nonviol/basicsat.html.

11. www.markshep.com/nonviolence/Understanding.html.

12. www.markshep.com/nonviolence/Understanding.html.

13. Olson, *Freedom's Daughters*, 155.

14. www.vernalproject.org/Opapers/WhyNV/WhyNonviolence3.html.

15. David Halberstam, *The Children* (New York: Random House, 1998), 78.

16. www.collegian.psu.edu/archive/2003/01/01-21-03dnews-09.asp.

17. Olson, *Freedom's Daughters*, 155.

18. Michelle Margaret Viera, "A Summary of the Contributions of Four Key African-American Female Figures of the Civil Rights Movement" (MA thesis, Western Michigan University, 1994), 27.

19. Olson, *Freedom's Daughters*, 156.

20. Olson, *Freedom's Daughters*, 156.

21. Ross, *Witnessing & Testifying*, 170.

22. Olson, *Freedom's Daughters.*

23. Olson, *Freedom's Daughters*, 156.

24. Olson, *Freedom's Daughters*, 157.
25. Olson, *Freedom's Daughters*, 157.
26. Olson, *Freedom's Daughters*, 157.
27. Olson, *Freedom's Daughters*, 157.
28. Olson, *Freedom's Daughters*, 158.
29. Ross, *Witnessing & Testifying*, 171.
30. Various sources suggest that the "jail, no bail" strategy was being used in several campaigns throughout the South—in Florida, South Carolina, and Tennessee at least—by 1960. It is unclear who first pioneered the strategy among student activists and which campaign, if any, set the example for others. What is clear is that it became an effective strategy throughout the movement. See also n15 in chapter 13 of this book.
31. Olson, *Freedom's Daughters*, 158.
32. Viera, "Summary of the Contributions," 29.
33. Olson, *Freedom's Daughters*, 160.
34. www.africanpubs.com/App/bios/1145NashDiane.asp?pic=none.
35. Ross, *Witnessing & Testifying*, 173.
36. Clayborne Carson, *In Struggle: SNCC and the Black Awakening of the 1960s* (Cambridge, Mass.: Harvard University Press, 1981), 23–24.
37. Viera, "Summary of the Contributions," 29.
38. Viera, "Summary of the Contributions," 33–35.
39. Viera, "Summary of the Contributions," 33–35.
40. Viera, "Summary of the Contributions," 33–35.
41. Viera, "Summary of the Contributions," 33–35.
42. word.cs.earlham. Edu/issues/XII/012398/comm731173a.html.
43. word.cs.earlham. Edu/issues/XII/012398/comm731173a.html.
44. www.collegian.psu.edu/archive/2003/01/01-21-03dnews-09.asp.

SUGGESTED READING

Ackerman, Peter, and Jack DuVall. *A Force More Powerful: A Century of Nonviolent Conflict*. New York: St. Martin's Press, 2000.
Ackerman, Peter, and Christopher Kruegler. *Strategic Nonviolent Conflict: The Dynamics of People Power in the Twentieth Century*. Westport, CT: Praeger Publishers, 1993.
Albert, David. *People Power: Applying Nonviolent Theory*. Philadelphia: Library Company of Philadelphia, 1985.
Bondurant, Joan. *Conquest of Violence*. Revised ed. Princeton, NJ: Princeton University Press, 1988.
Cooney, Robert, and Helen Michalowski. *The Power of the People: Active Nonviolence in the United States*. Philadelphia: Library Company of Philadelphia, 1977.
Dellinger, Dave. *Revolutionary Nonviolence*. New York: Anchor Books, 1971.
Deming, Barbara. *We Are All Part of One Another: A Barbara Deming Reader*. Gabriola Island, BC: New Society Publishers, 1984.
Gowan, Susanne, et al. *Moving Toward a New Society*. Gabriola Island, BC: New Society Publishers, 1976.
Irwin, Robert A. *Building a Peace System*. Washington, DC: Expro Press, 1989.

Lakey, George. *Strategy for a Living Revolution*. Revised ed. New York: Grossman Publishers, 1985.

McAllister, Pam, ed. *Reweaving the Web of Life: Feminism and Nonviolence*. Gabriola Island, BC: New Society Publishers, 1982.

Sharp, Gene. *Power and Struggle: The Politics of Nonviolent Action*. Manchester, NH: Porter Sargent Publishers, 1973.

———. *Social Power and Political Freedom*. Manchester, NH: Porter Sargent Publishers, 1978.

11

࿐

Mae Bertha Carter:
These Tiny Fingers

Constance Curry

*"Mae Bertha Carter: These Tiny Fingers" tells the story of the clear-eyed de-
termination, down-home grit, and sweet triumph of the Carter family of Sunflower County, Mississippi—African American sharecroppers who, in 1965,
sent their children to desegregate the previously all-white school system. It illustrates how local people, in spite of intimidation, harassment, and threats of
violence, were the ones truly responsible for the implementation of civil rights
legislation.*

Matthew and Mae Bertha Carter, as did their forebears, sharecropped on
cotton plantations in the heart of the Mississippi Delta. They were married in 1939 and had thirteen children, a great benefit for their work—many
pairs of hands to chop and pick the cotton. Mr. and Mrs. Carter each had
about a third-grade education, gleaned from a one-room schoolhouse or a
black church on the plantation, often used as a school. They were determined that their children would not suffer the indignities of an inferior education as they had.

The barriers to such determination had started in times of slavery when it
was against the law to teach a slave to read or write. Although it was partially
based on the belief that blacks were subhuman and really not able to learn, the
greater factor in this prohibition on education was the threat to the economic
system. If blacks got an education, they would be able to leave the fields and
the peonage of the sharecropping system. Thus, any attempts to provide
education for blacks were a shameful farce, and white political demagogues

continually incited their segregationist constituencies on the issue. As Mississippi Governor James Vardaman put it in 1899, "The Negro is not permitted to advance and their education only spoils a good field hand—it is money thrown away."[1]

These pronouncements and constant barriers did not deter some black families from their goal of a better life. In 1915, Mrs. Carter's mother, Luvenia Slaughter, had gone across the Mississippi River to West Helena, Arkansas, to attend Southland Institute. Established by the 56th Colored Regiment in 1866, Southland was the first permanent educational institution for blacks west of the Mississippi. Luvenia recalled that year as one of the happiest times in her life and often sang the songs she learned as she picked cotton back on the plantation with her family. A yellow fever epidemic prevented her and friends from returning to the school the following September. Matthew Carter's aunts were teachers, so both he and Mae Bertha were from families that knew that the only way out of the cotton fields was to get an education.

Mrs. Carter often told the story of the 1939 birth of their first child, Edna, and how beautiful that baby was. Her mother, Luvenia, would tell her that it was just because it was her baby. But Carter looked at Edna's perfect tiny fingers and told Matthew and her mother that those fingers would never pick cotton. Edna did pick cotton, as did the next four children, Naomi, Bertha, Matthew, and J. C., the "first batch," as Carter called them. They labored in the cotton fields on a "split session" schedule, which meant they attended school only when the cotton was chopped and picked, which usually added up to about seven instead of nine months. As the Carter children got older, they wondered why the shiny yellow school buses filled with white children were speeding by them as they worked in the burning sun of a Mississippi September. After they graduated from the "colored school," they all left Mississippi immediately. The daughters went to work and to stay with relatives and work in the North, and the two sons joined the armed services.

The 1954 Supreme Court's unanimous ruling in *Brown v. Board of Education* that segregated schools were unconstitutional barely made a ripple in the lives of black sharecroppers in the Delta, and white resistance intensified throughout the South. The threat of educated blacks exacerbated the already existing fear of miscegenation and specters of "race-mixing" among young children. Klan propaganda about "mongrelization" fanned white opposition, and in Indianola, the Sunflower County seat, two months after the decision, the segregationist Citizens' Council was organized. The council was composed of doctors, lawyers, and businessmen, and Mrs. Carter called them the "up-town Klan."[2] At the local and state levels, white politicians declared "never" to their constituencies and vowed to thwart the federal government's interference in their way of life.

By 1956, the Mississippi legislature passed additional laws designed to circumvent the court ruling, and that same year it established the State Sovereignty Commission to preserve segregation at all costs. The commission, which was state-funded, investigated persons who were believed to be subversive or a threat to the status quo. Meanwhile, violence and other attacks on African Americans intensified. In 1955, the Reverend George Lee, a leader in the Belzoni, Mississippi, chapter of the NAACP, was gunned down in his automobile, and he died on the way to the hospital. A few months later, several white men murdered black fourteen-year-old Emmett Till for allegedly whistling at a white woman in LeFlore County, not far from where the Carter family sharecropped on the Pemble Plantation in Sunflower County. Black people waited and hoped that change would soon be coming.

When civil rights workers arrived in the Delta beginning in 1961, Mae Bertha, Matthew, and the older Carter children started attending the mass meetings in nearby Cleveland. This was not a new thing for them because, in spite of the danger, they had stolen away in secret from the plantation after joining the NAACP in 1955. In fact, Mae Bertha and Matthew Carter had traveled through the Delta in their truck at night with their headlights turned off to avoid detection by whites as they tried to recruit new members. But there was a new burst of hope and enthusiasm with the arrival of young workers who told the black community about their rights and how to organize for voter registration and other battles. And always there was the music. At mass meetings in churches in the early 1960s, "Oh Freedom," "We Shall Overcome," and "This Little Light of Mine" echoed and inspired and bound people together in a manner that defies explanation. As Mrs. Carter said, "Just made us want to get up and do something."[3] Ruth and Naomi Carter went to Jackson in the summer of 1965 to march for voting rights and were arrested and jailed in the stockade at the fairgrounds where animals were kept. When asked about putting their children in the white school that fall, Carter always said, "We was already motivated."[4]

The Civil Rights Act of 1964, under Title VI, clearly mandated that school districts wanting to continue receiving federal funds were required to submit a school desegregation plan. Most of the all-white districts, particularly in rural areas, scrambled to find the least effective means possible of so doing. Drew Municipal School District submitted a "freedom of choice" plan that allowed all parents to choose whatever school they wanted to send their children to. They knew full well that none of the black families caught in the economic peonage of sharecropping would dare to choose a white school. But, as Carter said, "They just didn't know about us out on that plantation."[5]

When the choice forms arrived, Mae Bertha was visiting relatives in St. Louis, but when Ruth called, she came home right away. Ruth wanted to enter the eleventh grade at Drew High, and her six younger siblings were quite willing to follow her lead. Matthew and Mae Bertha signed the forms for all seven of the children to attend the formerly all-white schools. Mae Bertha told about the surprise and anger on the faces of the school principals at the

Children of Mae Bertha and Matthew Carter (Image courtesy of Rev. Maurice McCrackin.)

elementary and high schools in Drew when she and Matthew delivered the choice forms. Neither one of them could understand this reaction—after all, those white officials were the ones who had made the offer.

Mr. Thornton, the overseer on the Pemble Plantation, came to see Matthew Carter the next day and tried to talk him into withdrawing the children. Mrs. Carter overheard the conversation, and when Matthew came in to tell her about it, she instructed him as follows, "You go back out there and tell Mr. Thornton that I am a grown woman. I birthed those babies and bore the pain—that he can't be telling me where to send my children to school, and I'd be a fool to tell him where to send his children."[6] A few nights later, the family was awakened by the sound of trucks coming down the dirt road, flashing headlights, and the next thing they knew, gunshots exploded and bullets hit the walls and roof of their house. Matthew and Mae Bertha Carter ran to protect the children, and the family spent the rest of the night on the floor. The next morning, Mrs. Carter went to report the shootings to Amzie Moore, the NAACP leader in Cleveland, who called the FBI in Jackson. The deputy sheriff and other officials came out to investigate, but they never determined who fired the shots. Word of these incidents spread quickly, and by the opening day of school, the seven Carter children were the only black children to board the shiny new bus to the white school.

After the children left each morning, Mrs. Carter would go and lie across her bed and pray that God would take care of her children. Then, each afternoon, she would stand on the porch and count them, one by one, until all seven came down the steps of the bus. Then she would thank Jesus for taking care of them. This ritual went on for several months until she felt the children would be safe in spite of ill treatment at the school.

Soon after they enrolled the children, the plantation store cut off their credit, and the overseer plowed under their remaining cotton and let their animals out of the pen one night. Then, in 1966, when it became clear that the Carters were to be evicted from the plantation, they began to look for a house in or near Drew. They faced closed doors the minute they gave their names. Finally, the NAACP Legal Defense and Education Fund, the Unitarian Universalist Association, and the American Friends Service Committee joined together to purchase a house on a main street in Drew. Matthew and Mae Bertha Carter worked hard to repay the groups who had bought the house until the title to the house was theirs. Soon after the Carters moved into town, the white power structure knew that people from the "outside" were allied with the Carters and accepted the fact that the family was not going to be driven out by harassment or intimidation tactics.

Ruth Carter, entering the eleventh grade at the high school as the oldest of the enrolling children, was deeply affected by the taunts and treatment from the white students and teachers. They jumped out of her way in the halls and classes, called her "nigger," threw spitballs, or acted like she was not even there. Larry and Stanley Carter were pushed around as they climbed the stairs, and the white students often tried to trip them or push their books from under their arms. Beverly, in the third grade, spoke of standing against the wall at A. W. James Elementary School during play period watching the white girls jump rope. She was happy when they asked her to turn the rope one day. Thirty-five years later, she cried when she told an interviewer, "But they never let me jump."[7]

Fifth-grader Pearl could not believe her teacher's taunting her on "whether the NAACP had bought her eyeglasses." That same teacher isolated Pearl at a desk a little removed from the surrounding desks of white students and let them change their seats on a weekly basis. White first-graders called Deborah "walking Tootsie Roll" and refused to hold her hand when they were walking to lunch or to the bus. The humiliation and mistreatment continued for all of the children for five years until 1970, when the schools desegregated completely under court order. During those years, the children would come home after school and cry and talk with their mother about school that day, and they would often sing freedom songs. Matthew and Mae Bertha Carter would encourage them, pointing out that "it wasn't a white school, it was a brick school. It was their school—they paid taxes like everyone else."[8] And there was always another admonition from their mother—"you don't start something unless you plan to finish it."[9]

But perhaps Mae Bertha Carter's deepest lesson for her children, along with her total commitment to education, was her understanding of what "hating" does to a person. Sometimes Ruth would come home from school consumed with anger, telling her mother that she hated white people, she hated the school, and she hated Mississippi. She was especially vulnerable because she felt responsible when she listened to the stories and pain of her younger brothers and sisters who had followed her lead in choosing the white schools. But Carter wouldn't let any of the children talk about "hating people" and would talk to them about how that emotion can destroy the person who does the hating.

The children concentrated on their studies, remained focused, and refused to be diverted from their purpose of getting a good education. Stanley saw it as a continuing battle that they would lose if they dropped out or were expelled for any reason. They all graduated from Drew High School. Ruth moved immediately after graduation in 1968 to live with her grandmother in Toledo, Ohio. She had been held back from her normal graduation year, supposedly for failing English by four points. In 1967, Carl was the last Carter child to go to the previously all-white elementary school.

In the meantime, Mrs. Carter had been in touch with the NAACP Legal Defense and Education Fund in Jackson on the continuing harassment of her children in the schools, and their attorneys filed a suit. Finally, in 1969, a court order abolished the dual school system, and all black and white children in Drew were to attend the same elementary, middle, and high schools. Simultaneously, the white community rushed to establish private segregated academies, and most of the white students fled to the academies. While Carl and the other children no longer had to suffer the indignities and harassment of the first five years, they all noted the decline in social activities, in teaching abilities, and in course offerings.

Control of the public schools remained in the hands of a white school board. Some members had no children in the public school system—they sent them to the private academies—and one of Mae Bertha Carter's continuing battles was to get rid of Mr. DuBard, the school board chairman. Her other battles included challenging the dress codes (which at one point meant measuring the length of the Afro haircuts the black children were wearing), fighting for more black teachers, and raising questions about the private academies' using books that were meant for the public schools. She continued the fight for quality education for all children, pointing out always that getting an education meant that one could make choices in life.

With scholarship funds from the Herbert Lehman Fund and the NAACP Legal Defense and Education Fund, seven of the Carter children who graduated from Drew high school attended and graduated from Ole Miss.

Beloved by all of his children, Matthew Carter died in 1988. He was a good farmer and a gentle soul who was happy if his children were happy. When the family moved into Drew and he was barred from working at all the places where he applied, he stayed at home and took care of the house and children while his wife worked at Head Start. Later, he also worked for Head Start in Indianola. The daughters recall that their father learned to sew at an early age and would make their underpants from cotton sacks when they were little. He was always glad when there were little flowers or designs on the sack. Mrs. Carter knew that she could not have done it without him and always knew that black men in Mississippi were not as free to speak out— "they would just kill them, you know."[10]

Mrs. Carter continued her fight for quality education for all children. School officials appointed her daughter Beverly to the Drew school board in 1986. They told her that she might as well serve because her mother would be at all of the board meetings anyway. She was not reappointed in 1992— she had disagreed with most of the decisions made by the white board members and many of the policies that discriminated against a system by then composed predominantly of black children. She agreed with her mother on the need to oust William DuBard, the school board chair who sent his children to the private schools.

Mae Bertha Carter died quietly of cancer in April 1999, but she told me when I visited her in March of that year that she was not quite ready— there was too much yet to be done. She directed her disgust and discontent at the end of her life toward the fact that William DuBard was still the chair of the school board after some thirty years and that Senator Trent Lott was about to have an institute on leadership building at the University of Mississippi named for and dedicated to him. She was also concerned about the lack of interest among many black young people in registering to vote. Campaign meetings for worthy candidates often took place in her living room, and in 1991, Willie Simmons was the first black from that district to be elected to the state senate.

During her final weeks in Drew, she told the home help people to take her off the list if it meant she had to stay at home. She insisted on getting ice cream from Baskin-Robbins in Cleveland the day before she died.

The October after her death a tree was planted in her memory in the "Circle" at the University of Mississippi. This area is in front of the administration building and is where riots occurred when James Meredith, the first black admitted to the university, tried to enroll in 1962. When a group of black and white students suggested that a tree be planted in this area in memory of Mae Bertha, they were told that trees were not planted even for big donors or sports heroes. The young people insisted that Mae Bertha was another kind of hero and, instead of giving money to the university, she had given her children. The university agreed to allow the students to honor her.

Mae Bertha had thirteen children, thirty-four grandchildren, and sixteen great-grandchildren, and she knew them all by name. Many of them came to the tree planting, and some of the younger ones helped shovel the dirt back in around the tree. Beneath the graceful red maple, now growing quite tall, a plaque reads, "In memory of Mae Bertha Carter and her seven children who graduated from Ole Miss."

NOTES

1. James K. Vardaman, editorial, *Commonwealth* (Greenwood), June 30, 1899.
2. Mae Bertha Carter, personal interview, 1994.
3. Carter, personal interview, 1994.
4. Carter, personal interview, 1994.
5. Carter, personal interview, 1994.
6. Carter, personal interview, 1994.
7. Carter, personal interview, 1994.
8. Carter, personal interview, 1994.
9. Carter, personal interview, 1994.
10. Carter, personal interview, 1994.

SUGGESTED READING

Bolton, Charles. *The Hardest Deal of All: The Battle over School Integration in Mississippi, 1870–1980*. Jackson, MS: University Press of Mississippi, 2005.

Curry, Constance. *Silver Rights*. San Diego: Harvest Books, 1995.

Dittmer, John. *Local People*. Urbana: University of Illinois Press, 1995.

Hudson, Winson, and Constance Curry. *Mississippi Harmony*. New York: Palgrave MacMillan, 2002.

McMillen, Neil. *Dark Journey*. Urbana: University of Illinois Press, 1990.

Payne, Charles. *I've Got the Light of Freedom*. Berkeley: University of California Press, 1996.

12

&

Robert F. Williams: "Black Power" and the Roots of the African American Freedom Struggle

Timothy B. Tyson

The life of Robert F. Williams, though his role in the African American free-dom struggle is significant in its own right, suggests that violence and non-violence, civil rights and Black Power, are more complicated—and more closely intertwined—than traditional accounts portray them. Most black Southerners were prepared to defend their homes and communities by force if necessary. And much of what we associate with Black Power—an interna-tional analysis of white supremacy, an interest in things African, pride in African American culture and identity, an interest in creating a new black sense of self, and willingness to resort to "armed self-reliance" against white terrorism—were already present in the American South in the 1950s, long be-fore anyone chanted "Black Power."

"The childhood of Southerners, white and colored," Lillian Smith wrote in 1949, "has been lived on trembling earth."[1] For one black boy in Monroe, North Carolina, the earth first shook on a Saturday morning in 1936. Standing on the sidewalk on Main Street, Robert Franklin Williams witnessed a white policeman batter an African American woman. The po-liceman, Jesse Helms Sr., an admirer recalled, "had the sharpest shoe in town and he didn't mind using it." The police officer's son, Senator Jesse Helms, remembered "Big Jesse" as "a six-foot, two-hundred-pound gorilla. When he said, 'Smile,' I smiled."[2] Eleven-year-old Robert Williams watched in terror as "Big Jesse" flattened the black woman with his fist and then arrested her. Years later, Williams described the scene: Helms "dragged her off to the nearby jailhouse, her dress up over her head, the same way that a cave man would club and drag his sexual prey." He recalled "her tortured screams as her flesh was ground away from the friction of the concrete." The memory of this violent spectacle and the laughter of white bystanders haunted Williams. Perhaps the deferential way that African American men on the street responded, however, was even more deeply troubling. "The emasculated black men hung their heads in shame and hurried silently from the cruelly bizarre sight," Williams recalled.[3]

Knowledge of such scenes was as commonplace as coffee cups in the South that had recently helped to elect Franklin Delano Roosevelt. But for the rest of his life, Robert Williams, destined to become one of the most influential African American radicals of his time, repeated this searing story to friends, readers, listeners, reporters, and historians. He preached it from streetcorner ladders to eager crowds on Seventh Avenue and 125th Street in Harlem and to congregants in Malcolm X's Temple Number 7. He bore witness to its brutality in labor halls and college auditoriums across the United States. It fed the fervor of his widely published debate with Martin Luther King Jr. in 1960 and fueled his futile bids for leadership in the black freedom struggle. Its merciless truths must have tightened in his fingers on the night in 1961 when he fled an FBI dragnet with his wife and two small children, a machine gun slung over one shoulder. Williams revisited the bitter memory on platforms that he shared with Fidel Castro, Ho Chi Minh, and Mao tse-Tung. He told it over "Radio Free Dixie," his regular program on Radio Havana from 1962 to 1965, and retold it from Hanoi in broadcasts directed to African American soldiers in Vietnam. It echoed from transistor radios in Watts in 1965 and from gigantic speakers in Tiananmen Square in 1966. The childhood story opens the pages of his autobiography, "While God Lay Sleeping," which Williams completed just before his death on October 15, 1996. In the anguish of that eleven-year-old, we can find distilled the bitter history that shaped not only one of the South's most dynamic race rebels but thousands of other black insurgents. That moment marked his life, and his life marked the African American freedom movement in the United States.[4]

Robert Williams was born in 1925 to Emma C. and John L. Williams. His father was a railroad boiler washer in Monroe, North Carolina, a town of six thousand in the North Carolina piedmont.[5] Women born in slavery still tended vegetable gardens along the street where young "Rob" Williams grew up. His grandfather, Sikes Williams, born a slave in Union County, had attended Biddle Institute in nearby Charlotte after emancipation and became one of Union County's first black schoolteachers.[6] He enlisted as a Republican activist during the late nineteenth century and "traveled all over the county and the State making speeches and soliciting support for the Party." Sikes Williams also published a small newspaper called *The People's Voice*.[7] The "fusion" coalition of black Republicans and white Populists that he had labored to build won every statewide office in 1896. "The Chains of Servi-

NAACP Meeting, Monroe, North Carolina, 1957. Left to right: Edward S. Williams, Robert F. Williams, John H. Williams (kneeling), and Dr. Albert Perry. (Image courtesy of John Herman Williams.)

tude Are Broken," Williams and his white Populist allies in Monroe proclaimed to their black constituents that year. "Now Never Lick the Hand that Lashed You."[8] Two years later, however, white conservatives overthrew the democratic process. "Go to the polls tomorrow," soon-to-be mayor Alfred Waddell told white citizens of Wilmington, North Carolina, "and if you find

the negro out voting, tell him to leave the polls, and if he refuses, kill him."
In a campaign of fraud and violence all across the state in 1898, "Redshirt"
terrorists helped the party of white supremacy install what Democratic editor Josephus Daniels celebrated as "permanent good government by the
party of the white man."[9]

Robert's grandmother, Ellen Isabel Williams, lived through these struggles
and was a daily presence in his life as he grew toward manhood; Williams
remembered his grandmother as "my greatest friend."[10] He recalled that
"she read *everything*" and that she "specialized in history." Perhaps in part
because Robert so strikingly resembled her handsome late husband, she
would point to the iron printing press rusting in the shed and tell the young
boy stories of the crusading editor's political exploits. Herself born into slavery, she reminded her grandson that she had been conceived in the union of
her mother with their owner, Daniel Tomblin. Before she died, Ellen
Williams gave young Robert a gift that symbolized much that slavery and
the struggle for liberty had taught her: the ancient rifle that his grandfather
had wielded against white terrorists at the turn of the century.[11]

It would not be long before Williams, gun in hand, found himself facing a
new generation of white terrorists. In 1946, twenty-one-year-old Robert
Williams stepped down from a segregated Greyhound bus in Monroe wearing the uniform of his country. Four years earlier, Williams had moved to Detroit to work at Ford Motor Company. Coming home from Belle Isle Amusement Park on the evening of June 11, 1943, he and his brother battled white
mobs in one of the worst race riots in United States history.[12] Drafted in 1944,
Williams endured the ironies of marching for freedom in a segregated army.
When his government-issue shoe leather struck the same pavement where
ten years earlier he had seen "Big Jesse" Helms drag the black woman off to
jail, Williams was no longer a frightened eleven-year-old. Military training
had given black veterans "some feeling of security and self-assurance," he
recalled. "The Army indoctrination instilled in us what a virtue it was to
fight for democracy and that we were fighting for democracy and uphold-
ing the Constitution. But most of all they taught us to use arms." Like thousands of other black veterans whom John Dittmer has characterized as "the
shock troops of the modern civil rights movement," Robert Williams did not
come home to pick cotton.[13]

Another returning black veteran, a friend of Williams's named Bennie
Montgomery, did come home to raise cotton on the farm that his father operated as a sharecropper for W. W. Mangum, a white landowner near Monroe. Saturday, June 1, 1946, was a regular workday on the Mangum place,
but Montgomery asked Mangum for his wages at noon, explaining that he
needed to go to Monroe and have his father's car repaired. Mangum apparently kicked and slapped the young veteran, and Montgomery pulled out a
pocketknife and cut his employer's throat. The Ku Klux Klan wanted to
lynch the black sharecropper, but instead state authorities whisked Mont-

gomery out of town, tried and convicted him of murder, and ten months later executed him in the gas chamber at Central Prison in Raleigh.[14]

State authorities shipped the sharecropper's remains back to Monroe. Robbed of their lynching, however, the local klavern of "the invisible empire" let it be known that Bennie Montgomery's body belonged not to his family, but to the Ku Klux Klan. "They was gonna come and take Bennie's body out and drag it up and down the streets," J. W. McDow, another African American veteran, recalled. "I rather die and go to hell before I see that happen." A group of former soldiers met at Booker T. Perry's barbershop and made a battle plan. When the Klan motorcade pulled up in front of Harris Funeral Home, forty black men leveled their rifles, taking aim at the line of cars. Not a shot was fired; the Klansmen simply weighed their chances and drove away. Former U.S. Army PFC Robert F. Williams cradled a carbine that night. So did three of the men who would become key lieutenants in the "black militia" that Williams organized ten years later. "That was one of the first incidents," Williams recalled, "that really started us to understanding that we had to resist, and that resistance could be effective if we resisted in groups, and if we resisted with guns."[15]

Williams soon left the South for almost a decade, working briefly at Cadillac Motor Company in Detroit before using his GI Bill benefits to write poetry and study psychology at three different black colleges: West Virginia State College, Johnson C. Smith College, and North Carolina Central College for Negroes. "Someday," he vowed in an 1949 article for the Detroit edition of the *Daily Worker*, "I would return seasoned from the fight in the north and more efficient in the fight for the liberation of my people." In 1952, Williams wrote an essay for Paul Robeson's newspaper, *Freedom*, in which he predicted that African American college students would soon become "the most militant agitators for democracy in America today. They have nothing to lose and all to gain." At Johnson C. Smith College, Williams met one of his literary heroes, Langston Hughes, who considered Williams a promising poet and sent him handwritten poems as an encouragement.

In 1953, however, Williams ran out of money for college and reenlisted in the armed forces, this time in the United States Marine Corps.[16] Things did not go well for the young Marine. Objecting bitterly to racial discrimination, Williams clashed with his officers, spent much of his time in the brig, and received an undesirable discharge in 1955. His one bright moment as a Marine came on May 17, 1954, when he heard that the United States Supreme Court had struck down school segregation. "At last I felt that I was a part of America and that I belonged," he wrote. "I was sure that this was the beginning of a new era of American democracy."[17]

Upon his return to Monroe in 1955, Williams joined both the local branch of the NAACP and a mostly white Unitarian fellowship. In a Sunday sermon delivered to his fellow Unitarians in 1956, Williams hailed the Montgomery bus boycott and celebrated what he called "the patriots of passive revolution."

Invoking "the spirit of Concord, Lexington and Valley Forge," Williams declared from the pulpit that, as he put it, "the liberty bell peals once more and the Stars and Stripes shall wave forever."[18]

The atmosphere at the Monroe NAACP was less exuberant. In the wake of the *Brown* decision and the triumph at Montgomery, Ku Klux Klan rallies near Monroe began to draw crowds as big as fifteen thousand.[19] Dynamite attacks on black activists in the area were common and lesser acts of terror routine. "The echo of shots and dynamite blasts," the editors of the *Southern Patriot* wrote in 1957, "has been almost continuous throughout the South."[20] The Monroe NAACP dwindled to six members who then contemplated disbanding. When the newest member objected to dissolution, the departing membership chose him to lead the chapter. "They elected me president," Robert Williams recalled, "and then they all left."[21]

Finding himself virtually a one-man NAACP chapter, Williams turned first to the black veterans with whom he had stood against the Klan that night back in 1946. Another veteran, Dr. Albert E. Perry, MD, became vice president. Williams and Perry recruited from beauty parlors, pool halls, and street corners, building a cadre of roughly two hundred members by 1959. The largest group among the new recruits was African American women who worked as domestics.[22] The Monroe branch of the NAACP became "the only one of its kind in existence," Julian Mayfield wrote in *Commentary* in 1961. "Its members and supporters, who are mostly workers and displaced farmers, constitute a well-armed and disciplined fighting unit."[23] The branch became "unique in the whole NAACP because of a working class composition and a leadership that was not middle class," Williams wrote. "Most important, we had a strong representation of black veterans who didn't scare easily."[24]

In response to the drownings of several local African American children whom segregation had forced to swim in isolated farm ponds, the Monroe NAACP launched a campaign to desegregate the local tax-supported swimming pool in 1957. Not surprisingly, Ku Klux Klan terrorists blamed the affluent Dr. Perry for the resurgent black activism, and a large, heavily armed Klan motorcade attacked Dr. Perry's house one night that summer. Black veterans greeted the night riders with sandbag fortifications and a hail of disciplined gunfire. The Monroe Board of Aldermen immediately passed an ordinance banning Ku Klux Klan motorcades, a measure they had refused to consider prior to the gun battle.[25]

An even more vivid local drama dragged Monroe onto the stage of international politics on October 28, 1958. Two African American boys, "Fuzzy" Simpson and Hanover Thompson, ages eight and ten, met some white children in a vacant lot. A kissing game ensued in which the ten-year-old Thompson and an eight-year-old white girl named Sissy Sutton kissed one another.[26] Rarely in history has an incident so small opened a window so large into the life of a place and a people. The worldwide controversy that stemmed from the "Kissing Case" underlined the power of sexual questions in racial politics and demonstrated both the promise and the problems of Cold War politics for the African American freedom struggle.[27]

After the kissing incident, Sissy Sutton's mother reported that "I was furious. I would have killed Hanover myself if I had the chance." Sissy's father took a shotgun and went looking for the two boys. Neighbors reported that a white mob had roared up to the Thompson home and threatened not only to kill the boys but to lynch their mothers.[28] Later that afternoon, police officers spotted Hanover Thompson and Fuzzy Simpson pulling a red wagon loaded with soft drink bottles. "Both cops jumped out with their guns drawn," Thompson recalled. "They snatched us up and handcuffed us and threw in the car. When we got to the jail, they drug us out of the car and started beating us." The local juvenile court judge reported to Governor Luther H. Hodges that the police had detained the boys "for their own good, due to local feeling in the case."[29]

Authorities held the two boys for six days without permitting them to see parents, friends, or attorneys. Passing gunmen fired dozens of shots into the Thompson home. Klan terrorists torched crosses on the lawn. Hanover's sister found his dog shot dead in the yard.[30] For many white citizens, the case seemed to resonate with the sexual fears that accompanied their vision of where school desegregation would lead. "If [black children] get into our rural schools and ride the buses with our white children," one local woman wrote, "the Monroe 'kissing' incident is only a start of what we will have."[31] On November 4, Judge J. Hampton Price convened what he termed "separate but equal" hearings for the white parents and the black boys.[32] Denied the right to engage counsel or to confront their accusers, Hanover Thompson and Fuzzy Simpson were sentenced to Morrison Training School for Negroes. If they behaved well, Judge Price told the boys, it might be that they could be released before they were twenty-one.[33]

Robert Williams saw the "Kissing Case" as more than a local expression of the irrational sexual linchpin of white supremacy; the bizarre clarity of the case and the strange politics of the Cold War suggested a larger strategy. Like Martin Luther King Jr. and the Southern Christian Leadership Conference (SCLC) would do in Birmingham four years later, Williams and his friends in Monroe set out to use international politics of the Cold War as a fulcrum to push the United States government to intervene. Determined to make the "Kissing Case" a global metaphor for the American racial dilemma, they fired off press releases, pestered reporters, hounded the wire services, and put in motion what *Time* magazine called "a rolling snowball" of worldwide publicity.[34]

Williams addressed audiences at labor halls, liberal churches, and college auditoriums across the country. Soon the "Kissing Case" emblazoned front pages around the globe, forcing Governor Hodges to hire a team of professors from the University of North Carolina at Chapel Hill to translate the tens of thousands of letters that poured into his office.[35] John Shure, head of the United States Information Agency (USIA) at The Hague, reported that he himself had received more than twelve thousand letters "even though the response does not appear to have been organized."[36] While the White House and the State Department expressed alarm at the damage to U.S. foreign relations, Williams had a ready answer. "It is asinine for colored people to even think of sparing the U.S. State Department embarrassment abroad," he replied. "If the U.S. government is so concerned about its image abroad, then let it create a society that will stand up under world scrutiny."[37]

Governor Hodges soon launched a public relations campaign of his own to, as an aide urged the governor, "give the NAACP a taste of its own medicine . . . [and] place the whole Confederacy in your debt." The aide suggested to the governor that "by hitting directly at the communist connection, we might be able to convince people of the insincerity of these protests."[38] The Federal Bureau of Investigation informed Governor Hodges that "Robert Williams has been under investigation for a considerable period of time" and that "you would have access to this information if you desire."[39] The ensuing smear campaign asserted that the entire affair had been "a Communist-directed front," that the families of the boys were "shiftless and irresponsible," and that Hanover Thompson's mother had "a reputation for using her daughters in prostitution."[40] The USIA and the U.S. State Department broadcast these charges around the world, winning few minds and fewer hearts. Three and a half months after Hanover and Sissy had kissed each other, Governor Hodges announced under enormous political pressure that "the home conditions have improved to the extent that the boys can be given conditional release."[41]

The case furnished Williams not only with a network of seasoned activists in the American left but with a growing number of supporters among black nationalists in Harlem, including Malcolm X, minister at the Nation of Islam's Temple Number 7. "Every time I used to go to New York he would invite me to speak," Williams recalled. Malcolm would tell his congregation "that 'our brother is here from North Carolina, and he is the only fighting man that we have got, and we have got to help him so he can stay down there,'" Williams recounted.[42] Williams found ready support among other Harlem intellectuals and activists. "They all saw something in Monroe that did not actually exist—an immediately revolutionary situation," Harold Cruse observed.[43] Julian Mayfield, a Harlem writer and activist, later wrote an unpublished autobiography in which he disclosed that "a famous black writer made contact with gangsters in New Jersey and bought me two submachine guns which I took to Monroe." Williams was not the best-known black leader in the United States, but he may have been the best armed.[44]

The "Kissing Case" recruited new allies for Williams, but it launched him on a collision course with the NAACP hierarchy. Since the Scottsboro trials of the 1930s, the NAACP had steadfastly shunned so-called "sex cases" and political alliances that might leave the organization open to red-baiting.[45] Should the NAACP "ever get identified with communism," Kelly Alexander, head of the North Carolina Conference of Branches, told a reporter, "the Ku Klux Klan and the White Councils will pick up the charge that we are 'reds' and use it as a club to beat us to death."[46] Differences over strategy became bitter; Alexander complained to the national office that Williams "has completely turned his back on the one organization that is responsible for him being in the spotlight today," while Williams griped that Alexander "sounds more like a *Tom* than ever."[47] Roy Wilkins, executive secretary of the national organization, began to refer to Williams in private as "Lancelot of Monroe."[48]

Just as the "Kissing Case" headlines faded in the spring of 1959, two news stories from other parts of the South gripped black America. One was the lynching of Mack Charles Parker, accused of raping a white woman in Mississippi.[49] When Mississippi NAACP field secretary Medgar Evers heard that Parker had been dragged from his cell and murdered by a mob, he told his wife, "I'd like to get a gun and start shooting."[50] The other was the terrifying ordeal of four young black college students at Florida A&M. Their double date after a college dance was interrupted by four white men with guns and knives. The drunken assailants, who had vowed, as one of them testified in court later, "to go out and get some nigger pussy," forced the two eighteen-year-old black men to kneel at gunpoint while they undressed the two women and decided aloud which one they would kidnap and then gang-rape.[51] In the wake of these highly publicized outrages, NAACP Executive Secretary Roy Wilkins conceded in a letter marked "NOT FOR PUBLICATION" that "I know the thought of violence has been much in the minds of Negroes." By early May, Wilkins admitted, the NAACP found it "harder and harder to keep feelings from boiling over in some of our branches."[52]

Right on the heels of the Parker lynching and the terrors in Tallahassee, two pressing local matters brought Robert Williams and a crowd of black women to the Union County courthouse. B. F. Shaw, a white railroad engineer, was charged with attacking an African American maid at the Hotel Monroe. Slated for trial the same day, Lewis Medlin, a white mechanic, was accused of having beaten and sexually assaulted Mary Ruth Reid, a pregnant black woman, in the presence of her five children.[53] According to Williams, Reid's brothers and several of the black women of the Monroe NAACP had urged that the new machine guns be tried out on Medlin before his trial. "I told them that this matter would be handled through the law and the NAACP would help," Williams recalled, "[and] that we would be as bad as the white people if we resorted to violence."[54]

The proceedings against the two white men compelled Williams to reconsider his assessment. The judge dropped the charges against Shaw in spite of the fact that he failed even to appear for court.[55] During the brief trial of

Medlin, his attorney argued that he had been "drunk and having a little fun" at the time of the assault. Further, Medlin was married, his lawyer told the jury, "to a lovely white woman . . . the pure flower of life . . . do you think he would have left this pure flower for *that*?" He gestured toward Mary Ruth Reid, who began to cry uncontrollably. Lewis Medlin was acquitted in minutes. Robert Williams recalled that "the [black] women in the courtroom made such an outcry, the judge had to send Medlin out the rear door." The women then turned on Williams and bitterly shamed him for failing to see to their protection.[56]

At this burning moment of anger and humiliation, Williams turned to wire service reporters and declared that it was time to "meet violence with violence." Black citizens unable to enlist the support of the courts must defend themselves. "Since the federal government will not stop lynching, and since the so-called courts lynch our people legally," he declared, "if it's necessary to stop lynching with lynching, then we must resort to that method."[57] The next day, however, Williams disavowed the reference to lynching. "I do not mean that Negroes should go out and attempt to get revenge for mistreatments or injustice," he said, "but it is clear that there is no Fourteenth or Fifteenth Amendment nor court protection of Negroes' rights here, and Negroes have to defend themselves on the spot when they are attacked by whites."[58]

Banner headlines flagged these words as symbols of "a new militancy among young Negroes of the South." Enemies of the NAACP blamed this "bloodthirsty remark" squarely on the national office. "High officials of the organization may speak in cultivated accents and dress like Wall Street lawyers," Thomas Waring of the Charleston *News and Courier* charged, "but they are engaged in a revolutionary enterprise." That very morning, when he read the words "meet violence with violence" in a UPI dispatch, Roy Wilkins telephoned Robert Williams to inform him that he had been removed from his post as president of the Monroe NAACP.[59]

The fiftieth-anniversary convention of the NAACP that summer of 1959 became a highly public show trial whose central issue was whether the national organization would ratify Wilkins's suspension of Robert Williams. The national office printed up a pamphlet, "The Single Issue in the Robert Williams Case," and distributed it to all delegates.[60] As part of the coordinated effort to crush Williams, Thurgood Marshall visited the New York offices of the FBI on June 4, 1959, and urged agents to investigate Williams "in connection with [Marshall's] efforts to combat communist attempts to infiltrate the NAACP," an FBI memorandum stated.[61] Roy Wilkins twisted every available arm. Governor Nelson Rockefeller took the podium to congratulate the NAACP for "rejecting retaliation against terror" and "repulsing the threat of communism to invade your ranks."[62] Daisy Bates, the pistol-packing heroine of Little Rock, agreed to denounce Williams for advocating self-defense—after the national office consented to buy $600 a month in "advertising" from her newspaper.[63] "The national office not only controlled the platform," Louis Lomax wrote, but "they subjected the Williams forces to a heavy bombardment from the NAACP's big guns." Forty speakers, including Bates, King, Jackie Robinson, and dozens of distinguished lawyers, rose one after the other to denounce Williams. But when the burly ex-Marine from Monroe finally strode down the aisle to speak, he was neither intimidated nor penitent.[64]

"There is no Fourteenth Amendment in this social jungle called Dixie," Williams declared. "There is no equal protection under the law." He had been angry, they all knew; trials had beset him, but never had he intended to advocate acts of war. Surely no one believed that. But if the black men of Poplarville, Mississippi, had banded together to guard the jail the night that Mack Parker was lynched, he said, that would not have hurt the cause of justice. If the young black men who escorted the coed who was raped in Tallahassee had been able to defend her, Williams reminded them, such action would have been legal and justified "even if it meant that they themselves or the white rapists were killed." "Please," he beseeched the assembly, "I ask you not to come crawling to these whites on your hands and knees and make me a sacrificial lamb."[65]

And there the pleading stopped. Perhaps the spirit of his grandfather, Sikes Williams, the former slave who had fought for interracial democracy and wielded a rifle against white terrorists, rose up within him. Perhaps he heard within himself the voice of his grandmother, who had entrusted that rifle to young Robert. "We as men should stand up as men and protect our women and children," Williams declared. "I am a man and I will walk upright as a man should. *I will not crawl.*" In a controversy that the *Carolina Times* called "the biggest civil rights story of the year," the NAACP convention voted to uphold the suspension of Robert Williams.[66] The day after Daisy Bates had urged the assembly to censure Robert Williams for his vow to defend his home and family, she wired the attorney general of the United States to complain about dynamite attacks on her home in Little Rock: "We have been compelled to employ private guards," she said. Robert Williams wrote to Bates soon afterward: "I am sorry to hear that the white racists have decided to step up their campaign against you. It is obvious that if you are to remain in Little Rock you will have to resort to the method I was suspended for advocating."[67]

Against this backdrop of white lawlessness and political stalemate in 1959 and early 1960, Robert Williams moved to strengthen the local movement in Monroe and to reach out to a national audience. Though Williams underlined the fact that "both sides in the freedom movement are bi-racial," his emerging philosophy reinvigorated many elements of the black nationalist tradition whose forceful reemergence in the mid-1960s would become known as Black Power. His militant message was neither racially separatist nor rigidly ideological. Williams stressed black economic advancement, black pride, black culture, independent black political action, and what he referred to as "armed self-reliance." He connected the Southern freedom struggle with the anticolonialism of the emerging Third World, especially African nations. In the late 1950s, when other integrationists focused on lunch counters and voter registration, Williams insisted on addressing persistent black poverty: "We must consider that in Montgomery, where Negroes are riding in the front of buses," he said, "there are also Negroes who are starving." His approach was practical, eclectic, and improvisational. There must be "flexibility in the freedom struggle," he argued, and tactics must emerge from the confrontation itself. At the core of his appeal, however, stood his calls for absolute racial equality under a fully enforced U.S. Constitution, backed by an unyielding resistance to white supremacy.[68]

In pursuit of this uncompromising vision of interracial democracy, Robert Williams became an editor and publisher like his grandfather before him. Two weeks after the 1959 NAACP convention, FBI agents reported to J. Edgar Hoover that black children were "selling a newsletter known as *The Crusader* on the streets of Monroe."[69] Its title honored the late Cyril V. Briggs, Harlem organizer of the left-wing African Black Brotherhood, whose newspaper of the same name had issued a "Declaration of War on the Ku Klux Klan" in 1921.[70] *The Crusader*'s self-proclaimed mission was "advancing the cause of race pride and freedom." Soon sample mailings yielded several thousand subscribers across the country. Shortly after Williams began to spread his confrontational appeals in the *Crusader*, the first published biography of Martin Luther King Jr. appeared, written by a member of the SCLC's board of directors. The book was entitled *Crusader Without Violence*. Whether the title was intended as a direct rejoinder to Williams or not, it situated the book within a lively and important discussion.[71]

"The great debate in the integration movement in recent months," Anne Braden of the Southern Conference Educational Fund wrote in late 1959, "has been the question of violence vs. nonviolence as instruments of change."[72] Harry Boyte, soon to be Martin Luther King Jr.'s first white aide, observed that "the idea of striking back . . . meets a steady response among the downtrodden, grass roots of the southern Negro population." For several years, Boyte argued, Robert Williams "has succeeded in reaching these grass roots," exercising "great influence in Union County and beyond because of his militant position and refusal to submit to intimidation." Williams "poses a real threat to more peaceful and non-violent methods of solving our problems."[73] The FBI, too, remained uneasy about Williams's expanding range of contacts. Hoover's files, agents reported, "reflect numerous instances where groups in various sections of the country have proclaimed and demonstrated their sympathies with Williams and have sent him money."[74]

Not merely the FBI but also the most influential advocates of nonviolence felt compelled to deal with Robert Williams's growing reputation. In a widely reprinted debate first published in *Liberation* magazine, Williams faced Dr. Martin Luther King Jr. Again careful to endorse King's methods wherever they proved feasible, Williams advocated "armed self-reliance," explaining that among well-armed white vigilantes, "there is open defiance to law and order throughout the South today." Where law has broken down, he said, it was necessary and right to defend home and family. "Nonviolence is a very potent weapon when the opponent is civilized, but nonviolence is no repellent for a sadist," Williams noted. "Nowhere in the annals of history does the record show a people delivered from bondage by patience alone."

Dr. King conceded that white violence and white intransigence had brought the movement to "a stage of profound crisis." African Americans were frustrated, he said, and the "current calls for violence" reflected "a confused, anger-motivated drive to strike back violently." The Supreme Court's 1954 mandate and even the triumph at Montgomery had yielded small tokens, elaborate evasions, and widespread terror. Only three responses presented themselves. One could practice "pure nonviolence," King said, but this path "could not readily attract large masses, for it requires extraordinary discipline and courage." A position that encompassed legitimate self-defense was more practical. King pointed out that "all societies, from the most primitive to the most cultured and civilized, accept [self-defense] as moral and legal. The principle of self-defense, even involving weapons and bloodshed, has never been condemned, even by Gandhi." Here was where King the politician sensed his constituency. "When the Negro uses force in self-defense," King continued, "he does not forfeit support—he may even win it, by the courage and self-respect it reflects." This widely accepted position was, of course, precisely Williams's view— which was King's problem.

The third and most unacceptable position, King argued, was "the advocacy of violence as a tool of advancement, organized as in warfare, deliberately and consciously." Here, then, was the pale beyond which King sought to cast his adversary. "Mr. Robert Williams would have us believe that there is no collective or practical alternative," King insisted. "He argues that we must be cringing and submissive or take up arms." Essentially, Dr. King had invented his own Robert Williams, a kind of black Geronimo plotting military strikes against the white man, and then responded to *that* Robert Williams. Lacking theological training and combative in his manner, Williams made himself vulnerable to this caricature. But the philosophical position from which King centered his own argument—preferring nonviolence, but endorsing "the principle of self-defense, even involving weapons and bloodshed"—was precisely the place where Williams had taken his stand.[75] After the debate appeared in *Liberation* and began to resonate throughout the movement, W. E. B. Du Bois weighed in with a commentary, also entitled "Crusader Without Violence," in which he discouraged applause for King's critique of Robert Williams. In Montgomery, he wrote, King had "stood firm without surrender," but Du Bois considered it "a very grave question as to whether or not the slavery and degradation of Negroes in America has not been unnecessarily prolonged by the submission to evil."[76]

More than the persuasive skills of their elders, the bold actions of African American college students set these philosophical debates aside and gave the battalions of nonviolence their brief but compelling historical moment. On February 1, 1960, four students from North Carolina Agricultural and Technical College walked into Woolworth's in Greensboro, sat down at a segregated lunch counter, and asked to be served. Within two months, the sit-ins had spread to fifty-four communities across nine states of the old Confederacy, infusing the freedom movement with fresh troops and new tactics.[77] Only in 1960, when black students joined the movement in large numbers, did a truly broad-based movement to topple segregation become imaginable. Dr. King flew to Durham to encourage the students, but showed little inclination to lead a sit-in himself. On March 1, by contrast, Robert Williams followed a dozen black youths into Gamble's Drug Store in downtown Monroe and was the only person arrested. Marched down the street in handcuffs, a shotgun-toting guard on either side of him, Williams spoofed himself as "the dangerous stool-sitter bandit" and vowed that he had "never felt prouder in my life." Young insurgents in Monroe mounted an aggressive campaign of sit-ins that displayed its own unique style. "The Negroes remained in each store only a short time," the *Charlotte Observer* reported, "usually until management closed the counters." Under court orders to abide by the law or face imprisonment, Williams defied the judge and marched with his young troops. "We're using hit-and-run tactics," Williams told reporters. "They never know when we're coming or when we're going to leave. That way we hope to wear them down," he said, managing to sound like a platoon leader even while participating in a passive resistance campaign. "They were always doing something," the manager of Jones Drug Store recalled. "It's a wonder somebody didn't kill him." It was no mystery to Williams; the main difference between the sit-ins in Monroe and elsewhere was that "not a single demonstrator was even spat upon during our sit-ins," Williams claimed.[78]

The uneasy peace in Monroe would soon be broken, in large measure by followers of Dr. King. In 1961, the Reverend Paul Brooks of the SCLC and James Forman, soon to become president of the Student Nonviolent Coordinating Committee (SNCC), came to Monroe in the company of seventeen Freedom Riders fresh out of jail in Jackson, Mississippi. The young insurgents arrived in Monroe to launch a nonviolent campaign in Robert Williams's backyard, though Forman later denied any intention to undermine Williams. One of the Freedom Riders announced that he had come to Monroe because he considered "Mr. Robert F. Williams to be the most dangerous person in America." Another proclaimed: "If the fight for civil rights is to remain nonviolent, we must be successful in Monroe. What happens here will determine the course taken in many other communities throughout the South."[79]

Williams welcomed the Freedom Riders warmly but had a similar understanding of the stakes. "I saw it first as a challenge," he recalled, "but I also saw it as an opportunity to show that what King and them were preaching was bullshit."[80] Two weeks of picketing at the Union County Courthouse grew progressively more perilous for the Freedom Riders. Crowds of hostile white onlookers grew larger and larger. Finally, on Sunday afternoon, August 28, a mob of several thousand furious white people attacked the approximately thirty demonstrators, badly injuring many of them; local police arrested the bleeding protesters. In his classic memoir, *The Making of Black Revolutionaries*, James Forman later called this riot his "moment of death" and "a nightmare I shall never forget."[81] To the consternation of the SCLC, the nonviolent crusade swiftly deteriorated into mob violence; throughout the community, white vigilantes attacked black citizens and even fired fifteen shots into the home of former mayor J. Ray Shute, a white moderate who had befriended Williams.[82]

At the height of this violent chaos, a white married couple entered the black community for reasons that are unclear and drove straight into an angry black mob milling near Robert Williams's house. "There was hundreds of niggers there," the white woman stated, "and they were armed, they were ready for war." Black residents, under the impression that the demonstrators downtown were being beaten and perhaps slaughtered, threatened to kill the white couple. Williams, though busy preparing to defend his home, rescued the two whites from the mob and led them into his house, where they remained for about two hours. White authorities later charged Williams and several other people with kidnapping, although the white couple met two police officers on their way home and did not report their alleged abduction. The woman later conceded that "at the time, I wasn't even thinking about being kidnapped. . . . the papers, the publicity and all that stuff was what brought in that kidnapping mess."[83] During a long night of racial terror, Williams slung a machine gun over his shoulder and walked several miles with his wife and two small sons to where Julian Mayfield waited with a car. "I didn't want those racist dogs to have the satisfaction of legally lynching me," he explained to Dr. Perry.[84] The Williams family fled first to New York City, then Canada, then on to Cuba, to escape the hordes of FBI agents who combed the countryside in search of them. One of the agents assigned to search for Williams locally reported his frustrations to FBI Director J. Edgar Hoover: "Subject has become something of a 'John Brown' to Negroes around Monroe and they will do anything for him."[85]

The FBI dragnet never snared Williams, but it did not take Hoover long to hear from him. Every Friday night from 11 to midnight on Radio Havana, Williams hosted "Radio Free Dixie," a program that from 1961 to 1965 could be heard as far away as New York and Los Angeles.[86] During the early 1960s folk revival, Pete Seeger performed "Ballad of Monroe" all over the country—"Robert Williams was a leader, a giant of a man," the leftist troubadour sang.[87] From Cuba, Williams continued to edit the *Crusader* for a circulation that eventually grew to forty thousand copies.[88] In 1962, his book *Negroes with Guns*, published from Cuba, became the single most important intellectual influence on Huey P. Newton, soon to found the Black Panther Party in Oakland.[89] A play based on *Negroes with Guns*, Frank Greenwood's "If We Must Live," ran in Watts from July to December of 1965 to eager crowds and enthusiastic reviews.[90] Copies of the *Crusader* traveled down the Mississippi back roads with Student Nonviolent Coordinating Committee organizers: "this leaflet is being distributed by SNCC and COFO [Council of Federal Organizations] workers among U.S. Negroes," the Mississippi State Sovereignty Commission complained in the spring of 1964. Later that year, when SNCC began to veer away from nonviolence, members cited Williams approvingly in the fierce internal debates.[91]

As black activists began to reject even the tactical pretense of nonviolence, the influence of Robert Williams continued to spread. By the spring of 1962, "the example of the North Carolina militant," August Meier and Elliott Rudwick observe, had "had a profound effect" within the Congress of Racial Equality.[92] "Armed self-defense is a fact of life in black communities—north and south—despite the pronouncements of the 'leadership,'" a North Carolina activist wrote to Williams.[93] Long before the chants of "Black Power" that riveted national media attention in the late 1960s, most elements of that ambiguous slogan already were in place. "Your doctrine of self-defense set the stage for the acceptance of the Deacons For Defense and Justice," Lawrence Henry told Williams in the spring of 1966. "As quiet as it is being kept, the Black man is swinging away from King and adopting your tit-for-tat philosophy."[94]

Williams's influence was not limited to the South. "As I am certain you realize," Richard Gibson, editor of *Now!* magazine in New York wrote to Williams in 1965, "Malcolm's removal from the scene makes you the senior spokesman for Afro-American militants."[95] *Life* magazine reported in 1966 that Williams's "picture is prominently displayed in extremist haunts in the big city ghettos." Clayborne Carson names Williams as one of two central influences—the other being Malcolm X—on the 1966 formation of the Black Panther Party for Self-Defense in Oakland, "the most widely known black militant political organization of the late 1960s."[96] The Central Intelligence Agency exaggerated considerably in 1969 when it reported that Williams "has long been the ideological leader of the Black Panther Party." At that moment, Williams had already been named president-in-exile of two of the most influential revolutionary nationalist groups: the Revolutionary Action Movement, which the CIA believed to be "the most dangerous of all the Black Power organizations," and the Detroit-based Republic of New Africa, an influential group among nationalists with hundreds of members who sought to establish an independent black republic in Mississippi, Louisiana, Alabama, Georgia, and South Carolina.[97] "Despite his overseas activities," the CIA reported in 1969, "Williams has managed to become an outstanding figure, possibly *the* outstanding figure, in the black extremist movement in the United States."[98]

Even though he became friends with Che Guevara and Fidel Castro himself, Williams grew uneasy in Cuba: he yearned to return home. As the Soviet strings on the Cuban revolution shortened, Williams resisted pressure to make his own politics conform to the Soviet line. "I am under constant attack by the [United States Communist Party]," Williams wrote to a friend in the mid-1960s. "They are trying to cut off my facilities here in Cuba. One would think I am Hitler and Wall Street combined." An FBI informant as early as 1962 stated that Williams "has stubbed his toes" with Cuban Communists through his "criticism of [the] Communist Party for barring Negroes from leadership" and that he "may not be able to regain his footing." The Stalinists were "getting worse than the crackers in Monroe," Williams complained in 1964. "Things are about to the stage when I had to leave Monroe in a hurry."[99] Williams persuaded Castro to let him travel to North Vietnam in 1964, where he swapped Harlem stories with Ho Chi Minh and wrote antiwar propaganda aimed at African American soldiers.[100] In 1965, the Williams family relocated to Beijing, where Williams was "lionized and feted by top Peking leaders," according to CIA intelligence reports. The Williams family dined with Mao tse-Tung and moved in the highest circles of the Chinese government for three years.[101] Like the Black Power movement itself, as Williams got farther away from his roots in the South he sometimes drifted into apocalyptic nonsense; his 1967 essay, "The Potential of a Minority Revolution," for example, depicted a scenario in which black saboteurs and guerrilla enclaves could bring down the United States government.[102] Though Williams had been one of the best organizers in the black freedom movement, his isolation from any local constituency made him vulnerable to the same frustrations and delusions that plagued the rest of the movement in the last half of the 1960s.

In the late 1960s, when the Nixon administration moved toward opening diplomatic relations with China, Williams bartered his almost exclusive knowledge of the Chinese government for safe passage home and a Ford Foundation–sponsored post at the Center for Chinese Studies at the University of Michigan.[103] Not that the entire federal apparatus was happy to welcome him home: the Internal Security Division of the Department of Justice observed that "Williams could be the person to fill the role of national leader of the black extremists. We should offset attempts by him to assume such a position." Williams, however, wrote to a friend that "a lot of people are going to be surprised after my arrival not to find me fighting for leadership the way many others are doing."[104] Returning to family ties and local activism, Robert Williams spent the last twenty-seven years of his life in the small, trout-fishing village of Baldwin in western Michigan and died on October 15, 1996.

A week after his death, Rosa Parks climbed slowly into a church pulpit in Monroe, North Carolina. Beneath her lay the body of Robert F. Williams, clad in a gray suit given to him by Mao tse-Tung and draped with a black, red, and green Pan-African flag. Rosa Parks told the congregation that she and those who marched with Martin Luther King Jr. in Alabama had always admired Robert Williams "for his courage and his commitment to freedom. The work that he did should go down in history and never be forgotten."[105] Above the desk where Williams completed his memoirs just before his death, there still hangs an ancient rifle—a gift, he said, from his grandmother.

NOTES

1. Lillian Smith, "Foreword: A Letter to My Publisher," *Killers of the Dream* (1949; New York, 1961), 22. I am grateful to those who read drafts of this article or otherwise assisted in its preparation: David S. Cecelski, William H. Chafe, John Dittmer, Adam Fairclough, David Garrow, Raymond Gavins, Glenda Elizabeth Gilmore, Lawrence Goodwyn, Christina Greene, Herbert Hill, Gerald Horne, Stephen Kantrowitz, Danielle McGuire, Nellie McKay, Katherine Mellen, Perri Morgan, Syd Nathans, David Nord, Charles Payne, Richard Ralston, Robert Rubin, John Herd Thompson, Vernon C. Tyson, William L. Van Deburg, Craig Werner, Patrick Wilkinson, and Peter Wood.

2. Ernest B. Furguson, *Hard Right: The Rise of Jesse Helms* (New York, 1986), 30, 40.

3. Robert F. Williams, interview by Robert Carl Cohen, Dar es Salaam, Tanzania, 1968, transcript, 4–5, box 1, Robert Carl Cohen Papers, State Historical Society of Wisconsin, University of Wisconsin–Madison; *Crusader*, December 1967, 3; Timothy B. Tyson interview with Robert F. Williams, March 10, 1993, Baldwin, Michigan, audiotape, in possession of Timothy B. Tyson. See also Robert F. Williams, "While God Lay Sleeping: The Autobiography of Robert F. Williams," 1–4, unpublished typescript, in possession of Timothy B. Tyson. With respect to the "emasculated black men," the gender politics at work here is glaring and important, and central to the argument of my book *Radio Free Dixie: Robert F. Williams and the Roots of Black Power* (Chapel Hill, 1999). In the interest of presenting an abbreviated account of Williams's life, I have chosen to let this heavily gendered and sexualized language speak for itself in this context. I interpret it in some detail, however, in the work cited. I am grateful to the Williams family for sharing this manuscript and other family documents with me.

4. See Timothy B. Tyson, "Radio Free Dixie: Robert F. Williams and the Roots of Black Power" (PhD diss., Duke University, 1994); Marcellus C. Barksdale, "Robert F. Williams and the Indigenous Civil Rights Movement in Monroe, North Carolina, 1961," *Journal of Negro History* 69, no. 2 (Spring 1984): 73–89; Robert F. Williams, *Negroes with Guns*, ed. Marc Schlieffer (New York, 1962); and Williams, "While God Lay Sleeping."

5. Barksdale, "Robert F. Williams," 75; H. Nelson Walden, *History of Monroe and Union County* (Monroe, N.C., 1963), 15.

6. S. E. Williams, "Application Blank No. 15," original document in the possession of John Herman Williams, Detroit, Michigan. A photograph of the document is in the

possession of Timothy B. Tyson. I am grateful to Mr. Williams for sharing this and other family photographs and documents.

7. *Crusader*, July 18, 1959, 2; "History of Our Family Reunion," Williams Family Collection, Baldwin, Michigan; Williams transcript, box 1, 53, Cohen Papers. Due to a tragic fire, there are no known copies of *The People's Voice*, but its existence and politics are confirmed by both Williams family sources and by references to it in the local white newspaper. See *Monroe Enquirer-Journal*, "Monroe Historical Edition," September 1974, 4-B.

8. "To the Colored Voters of Union County," Black History File, The Heritage Room, Union County Courthouse, Monroe, N.C.

9. Glenda Elizabeth Gilmore, *Gender and Jim Crow: Women and the Politics of White Supremacy in North Carolina, 1896–1920* (Chapel Hill, 1996), 110–11. For Daniels's quotation, see J. Morgan Kousser, *The Shaping of Southern Politics: Suffrage Restriction and the Establishment of the One-Party South* (New Haven, 1974), 76. For the white supremacy campaigns of 1898 in North Carolina, see Helen G. Edmonds, *The Negro and Fusion Politics in North Carolina, 1894–1901* (Chapel Hill, 1951); Gilmore, *Gender and Jim Crow*; Eric Anderson, *Race and Politics in North Carolina, 1872–1901: The Black Second* (Baton Rouge, 1981); H. Leon Prather, *"We Have Taken A City": The Wilmington Racial Massacre and Coup of 1898* (Rutherford, N.J., 1984).

10. Robert Williams, "Someday I'm Going Back South," *Daily Worker* (Detroit edition), April 9, 1949, 7.

11. *Crusader*, July 18, 1959, 2; "The History of Our Family Reunion," Williams Family Collection; Timothy B. Tyson interview with Robert F. Williams, September 2, 1996, Baldwin, Michigan, audiotape in the possession of Timothy B. Tyson. The crucial role played by Ellen Williams, born a slave, in the ongoing political life of her family underscores the connection that Glenda Elizabeth Gilmore has drawn between African American women's activism during the late nineteenth and early twentieth centuries and the emerging African American freedom movement of the 1950s and 1960s. See Gilmore, *Gender and Jim Crow*, 224.

12. Williams transcript, box 1, 44, Cohen Papers. For a full account of what happened at Belle Isle that evening, see Robert Shogun and Tom Craig, *The Detroit Race Riot: A Study in Violence* (New York, 1976), 34–35. See also Dominic Capeci and Martha Wilkerson, *Layered Violence: The Detroit Rioters of 1943* (Jackson, MS, 1991).

13. Union County, North Carolina, Record of Military Discharges, vol. 7, 99, Monroe Public Library; John Dittmer, *Local People* (Urbana: University of Illinois Press, 1994), 1–9.

14. *Monroe Enquirer*, June 31, 1946, 1, and March 31, 1947, 1. See also Marcellus C. Barksdale, "The Indigenous Civil Rights Movement and Cultural Change in North Carolina, 1945–1965: Weldon, Chapel Hill, and Monroe" (PhD diss., Duke University, 1977), 42–43.

15. J. W. McDow interview with Timothy B. Tyson, September 17, 1993, Monroe, N.C., audiotape in the possession of Timothy B. Tyson; Woodrow Wilson interview with Marcellus Chandler Barksdale, box 9, Duke Oral History Collection, Perkins Library, Duke University, audiotape; B. J. Winfield interview with Marcellus Chandler Barksdale, box 9, Duke Oral History Collection, audiotape; transcript of the Robert F. Williams interview with James Mosby, 1970, Ralph Bunche Oral History Collection, Moorland-Spingarn Research Center, Howard University.

16. Williams, "Someday I'm Going Back South," 7; Robert F. Williams, "N. Carolina College Youth Calls for a Militant Generation," *Freedom* 11, no. 6 (June 1952): 5;

United States Senate, Committee on the Judiciary, *Testimony of Robert F. Williams: Hearings Before the Commmittee to Investigate the Administration of the Internal Security Act and Other Internal Security Laws of the Committee on the Judiciary*, Ninety-first Congress, Second Session, part 1, March 25, 1970, Exhibit No. 43, 211–12 (Washington, D.C., 1971); Williams transcript, box 1, 207, Cohen Papers.

17. U.S. Naval Intelligence, San Diego, Calif., Investigation Report, "21 Jan–28 Apr 1955 Intermittently," Robert F. Williams Federal Bureau of Investigation Subject File. I am grateful to the Williams family for sharing the complete file; parts of it are available in the Robert F. Williams Papers, Bentley Historical Library, University of Michigan, Ann Arbor. See also *Southern Patriot* 18, no. 11 (January 1960): 3; Williams's quotation is from Vincent Harding, introduction to "Awakenings, 1954–1956," in Clayborne Carson et al., eds., *The Eyes on the Prize Reader* (New York, 1991), 36.

18. Robert F. Williams, "Colonel Jim Crow's Last Stand: A Sermon Delivered at All Soul's Chapel Unitarian Fellowship, Monroe, North Carolina," March 25, 1956, 1–2, box 3, Williams Papers.

19. (Charleston) *News and Courier*, September 21, 1956, 1-B, reports attendance at a Union, South Carolina, rally at 12,000 to 15,000. *Monroe Enquirer*, March 17, 1958, 1, reported that in 1957 "cross-burnings and [Ku Klux Klan] meetings here attracted thousands."

20. *Southern Patriot* 15, no. 1 (January 1957): 1.

21. Williams interview with Mosby.

22. Robert F. Williams to the NAACP, March 11, 1957, box A333, National Association for the Advancement of Colored People (NAACP) Papers, Library of Congress, Washington, D.C.; Williams, *Negroes with Guns*, 50–51; McDow interview with Tyson; Winfield interview with Barksdale; Wilson interview with Barksdale; Williams interview with Tyson; Williams interview with Mosby. Membership reports indicate that the branch grew from 92 to 121 members in 1959, but Williams claimed and the records of the national office confirm that the Monroe branch declined to record many memberships "for the purpose of protecting those who join the NAACP who do not want their names known." See "Total Membership Received From Branches in North Carolina, January 1–October 1, 1959," box C113, NAACP Papers.

23. Julian Mayfield, "Challenge to Negro Leadership: The Case of Robert Williams," *Commentary* (April 1961): 298.

24. Williams, *Negroes with Guns*, 51.

25. "Citizens Fire Back at Klan," (Norfolk, Va.) *Journal and Guide*, October 12, 1957, 1; "Is North Carolina NAACP Leader a Marked Man?" *Jet*, October 31, 1957, 10–11; "Parades, Cavalcades, and Caravans" ordinance, in *Code of the City of Monroe* (Monroe, N.C., 1957), 473–75, North Carolina Collection, Louis Round Wilson Library, University of North Carolina at Chapel Hill.

26. Kelly Alexander to Roy Wilkins, "A Report of Activities of the North Carolina State Conference of Branches in Reference to the Case of David Simpson and James H. Thompson of Monroe, North Carolina," December 26, 1958, box 333A, NAACP Papers.

27. See Patrick Jones, "'Communist Front Shouts Kissing Case to the World': The Committee to Combat Racial Injustice and the Politics of Race and Gender during the Cold War" (master's thesis, University of Wisconsin–Madison, 1996).

28. George Weissman, "The Kissing Case," *Nation*, January 17, 1959, 47.

29. Gloster B. Current to Roy Wilkins, December 23, 1958, box A92, NAACP Papers. See also *Charlotte Observer*, January 12, 1959, 2-A; *Carolina Times*, January 10,

1959, 1; *Monroe Enquirer*, November 20, 1958, 1. See also James Hanover Thompson interview with Timothy B. Tyson, May 13, 1993, Durham, N.C., audiotape in possession of Timothy B. Tyson; J. Hampton Price to Luther H. Hodges, November 26, 1958, box 423, Governor Luther H. Hodges Papers, North Carolina Division of Archives and History, Raleigh, N.C.

30. Thompson interview with Tyson. See also "Attorney Bares Real Inside Story of North Carolina Kissing Case," *Chicago Defender*, January 17, 1959, 3.

31. Mrs. W. W. Rogers, letter to the editor of the *Charlotte Observer*, February 2, 1959, 2-B.

32. Chester Davis, "Press in North Gives Distorted Versions," (Winston-Salem) *Journal and Sentinel*, February 8, 1958, 1.

33. Writ of Habeas Corpus and Petition, Superior Court, Mecklenberg County, North Carolina, January 6, 1959, Laura Mola Papers, in possession of Timothy B. Tyson. See also "Transcript of Statements Made by Attorney Conrad Lynn During Interview on the 'Frank Ford Show,' Radio Station WPEN, Philadelphia, Pennsylvania on June 20, 1959, from 12:40 until 1:35 AM," box A92, NAACP Papers.

34. This strategy first emerged neither in Monroe nor in Birmingham, but appeared the moment that the Cold War did. "It is not Russia that threatens the United States so much as Mississippi," the NAACP declared in a 1947 petition to the United Nations, "not Stalin and Molotov but Bilbo and Rankin." See Mary Dudziak, "Desegregation as a Cold War Imperative," *Stanford Law Review* 41 (November 1988): 95 and n. 201. In Birmingham, Martin Luther King Jr. explained his strategic vision: "The United States is concerned about its image. Mr. Kennedy is battling for the minds and the hearts of men in Asia and in Africa, and they aren't gonna respect the United States of America if she deprives men and women of the basic rights of life because of the color of their skin." See Taylor Branch, *Parting the Waters: America in the King Years, 1954–1963* (New York: Simon and Schuster, 1988), 791. The *Time* story, which appeared in the international edition of the magazine, was reprinted in full in the *Monroe Enquirer*, February 9, 1959, 1.

35. Robert E. Giles to University of North Carolina President William C. Friday, February 6, 1959, box 423, Hodges Papers.

36. Shure's comments are excerpted in a letter from Representative Basil L. Whitener to Luther H. Hodges, March 2, 1959, box 423, Hodges Papers.

37. Williams recounted these remarks in *Crusader*, August 1962, 4.

38. John Briggs to Bill Sharpe, cc to Luther H. Hodges, February 23, 1959, box 423, Hodges Papers; Sharpe to Hodges, February 12, 1959, box 423, Hodges Papers; Hodges to Sharpe, February 19, 1959, box 423, Hodges Papers.

39. O. L. Richardson to Hodges, n.d., box 423, Hodges Papers.

40. Chester Davis, "Communist Front Shouts 'Kissing Case' to the World," (Winston-Salem) *Journal and Sentinel*, February 8, 1959, 1.

41. *Monroe Enquirer*, February 16, 1959, 1.

42. Williams, transcript, box 1, 382–83, Cohen Papers. The Federal Bureau of Investigation found the alliance alarming; director J. Edgar Hoover warned his Charlotte, North Carolina, office about Williams's "recent activities in connection with the Nation of Islam at New York" and ordered that a file be opened with respect to the Nation of Islam and Williams. See Director to Charlotte SAC, June 18, 1959, Robert F. Williams Subject File.

43. Harold Cruse, *The Crisis of the Negro Intellectual* (New York: New York Review of Books, 2005), 358–59.

44. Julian Mayfield, "Tales from the Lido," unpublished autobiography draft, Julian Mayfield Papers, Schomberg Center for the Study of Black Culture, New York Public Library. I am grateful to Kevin Gaines for sharing these materials. Though it is merely speculation, Amiri Baraka (then Leroi Jones) is a "famous black writer" who admired Williams greatly and in 1959–1960 not only had "rejected Martin Luther King's philosophy" but had written "A Poem Some People Will Have to Understand," the last line of which is "Will the machinegunners step forward?" See Amiri Baraka, *The Autobiography of Leroi Jones* (Chicago, 1997), 237.

45. Dan T. Carter, *Scottsboro: A Tragedy of the American South* (Baton Rouge, 1969). See also James Goodman, *Stories of Scottsboro* (New York, 1994).

46. Davis, "Communist Front," 1.

47. Kelly M. Alexander to Roy Wilkins, "A Report of Activities of the N.C. Conference of Branches in Reference to the Case of David Simpson and James Thompson of Monroe, N.C.," box A333, NAACP Papers; Robert F. Williams to George Weissman, December 17, 1958, box 1, Committee to Combat Racial Injustice Papers, State Historical Society of Wisconsin, University of Wisconsin, Madison.

48. Roy Wilkins to P. L. Prattis, "Personal, Not for Publication," May 28, 1959, 1, box A333, NAACP Papers.

49. Howard Smead, *Blood Justice: The Lynching of Mack Charles Parker* (New York, 1986).

50. Mrs. Medgar Evers with William Peters, *For Us, the Living* (New York, 1970), 194.

51. Roy Wilkins, "Report of the Secretary to the Board of Directors for the Month of April 1959," box A333, NAACP Papers. See also *Washington Post*, May 3, 1959, 4; (Durham) *Carolina Times*, May 23, 1959, 1; *New York Times*, May 7, 1959, 22; *Pittsburgh Courier*, June 20, 1959, 3; *Charlotte Observer*, May 3, 1959, 1.

52. Wilkins to Prattis, "Personal, Not for Publication"; Roy Wilkins, *Standing Fast: The Autobiography of Roy Wilkins* (New York, 1982), 265.

53. *Monroe Enquirer*, January 26, 1959, 1; *Monroe Enquirer*, March 9, 1959, 1; *New York Post*, January 27, 1959, 4; *New York Post*, May 7, 1959, 1; *New York Post*, November 11, 1959, 1; *Crusader*, April 1963, 4; *Carolina Times*, February 7, 1959, 2; *Carolina Times*, January 31, 1959, 1.

54. Williams interview with Mosby.

55. *Southern Patriot* 18, no. 11 (January 1960): 3.

56. *Monroe Enquirer*, May 7, 1959, 1; Jones, "'Communist Front Shouts Kissing Case to the World,'" 127; Williams interview with Mosby.

57. "Rec'd via phone from UPI—May 6, 1959," box A333, NAACP Papers. See also "N.A.A.C.P. Leader Urges Violence," *New York Times*, May 7, 1959, 22.

58. "Roy Wilkins, Executive Secretary, Complainant, Against Robert F. Williams, Respondent, Brief for Respondent," 1–2, box A333, NAACP Papers.

59. "N.A.A.C.P. Leader Urges Violence," *New York Times*, May 7, 1959, 22; "Negro Calls for Lynch of Whites," (Jackson, Miss.) *State-Times*, 1; (Charleston, S.C.) *News and Courier*, May 7, 1959, 1; telegram from Roy Wilkins to Robert Williams, May 6, 1959, box A333, NAACP Papers.

60. "The Single Issue in the Robert Williams Case," box 2, Committee to Combat Racial Injustice Papers.

61. Telegram from SAC, New York, to Director, June 5, 1959, Thurgood Marshall Federal Bureau of Investigation Subject File. My thanks to Alex Charns for sharing these documents obtained under the Freedom of Information Act.

62. *New York Times*, July 14, 1959, 1.

63. Daisy Bates to Roy Wilkins, July 23, 1959, box 1, Bates Papers, State Historical Society of Wisconsin, University of Wisconsin, Madison.

64. Louis Lomax, *The Negro Revolt* (New York, 1962), 112–14.

65. *Crusader*, July 25, 1959, 1.

66. *Pittsburgh Courier*, July 25, 1959, 1; *Crusader*, July 25, 1959, 1. "Year in Review," *Carolina Times*, January 5, 1960, 1. With respect to the obvious gender politics at work here, see note 3 above.

67. Daisy Bates, *The Long Shadow of Little Rock: A Memoir* (New York, 1962), 162; Robert F. Williams to Daisy Bates, August 19, 1959, box 2, Bates Papers.

68. Andrew Myers, "When Violence Met Violence: Facts and Images of Robert F. Williams and the Black Freedom Struggle in Monroe, North Carolina" (MA thesis, University of Virginia, 1993), 44–45; Williams, *Negroes with Guns*, 40. Cruse, *The Crisis of the Negro Intellectual*, 358–59 and 382–401, attacks Williams for being insufficiently ideological. Without examining Williams's political activism in any detail, Cruse dismisses him as merely an integrationist with a gun whose idea of revolution would be unacceptable to any American Marxist. Given the political achievements of Marxist theorists in the interim, this seems more a strength than a weakness. It is time to reconsider the kind of provisional and eclectic homegrown radicalism that black Southerners developed in the late 1950s and early 1960s. For a succinct and persuasive analysis in this vein, see Clayborne Carson, "Rethinking African-American Political Thought in the Post-Revolutionary Era," in Brian Ward and Tony Badger, eds., *The Making of Martin Luther King and the Civil Rights Movement* (New York, 1997), 115–27. For a well-documented and compelling historical account that points to some of the same conclusions, see Charles Payne, *I've Got the Light of Freedom* (Berkeley: University of California Press, 1995).

69. "From Charlotte SAC to Director," July 31, 1959, Robert F. Williams Federal Bureau of Investigation Subject File.

70. It is not surprising that Briggs appealed to the firebrand from Monroe: "With the murderer clutching at our throats," Briggs wrote in the hooded order's heyday, "we can ill afford to choose our weapons but must defend ourselves with what lies nearest, be it poison, fire, or what." See Cyril V. Briggs, "Declaration of War on the Ku Klux Klan," *Crusader*, January 1921, quoted in Shapiro, *White Violence and Black Response*, 208–9 and 495n. Williams told historian Robert A. Hill that "many years ago I heard of Cyril V. Briggs and his *Crusader*" and that he had adopted the name in honor of Briggs. See Cyril Briggs, *The Crusader, Cyril V. Briggs, Editor*, ed. Robert A. Hill (New York, 1987), xlviii.

71. L. D. Reddick, *Crusader Without Violence: A Biography of Martin Luther King, Jr.* (New York, 1959).

72. *Southern Patriot* 18, no. 11 (January 1960): 3.

73. Harry Boyte, "Education and the Unfinished Business of Democracy," draft, n.d., Box 26, Boyte Family Papers.

74. Groups cited include chapters of the NAACP and the Congress of Racial Equality, the Nation of Islam, and the Fair Play for Cuba Committee. See "Director to Charlotte SAC," September 18, 1961, Robert F. Williams Federal Bureau of Investigation Subject File.

75. *Liberation*, September 1959; *Liberation*, October 1959. Williams and King appear side by side in *Southern Patriot* 18, no. 11 (January 1960): 3, with an excellent

commentary by Anne Braden. Abbreviated versions may be found in Carson et al., eds., *The Eyes on the Prize Reader*, 110–13.

76. W. E. B. Du Bois, "Crusader Without Violence," *National Guardian*, November 9, 1959.

77. William Chafe, *Civilities and Civil Rights: Greensboro, North Carolina and the Black Struggle for Freedom* (Oxford, New York: Oxford Univeristy Press, 1981), 71–72. This account remains the definitive work on the sit-ins and one of the best local studies of the freedom movement.

78. Criminal Record #75CR9796, March 11, 1960, Union County Courthouse, Monroe, N.C.; *Charlotte Observer*, March 9, 1960, 1, and March 22, 1960, 7-A; *Crusader*, May 14, 1960, 1–2; W. R. May telephone interview with Timothy B. Tyson, May 26, 1994, Monroe, N.C.; Williams, *Negroes with Guns*, 68.

79. *Crusader*, August 21, 1961, 3; James Forman telephone interview with Timothy B. Tyson, January 17, 1997, audiotape in possession of Timothy B. Tyson. "We have been friends with Mr. Williams," Joseph McDonald, a Freedom Rider from New York, told reporters, "but we have no real connection with him, because he believes in the defensive violence technique. That is to say, he would defend his home." See *News and Observer*, August 29, 1961, 1.

80. Williams interview with Mosby.

81. James Forman, *The Making of Black Revolutionaries* (1972; Seattle, 1997), 193–98.

82. Harry G. Boyte to Truman Nelson, August 23, 1962, box 26, Boyte Family Papers.

83. Mabel Stegall interview with Algernon Watt, c. 1962, audiotape in possession of Timothy B. Tyson. In this and other interviews with the press in 1961, Stegall confirmed that Williams had tried to prevent them from being hurt and that he had done nothing to detain them. See *Monroe Enquirer*, August 31, 1961, 1; *News and Observer*, August 29, 1961, 1. State investigative records generally confirm Williams's accounts of these events. See Walter Anderson, State Bureau of Investigation, to Hugh Cannon, Office of the Governor, September 14, 1961, Box 111, Governor Terry Sanford Papers, North Carolina Division of Archives and History, Raleigh, N.C. The national office of the NAACP conducted its own investigation, and John Morsell, no admirer of Williams, wrote that "we believe . . . that the charges of kidnapping against the so-called Monroe defendants are probably without genuine substance. . . . the charge of Kidnapping was leveled vindictively." John Morsell to Clore Warne, March 15, 1963, box A279, NAACP Papers. "In my own mind," the SCLC's Harry Boyte wrote, "I have no doubt that Robert Willams and any of the others who have been charged are innocent of kidnapping." See Harry Boyte to Truman Nelson, August 23, 1962, box 26, Boyte Family Papers. The charges were later dropped.

84. Robert F. Williams to "Doc," n.d., box 1, Williams Papers. The escape from Monroe has been shrouded in mystery for decades. Some black residents of Monroe still maintain that Fidel Castro sent helicopters for him. Others tell of how he escaped in a hearse owned by a black funeral director from Charlotte. Williams himself was reluctant to speak on this point, explaining that he had pledged to protect the many people who had helped his family. Before he died, however, he confirmed the larger outlines of this story for me in an untaped interview on September 2, 1996. Julian Mayfield, undoubtedly one of the persons whom Williams had protected by his secrecy, tells the story in some detail in his unpublished memoir, "Tales from the Lido," Julian Mayfield Papers.

85. Teletype, Charlotte SAC to Director, August 30, 1961, Robert F. Williams Federal Bureau of Investigation Subject File.

86. Williams transcript, box 1, 622–23, Cohen Papers. An FBI report states that "Radio Free Dixie" had "a very strong signal which can be heard very clearly throughout the southern states." Charlotte SAC to Director, June 6, 1963, 7, Robert F. Williams Federal Bureau of Investigation Subject File. An activist in Watts, Los Angeles, wrote to Willliams in 1962 that "I am letting my other nationalist friends make copies [of the tapes] and telling each of them to let someone make a copy of theirs." See Robert Perkins to Robert F. Williams, December 15, 1962, box 1, Williams Papers; Kay Greaves, KPFA Radio, to Robert F. Williams, August 19, 1963, Williams Papers. The Williams Papers hold hundreds of letters from listeners, many of them in Los Angeles and some as far away as the state of Washington, and taped copies of the broadcasts.

87. "Bill" to Robert F. Williams, April 29, 1962, box 1, Williams Papers; Gary Green to Robert F. Williams, n.d., Williams Papers. "Bill" writes: "Pete Seeger has composed a 'Ballad of Monroe'—very good. He played it tonight at a reception prior to the benefit concert."

88. U.S. Senate, *Testimony of Robert F. Williams*, Part 1, February 16, 1970, 39. Williams explains that the *Crusader*, which began as a newsletter mailed from Monroe, was shipped in bulk to Canada, packed in bundles, and shipped out from Vancouver, Toronto, and Montreal and sometimes from Mexico. See Williams transcript, box 1, 623–24, Cohen Papers. Extensive correspondence concerning the day-to-day logistics of the distribution may be found in the Williams Papers.

89. David Horowitz, *Destructive Generation: Second Thoughts about the Sixties* (New York: Summit, 1989), 146. Horowitz, a bitter and vituperative critic of Newton, describes Williams's book as the single most important intellectual influence on Newton. Hugh Pearson, a critic who shows far more sympathy, confirms in *Shadow of the Panther* (Reading, Mass.: Addison-Wesley, 1994), 28, that *Negroes with Guns* "fascinate[d]" Newton. Gilbert Moore, an uncritical admirer of Newton, traces the Black Panther leader's political awareness to his discovery of Robert Williams. See Gilbert Moore, *A Special Rage* (New York, 1971), 4.

90. Anne Leslie, "Exciting in Form, Ugly in Content," (Los Angeles) *People's World*, July 3, 1965, 3. "LIVE is only running out of bookings now," author Frank Greenwood wrote to Robert Williams six months after the review. "We appeared in Watts and really shook up and inspired the brothers out there. . . . The reception was something else, Bob. My folks are ready, man! And particularly the young ones. . . . We did a free show for Watts and Venice teenagers at the center and afterwards they got up en masse and applauded!" See Frank Greenwood to Robert F. Williams, December 1, 1965, box 1, Williams Papers. The *Crusader* was popular in Watts, though it is absurd to blame Williams for the Watts riot as many right-wing observers did. Gerald Horne, *Fire This Time: The Watts Uprising and the 1960s* (Charlottesville, VA, 1995), 265, 268.

91. The observation is attached to a copy of the *Crusader* found in box 135, Johnson Family Papers, University of Southern Mississippi Manuscript Collections, Hattiesburg, Mississippi. My thanks to Elizabeth A. Corris for locating these materials for me. According to an FBI report, "five Negro employees of the Student Non-violent Coordinating Committee were arrested for speeding" in Columbus, Mississippi, on June 8, 1964, and "charged with possession of Communist literature, due to their possession of 'The Crusader,' which was published in Cuba by Robert Williams." See "Supplemental Correlation Summary," April 19, 1969, Robert F. Williams Federal Bureau of Investigation Subject File. For transcripts of SNCC deliberations in which Williams was cited, see Danny Lyons, *Memories of the Southern Civil Rights Movement* (Chapel Hill, 1992), 147.

92. August Meier and Elliott Rudwick, *CORE: A Study in the Civil Rights Movement, 1942–1968* (Urbana, Ill., 1975), 202–4.

93. Clyde Appleton to Robert F. Williams, September 20, 1965, box 1, Williams Papers.

94. Slater King to Robert F. Williams, November 10, 1963, box 1, Williams Papers; Lawrence Henry to Robert F. Williams, March 31, 1966, Williams Papers.

95. Richard Gibson to Robert F. Williams, March 5, 1965, box 1, Williams Papers.

96. Russell Sackett, "Plotting a War on Whitey," *Life*, June 10, 1966, 100; Clayborne Carson, "The Black Panther Party," in Mari J. Buhle et al., *Encyclopedia of the American Left* (New York: Garland Publishers, 1990), 96.

97. Central Intelligence Agency Report, "Revolutionary Action Movement," August 8, 1968, Robert F. Williams Federal Bureau of Investigation Subject File; William L. Van Deburg, *New Day in Babylon* (Chicago: University of Chicago Press, 1992), 144–49.

98. This claim is probably an exaggeration, though its degree of validity reflects not only Williams's appeal among increasing radical black youth but also, as the report noted, "the apparent diminution in the leadership of Stokely Carmichael, H. Rap Brown, Eldridge Cleaver, and other black leaders; one wonders if Williams is about to claim the center of the Black Power stage." See Central Intelligence Agency Report, "Robert Franklin Williams," August 28, 1969, 2, Robert F. Williams Federal Bureau of Investigation Subject File.

99. Memorandum from A. B. Eddy to Mr. Evans, May 14, 1962, Robert F. Williams Federal Bureau of Investigation Subject File; Robert F. Williams to "Harry," n.d., box 1, Williams Papers; Robert F. Williams to Julian Mayfield, n.d., c. 1964, Williams Papers.

100. Sidney Rittenberg to Timothy B. Tyson, "Recollections of Robert Williams," May 4, 1997, typescript in possession of Timothy B. Tyson. See also Williams transcript, box 1, 312, Cohen Papers. Copies of a printed and illustrated version of Williams's broadcasts to African American soldiers, "Listen, Brother," may be found in the Williams Papers. Questions have been raised about the veracity of Ho Chi Minh's stories of his connection to Harlem and the Garvey movement, and I have no evidence to add here except that the North Vietnamese leader retold these stories to Williams.

101. Rittenberg to Tyson, "Recollections of Robert Williams," 3.

102. *Crusader*, September–October 1967, 1.

103. Rittenberg, "Recollection of Robert Williams," 3. See also Williams, "While God Lay Sleeping," 237–319.

104. Department of Justice Memorandum, J. Walter Yeagley, Assistant Attorney General, Internal Security Division, to Will R. Wilson, Assistant Attorney General, Criminal Division, August 8, 1969, Robert F. Williams Federal Bureau of Investigation Subject File. See also Myers, "When Violence Met Violence," 73–74; Robert F. Williams to Robert Carl Cohen, April 26, 1969, box 1, Cohen Papers.

105. Mrs. Rosa Parks, eulogy for Robert Williams, November 22, 1996, Central Methodist Church, Monroe, N.C., written notes of Timothy B. Tyson; videotape in Williams Family Collection.

V

&

THE BORNING MOVEMENT

13

ઉ

Judith Brown:
Freedom Fighter

Carol Giardina

The resurgence of the women's liberation movement in the 1960s from the black freedom struggle is shown through the life of one activist, women's liberation founder Judith Benninger Brown. Brown's first movement experiences were in the fight for black civil rights in the Black Belt South. In that struggle, she lived on a cutting edge of gender democracy far exceeding that in the mainstream society. The militancy of Patricia Stephens Due and Bettie Wright, the two black civil rights leaders whose leadership she followed, was instrumental in Brown's development as a feminist. So was the knowledge of the very real possibilities of changing the world because everyday people would and could organize and stand up for their rights against great odds and at the risk of their lives. These newly learned lessons, not a reaction to male chauvinism or a flight from it, impelled and emboldened Brown to organize for women's freedom.

The continuity of Brown's activism with suffragists and other progressives is traced through her family from the turn of the century through the 1950s. A tradition of struggle passed on in activist families, was, in addition to the civil rights movement, a central influence in the start of the women's liberation movement.

My first two movement experiences were in militant civil rights groups led by black women. . . . I was used to seeing a woman lead, be outspoken, take risks, confront men on male supremacy and confront white people on racism. I worked with Patricia [Stephens Due] for a year. . . . she had taught me a very high degree of militancy. . . . this was my best model.[1]

In 1963 most of Florida was segregated—hospitals, schools, libraries, restaurants, other public accommodations, and just about everything else. Whether by law or by custom, segregation was backed up with violence and with the threat of violence. Whites could expect passing blacks to look away and to walk off the sidewalk into the street, and many did. North Florida, a sparsely populated land of tobacco plantations, pecan groves, turpentine camps, and lumber and pulpwood industries, was sharply divided between the small, wealthy, landholding elite and those who worked for them for far below minimum wage because Florida agribusiness was exempt from federal labor law. By Northern standards, the middle class was almost nonexistent. Confederate flags flew in courthouse squares, public schools were named for Ku Klux Klan founders and Confederate generals, audiences rose to sing "Dixie" at public events, and billboards reading "Impeach Earl Warren" (then chief justice of the Supreme Court) dotted the highways. Even in South Florida, which was more developed, some towns enforced curfews against blacks on the street after sundown.

Indeed, although blurred in the Northern mind with Miami, most of Florida was no less racist than its Deep South neighbors. Declaring it a "great mistake," the Florida Supreme Court had voted down the Supreme Court's *Brown v. Board of Education* ruling.[2] Eight of Florida's ten congressmen signed the Southern Manifesto pledging massive resistance to the *Brown* ruling. Public schools remained segregated. Signed oaths supporting "the race segregation laws of this state" were required of public employees.[3] Representing only a small fraction of the state's electorate, a handful of diehard segregationist rural lawmakers known as the "Pork Chop Gang" controlled the state legislature.

Discrimination against Florida's female citizens was, of course, different from racial discrimination. Still, like their sisters across the nation, women in Florida faced arbitrary and undemocratic treatment by accident of birth. Newspaper advertisements for "help wanted" were segregated by sex as well as by race. To purchase on credit, even a wage-earning woman had to document her husband's permission. State universities subjected women to curfews and dress codes. Abortion was illegal, birth control was hard to come by, and a woman earned fifty-nine cents to a man's dollar. Florida had not supported the Nineteenth Amendment for women's suffrage and, indeed, failed to ratify it until 1969. The state continued to oppose women's rights by withholding support for the Equal Rights Amendment (ERA).

Judith Benninger Brown (1941–1991) was a leading figure of the Southern civil rights struggle and an internationally recognized pioneer of the worldwide feminist revival, from the 1960s until 1991. Contemporaries credited "Toward a Female Liberation Movement," the paper that she coauthored with Beverly Jones in 1968, with starting the women's liberation movement.[4] She put her life in the movement against white supremacy and found there the courage and consciousness to take on male supremacy. Characteristically, she fought both with everything she had.

Judith Brown staffs a Gainesville, Florida, Women's Liberation literature table at a 1986 "Take Back the Night" event. (Image courtesy of Carol Giardina.)

In 1963, Judith Benninger, blond and blue-eyed in a shirtwaist dress, was, for all appearances, the quintessential Southern college girl. Born in Tulsa, Oklahoma, Judith moved with her family to the small north-central Florida town of Gainesville from Tuscaloosa, Alabama, when she was fifteen. She graduated from segregated Gainesville High School and thrived as a Girl Scout. Staying in her hometown for college, she attended the University of Florida, which was segregated throughout most of her undergraduate years. She was preparing to enter graduate school there that fall on a Ford Foundation fellowship.

The future would change irrevocably, however, on a hot June night in 1963, when Judith Benninger, then twenty-two, walked downtown to have dinner with friends. Leaving the restaurant, they found themselves in the middle of an angry white mob. Across the street, in the direction in which the crowd was throwing things, Judith saw two well-dressed black men about her age trying unsuccessfully to purchase tickets at the Florida Theater, a local movie theater. She guessed immediately that the young men sought to integrate the segregated movie house. "I felt I had to choose to stand in support of them or stand with the hecklers," she said, "so I walked across the street."[5] Now Judith too was in the line of fire. "I got hit," she said. "There were no police."[6]

Later, back in her dormitory on campus, Judith found herself wanting to find the people with whom she had lined up at the ticket booth. "They had a light in their eyes," she said, "a look of deep sincerity and intelligence—the bravest—unlike any other people I knew."[7] She asked around until a friend of her father's took her to a mass meeting in Gainesville. Led by the Youth Council of the National Association for the Advancement of Colored People (NAACP), a thousand people, packed tightly into a church, sang, testified, and debated whether to continue demonstrating at the theater. Judith, one of three whites in the church, joined the NAACP that night.

Soon afterward she helped organize the Student Group for Equal Rights (SGER), the first civil rights group at the University of Florida. That fall, across from campus at a segregated restaurant serving thousands of students a day, SGER, or the Student Group, as it was known, would call a boycott and set up picket lines.

Earlier in that summer of 1963, a civil rights worker had been brutally beaten in the jail in nearby Ocala, home base of Florida's White Citizens' Council. The newly organized Student Group joined the pickets there. Then, it was south to Dunnellon, Florida, to help desegregate the little town's only theater. Leaving Ocala and Dunnellon to return home, Judith and the other students kept an anxious watch on the carloads of armed white men that followed them to the county line. They also had black escorts—among them Bettie Wright, the founder and president of the Dunnellon chapter of the Congress of Racial Equality (CORE). Wright, it seemed, felt a responsibility to protect the students who had come to help.

Bettie Wright, also a student, had started out as a member of the Tallahassee CORE chapter at Florida Agricultural and Mechanical University (FAMU), a traditionally black college in Tallahassee, the state capital. Throughout the spring, Tallahassee CORE led demonstrations to desegregate the movie theaters, and Wright, an ardent participant, had been teargassed and jailed. When FAMU adjourned for the summer, "there was just too much momentum," as Wright put it, and so back home in Dunnellon, she immediately organized a CORE chapter that began picketing the town's segregated theater.[8] Judith Benninger met Wright when Gainesville's Student Group, Judith among them, joined the Dunnellon pickets.

According to Dan Harmeling, a white University of Florida student who was part of SGER, Bettie Wright, then twenty-one, was respected as the CORE leader by older men and women in Dunnellon and also by the students from Gainesville. Harmeling called Wright "dynamic—clearly someone who would inspire people."[9] Judith, Harmeling said, admired her and spent the summer working with her. Judith described Bettie Wright as "proud, dignified, and militant."[10] "It meant something to me that she was a woman," she said. "I'd never seen a woman take leadership like that."[11] Wright was one of the two civil rights leaders—indeed, the first—to whom Judith attributed her own rising militancy. And Wright said Judith was "part of my support. We got a lot done in the summer of 1963."[12]

When she returned to school in the fall, Betty Wright took Judith with her to a night CORE rally in Tallahassee. There, Wright introduced her to Patricia Stephens Due, who had recruited Wright to Tallahassee CORE. Later that year, Judith would join Patricia Due in a CORE voter education project in the Florida panhandle. Judith's transformation into a freedom fighter, already underway with Wright, would continue as she worked with Patricia Due, a twenty-three-year-old student whose reputation was already legend.

Due was born in Quincy, Florida, the county seat of a majority-black panhandle county. Nineteen when she began organizing, Due was called a "sparkplug" and was known for "boundless energy and remarkable poise."[13] In 1959, while a junior in college, Due, with her sister Priscilla, had organized the CORE chapter at FAMU. On February 13, 1960, twelve days after the Greensboro sit-ins ignited a national chain reaction, Due led a sit-in at Woolworth's lunch counter. This made Tallahassee the third town outside of North Carolina to stage sit-ins.

Faced with mobs armed with knives, ax handles, and guns, Tallahassee CORE continued the sit-ins for a month. "Fill the jails, if necessary," Due urged as the marchers grew to one thousand strong and students were beaten and arrested.[14] At their trials, eight of the defendants, including Due and her sister Priscilla, accepted jail sentences rather than pay the fines. They were among the first demonstrators in the sit-in movement to use the "jail-in" strategy.[15] From her cell, Due wrote a widely circulated letter, "Through Jail to Freedom." "We could be out on appeal," she said, "but we all strongly believe that Martin Luther King was right when he said, 'We've got to fill the jails in order to win our equal rights.'"[16]

The "jailbirds," as they called themselves, came to the attention of the national media and began to receive mail from all over the world.[17] Martin Luther King Jr. wrote to them, saying: ". . . your valiant witness is one of the glowing epics of our time."[18] As pioneers of the jail-in, the sisters and three others embarked on a national tour. They were hosted by Eleanor Roosevelt and Jackie Robinson, and spoke at Adam Clayton Powell's Abyssinian Baptist Church in New York. They returned to Tallahassee to continue direct action activities.

In late 1963, Due initiated the CORE voter registration project. Judith Benninger became her right hand in the project. The September night rally and the tumultuous months that followed readied Judith for this work.

At the rally, Judith, along with Dan Harmeling, her SGER co-worker, joined five whites from Florida State University and hundreds of black students from FAMU. The Tallahassee students, under Due's leadership, had been working all spring to integrate the town's segregated movie theaters. Now, Due asked the rallying students to march on the theater. Singing at the top of their lungs, the students marched down the main street in Tallahassee directly into a large crowd of white men armed with ax handles and chains. Harmeling described what followed:

> Judy and I were walking to the Florida theater. Judy squeezed my hand. . . . the vicious beating of a white civil rights worker in the Ocala jail had us worried. We were too far in front to turn back and ahead a jeering white mob. Judy stepped forward, lifted her sign, and began the picket. . . . 348 people arrested . . . days in jail . . . a trial . . . guilty verdicts, more jail time and Judy lost her financial aid for graduate school.[19]

This was Judith's first arrest. It was the eve of Birmingham Sunday. The next day the jailed civil rights workers learned that four black children, Denise McNair, Cynthia Wesley, Carole Robertson, and Addie Mae Collins had been killed in Sunday school when the Sixteenth Street Baptist Church in Birmingham was dynamited. Reflecting on the arrest, Judith said:

> When I saw her [Patricia Due] getting dragged and kicked to a police car, I instantly changed my mind about not being arrested, and spent my first full day in jail on Birmingham Sunday. When we heard about the bombing that day, I was filled with gratitude to be in jail. I changed overnight. . . . I don't know if I would have followed a man to jail.[20]

Though grateful to be in jail, Judith was badly frightened there. She and three other female civil rights workers were packed into a cell for the night, while white female inmates jailed for nonpolitical reasons were freed from their cells. These inmates pushed broomsticks tipped with razor blades through the bars at Judith and her comrades, who barely escaped being cut by huddling at the far end of the cell. Their attackers, later fast friends with the civil rights workers, said the jailers put them up to the attack. Although frightened, the demonstrators adopted the "jail, no bail" strategy and remained in jail for weeks. FAMU students brought them food and massed in the streets outside, singing freedom songs and demanding their release.

Judith Benninger and Dan Harmeling were the first University of Florida students arrested for civil rights agitation. When Judith was convicted of contempt for defying an injunction against mass picketing at the theater, the university expelled her and took away her Ford Foundation fellowship for graduate school. However, with support from her family and from students and faculty, her punishment was reduced to suspension and then to permanent disciplinary probation. The university did not restore the fellowship.

But Judith had already decided she wanted to work with Due on the voter registration project and wasted no time attempting to convince Due that she could do it. "How much effort and thought and change I had to go through to pursue her so she would allow me to follow her," she said.[21]

Judith was now traveling back and forth to Tallahassee weekly. She participated in sit-ins with Tallahassee CORE and worked with Due on a grant proposal for the voter registration project. Due had carefully researched voter registration statistics and demographics and chose Florida's Black Belt counties to locate the project. She chose these counties over the advice of older civil rights advocates who considered the area too dangerous.

The Southern Regional Council funded the project. CORE opened an office in Tallahassee, and the Big Bend Voter Education Project began in Leon and Gadsen counties. Tallahassee was the county seat of Leon County, where blacks, about 33 percent of the eligible voters, were less than half of those registered. In neighboring Gadsen County, blacks outnumbered whites two to one, but only 3.7 percent were registered to vote.

Judith moved to Tallahassee and became second in command of the Project under Due, who had been appointed CORE field secretary for North Florida. The two young women, Patricia, twenty-three, and Judith, a year younger, made a striking interracial pair in the otherwise segregated city. They traveled together to talk about voter registration in black churches, restaurants, barbershops, and just about anywhere they could find listeners. They were often accompanied by Freedom, Patricia's large, protective German shepherd. Before long they were canvassing in black neighborhoods with some thirty Project volunteers, many of them students from FAMU and Florida State University (FSU).

The white power structure was not long in responding. These activities came to the attention of the notorious Johns Committee, Florida's equivalent of the House Un-American Activities Committee. In March 1964 the committee sent investigators to interrogate Judith about her personal life and her political views. Not long after the visit from the Johns Committee, Judith began to receive telephone calls and letters from the Tallahassee Health Department identifying her as a venereal disease carrier. In April sixty letters making this claim were handed out in the neighborhood of the Project office. A representative of the health department visited Judith's family in Gainesville and told them their daughter had syphilis. She was threatened with arrest if she did not submit to a blood test. No sooner had this situation been resolved (Judith tested negative) than she found her health insurance and car insurance canceled.

In spite of these and other dirty tricks, and ongoing harassment and threats of violence, Judith was exultant. Black voter registration in Leon County had nearly doubled, and in Gadsen County it had more than doubled. The Project was approved for expansion, and additional support was on its way.

At Due's request, Judith set out to recruit out-of-town volunteers for a summer voter registration drive. The volunteers received no salary but lived with local black families or in a Freedom House in a black neighborhood.

Five of her recruits were men who came to live in the Freedom House in Quincy, the new base of operations for the expanded project. Quincy was the county seat of Gadsen County, one of five in Florida listed by the U.S. Civil Rights Commission for disfranchisement of blacks and violent repression of black civil rights.

Judith was arrested at her first presentation on voter education in Gadsen County. She was jailed for three days along with another white female civil rights worker. Guards put the two into a cell with eight male inmates and encouraged the male inmates to rape the two young women. Fortunately the men refused to go along with the jailers.

Patricia Due compared civil rights work in Gadsen County with "going into a lion's cage without a weapon."[22] For Patricia, Judith, and the other volunteers, nights in the Freedom House brought no relief from the violence of their days. Volunteers were trained in nonviolence and pledged to maintain it. But black neighbors armed with shotguns guarded the Freedom House at night. During the course of the summer, night riders shot into the house. One of Judith's recruits, a white Marine veteran, was seriously injured when the white attackers hit him in the face with a rifle. Judith wrote about night in the Freedom House:

> By night the dark draws down its awful curtain, and all the specters begin to walk. . . . Tonight, there are grown men playing a game in the bushes. They wait. . . . Seven rifles are aimed into my house. We wait. . . . Scott runs into the house with his face laid raw. "I'm a Marine, you know. . . . I was taught to disarm and kill a man with a rifle. . . . I could do it blind, and I let him hit me." I call the mayor, mumbling bloodshed, men with guns, "God, oh God they are still outside my house." The night is clear again, quiet—all of our people in the hundred mile range are accounted for. The lights are turned off. . . . 3 a.m. and I hear a shot. . . . "My God, Pat, they are shooting at us now."[23]

To provide even minimal protection, the Project maintained a strict system for volunteers to check in at regular intervals. Remarkably, with no authority other than that vested in her by Due, Judith often found herself accounting for the whereabouts of volunteers before the Freedom House shut down for the night. For the male volunteers, the experience of reporting to women was undoubtedly their first.

The Project continued for more than a year (1964–1965) and included, at its peak, eight counties in the Florida panhandle, four in the Black Belt or "Old South" section bordering on Georgia and Alabama. In these areas many black families lived on large tobacco plantations under almost feudal conditions. In two of the counties, ironically named Lafayette and Liberty, there had never been a black voter.[24]

When the project ended in 1965, North Florida saw more newly registered black voters than any other region in the South.[25] Among these voters was Mrs. Pearlie Williams, a 109-year-old woman who had been born a slave. It was "about time," she said, for her to register and vote.[26] But as black registration rose, so did the violence directed at the civil rights workers. Cars were firebombed, staff beaten and threatened with death, shots fired into the Freedom House, and crosses burned at the homes of African Americans. Judith reflected:

> I was not in the Civil Rights Movement as an office worker in a "white" thing. I was in the field in small towns in dangerous situations. It scared the shit out of me, but although we got pushed around, shot at, arrested a lot, we made it out alive and we accomplished our goals. So my experience was very positive.[27]

Thus Judith learned from Bettie Wright and Patricia Due the fundamental lesson of the effectiveness of militant female leadership. Wright and Due led with their courage, they directed political strategy for the campaigns they waged, and although they were just about Judith's age and sometimes younger than their recruits, many of whom were men, they led the groups they had organized. The experience of female leadership in the civil rights movement shaped Judith Benninger's view that the women's liberation movement was built on the strengths of the civil rights movement. One of the many founders of women's liberation first active in the civil rights movement, Judith learned, as she put it, to "confront men on male supremacy and confront white people on racism."[28]

Judith's start in the movement was in organizations that in 1963 were like few if any others in the larger white society. Organizations made up of both men and women, but female-led, such as Dunnellon and Tallahassee CORE, were vanguards of sexual equality. Thus her experience was, as she said, not only "positive," but one that afforded singular preparation for women's liberation.

For almost a year, Judith Benninger had lived on an intense, dangerous cutting edge where conditions more nearly approximated equality between the sexes than any she had known. And she had experienced men following women's leadership, including her own, even at times when their lives were threatened. Soon, she would seek to re-create this democratic situation in the larger society by helping to jump-start a movement for women's liberation.

Along with discovering the possibility of democratic relationships between men and women, Judith also developed confidence in the very real possibilities of changing the world. In July 1964, the Civil Rights Act, one of the movement's significant achievements, made equal access to public accommodations and schools the law of the land. On September 14, 1964, the anniversary of CORE's march on the segregated Tallahassee theater where she was first arrested, Judith returned with several of the original group. Recalling the violence and hatred that marked the earlier occasion, she called the difference an "amazing change."[29] This time, she reflected proudly, the interracial group was admitted without any problems. The following year, the Voting Rights Act (1965), another victory of the movement, made good the accomplishments of the Big Bend Voter Education Project.

The civil rights movement transformed Judith Benninger into a feminist freedom fighter because it provided her with ideological and practical weapons with which to oppose male supremacy. She had gained confidence in her courage and perseverance in the face of almost paralyzing fear. She learned the effectiveness of mass action and came to the understanding that everyday people would and could organize and stand up for their rights against great odds. She also learned that one need not have establishment "credentials" to be expert enough to figure out how to take on the establishment. At the same time, she honed practical skills like speaking out, writing press releases, and recruiting. She had become a confident organizer with a new standard of equality and respect for women.

But if the distinctively democratic aspects of the civil rights movement helped make Judith a freedom fighter for women's liberation, how did she come to be in the civil rights movement in the first place? Why did she cross the street to stand with the young men who sought to integrate the Gainesville theater on that June night in 1963? Why had she gone with Bettie Wright to the CORE night rally in Tallahassee? Why had she marched on the theater? Wright seemed to know that Judith's readiness to fight injustice had earlier roots. As Wright said, "Something had to be there already for her to even be there with me."[30]

Like Bettie Wright, Julian Brown knew this too. Julian, a civil rights and antiwar activist, and Judith were married in 1966. Reflecting on how they came to be in the movement that brought them together, "Brownie," as he was known, recalled with shameless male chauvinist adoration: "she was a queen, with truly royal bearing—tall, straight, blond, aloof. She also had the finest legs I'd ever seen on a woman. I loved walking behind her on a picket line."[31] But, he said, the combination of physical beauty and acute awareness of "anything that was unfair" intimidated men even as it left him "awestruck" and "honored" to win her hand.[32]

Of his wife's perception of unfairness, Brownie said, "She would see this in men. And see the specifics in perspective; in the bigger picture." According to Brownie, his wife learned the "bigger picture" from her family. "It's in my genes," Judith once exclaimed to him, retelling an incident from her teenage years.[33] Her mother, ironing clothes while watching the McCarthy hearings on television, had hurled her iron at the set. And not long after Judith witnessed her mother's reaction to McCarthyism, Judith saw her family subjected to its Southern variety. Her father, a professor at the then segregated University of Alabama in Tuscaloosa, was fired for supporting the admission of Autherine Lucy, the first black student to enroll there. "My father," she remembered, ". . . got up in the faculty senate and suggested that her admission be based on her [Lucy's] qualifications which seemed rather good."[34]

Autherine Lucy was admitted to the University of Alabama in 1956 under a court order resulting from an NAACP lawsuit. During her brief attendance she faced hostile mobs of white students and townspeople who threatened her life and assaulted her. Judith's mother took Judith and her younger brother, Christopher, to watch the brave young woman make her way through the mob onto the campus. As they watched tensely from the sidelines, Judith's mother told them that this was "like fascism."[35] The university soon expelled Autherine Lucy. The national media quoted Judith's father as being in favor of Lucy's admission, and the university fired him from his teaching position.

Despite his support for Autherine Lucy, Professor Benninger, fearing that his daughter's career would be jeopardized as his had been, opposed her participation in the civil rights movement. On her mother's side of the family, however, she was encouraged by her aunts, Roxane and Jane Eberlien, whom she had known since childhood as opponents of white supremacy and male supremacy. Indeed, her aunt Jane was a contemporary in the civil rights movement who blocked streets during the 1964 Democratic National Convention to protest the failure to seat the delegation from the Mississippi Freedom Democratic Party.

Neither Jane nor Roxane had children of their own, and Judith and her brother were the only children in this close extended family. Upon learning of Judith's birth, Roxane, who remained single and took a particular interest in her niece, wrote, "How I would like to have her where I could . . . submit her to the most rigorous training."[36] As a child, Roxane herself had been trained by some of the leading activists of her day. And she would pass this on to her niece.

The Eberlien sisters grew up in Free Acres, a single-tax colony in New Jersey based on principles of racial and sexual equality. Years before the passage of the Nineteenth Amendment, women had full voting rights in colony affairs. Established in 1910 by Bolton Hall, attorney for Emma Goldman and follower of Henry George, Free Acres attracted radicals and artists such as Paul Robeson, Michael Gold, and Alexander Calder. Hall, a friend of the Eberlien family, had been arrested for distributing birth control leaflets with Margaret Sanger. Roxane and Jane maintained the family home well into Judith's adulthood. Immersed in her family's political history, Judith was a frequent guest, even spending her honeymoon at Free Acres.

Judith's maternal grandparents, Ernest and Undena Eberlien, were lifelong activists. Ernest was an officer and organizer in the lithographers' union and membership chair of the Socialist Party branch to which his wife, Undena, also belonged. The couple held Party meetings in their home. Before they moved to Free Acres, the Eberliens were among the first residents of Helicon Hall, a collective established by Upton Sinclair in Englewood, New Jersey. As children, the Eberlien sisters learned feminism from their mother, an ardent reader of Charlotte Perkins Gilman and an active suffragist. The children had been jailed with Undena when she attempted to vote. Their father, also a suffrage supporter, came to get the family out of jail.

The longtime Free Acres administrator, Ami Mali Hicks, was described by neighbors as a "forbidding feminist" who could "vanquish a man with ten words and who held sway here."[37] Hicks was a member of the Women's Political Union, the militant suffrage group modeled on the tactics of the British movement and organized in the United States by Harriet Stanton Blatch, Elizabeth Cady Stanton's daughter. Hicks was particularly influential with Judith's aunt Roxane, who in turn helped to "train" Judith. As suffrage agitation peaked in 1920, Roxane Eberlien, then only ten, was living in New York City with Hicks. Theirs was a lifelong friendship. When Hicks became elderly and could no longer work, Roxane stood by her and provided financial support.

Roxane was also close to Lola Kessler, whom Judith called "my patroness."[38] Lola and her husband, Max, were Jewish refugees from Nazi-occupied Austria who were assisted by Roxane Eberlien. Roxane, an American State Department decoder in Switzerland during World War II, had secretly used classified information to assist Jewish friends, including the Kesslers. The Kesslers worked for the World Woman's Party, an international project of Alice Paul, leader of the National Woman's Party. As a teenager Judith visited Lola Kessler in New York City, where Lola lavished attention upon her.

In addition to Lola Kessler, Judith met other influential reformers through Roxane Eberlien. Judith's brother, Christopher, recalled visits to Aunt Roxane during the late 1950s and early 1960s when she worked as assistant to Adlai Stevenson. While visiting at Stevenson's, Judith and Christopher met women such as Eleanor Roosevelt and Helen Keller. Summing up Roxane's influence, Christopher said she had imbued in niece and nephew alike the idea that they "could change the future."[39]

Thus Judith's activist family was the "something" that, as Bettie Wright put it, had been "there already" when Judith crossed the street to stand with the members of the NAACP Youth Council that night in June 1963. Her civil rights experience in the vanguard of gender democracy combined with the family tradition, and she was attracted to the early stirrings of women's liberation.

In 1965, Judith heard the first call for women's liberation when her soon-to-be husband Brownie was working with the Southern Christian Leadership Conference (SCLC) in Chicago. There he encountered "Sex and Caste," the early feminist position paper by Casey Hayden and Mary King. Sensing its importance, Brownie read "Sex and Caste" over the telephone to his fiancée in Gainesville. A year later, a workshop on Simone de Beauvoir's *The Second Sex* put on by Gainesville's Students for a Democratic Society (SDS) also raised Judith's feminist consciousness.

Then in 1968, with civil rights coworker Beverly Jones, Judith, now Judith Brown, coauthored "Toward a Female Liberation Movement," a founding document of the independent movement that has been credited with starting it. This historic manifesto called for a completely independent women's movement and set forth emphatically the principles on which to build it. Women's liberation pioneer Kathie Sarachild said that "it was—and is—the most powerful single women's liberation statement after Simone de Beauvoir's *The Second Sex*."[40]

Naomi Weisstein, cofounder in 1967 of the first women's liberation group in the nation, recalled the galvanizing effect of "Toward a Female Liberation Movement," soon known as the Florida Paper:

> After we got started, for months we were paralyzed with doubt: was there any need for an independent women's movement? Then the paper came out. It transformed our thinking. Here was a vision of the liberation of women so real, palpable, and compelling we forged ahead. After that paper, there would be no turning back for us or for the rest of the movement.[41]

Thus attributed with transforming the paralysis of the first women's liberation group into forward motion, indeed with setting the course of the whole early movement, the Florida Paper provided the crystallizing idea needed by the emerging movement and made Gainesville a flashpoint of national social change. Women must fight their own battles, said Jones and Brown, taking a lesson from Stokely Carmichael's Black Power injunction to whites to "fight your own oppressor." Naming men the oppressor, the paper proclaimed that women must form their own movement. It set forth in detail the overwhelming oppression of women in this male-dominated society. And it proposed measures to defeat this oppression and work toward complete freedom.

Other contemporaries agreed. "Dear Judy . . .Your pamphlet has become a kind of 'what is to be done' for the movement . . ." wrote the editor of the *New South Student*, the journal of the Southern Student Organizing Committee (SSOC), the Southern counterpart of Students for a Democratic Society (SDS).[42] As activist-scholar Marlene Dixon put it, "That paper started it if anything written started it. That paper just laid it on the line."[43] Published by Jones and Brown themselves, the Florida Paper spread like wildfire across the United States. It was distributed by the SSOC and the New England Free Press and published by the mainstream press in part and in whole in at least nine anthologies of women's liberation. By December 1968 the paper had crossed the Atlantic to Sweden, where a Swedish magazine, *Ord & Bild*, published portions of it. "An inquiry makes it clear that your views do have considerable impact on women . . ." the Swedish editor of *Ord & Bild* wrote Brown.[44]

But putting out a call for a women's liberation movement was only a first step. Now Brown and Jones began to organize one. They joined forces with a handful of women to organize the first national meeting of the emerging movement. This historic meeting took place in Sandy Springs, Maryland, in

August 1968. Bringing together early women's liberation theoreticians and organizers, the meeting clarified that a new social movement of national proportion was forming. City after city reported its activities, breaking the isolation of local organizing. Local work assumed the full measure of its significance: a movement for the liberation of women was in birth.

At Sandy Springs, Gainesville feminist pioneers forged an alliance with Kathie Sarachild (Amatniek) and Carol Hanisch based on a range of hotly debated issues on which the women agreed. Sarachild and Hanisch, also veterans of the Southern civil rights movement, were early members of the nation's second women's liberation group, New York Radical Women, which had initiated the practice of feminist consciousness-raising. Consciousness-raising was a concept that would become a vital tool in organizing the movement.

Consciousness-raising involved women giving testimony from their daily lives—"recalling and sharing our bitter experiences," as Sarachild put it. Participants took turns answering questions on particular topics, questioning the testimony, and looking for the root of different feelings and experiences.[45] Sarachild also saw consciousness-raising as a way to develop radical feminist theory, as it involved

> understanding oppression wherever it exists in our lives—our oppression as black people, workers, tenants, consumers, children, . . . as well as our oppression as women . . . analyzing whatever privileges we may have—the white skin privilege, the education and citizenship of a big power (imperialist) nation privilege, and seeing how these help to perpetuate our oppression as women, workers.[46]

Judith Brown learned consciousness-raising from Sarachild and Hanisch. She immediately used the method in organizing Gainesville Women's Liberation, the first women's liberation group in the South and a front-runner in the resurgence of the movement nationally. Gainesville soon became the Southern base of a North-South organizing partnership that participants called "The Life Group."[47] This collaboration, a kind of "grass-roots think tank," was responsible for the national launching of consciousness-raising, the first program of the women's liberation movement, at the larger national women's liberation conference in Lake Villa, Illinois, that fall.[48]

The consciousness-raising program was a leap for the new movement going on the offensive with mass organizing. Letters came to Gainesville from housewives with no connection to the student movement, many asking, "I want to organize a group: can you help me?"[49] Brown helped form a number of women's liberation groups by teaching consciousness-raising to women who went on to be organizers.

She attributed her early affinity for consciousness-raising to Patricia Due's insistence that in the many mass meetings of the Big Bend project, she speak from personal experience. This was difficult at first because, as Brown said, "this exercise that Pat put me through was entirely unfamiliar to me. . . . I took to consciousness-raising as legitimate because of what I slowly learned in this manner."[50]

Thus the continuity between Brown's work for black civil rights and women's liberation was more than a matter of roots; it was a guide for on-going activity—including alliances. For example, in 1970 Gainesville Women's Liberation and the Black Student Union at the University of Florida jointly sponsored a rally to oppose the nomination of then President Nixon's appointee to the Supreme Court, G. Harrold Carswell. Carswell had established a "clear cut record of sex discrimination," said national feminist leader Betty Friedan.[51] His ruling that denied employment to women on the grounds that they had children and so should stay at home exemplified this record.

Carswell's record against black civil rights was also well known, and Brown remembered him from CORE days. As a federal district judge for the counties in the Big Bend project, he had ruled against an appeal by students jailed for demonstrating at the segregated Tallahassee theater. His ruling, later overturned, assured that the demonstrators, Brown and Due among them, would be harshly disciplined by their respective universities. He also ruled against one of the Project volunteers, who was viciously beaten because he had talked about registering to vote with black workers on a tobacco plantation.

Gainesville Women's Liberation and the Black Student Union were part of a national coalition that defeated Carswell's appointment. The flyer for the Gainesville rally featured the women's symbol next to the word "Sexist" in large print and a fist clenched in the Black Power salute next to the word "Racist," also in large print. The flyer declared the two groups' opposition to the "decimation of the Black Panther Party" and to the torture of "imprisoned Panther sisters." At the same time it demanded "child care for working mothers" and "repeal of Florida's murderous abortion law."[52] This joint protest linked two freedom movements in which Brown worked throughout the 1960s.

In addition to her pioneering work for civil rights and women's liberation, Brown was active in support of Black Power and academic freedom. She also actively opposed the war in Vietnam. The Federal Bureau of Investigation (FBI) compiled nearly five hundred pages that detailed her work in these movements. Among the documents released to her under the Freedom of Information Act (FOIA) were pages of an FBI "Agitator Index."[53] The Agitator Index showed Brown's rank as an agitator, indicating the FBI's consideration of her as a threat to the establishment.

Despite the FBI and Judge Carswell, Brown succeeded in regaining admission to the University of Florida. She took a master of arts degree in English literature in 1968 and wrote a thesis on acclaimed black Florida writer Zora Neale Hurston, who had not yet been rediscovered. Later, with the help of her husband, Brown went to law school. Although they were divorced in 1971, Brownie helped Judith with financial support for law school as she had earlier supported him.

In 1974 Brown began practicing law in Gainesville. Her law practice was a part of her ongoing commitment to social justice. She sued the campus newspaper for sex discrimination and won equal pay for female journalists. She successfully defended students arrested for demonstrating against the university's investment in apartheid South Africa, and she represented students disciplined by the university for abortion-rights protest. She also did pathbreaking work in disability law and in defense of those fighting child sexual abuse. At the same time, she kept up with routine movement work such as mailing postcards for meetings and marching in demonstrations. In 1985 she reorganized Gainesville Women's Liberation into an organizer school for women's liberation.

In addition to working for justice, Judith Brown led a full life. She was active in the Girl Scouts for many years and served as a camp counselor. She loved the outdoors and was an enthusiastic mountain hiker. She was on city-league teams for volleyball, softball, and intramural basketball, which she also coached. She often played freedom songs on her guitar for sing-alongs with friends. An accomplished writer, she wrote poems and prose about everything that engaged her. Along with family and friends, her house contained a succession of dogs and cats named Freedom. In 1991, at only fifty, she died after a three-year struggle against breast cancer and pain.

Upon her death, fellow activists set up a scholarship in her name at the University of Florida to help carry on the work that was the purpose of her life: the fight of people, and of women in particular, for dignity, equality, freedom, and a democratic society. The Judith Brown Scholarship, along with the ongoing achievements of the civil rights movement and the women's liberation movement, continues the legacy of Judith Brown. The scholarship helps to support upcoming freedom fighters, many of whom are getting started at about the same age as Judith was when her scholarship was taken away. The Judith Brown Scholarship is awarded *for* activism.

Every year the Gainesville movement commemorates Judith's work by holding a daylong seminar to study ways to protect and defend freedom fighters. And when the people gather, they always speak of Judith in the words of Woody Guthrie: Wherever people are fighting for their rights, that's where Judith Brown will be.

NOTES

1. Judith Brown, Gainesville, to Kathie Sarachild (Amatniek), New York, July 15, 1985, Redstockings Women's Liberation Archives for Action, New York, N.Y.

2. Stetson Kennedy, *Jim Crow Guide to the U.S.A.* (London: Lawrence & Wishart, 1959), 98.

3. Kennedy, *Jim Crow Guide*, 35.

4. A facsimile of the original pamphlet by Beverly Jones and Judith Brown, "Toward a Female Liberation Movement," is available from Redstockings Women's Liberation Archives for Action. See www.Redstockings.org.

5. Judith Brown, interview by the author, video recording, tape 1, Gainesville, Fla., April 8, 1990.

6. Judith Brown, interview by the author.

7. Judith Brown, interview by the author.

8. Betty Wright, interview by the author, tape recording, Salisbury, Md., September 10, 2000.

9. Dan Harmeling, interview by the author, tape recording, Gainesville, Fla., September 4, 2000.

10. Judith Brown, interview by the author.

11. Judith Brown, interview by the author.

12. Betty Wright, interview by the author.

13. Glenda Alice Rabby, *The Pain and the Promise: The Struggle for Civil Rights in Tallahassee, Florida* (Athens: University of Georgia Press, 1999), 120.

14. August Meier and Elliott Rudwick, *CORE: A Study in the Civil Rights Movement, 1942–1968* (Urbana: University of Illinois Press, 1975), 106.

15. Meier and Rudwick, *CORE*, 107. According to Meier and Rudwick, Tallahassee CORE's demonstrations in February and March 1960 were "notable because . . . they introduced a militant new tactic—the jail-in." Going to jail instead of paying their fines, Due and four other defendants "chose to remain in the county jail for sixty days, thus becoming the first activists to undertake a jail-in." (106–7). Due, speaking on the group's decision to go to jail rather than pay the fines, said, "If we went to jail, I thought, all of America might learn the truth about the South. . . . It was the first time any activities in the student sit-in movement had chosen jail rather than pay their fine. We pioneered the tactic, becoming the first jail-in of the student protest movement of the 1960s." Tananarive Due and Patricia Stephens Due, *Freedom in the Family: A Mother-Daughter Memoir of the Fight for Civil Rights* (New York: One World Ballantine Books, 2003), 70.

16. Patricia Stephens Due, "Through Jail to Freedom," letter, transcript in James Peck, *Freedom Ride* (New York: Simon and Schuster, 1962), 79.

17. Rabby, *The Pain and the Promise*, 106.

18. Rabby, *The Pain and the Promise*, 106.

19. Dan Harmeling, Gainesville, Fla., to Carol Giardina, Gainesville, Fla., June 29, 1991, transcript in the hands of Carol Giardina, Judith Brown Endowment, Gainesville, Fla.

20. Judith Brown, Gainesville, Fla., to Kathie Sarachild (Amatniek), New York, August 15, 1985, Redstockings Women's Liberation Archives for Action.

21. Judith Brown, Gainesville, Fla., to Kathie Sarachild (Amatniek), New York, November 21, 1988, Redstockings Women's Liberation Archives for Action.

22. Rabby, *The Pain and the Promise*, 174.

23. Judith Brown, "CORE Voter Registration Drive," Quincy, Fla., 1964, 42–45, Judith Brown's notebook of the Big Bend Voter Education Project, Judith Brown Endowment.

24. Rabby, *The Pain and the Promise*, 173.

25. Rabby, *The Pain and the Promise*, 178.

26. Judith Brown, "Freedom Day Last Monday in Quincy," *Gadsen County Free Press*, August 1, 1964, Judith Brown Endowment.

27. Judith Brown, Gainesville, Fla., to Kathie Sarachild (Amatniek), New York, August 15, 1985, Redstockings Women's Liberation Archives for Action.

28. Judith Brown, Gainesville, Fla., to Kathie Sarachild (Amatniek), New York, July 15, 1985, Redstockings Women's Liberation Archives for Action.

29. Judith Brown, interview by the author.

30. Betty Wright, interview by the author.

31. Julian Brown, Pierre, S.D., to Carol Giardina, Gainesville, Fla., June 29, 1991, Judith Brown Endowment.

32. Julian Brown to Carol Giardina, June 29, 1991.

33. Julian Brown, interview by the author, tape recording, Gainesville, Fla., January 29, 2001.

34. Judith Brown, Gainesville, Fla., to Kathie Sarachild (Amatniek), New York, July 13, 1985, Redstockings Women's Liberation Archives for Action.

35. Judith Brown, interview by the author.

36. Roxane Eberlien, diary entry, Bern, Switzerland, March 16, 1941, in Laurel Hessing, *Treasures of the Little Cabin: A Free Acres Cabin Tells the Stories of Those Who Loved It and Sought Its Shelter* (Free Acres, NJ, 1999), 316. Source documents compiled, edited, and annotated by Laurel Hessing.

37. Martin A. Bierbaum, "Free Acres: Bolton Hall's Single Tax Experimental Community," *New Jersey History* 102 (Spring/Summer 1984): 47.

38. Judith Brown, Gainesville, Fla., to Kathie Sarachild (Amatniek), New York, December 11, 1985, Redstockings Women's Liberation Archives for Action.

39. Christopher Benninger, interview by the author, tape recording, New York, December 8, 1999.

40. Kathie Sarachild, quotation on the jacket of "Toward a Female Liberation Movement," Redstockings Women's Liberation Archives for Action.

41. Naomi Weisstein, New York, to Carol Giardina, Gainesville, Fla., June 23, 1991, transcript in the hands of Carol Giardina, Judith Brown Endowment.

42. Dave Nolan, Nashville, Tenn., to Judith Brown, Gainesville, Fla., September 21, 1968, transcript in the hands of Carol Giardina, Judith Brown Endowment.

43. Marlene Dixon, "An Interview with Marlene Dixon: On the Beginnings," interview by Joan Robins in Joan Robins, *Handbook of Women's Liberation* (North Hollywood, Calif.: Now Library Press, 1970), 105.

44. Lars Backstrom, Stockholm, Sweden, to Judith Brown, Gainesville, Fla., December 25, 1968, transcript in the hands of Carol Giardina, Judith Brown Endowment. Additionally, significant sections of the paper appeared in England and across the United States in Germaine Greer's bestseller, *The Female Eunuch*, in 1970 and 1971.

45. Kathie Sarachild, "A Program for Feminist Consciousness-Raising," in Redstockings, ed., *Feminist Revolution* (New York: Random House, 1978), 202–3.

46. Sarachild, "A Program," 202–3.

47. Judith Brown, Gainesville, Fla., to Kathie Sarachild (Amatniek), New York, November 22, 1985, Redstockings Women's Liberation Archives for Action.

48. Redstockings, the early women's liberation group, is today a "grass-roots think tank." The phrase is borrowed from Redstockings, Redstockings Catalog, Redstockings Women's Liberation Archives for Action.

49. Judith Brown, Gainesville, Fla., to Carol Hanisch, New York, August 27, 1968, Redstockings Women's Liberation Archives for Action.

50. Judith Brown, Gainesville, Fla., to Kathie Sarachild (Amatniek), New York, n.d., Redstockings Women's Liberation Archives for Action.

51. Betty Friedan, *It Changed My Life: Writings on the Women's Movement* (New York: W. W. Norton, 1985), 129.

52. Anti-Carswell Rally flyer, February 23, 1970, Selected Documents from Gainesville Women's Liberation History and Organizing, Judith Brown Endowment.

53. Agitator Index, FBI file of Judith Brown, released in 1986 Freedom of Information Act (FOIA), Judith Brown Endowment.

SUGGESTED READING

Primary Sources

Due, Tananarive, and Patricia Stephens Due. *Freedom in the Family: A Mother-Daughter Memoir of the Fight for Civil Rights*. New York: One World Ballantine Books, 2003.

Evans, Sara. *Personal Politics: The Roots of Women's Liberation in the Civil Rights Movement and the New Left*. New York: Vintage, 1979.

Giardina, Carol. "Origins and Impact of Gainesville Women's Liberation, the First Women's Liberation Organization in the South." In *Making Waves: Female Activism in Twentieth-Century Florida*, edited by Kari Frederickson and Jack Davis. Gainesville: University Press of Florida, 2003.

Jones, Beverly, and Judith Brown. "Toward a Female Liberation Movement." Gainesville, Fla., June 1968. Redstockings Women's Liberation Archives for Action, New York, N.Y. (hereafter, Redstockings Archives). See www.Redstockings.org.

Redstockings, ed. *Feminist Revolution*. New York: Random House, 1978. Redstockings Archives.

Sarachild, Kathie. "The Civil Movement: Lessons for Women's Liberation." Transcript of a speech at The Sixties Speak to the Eighties: A Conference for Activism and Social Change, University of Massachusetts at Amherst, October 22, 1983. Redstockings Archives.

Secondary Source

Rabby, Glenda Alice. *The Pain and the Promise: The Struggle for Civil Rights in Tallahassee, Florida*. Athens: University of Georgia Press, 1999.

14

༄

José Angel Gutiérrez: *La Raza Unida* and Scholarship for Social Justice

David J. Libby

This chapter explores the work of José Angel Gutiérrez, who as a graduate student studied the poverty and inequality of his hometown of Crystal City (or Cristal), Texas. Based on his studies and his experience as a grassroots political activist, Gutiérrez worked with community leaders to establish a new political party. The result of this effort was a revolutionary political transformation that brought down the existing power structure and created a new government under the control of the city's Mexican American majority.

South Texas during the 1960s was a region wracked by poverty and inequality. The southern counties of Texas, if separated from the rest of the state, had the demographic profile of a Third World country, with alarmingly high rates of poverty, malnutrition, unemployment, and illiteracy. The region was also sharply divided along racial lines, with the Anglo-American population firmly in control of political power and economic resources. The underclass was composed primarily of Mexican Americans, many of whose ancestors had lived in Texas before it was part of the United States. In many counties, Mexican Americans constituted the majority of the population. During the first half of the twentieth century, indiscriminate murders of Mexican Americans paralleled the lynching of African Americans in the Jim Crow South. The region had a long history of racial inequality that excluded all but a small number of Mexican Americans from the power structure.

While the region's economic capital of San Antonio mirrored the inequality of south Texas, the tendencies toward racial violence were muted. Numerous factors contributed to the difference. San Antonio's white population was more diverse, with German, Czech, Irish, and other immigrant groups, which were not as vested in the ideology of white supremacy. San Antonio's racial divisions came to a head during the 1930s as the result of a pecan-sheller strike led by Emma Tenauyunca. The strike's success was limited, but it demonstrated the power of a unified Mexican American population. Two decades later, in response to signs that a larger civil rights movement was underway, religious leaders from the city's Catholic, Protestant, and Jewish communities publicly denounced segregation and called for immediate and peaceful integration. The larger community did not immediately comply, and most of San Antonio's Mexican American population continued to live in poverty. Still, the city avoided much of the urban violence that many other cities in the United States experienced. San Antonio's history and demographics set it apart from most other Southern cities at the beginning of the civil rights movement, and it became the training ground for a movement to address the political and economic inequalities of south Texas.

Located in the primarily Mexican American west side of San Antonio, St. Mary's University had a long tradition of educating the leaders of San Antonio and south Texas. Many of San Antonio's political leaders, judges, and business leaders attended St. Mary's as undergraduates and as law students. St. Mary's educated not only the city's elite, but a sizable population of impoverished Mexican American and Anglo students. A large segment of St. Mary's students hailed from smaller towns in south Texas. Each town had its own political structure, but inequality dominated all, rooted in racial divisions and preserved by decades-old concentrations of power and wealth.

José Angel Gutiérrez was a native of Crystal City, Texas, a town that in the 1960s became the epicenter for the Mexican American movement for civil rights in Texas. Nearly 90 percent of Crystal City's population was Mexican American, and in 1963 the town gained national attention when the all-Anglo city government was defeated by a ticket of Mexican American candidates. This election signaled the success of grassroots politics; however, the political terrain of Crystal City would remain contested throughout the 1960s.

Gutiérrez had become a radical during his youth. After the death of his father, prominent as the local Mexican physician, his family's economic and social standing declined steeply, and "the Anglo social doors in Cristal shut tightly on us." His mother was only able to find work in the fields. Gutiérrez wrote later, "I was now, without my doctor father, just another Mexican."[1] Steeped in the tradition of grassroots activism, Gutiérrez participated in the Mexican American victory of 1963. He became well known locally for his speaking abilities, which attracted the interest of Mexican American community organizers and the local political machine. Gutiérrez attended community college in Uvalde, Texas, before transferring to Texas A&I University (now Texas A&M–Kingsville). At A&I, Gutiérrez continued his involvement

José Angel Gutiérrez (Image courtesy of K. Cecilia Lugo.)

in student political organizations. He worked to forge coalitions addressing the interests of Mexican American, African American, and Anglo students. After graduating, Gutiérrez enrolled in the master's program in government at St. Mary's University.

Gutiérrez met a number of other Mexican American students at St. Mary's whose experiences in grassroots political activism were similar to his own. Their discussions ranged from immediate political conditions in south Texas to the activism of civil rights leaders such as Stokely Carmichael and Cesar Chavez. They also studied works by revolutionary leaders from Cuba and Mexico, including Che Guevara and Ricardo Flores Magón. They read and discussed books on these topics in each other's homes, in local parks, and over beers at the Fountain Room, a tavern near the university. The students organized themselves into a political organization called the Mexican American Youth Organization (MAYO). MAYO reached out to Mexican Americans in San Antonio to help identify particular issues and address them through political action. During semester breaks, MAYO activists traveled to work among Mexican American communities in Texas and as far away as Los Angeles, Chicago, Atlanta, and New York. MAYO reached out to Mexican American communities to study social conditions, establish a dialogue among grassroots political groups, and learn from their experiences. In 1967,

MAYO began organizing "issues conferences" to gather community representatives and continue the political conversations. Starting in 1968, MAYO focused on organizing and staging high school walkouts to bring about change in the educational system. This activity organized high school students and developed in them a political consciousness, but most of the walkouts had limited results.

Gutiérrez paralleled his organizing activities in his course work as a graduate student at St. Mary's. His academic studies analyzed the extreme poverty in south Texas. He completed a master's thesis titled *"La Raza* and Revolution: The Empirical Conditions of Revolution in Four South Texas Counties." The title, *La Raza,* was Spanish for "the people" and also referred to *"La Raza Unida,"* which was the slogan MAYO chose to express unity among Mexican Americans. Gutiérrez's approach was a standard social science study, although focused on events that were immediate to his circumstances. Despite his own involvement in grassroots politics, his thesis is remarkable for its scholarly detachment. This scholarly tone is especially notable in light of Gutiérrez's admission, decades later, that his own resentment was growing at the time he composed the study. However, his research was balanced, and Gutiérrez only revealed his political perspective in his analysis of the evidence he presented.

In his thesis, Gutiérrez studied revolutions as social phenomena that result in radical transformations of the society. While revolutions are commonly assumed to be violent, Gutiérrez neither made a call for violence nor predicted that violence would ensue. Instead he documented the conditions in which Mexican Americans lived by studying the economic, social, and political realities of daily life. Confronting this reality, Gutiérrez drew the conclusion that change was necessary.

Gutiérrez argued that the economic conditions of south Texas stood in sharp contrast to the rest of the United States. The study focused on statistical levels of economic development including incomes, education levels, and other signs of prosperity. Gutiérrez found that if most of the United States compares favorably to western Europe, the favorable comparison for south Texas would be Latin American dictatorships. He drew the conclusion that the social conditions did not support the existing political structure. Put another way, the poverty and inequality of south Texas did not constitute a democracy. The racial dimension of inequality could best be seen by comparing the number of Mexican American and Anglo large landowners. In the four counties Gutiérrez examined, only four Mexican Americans owned more than 300 acres, compared to fifty-three Anglos. As a result, in many rural areas, Mexican Americans worked as temporary migrant laborers. Gutiérrez added another contrast to the condition of Mexican Americans by comparing levels of employment, education, and overcrowding in San Antonio's west side to the Watts neighborhood of Los Angeles, which had recently been devastated by riots. The statistics showed that the conditions in

San Antonio's west side were worse than Watts, with similar rates of unemployment and underemployment, higher rates of overcrowding, and a lower median income.

The social reality that Gutiérrez documented in his thesis provided evidence that, in addition to economic and political power, the social institutions in south Texas segregated and excluded Mexican Americans. Gutiérrez drew on his own experiences growing up in Crystal City, as well as interviews with dozens of Mexican Americans in the four counties he studied. His findings documented that Mexican American children were socialized into a segregated world. Spanish was discouraged, and most students were steered toward vocational courses in high school. Counselors rarely considered college a viable option for Mexican American students. The subtle and overt forms of bias fostered a disproportionately high dropout rate, which limited the employment opportunities of young Mexican Americans. Socially, Anglos and Mexican Americans were almost entirely segregated, with separate social clubs and strong taboos on interracial dating. Public services, ranging from police protection to health services to utilities, were second-rate for Mexican Americans in south Texas. In addition, hiring discrimination forced many Mexican Americans into marginal employment as day laborers and migrant farm workers.

The political picture that Gutiérrez drew of south Texas was equally disturbing. Gutiérrez described a region where decades of corrupt politics prevented Mexican Americans from having a political voice. Machine politics based on patronage and personal loyalty dominated the region. Most participants in the electoral system supported a *patrón* in exchange for some economic benefit, usually continued employment. Employers bought votes by paying their workers' poll taxes. Election observers confirmed that voters supported their *patrón*. The resulting electoral system did little more than support the political machine. Few participated besides those who benefited from supporting a *patrón*. The impoverished migrant workers could not afford the $1.75 poll tax, least of all in an election that was rigged. When in 1966 the poll tax was repealed by court order, 600,000 Mexican Americans were added to the state's voter registration rolls, but because of new voting regulations, their participation continued to be limited. A ten-month waiting period excluded many migrant laborers from voting. Steep filing fees prevented Mexican Americans from running for office. And fraud and intimidation continued to undermine the legitimacy of elections.

Confronted with these obstacles, many Mexican Americans continued to avoid participating in politics. Gutiérrez observed, however, that a grassroots political movement was underway, organized by Mexican Americans who rejected out of hand the power structure as it existed:

> Having been excluded from participation in the traditional political process, the Mexican American is developing a new approach and viewpoint about political

affairs. This new approach is to reject assimilation into the Anglo controlled political system and seek, through organized political movements, the radical redistribution of political power to include Mexican Americans. These political movements will attempt to produce constituencies of Mexican American voters of sufficient size to elect Mexican Americans to offices who will promote the interests of Mexican Americans only. Should these constituencies be closely knit and if Mexican American voters constitute the majority, a third political party for Mexican Americans should be formed.[2]

Gutiérrez suggested that a third party not only was possible but could be a viable alternative to the rigged political structure of south Texas. In making this assertion, Gutiérrez recognized that there were limitations to this vision. First, Mexican Americans were not mobilized as a whole. While some had been mobilized, others had not. In addition, the personality-driven machine politics of south Texas created a pattern of Mexican American voters supporting individuals rather than issues. As Gutiérrez observed, personality politics could have a powerful effect on politics in south Texas. In the senatorial election of 1960, state attorney general Waggoner Carr had offended many Mexican Americans because of his opposition to a strike organized by Mexican American workers in New Braunfels. Carr lost to the Republican candidate, John Tower, because he lost the support of Mexican American voters. The outcome of this election would prove instructive, for the state's political establishment did not adapt to the reality that a united Mexican American vote could undermine the state's power structure. The effect would indeed be revolutionary.

Concluding his thesis, Gutiérrez asserted that the empirical conditions supporting revolution truly existed in south Texas. The levels of economic and political inequality paralleled those in dictatorships such as Haiti and the Dominican Republic. Social segregation mirrored the experience of African Americans in the Southern states and in cities that experienced riots. In illustrating these parallels, Gutiérrez carefully measured his terms by emphasizing that revolution would consist of creating a new political power structure in which Mexican Americans had a voice. Gutiérrez never called for overt violence in "*La Raza* and Revolution"; instead, he predicted the change would come about as the result of grassroots political organization. Perhaps the most significant aspect of his analysis was his call for the creation of a third political party as a step toward wider distribution of political power.

Gutiérrez worked with several other graduate students to move *La Raza* from an ideal to a reality. He returned to Crystal City and began a new organizational push. The tensions between Anglo elites and the Mexican American majority had continued while he was pursuing his education. Economic intimidation and violence replaced poll taxes as means of reasserting Anglo control over the power structure. In this environment, the smallest challenges became significant victories. As had occurred in the early 1960s, Crystal City High School served as a stage for numerous challenges to the racial order. Mexican American students participated in school activities that fostered ethnic pride. The Spanish club, previously led by Anglo students chosen by teachers, held elections that voted in Mexican American officers. In 1969, administrators rejected student demands for Mexican American cheerleaders. The school administration excluded Mexican American students from the cheerleading squad by requiring that cheerleaders' parents had to have graduated from Crystal City High School. Few Mexican American students qualified because of the high dropout rate fostered by teacher and administrative bias. With the help of Gutiérrez and other MAYO organizers, students protested this rule by going on strike in early December 1969. This was the thirty-ninth walkout organized by MAYO, and by far the most successful. As the strike stretched from days into weeks, political tensions heightened. MAYO volunteers assembled a curriculum of "liberation classes" taught by Mexican American educators from communities as far away as San Antonio, similar to the "Freedom Schools" organized by the Student Nonviolent Coordinating Committee in the Mississippi Freedom Summer of 1964. Meanwhile, school administrators found that the absence of nearly seventeen hundred students sharply reduced the level of funding from the Texas Education Agency.

With political tensions growing, Gutiérrez, along with other members of MAYO, saw their opportunity. The movement continued with boycotts of businesses that opposed the student movement. MAYO leaders had researched the requirements on organizing a third party in the hopes of providing the information necessary to political leaders of grassroots organizations. This work included creating how-to manuals and providing copies of necessary paperwork to be filed. With the success of the school and business boycotts, and a successful voter registration drive underway, the leaders of MAYO began to organize a third political party. In January 1970, *La Raza Unida* filed papers in Zavala County to become a recognized political party. On April 3, 1970, candidates from *La Raza Unida* won control of the school board, with Gutiérrez elected school board president. In coming years, *La Raza Unida*'s effect on Texas politics would be seismic.

La Raza was founded based on the contention that neither of the mainstream political parties served the interests of Mexican American voters. This contention was certainly open to debate, even among Mexican American activists. Democrat Henry B. González was involved in politics as a state senator in the 1950s, running for governor in the 1958 primary and receiving nearly 19 percent of the vote. Two years later, González was elected to the United States House of Representatives. González had been critical of the students of MAYO. He denounced them on the floor of Congress as "Brown Bilbos," making a reference to the Mississippi racial demagogue and former senator Theodore Bilbo. González, ultimately, was assimilationist, preferring to work from within the system and within the Democratic Party. Adopting a separatist political stance would distance him from the Johnson administration, and may also have cost him the support of Anglo voters who, along with Mexican Americans, sent him to Congress. There was little common ground between assimilationists such as González and the leaders of MAYO and *La Raza Unida*.

While the opposition of assimilationist Mexican American leaders such as Henry B. González undermined Gutiérrez's call for unity, he faced more formidable opposition as well. Gutiérrez's activism made him a target of government agencies that saw him as a troublemaker. Efforts to discredit, undermine, or simply get rid of Gutiérrez continued through his career as an activist. Although eligible for a deferral from the Vietnam draft on numerous grounds, including being married with a child and being enrolled in graduate school, Gutiérrez continued to be classified 1A, which was the most eligible for the draft. He joined the Army reserve to avoid leaving his wife and child, and this move forced him to postpone his doctoral studies at the University of Texas. Gutiérrez also reported being followed, probably by FBI agents. As he organized protests and formed *La Raza Unida*, Gutiérrez faced regular harassment from local police and Texas Rangers.

Gutiérrez's struggles continued beyond his political organizing activities. As a graduate student, he faced a dissertation committee that demanded he use the academic language of social science, rendering his work inaccessible to many of the people he studied and represented. Gutiérrez had his revenge when he published in Mexico a small volume of vignettes from his fieldwork with the tongue-in-cheek title *A Gringo Manual on How to Handle Mexicans*. The *Gringo Manual* named 141 "tricks" that gringos employ against Mexican Americans, divided into nine different categories. Tricks 107 through 109 describe efforts to reserve public facilities:

Trick Number 107: Can't Have the Park

Public facilities are administered by the public bodies. Therefore, permission to use the facilities must be granted by the administrators in charge.

You are urged caution in attempting to obtain the use of a public facility. Many a group has gone to ask for a park or hall and been turned down because "another group has it reserved for that day."

Should that happen to you once, try sending a fake inquiry about the availability of the facility before your real group applies.

Trick Number 108: Can't Have the Park

The administrator in charge of the public facilities gets smart after you get him once or twice.

He retaliates by telling you that confirmation will be witheld for 24 hours "because so-and-so also asked for the park for some group or another, whose name I can't remember right now. But call me tomorrow at 10 a.m." Sure enough. You are informed when you call that so-and-so did call and what's-its-name was the local fraternal, "Order of Wingless Ding Bats."

Trick Number 109: Can't Have the Park

You catch on to the Can't Have the Park—Part I and Part II. What can you do?

Try calling the Fraternal Order of the Wingless Ding Bats and see if they *are* having a function. Don't expect the administrator not to have called them also. Should you succeed in proving that you are being denied access to the public facility, be careful you don't fall into Step III.

That being the catch all trick that because of the nature of your group and the ill-will it causes, you are denied. "We don't want to divide the community, you understand."[3]

This volume was in print and distribution before his dissertation was on file at the University of Texas. Here again, Gutiérrez faced another gringo trick. He used an inexpensive printer across the border in Piedras Negras to publish the book. When he attempted to bring the finished product back to the United States, it was turned back as subversive material. Only by breaking the press run into smaller quantities could Gutiérrez smuggle it in, with the help of some friends.

Beyond the harassment of law enforcement, Gutiérrez confronted an organized effort to discredit his character. Most significantly, his opponents orchestrated an effort to brand him a racist and an advocate of violence. Gutiérrez often used the term "gringo" to describe a mind-set that Mexican Americans were inferior. Toward people who held that gringo mind-set, he expressed contempt. His use of this term, a relatively mild epithet that primarily conveyed disrespect, offended his opponents. Gutiérrez's impassioned rhetoric was often used in attempts to discredit him and the cause. Under the headline "MAYO Leader Wants Change, 'Eliminate' the Gringo," an Odessa, Texas, newspaper reported in 1970 that speaking at a MAYO meeting, Gutiérrez told attendees that they needed to let gringos know "1. We don't like you; 2. We're going to get rid of you, and 3. We are going to stand right on top of you, and you better leave while you can."[4] The invective did little to turn away his support base but angered his opponents. To Gutiérrez, people offended by such oratory had some sense of the offense he took when Mexican Americans were excluded from political processes and economic opportunities. Although he was at times bombastic in his public speeches, Gutiérrez emphasized revolution through political reform and peaceful change. The fact that *La Raza Unida*'s efforts in Crystal City never involved violence stands as evidence that his approach to revolution was peaceful.

Among the first steps Gutiérrez took to implement the revolution was a series of educational reforms designed to eliminate bias in the schools. The school board imposed a retirement age of sixty-five, forcing the retirement of thirteen teachers and administrators. They introduced bilingual education programs in elementary schools that required student proficiency in Spanish and English, and required all teachers to learn Spanish. The board paid for funding increases by raising property tax valuations and by applying for federal grants. In two years, the new school board nearly tripled the education budget. Increased spending supported teacher education in graduate programs, as well as the construction of new school buildings. By the end of Gutiérrez's term, the dropout rate was reduced by half, and more graduates were being admitted to college and receiving scholarships. Meanwhile, additional grant money came from foundations to support teacher development.

The schools also instituted symbolic changes to reflect the culture and traditions of the majority of its students. The high school marching band replaced John Philip Sousa marches with traditional Mexican folk music. In one halftime show, the band marched into a formation that spelled the word R-A-Z-A on the football field. Meanwhile, football players and band members alike began using a raised fist as a salute during football games. These changes elicited controversy—especially when performed on opposing teams' fields in neighboring towns. Still the student enthusiasm for the new routines resulted in several awards for the band's halftime show. By the mid-1970s, the band developed a halftime show that reenacted the walkout of 1969.

Such radical changes caused a backlash. In 1971, white parents pooled their funds to open a private school. The leader of this group, former school superintendent C. R. Tate, stated that the school was opened "for the purpose of reintroducing the type of education and curriculum that had existed in the past."[5] Students were taught in classrooms at the First Methodist and First Baptist Churches by teachers who were either retired or fired from the public schools. Other parents transferred their children to schools in neighboring towns.

Because *La Raza* was organized as a party that promised to serve the interests of Mexican American voters, it drew strong support and grew rapidly. Chapters were established in Colorado, California, New Mexico, and elsewhere. A statewide convention met in San Antonio. It nominated Ramsey Muñiz for governor and a slate of candidates for state and local offices. Later that year, *La Raza Unida* held a national convention in El Paso, Texas. Large delegations came from across the southwestern states, with additional delegates from all over the country. The convention, initially called with the intent of endorsing a presidential candidate, resolved instead that neither candidate deserved the party's endorsement. In the 1972 election Muñiz won more than two hundred thousand votes in the election. While the vote amounted to about 6 percent of the total, it nearly changed the outcome of the election. Democrat Dolph Briscoe received 48 percent of the vote, which put Republican Hank Grover within reach of victory, although Briscoe prevailed. Much like the 1960 senatorial election, the 1972 gubernatorial election stood as evidence that a united Mexican American vote had the power to tip the balance of power in state politics. In twenty-two south Texas counties, *La Raza Unida* candidates won offices.

The revolution in Crystal City continued. A slate of *La Raza Unida* candidates won control of the Zavala County Court in 1974. Gutiérrez was elected county judge (the chief administrative post in Texas counties) and held the post until 1981. During Gutiérrez's administration, county policies attempted to address the inequality of county services and living conditions. Gutiérrez and the county court invested in road and bridge improvement, focusing on unpaved roads in impoverished areas. They expanded ambulance services and built a health center for migrant laborers. To pay for these services, they equalized property tax valuations for the first time in decades. Zavala County leaders also sought federal grant funds for community development initiatives. Grants were approved to fund urban renewal programs and establish a nonprofit economic development corporation to support agricultural cooperatives. Public services improved, and hiring practices created a workforce that represented the county's demographic profile. Symbolic actions also gave Zavala County's Mexican American residents pride, most notably when Crystal City was renamed Cristal.

Gutiérrez faced significant problems during his tenure. Democratic governor Dolph Briscoe led a campaign to prevent federal grant money from arriving in Zavala County. He had described the economic development corporation as the "making of a little Cuba on Texas soil."[6] The state's Democratic Party establishment, including several Mexican American congressmen, supported Briscoe's campaign. *La Raza Unida* leaders ironically found themselves turning to Republican Senator John Tower for support from the Ford administration. The victory of Jimmy Carter in 1976 gave Briscoe greater influence in federal funding decisions. Grant funds of approximately $1.5 million, approved in 1975, were tied up in bureaucracy and ultimately canceled in 1979. Zavala County also faced the cutoff of natural gas service during the energy crisis of the 1970s, eventually suing the Lo Vaca gas company over pricing.

Compounding the mixed successes in policy, the unity of *La Raza Unida* was beginning to falter. Internal factions began to develop as leaders competed for party loyalty. The local split mirrored growing factionalism in the national organization. Many Mexican American voters returned to the Democratic Party. Gutiérrez won a second term as county judge in 1978, but by 1980 a group of commissioners hostile to his leadership cut his salary and began disregarding his authority by meeting in secret. Eventually the commissioners attempted to discredit him through judicial proceedings. Seeing his limited chances for success, Gutiérrez negotiated the terms for his resignation and left office in January 1981.

By the time Gutiérrez resigned, *La Raza Unida* no longer functioned as a political party. After failing to receive 2 percent of the statewide vote in 1978, the party was automatically decertified. Its political high point was the governor's election in 1972, when the Democratic Party found it was unable to count on the Mexican American vote. In the years that followed, the state's power structure adapted in ways that addressed issues significant to Mexican American voters. Improved electoral access, the breakdown of *patrón* politics, and continued grassroots activism made government more responsive to the needs of Mexican Americans.

The legacy of José Angel Gutiérrez's vision of a people united, standing up, and demanding equality remains a work in progress. Since the election of 1972, Mexican Americans in Texas have held major offices in both political parties. San Antonio elected its first Mexican American mayor in modern times in 1978. Local universities—private and public—increasingly reflect the demographic profile of the city and the region at large. Many have established programs for students to study the history, literature, and culture of Mexican Americans. Access to university education has created greater opportunities for Mexican American students. By the 1990s, St. Mary's University—where Gutiérrez's thesis adviser Charles Cotrell was installed as president in 2000— sent more Mexican American graduates to medical school than any other college in the United States. Despite these successes, many Mexican Americans in south Texas continue to struggle against poverty. The significant difference is the degree to which Mexican Americans exert their political clout. While the economic inequalities that Gutiérrez documented in his thesis continue in many counties in south Texas, a Mexican American political voice is working to address them.

NOTES

1. José Angel Gutiérrez, *The Making of a Chicano Militant: Lessons from Cristal* (Madison: University of Wisconsin Press, 1998), 31, 33.
2. José Angel Gutiérrez, "*La Raza* and Revolution: The Empirical Conditions of Revolution in Four South Texas Counties" (MA thesis, St. Mary's University, 1968), 49.
3. José Angel Gutiérrez, *A Gringo Manual on How to Handle Mexicans* (Crystal City, Tex.: Wintergarden Publishing, 1974), 75–77.
4. *Odessa American*, February 28, 1970, quoted in Armando Navarro, *The Cristal Experiment: A Chicano Struggle for Community Control* (Madison: University of Wisconsin Press, 1998), 67.
5. Navarro, *The Cristal Experiment*, 238.
6. Gutiérrez, *The Making of a Chicano Militant*, 256.

SUGGESTED READING

José Angel Gutiérrez completed his PhD at the University of Texas. After his six-year tenure as Zavala County judge, he attended law school at the University of Houston.

His published works include *La Raza and Revolution: The Empirical Conditions of Revolution in Four South Texas Counties*. Originally his MA thesis at St. Mary's University in San Antonio, this work was published in 1972 (San Francisco: R and E Research Associates). He also authored two tongue-in-cheek books on interracial dynamics, *A Gringo Manual on How to Handle Mexicans* (Crystal City, Tex.: Wintergarden Publishing, 1974; revised edition, Houston: Arte Publico Press, 2001); and *A Chicano Manual on How to Handle Gringos* (Houston: Arte Publico Press, 2003). His memoir on his activism is *The Making of a Chicano Militant: Lessons from Cristal* (Madison: University of Wisconsin Press, 1998). He is now a professor of political science at University of Texas at Arlington and practices law in Dallas.

For more information on Gutiérrez and La Raza, in addition to his publications, see Armando Navarro, *The Cristal Experiment: A Chicano Struggle for Community Control* (Madison: University of Wisconsin Press, 1998) and *La Raza Unida Party: A Chicano Challenge to the U.S. Two-Party Dictatorship* (Philadelphia: Temple University Press, 2000); Armando Trujillo, *Chicano Empowerment and Bilingual Education: Movimiento Politics in Crystal City, Texas* (New York: Garland, 1998); John S. Shockley, *Chicano Revolt in a Texas Town* (South Bend, Ind.: Notre Dame University Press, 1974); and Ignacio M. Garcia, *United We Win: The Rise and Fall of La Raza Unida Party* (Tucson: Univeristy of Arizona Mexican American Studies and Research Center, 1989).

15

ℰ

Leonard Peltier:
A Small Part of a
Much Larger Story

Crystal S. Anderson

Leonard Peltier exemplifies a brand of civil rights activism defined by a relationship to the indigenous community at large and contextualized by the historical treatment of Native Americans in the United States. Peltier's activism finds roots in the treaty violations, the reservation system, and the suppression of Indian culture that go back to the nineteenth century. Growing up, he likened reservation authorities and boarding school officials to agents of the Bureau of Indian Affairs and Christian missionaries encountered by his ancestors. His worldview, grounded in Indian cultural ways, often resulted in brushes with law enforcement, but it also laid the groundwork for his increasingly activist consciousness, a consciousness attuned to the plight of all Indians. As a teenager, Peltier recognized the economic and government forces behind Indian policy. Emulating black activists of the 1960s, he put his thoughts into action by participating in large-scale protests such as the takeover of Alcatraz by Indians of All Tribes in 1969 and the "Trail of Broken Treaties" march to Washington in 1972. Such high-profile activism made him a target for law enforcement seeking to quell social unrest and culminated in his arrest and conviction for the murder of two FBI agents on an Indian reservation in 1975. Peltier insisted he had nothing to do with the murders and attributed the government's prosecution to part of a campaign to silence his critique of the government's treatment of Indians. Information and documents have surfaced since the conviction casting serious doubt on the government's case against Peltier, yet his appeals have all been denied and he remains in prison serving consecutive life sentences. In spite of his continued imprisonment, Peltier still insists on working for Indian rights.

I am ordinary. Painfully ordinary. This isn't modesty. This is fact. Maybe you're ordinary, too. If so, I honor your ordinariness, your humanness, your spirituality. I hope you will honor mine. That ordinariness is our bond, you and I. We are ordinary. We are human. The Creator made us this way. Imperfect. Inadequate. Ordinary. . . . We're not supposed to be perfect. We're supposed to be *useful*.

Leonard Peltier, Prison Writings: My Life Is My Sun Dance

When we think of the civil rights movement, certain images may come to mind: black students sitting at lunch counters, black and white Freedom Riders traveling on buses, large crowds marching in protest. Such images tell a powerful story of struggle for freedom, but they tell only one story. Other ethnic groups, like American Indians, have their own tales to tell about their quest for justice and their search for freedom, and few figures provide as compelling a story as Leonard Peltier. As the epigraph to this chapter indicates, Leonard Peltier considers himself to be ordinary. Rather than a rationalization for complacency, such ordinariness functions as a call to personal action and community activism. It is this duty to his people that guided Peltier through most of his life and eventually catapulted him to the center of Indian activism during the 1960s and 1970s. He continues to underscore his personal commitment to the issues that affect Indians as he serves his consecutive life sentences in the federal justice system. Moreover, he links the plight of his people with that of indigenous people everywhere, suggesting that the Native American struggle incorporates all of humanity. By doing so, Peltier has fulfilled the prime directive of his life: to be useful.

Leonard Peltier entered into the country's imagination largely through his activism on the part of the American Indian Movement and his imprisonment for the murder of two FBI agents. However, these events do not represent the sum total of his life, nor do they completely explain his significance as an individual committed to justice and equality for his people. The seeds of Peltier's activism began not with his birth and childhood experiences, but with the lives and deaths of his ancestors in their acts of resistance against encroaching federal government interests. Peltier acknowledges that "my own personal story can't be told . . . without going back long before my own birth on September 12, 1944, back to 1890, and to 1876 and to 1868 and to 1851 and, yes, all the way back through all the other calamitous dates in the relations between red men and white, back to the darkest day of all in human history: October 12, 1492, when our Great Sorrow began."[1] The historical treatment of Indian peoples that resulted in treaty violations, the reservation system, and denial of sovereign tribal rights colored Peltier's understanding of himself and his purpose in the world. Born into families of the Ojibway and Dakota Sioux, Peltier married into the Lakota Sioux people. As a result, he experienced firsthand conditions crafted by years of federal Indian policy aimed more at the assimilation of Indians than at preservation

Leonard Peltier (Image courtesy of the Leonard Peltier Defense Committee.)

of their culture and concern for their well-being. In order to understand that world and the ways in which Peltier's actions continued the centuries-old tradition of Indian resistance, one must understand the historical relationship between native peoples and the federal government.

While a history of the relations between the federal government and American Indian tribes is too detailed to discuss here, it is significant to note that most of the Indian policy enacted by the government reflected disdain and active disrespect for Indians and their way of life. Although Thomas Jefferson noted in 1791 that Indians within state boundaries should be left alone, following the purchase of the Louisiana Territory in 1803, he proposed the beginnings of Indian relocation.[2] Historian Ronald Takaki describes Andrew Jackson as a significant purveyor of Indian policy who was driven by his own economic and political interests in divesting Indians of their land. Enraged by the losses he suffered in his campaign against the Creeks in 1814, Jackson nevertheless justified this and subsequent actions toward Indians using rhetoric that revealed a sense of superiority:

> They have disappeared from the face of the Earth. In their places a new generation will arise who will know their duties better. The weapons of warfare will be exchanged for the utensils of husbandry; and the wilderness which now withers in sterility and seems to mourn the desolation which overspreads it, will blossom as the rose, and become the nursery of the arts. . . . How lamentable it is that the path to peace should lead through blood, and over the carcases of the slain!! But it is in the dispensation of that providence, which inflicts partial evil to produce general good.[3]

In this passage, Jackson articulated a general sense that the fate of the Native Americans was inevitable. Their elimination resulted from some unknown calamity rather than from the intervention by the government on behalf of whites intent on acquiring Indian land. By praising the next generation for their willingness to submit to American cultural values, Jackson denigrated the native way of life. He clearly privileged the farming of land performed by American whites over the symbiotic relationship nomadic tribes had with the land. In the end, Jackson rationalized that injustices borne by Indians were a small price to pay for the benefits that accrued to whites. Statements like these demonstrated the federal government's disdain for Indian ways.

The underlying ideas behind statements of denigration translated into more overt action. The Indian Removal Act of 1830 had already sanctioned the relocation of large groups of Indians farther west. When it became apparent that the concept of keeping Indian territory separate from whites was a failure, the government established reservations and placed them under the control of the Bureau of Indian Affairs (BIA). Takaki describes Francis Amasa Walker as the father of the reservation system who, like Andrew Jackson, envisioned Indian submission to assimilation on these sites: "According to his plan, warlike tribes would be corralled onto reservations, and all Indian bands outside their boundaries would be 'liable to be struck by the military at any time, without warning'. . . . Indian tribes would be consolidated into one or two 'grand reservations' with railroads cutting through them here and there, leaving the rest of the territory open for white settlement, free from Indian 'obstruction or molestation.'"[4] Like resettlement, the use of reservations represented a failure to validate Native American culture. It also demonstrated an attempt to separate Indians from their land for the gain of others. Such policies undermined Indian culture, which revolved around reverence for the land, not its exploitation for financial gain.

One could argue that government forces stripped Leonard Peltier of his agency and relocated him to a modern-day reservation in the federal system, just like his ancestors. Yet long before Peltier was designated U.S. Prisoner #89637132, he was born Leonard Peltier, also known as Gwarth-ee-lass ("He Leads the People") among Native Canadian Indians, later known as Tate Wikuwa ("Wind Chases the Sun") among the Sioux, on September 12, 1944, in Grand Forks, North Dakota. The multiple designations are significant to Peltier, for he says they represent "total freedom and total commitment."[5] His father, Leo Peltier, was Chippewa and French, and his mother, Alvina Showers, was Dakota Sioux and Chippewa. When he was four years old, Peltier's parents divorced, and he and his sister went to live with his paternal grandparents, Alex and Mary Dubois-Peltier, on the Turtle Mountain Reservation near Belcourt, North Dakota.

Peltier's earliest experiences confronted the consequences of Indian treatment at the hands of reformers, for the federal government was not the only entity that sought to assimilate the Indian. In 1870, President Grant bestowed the task of Indian religious instruction and assimilation on Christian denominations. As part of their charge, missionaries had virtual control over the reservation Indians and repressed their religious freedom as they attempted to convert them.[6] Historian Michael C. Coleman asserts that Presbyterian missions advanced the "civilizing" benefits of the gospel as evident in the Princeton Theology, which "was a theology of rigid exclusivity, with obvious implications for those who had not yet heard its message. Such heathens could not save themselves through their own deficient standards. Yet as human beings they were responsible for the choices they made in life, and ultimately they had but two: accept the Gospel or be damned."[7] While Catholics proselytized Peltier, they, like the Presbyterian missionaries, used their mission to civilize "heathen" groups, which necessitated destroying the Indian portion of their identity.

Peltier was brought up with both Christian religion and traditional Indian religion through his grandmother, yet he felt alienated by the Catholic religion imposed by missionaries:

> That was something I lost faith in at an early age. I must have been about nine years old. I remember thinking to myself that I could never be a good, believing Catholic; it all seemed so harsh and far removed and devoid of human caring, at least where Indians were concerned. . . . I always felt more at home, more at ease with Indian religion; it made me feel like I belonged, like I was wanted *as* an Indian, and it also seemed loving and caring and wonderfully mystical and bound to our Mother the Earth and our Grandfather the Sky and to Wakan Tanka, the Great Mystery.[8]

Even as a child, Peltier perceived the Catholic faith as antagonistic to his identity as an Indian. Instead, he found a greater connection to Indian religion, as it was more compatible with Indian values.

By the age of six, Peltier became more cognizant of the injustice inflicted upon Indians on a daily basis. His grandfather almost moved the family to Montana following an incident where Peltier hit a white child in the head with a rock in response to taunts. Although the rock only resulted in a small wound, Peltier recalls that the white child's mother came to their house, "yelling and screaming and carrying on, warning she was going to have me put away in the reformatory . . . [and that] she was going right to the police, have the whole 'dirty bunch' of us thrown in jail."[9] Peltier feared this threat because he knew that Indians were not treated fairly by law enforcement, particularly in a dispute involving a white person. It was daily incidents like this that informed his later activism: "I trace the roots of my own political activism to the rank racism and the brutal poverty I experienced every day as an Indian child growing up on the Turtle Mountain Chippewa and Fort Totten Sioux reservations in North Dakota."[10]

Threats like those offered by the white woman soon materialized into reality for Peltier. After his grandfather died, Peltier experienced the power of the Bureau of Indian Affairs in North Dakota firsthand. In 1953, authorities declared his grandmother incapable of raising them on her own and took Peltier, his siblings, and his cousins to a boarding school in Wahpeton, North Dakota. Such institutions sought to eradicate bonds the children had to Indian culture. Most of these schools were deliberately located far from the Indian places where the children grew up. Peltier says this was more than an introduction to non-Indian life: "I consider my years at Wahpeton my first imprisonment, and it was for the same crime as all the others: being an Indian."[11] Peltier's characterization was wholly accurate. Many of the schools were renovated prisons. Scholar David Wallace Adams asserts that through the elimination of school vacations and the erection of physical barriers between children and members of tribes, reservation officials used the desolate locations to lessen the ties between Indian children and their families.[12]

The reception that Peltier and his relatives received was decidedly inhospitable, for they endured many policies aimed at destroying the children's identification with Native American culture. Appearance was the first target. According to Peltier, officials stripped them, bathed them, and powdered them with DDT. Their long hair was cut because, as Adams explains, it "was symbolic of savagism; removing it was central to the new identification with civilization."[13]

The corporal punishment endured by Peltier and his relatives reflected standard operating procedure at boarding schools that housed Indians. The institutions used such punishment to control behavior they deemed unseemly. Adams notes that while "the official position of the government was that corporal punishment should be resorted to 'only in cases of grave violation of rules,' . . . [f]or students twelve years and older, however, who were 'guilty of persistently using profane or obscene language; of lewd conduct; stubborn insubordination; lying; fighting; wanton destruction of property;

theft; or similar misbehavior'—in other words, just about everything—superintendents were permitted to inflict corporal punishment and even to imprison students in the guardhouse."[14] Failure to speak English was an offense that often resulted in assault. Historian Joel Spring argues that "the attitude of many white educators . . . was [that] the elimination of tribal languages and the learning of English would lead to the absorption and practice of white values by Indians."[15] Despite the abuse, Peltier remembers that such measures were not effective: "We were beaten if we were caught speaking our own language. Still, we did. We'd sneak behind the buildings, the way kids today sneak out to smoke behind the school, and we'd talk Indian to each other. . . . And you could say that the first infraction in my criminal career was speaking my own language."[16]

After finishing the ninth grade in Flandreau, South Dakota, Peltier returned to the Turtle Mountain Reservation in North Dakota in 1957. During this period of time, Peltier became acutely aware of the cultural strains placed on young Indians on the reservation: "I attended lots of powwows and religious ceremonies, but I also went to the largely white school dances and listened to a lot of rock radio. . . . I was drawn to both cultures. I found myself spread-eagled between them, really, and, like many of my Indian brothers and sisters, I was nearly torn apart by the contradictions and conflicts between the two that I both saw in the outside world and felt within myself."[17] Contrary to popular belief, Indians were not out of touch with the world around them. Indians of Peltier's generation, coming of age during the 1950s and 1960s, faced the dilemma of being Indian in an increasingly American world.

Yet such Native Americans often interacted with that American world with negative results. In 1958, Peltier had his first brush with the law. Like this initial encounter, Peltier's subsequent interactions with law enforcement would continue to center on his identity as an Indian. Law enforcement officers arrested and incarcerated Peltier for stealing fuel from an army depot to heat his grandmother's house. He explains that he was motivated by the plight of those around him: "The younger children would be begging for scraps of bread—baking powder bread, because yeast bread was a treat for many of us. What hurt most was to see the look on the mothers' and fathers' faces when there wasn't even bread to give the kids."[18] This lack of basic resources translated into not just physical deprivation, but emotional deprivation as well. Indians lacked the agency to provide for their own families. Instead of recognizing Peltier's theft as a response to severe poverty, Peltier was "considered 'incorrigible' . . . a 'hardened criminal' [who] was already well" on his way.[19] Exercising his identity as an Indian would become an exercise of his civil rights, and Peltier would be met consistently with punishment by law enforcement.

Bad treatment at the hands of local law enforcement officers and deplorable living conditions represented just a few factors that prompted Indians like

Peltier to eventually leave the reservations. Journalist Peter Matthiessen notes that the BIA enacted a policy of withholding food for those who refused to leave under the federal relocation program.[20] The relocation policy mirrored the administration's desire to end federal responsibility for Indians. More importantly, under the policy, tribes lost what little political autonomy and control over natural resources on their lands they had left.

Peltier saw such policies as further attempts to undermine Indian culture and traditions: "Those suddenly became the most important, the most feared, words in our vocabulary: 'termination' and 'relocation.' . . . To us, those words were an assault on our very existence as a people, an attempt to eradicate us."[21] But like many natives, Peltier participated. In 1959, his mother moved to Portland under the program, and he followed her there. After working as a migrant worker, Peltier co-owned an auto body repair shop in Seattle, where he also did repairs way below cost for friends. The second floor of the shop doubled as a halfway house. Eventually, the shop folded, for as Peltier puts it: "My one attempt at capitalism was over, scuttled by that old Indian weakness: *sharing* with others. It's a practice that means we're rich as a people, but poor as individuals."[22] For Peltier, the bottom line was not financial, but cultural. His experience as a reservation refugee caused him to view the policy of termination as anything but a benign act.

While Peltier felt a definite sense of outrage at his treatment, his activist consciousness toward the plight of other Indians was not awakened until he was fourteen. While attending a meeting, he was profoundly moved by a cousin's speech about the hunger of Indian children:

> It was like a revelation to me—that there was actually something worthwhile you could *do* with your life, something more important than living your own selfish little life day by day. Yes, there was something more important than your poor miserable self: your *People*. You could actually stand up and fight for them! Now *that* was something I had never learned in school or heard about on the radio. . . . Yes the People, the Tiospaye as the Lakota call the extended family, and, by extension, as I would come to see in later years, *all* Indian people, all indigenous people, all human beings of good heart.[23]

Peltier saw his life intricately connected with the lives of other Indians.

Such a realization resulted in a shift in Peltier's worldview. Suddenly, he saw his plight as the plight of all Indians, past and present. This can be seen in his concern over the rights of Indians as indigenous people with binding treaties with the United States government. While watching television, Peltier learned of the question of tribal sovereignty: "Utterly outraged, I learned that these Native peoples of the Northwest were simply trying to maintain the rights clearly guaranteed to them under formal and still-binding treaties with the U.S. government."[24] Tribal sovereignty was intimately connected with the land. Some scholars argue that unlike other minority groups, Indian nations had "a land base and the legal sovereignty necessary to protect it."[25] The desire for unfettered access to Indian land motivated the federal government to renege on recognizing tribal sovereignty and create the reservation system. Initially, the United States government treated tribes like sovereign nations, but the Supreme Court decision *Cherokee Nation v. State of Georgia* (1831) changed all that by creating a category of "domestic dependent nations." By 1871, Congress ceased the practice of treaty negotiation with tribal nations, and Indian tribes became the wards of the Bureau of Indian Affairs. Historian Klaus Frantz argues that "an era now began in which the American Indian was deprived of political, economic and cultural autonomy and subjected to very strong pressures to assimilate. 'Kill the Indian in him and save the man' was the slogan, and any means to this end seemed acceptable."[26]

In addition, Peltier also became aware of the monied interests that often drove such policies: "The sportsmen and commercial fishers were complaining. They said that Indians were harvesting too many fish. . . . They demanded it be stopped, regardless of whether or not these Native people had a legal right to fish the lakes and rivers, and regardless of the fact that, in exchange for that legal right and little else, they'd given away virtually the whole of the Pacific Northwest."[27] Fishing rights were just as central as issues surrounding the land because water had become increasingly valuable. Frantz notes that the growing scarcity of water affected metropolitan areas, and water shortages contributed to problems in irrigation farming. Unlike previous treaty violations, Indians continued to challenge illegal uses of these laws: "Despite all the measures the BIA took to improve farming and despite the framework of water rights established for the protection of reservation Indians, the fact remains that the western states generally ignored the Winters Doctrine and continued to allocate large amounts of water to non-Indians, even more water than actually existed."[28]

Peltier identified the heady times of revolt and rebellion of the 1960s as the backdrop for his early participation in the fight for civil and human rights. The federal policy aimed at undermining Indians' bond to their culture inadvertently contributed to their political awareness. The efforts at cultural erasure of Indians paralleled the segregation experienced by African Americans, for both emerged as socially sanctioned attempts to minimize the presence of both groups in the social landscape. The experiences of African Americans seemed even more profound for the Indian cause when mass relocation placed Indians in urban areas peppered with activists: "This was the time, remember, of the anti–Vietnam War movement and the New Left, of Black Power and Kent State and Watergate, of the Symbionese Liberation Army and the Weathermen. The notion of Red Power was inevitable. We didn't even have to invent a cause. We had one we'd been born with: the very survival of our people as a People."[29] Peltier took inspiration from black civil rights activists and others who had been intimidated into silence. It is important to recall that individuals involved in the black struggle for freedom perfected a successful response to large-scale discriminatory treatment. Their critique of government policies inspired Indians like Peltier to action.

Rather than just talking about deplorable conditions on the reservations and the general disdain individual whites had for Indians, Peltier began to articulate specific grievances as a result of his contact with activists: "Instead of reacting defensively to white man's chosen terms like 'termination' and 'relocation,' Indians on and off the rez began talking seriously and passionately about 'sovereignty' and 'treaty rights,' about 'reparations' as well as the 'return of ancestral lands.'"[30]

While nearly every Indian group had a history of exploitation to tell about the U.S. government, Peltier knew that the Sioux on the Pine Ridge Reservation had an especially strong case for many of their political grievances, many of which centered on land and trampled rights. Several scholars note the federal government's interest in the land held by Indians going back to 1868. Under Red Cloud, the Oglalas, the largest of the seven groups of Lakota Indians, made a unified military response to the United States invasion designed to open up a route to Virginia City that ultimately threatened the buffalo economy. The Oglalas succeeded in halting all traffic along the route, and Red Cloud used this leverage to get the federal government to sign the 1868 Laramie Treaty, which allowed the Lakotas a homeland in perpetuity, including the Black Hills, which they considered sacred. Under the provisions of the agreement, the treaty could not be altered except by the permission of the Lakotas.

However, alteration of the treaty became imminent when the press reported massive mineral resources located in the Oglala territory. In 1872, Congressman Moses Armstrong drafted a bill providing for the purchase of the Black Hills from the Lakota. When gold was actually discovered in 1874 and the Lakota refused to sell the Black Hills, the United States War Department authorized General Philip Sheridan to begin operations against the Sioux. However, by 1876, in exchange for desperately needed rations, the Lakotas signed away the title to the land. Yet, under the terms of the treaty, the government failed to secure that permission in a legal fashion, thus rendering the transaction illegal and void in the eyes of the Lakotas. Nevertheless, in 1877, Congress incorporated this land into U.S. territories. Scholars contend that "with the Lakota safely disarmed and immobilized, their leadership co-opted, killed in battle, assassinated or driven into exile, and the bulk of their land expropriated, the government launched an offensive intended to undercut their cultural integrity and free even more territory for 'settlement.'"[31]

The allotment system further destabilized the Sioux relationship to the land. In 1887, the General Allotment Act, also known as the Dawes Act, declared that private ownership of tribal lands became the federal government's official policy, a policy that was eagerly supported by private land speculators, natural resource industries, and cattle ranchers: "In their opinion only a healthy egoism, an 'intelligent greed,' and the desire for individual landownership could free Indians from their 'barbarous' condition. Reformers believed that abolishing reservations would result in Indian personal responsibility, while lobbyists reasoned Indians didn't need the land."[32] Allotment gave each Indian (except married women) a certain number of acres, and land not allotted was made available to whites. This profoundly affected the Sioux, for the Laramie Treaty of 1868 had given lands to the Western Sioux in perpetuity. The allotment divided this land into six smaller reservations, which violated the terms of the Laramie Treaty.

In addition to the land issue, government interaction radically changed the cultural lives of the Sioux. In 1883, Congress outlawed a range of Lakota spiritual ceremonies, including the Sun Dance, Lakota rites for burying the dead, and sweat lodges. In 1885, the Major Crimes Act usurped Indian sovereignty by giving the federal government jurisdiction over major felonies, which gave it license to control the justice system on the later-established reservations. No longer did Native American values hold sway in judicial decisions. The General Allotment Act eliminated the Indian custom of holding land communally, undermining collective consciousness and values of sharing among Indians: "In the view of this pressure to share one's possession with others, it is understandable that many reservation Indians have no great motivation for strenuous work to earn a large income or provide themselves with surplus reserves of money and material goods."[33]

Understanding the dynamic between the Sioux and the government in the 1880s is crucial to understanding the dynamic that led to their clash in the 1960s, for contemporary Indian activists framed their actions as a response to the historic discrimination practiced by the government. This type of Indian activism took its cue from the black civil rights movement. Black activists used the historical treatment of blacks to bolster their political and economic demands for justice. They often pointed to the degradation of centuries of backbreaking, unpaid labor and denial of educational opportunities, and showed that such forces continued to have a negative effect on African Americans in the 1960s. By articulating such connections, black activists spurred others to change the society. In the 1960s, Indians saw the success black activists had in acting in response to historic discrimination practiced by the government. This can be seen in the takeover by Indians of Alcatraz in 1969, an event that marked one of the first notable instances of Indian activism. Using the federal provision that allowed Indians first claim on surplus federal land, Richard Oakes led the takeover of Alcatraz. The group holding the island called themselves Indians of All Tribes, a political group that signified a pan-Indian movement, which distinguished these activists from national Indian organizations of the time. Scholars suggest that organizations such as the National Congress of American Indians held to the idea that Indians distinguished themselves from other groups by not overtly demonstrating.

However, student groups like the one led by Oakes were working to raise consciousness.[34] While Indians did not realize their goal of transforming Alcatraz into an Indian educational center, their protest demonstrated that Native Americans were ready to address publicly the circumstances of their lives.

The groups that participated in the Alcatraz takeover provided lessons for other Native American activist groups such as the American Indian Movement (AIM), which Peltier joined in 1968. His activities with AIM and other similar groups demonstrated his commitment to the betterment of his people. Peltier was active in efforts to enforce Indian fishing rights, the antiwar movement, and reappropriation of surplus Indian land. It is important to note that Peltier saw his political activities as an extension of his responsibility to his people: "This wasn't anti-*any*thing. This was *pro*-Indianism. Something new, an intertwining of traditional Indian Way and spiritual values with urban political savvy and an absolute dedication to our cause."[35]

Perhaps because of this distinction, Peltier saw AIM more as a movement made up of dedicated individuals working for a common goal and less as an organization: "There are no followers in AIM. We are all leaders. We are each an army of one, working for the survival of our people and of the Earth, our Mother. This isn't rhetoric. This is commitment. This is who we are."[36] Rather than being beholden to official leaders, AIM members relied on the wisdom of the elders. Peltier notes that AIM learned this lesson early on: "We never bothered with invitations from the traditional leaders the way we should have. . . . [Later] all that changed; we never went anyplace again without being invited by the elders."[37]

Thus began the more public phase of Peltier's activist life. In November 1972, Peltier joined AIM and participated in the "Trail of Broken Treaties" march to Washington. AIM sought to dialogue with government agencies on a range of issues, including a reorganization of the BIA and investigations into treaty violations. The event escalated when government security guards roughly handled women and elders in the group. In response, Peltier and others seized the BIA building, barricaded doors with furniture, and searched for files that would substantiate their claims of government deception in Indian relations. The group elected Peltier to be part of the security force for the activists to protect the elders and children. The standoff ended when the government made overtures to address the Indians' demands.

AIM intended for the siege of the BIA building to raise awareness about the plight of Indians. However, the siege mainly succeeded in making the organization and Peltier targets of the Federal Bureau of Investigation. While the protesters believed their actions were noble, the press portrayed them as violent and dangerous. According to a white paper by the Justice Department, "An Indian seated behind a bureaucrat's desk did not look like a civil rights protester. He looked like a burglar."[38] The FBI used the incident to identify Peltier as a key leader and extremist in AIM. Some historians assert that the fundamental task of the FBI since its inception was to function as "a mechanism to forestall, curtail and repress the expression of political diversity within the United States."[39]

Peltier's activist life increasingly became an expression of his political as well as spiritual life. Working at the grassroots level, Peltier helped to find employment for native people and worked in a rehab program overseen by the Milwaukee AIM group following the AIM siege. For Peltier, this was just the extension of his commitment to his people: "I also became increasingly involved in the spiritual side of AIM, the spiritual basis of the political work we were doing. You really can't separate the two in Indian Way. The political and spiritual side are one and the same. . . . In Indian Way, if you see your people suffering, helping them becomes absolutely necessary. It's not a social act of charity or welfare assistance; it's a spiritual act, a holy deed."[40] In August of 1973, Peltier attended his first Sun Dance, where he was pierced, a ritual that he credits for his ability to endure his treatment as an activist.

This integration of the spiritual and the political became greater for Peltier as his encounters with law enforcement began to escalate. In 1973, Peltier encountered two off-duty policemen who baited him in a local restaurant. They drew their weapons and found an inoperational gun on Peltier. Beaten and arrested on false charges of attempted murder, Peltier was imprisoned in a Milwaukee jail. Peltier fled the country and missed his pretrial hearing. A warrant was issued for his arrest. However specious, the murder charges were significant because they placed him even more prominently on the FBI's radar. The agency placed him on its most wanted list. Some historians argue that harassment arrests were used by the FBI toward civil rights activists to curtail their activities rather than in the interests of justice: "The repeated arrest of targeted individuals and organization members on spurious charges was carried out, not with any real hope of obtaining convictions (although there was always the possibility, assuming public sentiment had been sufficiently inflamed), but to simply harass, increase paranoia, tie activists up in a series of pre-arraignment incarcerations and preliminary courtroom procedures and deplete their resources through the postings of numerous bail bonds (as well as the retention of attorneys)."[41]

While on the run, Peltier remained active in Indian causes: fishing rights in Washington, protection at funerals for fallen Indian activists, protests involving Indian employees and manufacturers in Arizona. But 1975 marked the beginning of events that would catapult Peltier into the consciousness of mainstream America and test his commitment to his people and the cause of Indian rights. These events began with the situation on the Pine Ridge Reservation, which had been a hotbed of conflict for years as a result of tensions between the traditionals and the elected representatives. Journalist Jim Messerschmidt notes that when tribal chairman Dick Wilson was elected in 1972, he ignored the demands of traditional Indians. He used federal money to support the political police known as the Guardians of the Oglala Nation, or GOONs, who often attacked residents. Wilson demonstrated his complete lack of concern for Indian opinion when he signed away one-eighth of the reservation to the Badlands National Monument and attempted to sell the Black Hills.[42] It was his attempt to sell this sacred site that prompted Wounded Knee II, one of the most prominent Indian protests in contemporary times.

Peltier suggests that the federal government's presence on the Pine Ridge Reservation was linked to the lucrative natural resources on the reservation: "I have no doubt whatsoever that the real motivation behind both Wounded Knee II and the Oglala firefight, and much of the turmoil throughout Indian Country since the early 1970s, was—and is—the mining companies' desire to muffle AIM and all traditional Indian people, who sought—and still seek—to protect the land, water, and air from their thefts and depredations."[43] Peltier assumed, like many Native Americans, that the government would not stop until it had secured those resources, nor would the government stand idly by and allow militant Indians to dictate policy.

Presumably to that end, law enforcement used its considerable power to secure its authority on the reservation. Harassment and violent encounters between law enforcement and residents at Pine Ridge dramatically increased. Between 1973 and 1975 the General Accounting Office documented sixty murders of Indians during that time. No one was ever held responsible for the homicides. Residents referred to this time as the "reign of terror," and in response, the elders of the Oglala Lakotas asked AIM members to help protect Indians from attacks by GOONs. Peltier insisted that "we weren't there to attack or kill or intimidate anybody, only to stand between the GOONs and the traditionalists with our bodies, our prayers, and a small supply of defensive arms. We called ourselves a spiritual camp, and that's what we truly were."[44] Peltier and other AIM members set up their headquarters near the home of Harry and Cecelia Jumping Bull.

During this time, Peltier and other AIM members discussed the rights for Indians to live their way of life: "In Oglala, the AIM people combined talks on the 1868 Treaty and the struggle for sovereignty with community service: they chopped firewood for stoves of the elderly, planted trees and a community garden to offset the unhealthy welfare food, reroofed a store that had burned down and provided counseling to alcoholics."[45] AIM activists were also engaged in political discussions about the future. Indian activist Jean Day recalled that "we also met with the elders and the traditional people and many, many families, and we discussed the realities of sovereignty. What does it mean, and how can we live it? We'd talk about, What Does the Treaty Mean? There was a lot of learning and teaching going on at that time."[46]

According to Peltier, early on the morning of June 26, 1975, he heard gunshots emanating from the Jumping Bull home, then screams. Unsure of what was going on, he grabbed a rifle and ran toward the house. The Jumping Bulls were not there, but he walked into the middle of a firefight involving unknown participants. Fearing for the lives of children, Peltier and other Indians fired some warning shots over the strangers' heads. A little while later, Peltier and the others discovered the dead bodies of federal agents Jack Coler and Ronald Williams slumped behind the wheel of their car, as well as the body of Indian Joe Killsright Stuntz, whose murder was never investigated. Peltier immediately realized the significance of the situation: "If those agents were dead, we—those of us Indians at the Jumping Bull property that day, whether man, woman and child—were as good as dead, too."[47] Peltier and the others fled and were captured in the midst of what was called the largest manhunt until that time.

The FBI and those who support their handling of the case against Peltier told a different story. According to journalist Mark Tooley, two FBI agents, Jack Coler and Ronald Williams, were pursuing a suspect, Jimmy Eagle, when Williams reported that individuals appeared from the van with rifles, poised to fire. The agents' car was hit more than one hundred twenty times by bullets from a range of firearms, and the agents managed to get off only a few shots of their own. Coler was shot in the initial firefight, but both Coler and Williams were killed at close range. The FBI argued that a witness identified Peltier as the driver of the van and found Peltier's thumbprint on Coler's gun. They also recovered other firearms and explosives in the van they say Peltier drove. In the end, the government contended that Peltier was a longtime criminal and represented a dangerous and disruptive force on the reservation and that Peltier killed the two FBI agents with malice and without mercy. He was captured while fleeing the scene.[48]

While four individuals were indicted for the deaths of the two agents, only three individuals went to trial. Charges were dropped due to insufficient evidence against Eagle; Dino Butler and Bob Robideau went to trial in Cedar Rapids, Iowa, in July 1976, where they were acquitted. Peltier became the last suspect left to convict for the deaths of the two agents. Fearing that he could not receive a fair and impartial trial from the U.S. government, Peltier fled to Canada to seek sanctuary during the trials of Butler and Robideau. Peltier was arrested February 6, 1976, and held in the Okalla Prison in Vancouver, British Columbia, when the U.S. government produced an affidavit from Myrtle Poor Bear, who swore that she overheard a plot to kill agents and saw Peltier shoot the agents. Upon this affidavit and other evidence later determined to be false, the government convinced Canadian courts to extradite Peltier to the United States, where he was certain to be convicted.

Many of Peltier's supporters contend that the government's case was riddled with lies and misrepresentations. Some historians argue that fabrication of evidence, withholding of exculpatory evidence, and intimidation of witnesses were widely used FBI tactics.[49] Requests via the Freedom of Information Act demonstrated that the FBI falsely reported matches between Peltier's rifle and a casing found in the FBI agents' car. Poor Bear's affidavit was later proved to be coerced by FBI agents who showed her a picture of a dead Indian woman's hands and told her that she would end up the same way unless she cooperated.[50] She had never seen Peltier and was not at the Jumping Bulls' house on the Pine Ridge Reservation.

The Canadian government extradited Peltier back to the United States in December 1976. In March 1977, Peltier's trial was moved from Cedar Rapids, Iowa, to Fargo, North Dakota, which he described as "an openly hostile court."[51] Peltier cited irregularities with his trial, including the introduction of illegal evidence, misconduct on the part of the government regarding witnesses, and judicial misconduct when the judge prevented him from pleading self-defense. On July 1, 1977, Peltier was sentenced to two consecutive life terms in the U.S. penitentiary at Leavenworth, Kansas, by an all-white jury after eight hours of deliberation. In a statement in court, Peltier accused the court of perpetuating the long history of discrimination against Indians: "You are about to perform an act which will close one more chapter in the history of the failure of the United States to do justice in the case of a Native American. After centuries of murder of millions of my brothers and sisters by white racist America, could I have been wise in thinking you would break that tradition and commit an act of justice?"[52] Once again, Peltier placed his fate within the context of his ancestors and his people.

Peltier's incarceration initiated a new chapter of his struggle for equal treatment. In 1979, Peltier recalls that he was inexplicably moved from a maximum-security prison in Marion, Illinois, to a low-security prison in Lompoc, California. There, he discovered an assassination plot against his own life. He unsuccessfully attempted to escape and received an additional seven years added to his consecutive life sentences for his trouble.

Peltier's legal wrangling with the government continued after his conviction. On March 5, 1979, the Supreme Court refused to review his case. On October 1, 1984, hearings for a new trial began in Bismarck, North Dakota, before the same judge who presided over Peltier's original trial. In 1985, this judge denied Peltier's appeal for a new trial. In 1986, the Eighth Circuit Court of Appeals acknowledged misconduct on the part of the government involving evidence and witnesses, yet it denied Peltier's appeal. In 1992, Peltier was still considered guilty of aiding and abetting a murder despite the court's acknowledgment of the lack of credible evidence to prove his guilt of murder and the government's admission that it did not know who killed the FBI agents. In late 1993, former U.S. attorney general Ramsey Clark submitted a formal application for clemency on behalf of Peltier—it was denied. In 1998, the U.S. Parole Commission rejected his bid for parole; he can apply again in 2008. Peltier believes that "the fact that I was convicted without any credible evidence of guilt, and that no amount of genuine evidence to the contrary, however overwhelming, seems to be enough to win my release or even a retrial much less parole after nearly a quarter of a century, is precisely why I am often called—no doubt to the great embarrassment of the United States government—a 'political prisoner.'"[53]

Despite failing health and abuse from the prison system, Peltier continues to serve his people. He participates in a weekly sweat lodge with fellow Indian prisoners. He has organized charitable drives. He has sponsored campaigns for improving the health care system on the Rosebud Reservation and economic reform at Pine Ridge. His current work on winning religious rights for Native American prisoners represents his continued struggle on behalf of Indians. Even though the federal government prides itself on the religious freedoms imbedded in the Constitution, historian Lyman H. Legters notes that the government still seems reluctant to enforce that freedom for Indians: "So far as the narrower issue of religious freedom is concerned, the promise of the American Indian Religious Freedom Act (AIRFA) has been systematically thwarted by the executive and judicial branches as they converted a substantive intent into a procedural charade."[54]

Peltier's mode of activism mirrored two themes that historian Raymond D'Angelo uses to describe black civil rights activity. On one hand, Peltier's actions represented the embodiment of the intersection of private lives and public events: "The movement offers us a case study of the problem of injustice, which was not simply an individual trap but the result of the destructive historical condition of segregation reaching beyond ordinary citizens. Personal problems of victimization by racism and discrimination became a 'public issue' with the widespread recognition that the aggregate number of individual problems threatened American society as a whole."[55] During his activism, Peltier stressed that his actions were not just sparked by his own experience, but by the realization that his life as an Indian was contextualized by the larger legacy of white-Indian relations.

On the other hand, D'Angelo also points to an alternative model of civil rights activity by suggesting that "the civil rights movement was driven by the courage and conviction of ordinary citizens who listened to leaders, and at times pushed them in the right direction."[56] Peltier rarely describes himself as a leader or hero, just as an ordinary person engaged in a struggle for justice. Often, his explanations of key events in his activist life focus on the inevitability and inherent rightness of his actions. Using these two critical lenses provided by D'Angelo, Peltier's life represents not just the actions of a revolutionary from the heyday of the sixties, but also a model that shows that individuals can affect the course of events for the better, even when such actions extract a high toll for the individual.

After all of his literal trials and tribulations, Peltier still wants what he has always wanted: "No one can bring the dead back. But we can do something for the living. Economic reparations to Native Americans are absolutely essential for a just future, as is the return of sacred sites and significant pieces of ancestral territory, as well as a fair share of the natural resources on lands taken in violation of treaties. . . . The law I look to for justice for my people is not the white man's law, the unnatural law, the man-given law. The law my people and I look to is the law of the Great Spirit, which never ceases to work."[57] To this day, Peltier works on the premise that he was not put here to be perfect—he was put here to be useful to his people everywhere.

NOTES

1. Leonard Peltier, *Prison Writings: My Life Is My Sun Dance* (New York: St. Martin's Griffin, 1999), 50.
2. Howard Zinn, *A People's History of the United States, 1492–present*, rev. ed. (New York: HarperPerennial, 1995), 125.
3. Andrew Jackson, quoted in Ronald Takaki, *A Different Mirror: A History of Multicultural America* (Boston: Little, Brown, 1993), 85–86.
4. Takaki, *A Different Mirror*, 233.
5. Peltier, *Prison Writings*, 61.
6. Klaus Frantz, *Indian Reservations in the United States: Territory, Sovereignty, and Socioeconomic Change* (Chicago: University of Chicago Press, 1999), 21.
7. Michael C. Coleman, *Presbyterian Missionary Attitudes toward American Indians, 1837–1893* (Jackson and London: University Press of Mississippi, 1985), 36.
8. Peltier, *Prison Writings*, 73.
9. Peltier, *Prison Writings*, 76.
10. Peltier, *Prison Writings*, 58.
11. Peltier, *Prison Writings*, 78.
12. David Wallace Adams, *Education for Extinction: American Indians and the Boarding School Experience, 1875–1928* (Lawrence: University Press of Kansas, 1995), 35.
13. Adams, *Education for Extinction*, 101.
14. Adams, *Education for Extinction*, 121.
15. Joel Spring, *Deculturalization and the Struggle for Equality: A Brief History of the Education of Dominated Cultures in the United States* (New York: McGraw-Hill, 1994), 20.
16. Peltier, *Prison Writings*, 78.
17. Peltier, *Prison Writings*, 79.
18. Peter Matthiessen, *In the Spirit of Crazy Horse* (New York: Viking, 1991), 46.
19. Peltier, *Prison Writings*, 84.
20. Matthiessen, *Crazy Horse*, 48.
21. Peltier, *Prison Writings*, 80.
22. Peltier, *Prison Writings*, 89.
23. Peltier, *Prison Writings*, 83.
24. Peltier, *Prison Writings*, 90.
25. John Sanchez, Mary E. Stuckey, and Richard Morris, "Rhetorical Exclusion: The Government's Case Against American Indian Activists, AIM and Leonard Peltier," *American Indian Culture and Research Journal* 23, no. 2 (1999): 30.
26. Frantz, *Indian Reservations*, 17.
27. Peltier, *Prison Writings*, 91.
28. Frantz, *Indian Reservations*, 215.
29. Peltier, *Prison Writings*, 94.
30. Peltier, *Prison Writings*, 92.
31. Ward Churchill and Jim Vander Wall, *Agents of Repression: The FBI's Secret Wars Against the Black Panther Party and the American Indian Movement* (Boston: South End Press, 1988), 110.

32. Frantz, *Indian Reservations*, 23.

33. Frantz, *Indian Reservations*, 170.

34. Paul Chaat Smith and Robert Allan Warrior, *Like a Hurricane: The Indian Movement from Alcatraz to Wounded Knee* (New York: The New Press, 1996), 37.

35. Peltier, *Prison Writings*, 94.

36. Peltier, *Prison Writings*, 98.

37. Matthiessen, *Crazy Horse*, 50.

38. Matthiessen, *Crazy Horse*, 54.

39. Churchill and Vander Wall, *Agents of Repression*, 12.

40. Peltier, *Prison Writings*, 103.

41. Churchill and Vander Wall, *Agents of Repression*, 44.

42. Jim Messerschmidt, *The Trial of Leonard Peltier* (Boston: South End Press, 1983), 3.

43. Peltier, *Prison Writings*, 117.

44. Peltier, *Prison Writings*, 113.

45. Matthiessen, *Crazy Horse*, 142.

46. Matthiessen, *Crazy Horse*, 143.

47. Peltier, *Prison Writings*, 126.

48. Mark Tooley, "The Unpardonable Leonard Peltier: Why Does the Left Want to Release the Murderer of Two FBI Agents?" *The Weekly Standard*, December 20, 1999, 20.

49. Churchill and Vander Wall, *Agents of Repression*, 51.

50. In September 1975, Anna Mae Aquash was arrested with other AIM activists and, according to Aquash, was threatened by FBI to give false testimony against Peltier and refused. On February 24, a Jane Doe later identified as Aquash was found dead on the Pine Ridge Reservation. The BIA coroner declared that she died of exposure, and her hands were cut off and taken by the FBI for identification, but they already knew her identity. After the body was exhumed by Aquash's family, a new coroner discovered that she was shot in the back of the head.

51. Peltier, *Prison Writings*, 159.

52. Peltier, *Prison Writings*, 238.

53. Peltier, *Prison Writings*, 163.

54. Lyman H. Legters, "Indian Religion, the First Amendment, and the State," in Lyman H. Legters and Fremont J. Lyden, eds., *American Indian Policy: Self Governance and Economic Development* (Westport, Conn.: Greenwood Press, 1994), 92.

55. Raymond D'Angelo, preface to *The American Civil Rights Movement: Readings and Interpretations* (New York: McGraw-Hill, 2001), xiii–xiv.

56. D'Angelo, preface to *The American Civil Rights Movement*, xiv.

57. Peltier, *Prison Writings*, 204, 205.

SUGGESTED READING

Adams, David Wallace. *Education for Extinction: American Indians and the Boarding School Experience, 1875–1928*. Lawrence: University Press of Kansas, 1995.

Churchill, Ward, and Jim Vander Wall. *Agents of Repression: The FBI's Secret Wars Against the Black Panther Party and the American Indian Movement*. Boston: South End Press, 1988.

Coleman, Michael C. *Presbyterian Missionary Attitudes toward American Indians, 1837–1893*. Jackson and London: University Press of Mississippi, 1985.

D'Angelo, Raymond. Preface to *The American Civil Rights Movement: Readings and Interpretations*. New York: McGraw-Hill, 2001.

Frantz, Klaus. *Indian Reservations in the United States: Territory, Sovereignty, and Socioeconomic Change*. Chicago: University of Chicago Press, 1999.

Legters, Lyman H. "Indian Religion, the First Amendment, and the State." In *American Indian Policy: Self Governance and Economic Development*, edited by Lyman H. Legters and Fremont J. Lyden. Westport, Conn.: Greenwood Press, 1994, 91–102.

Matthiessen, Peter. *In the Spirit of Crazy Horse*. New York: Viking, 1991.

Messerschmidt, Jim. *The Trial of Leonard Peltier*. Boston: South End Press, 1983.

Peltier, Leonard. *Prison Writings: My Life Is My Sun Dance*. New York: St. Martin's Griffin, 1999.

Sanchez, John, Mary E. Stuckey, and Richard Morris. "Rhetorical Exclusion: The Government's Case Against American Indian Activists, AIM and Leonard Peltier." *American Indian Culture and Research Journal* 23, no. 2 (1999): 27–52.

Smith, Paul Chaat, and Robert Allan Warrior. *Like a Hurricane: The Indian Movement from Alcatraz to Wounded Knee*. New York: The New Press, 1996.

Spring, Joel. *Deculturalization and the Struggle for Equality: A Brief History of the Education of Dominated Cultures in the United States*. New York: McGraw-Hill, 1994.

Takaki, Ronald. *A Different Mirror: A History of Multicultural America*. Boston: Little, Brown, 1993.

Tooley, Mark. "The Unpardonable Leonard Peltier: Why Does the Left Want to Release the Murderer of Two FBI Agents?" *The Weekly Standard*. December 20, 1999, 20.

Zinn, Howard. *A People's History of the United States, 1492–present*. Rev. ed. New York: HarperPerennial, 1995.

16

&

Sylvia Rivera:
Fighting in Her Heels:
Stonewall, Civil Rights,
and Liberation

Layli Phillips and Shomari Olugbala

This chapter details the life and legacy of Sylvia Lee Rivera (1951–2002), a life-long activist for the rights and visibility of gay, lesbian, and transgender people, gender nonconformists, and homeless street youth. Through her role in the 1969 Stonewall Rebellion, she became a pivotal figure in and an icon of two movements: gay liberation and transgender rights. "Punctum theory" is defined and presented as a means for understanding critical moments in history, using both Brown v. Board of Education *and the Stonewall Rebellion as illustrations. Critical moments in Sylvia Rivera's development as an activist are also chronicled. Finally, Sylvia Rivera's lasting contributions to American culture and society are examined.*

> When I was young, I never thought I was going to be a part of gay history—
> I didn't even expect that gay history would be in existence. So there's a lot
> of joy in my heart. . . . But I do get depressed when this time of year comes
> around: for 30 years I've been struggling and fighting, and I still feel like an
> outcast in the gay community.
>
> Sylvia Rivera[1]

Sylvia Lee Rivera (1951–2002), born Ray Rivera Mendoza to parents of Puerto Rican, Venezuelan, and Mexican descent, was a lifelong activist for the rights and visibility of gay, lesbian, and transgender people, gender nonconformists, and homeless street youth. In her lifetime, she achieved status as an icon of the gay rights movement due to her pivotal role in the

1969 Stonewall Rebellion. After the Stonewall Rebellion, Sylvia continued to engage in "street activism" as well as leading and participating in organized efforts to advance gay and transgender liberation. Throughout her lifetime, Sylvia advocated for homeless street youth, many of whom were gay or transgender themselves. In 1970, she founded S.T.A.R., or Street Transvestite Action Revolutionaries, later Street Transgender Action Revolutionaries, and the S.T.A.R. House, a residence for transgender street youth in New York City, with fellow activist Marsha P. Johnson. By the time of her death, Sylvia had received numerous accolades and awards recognizing her lifetime of activism, although ironically, much of her life she had been shunned and ignored by the mainstream gay community for her radical politics and unabashed transgenderism and gender nonconformity. During her lifetime, she also faced many personal obstacles, including childhood sexual abuse, homelessness, drug addiction, depression, and attempted suicide, which complicated her public life and led to periods of relative inactivity. Like many great historical figures whose importance is fully recognized only after their deaths, Sylvia lived in near obscurity during the latter decades of her life. Nevertheless, today her significance to the gay and lesbian as well as transgender rights movements is affirmed and celebrated by numerous historians, activists, and members of the general public.

In this chapter, we will discuss the significance of the Stonewall Rebellion and its link to the civil rights movement. In addition, we will discuss the role of Sylvia Rivera during the Stonewall Rebellion and related aftermath. We will present biographical information about Sylvia Rivera and discuss her legacy with regard to both civil rights and liberation for gay, lesbian, and transgender people as well as people of color. Before proceeding to these topics, however, we will begin with a model for interpreting important historical events. This model will serve as a foundation for interweaving the numerous themes addressed in this chapter.

THINKING ABOUT CRITICAL MOMENTS IN HISTORY

History can be thought of as a series of critical moments in time wherein noteworthy transformations in society took place. Whether to deem particular events or developments noteworthy is, of course, hotly debated by historians and others. Regardless, the societal transformations in question are all produced by a unique confluence of antecedent factors, many of which can be identified and examined. In addition, each of these societal transformations produces multiple and divergent aftereffects, which, likewise, can be named and observed. The work of history, then, can be thought of as, among other things, a process of deconstructing events and developments in human society on the basis of things that came before and after them. It should be

Sylvia Rivera (Image courtesy of Lina Pollata.)

remembered that all such events are subject to interpretation, and that not all historians interpret the same event the same way.

Our purpose in this chapter is to interpret and deconstruct a particular historical event, namely, the 1969 Stonewall Rebellion, in ways that relate it to the civil rights movement of the latter half of the twentieth century in the United States. In interpreting and deconstructing the Stonewall Rebellion, we will focus on the figure of Sylvia Rivera, a key actor in, and later icon of, that event. We will analyze both the antecedents and sequelae of the Stonewall Rebellion in light of Sylvia Rivera's personal history and participation, noting the intersecting strands of race, class, gender, nationality, and sexuality-based politics in the production of this event's meaning and potential.

Chela Sandoval, Chicana feminist and history-of-consciousness scholar, has used the term *punctum* to describe a point in history where the status quo ruptures and new possibilities become thinkable and workable.[2] These moments of possibility are at the heart of socially transformative events like those described in the preceding paragraphs. They occur when the convergence of competing social forces produces events that surprise or even shock the larger society, making for unprecedented windows of opportunity with regard to social change. A punctum can be visualized as a bursting bubble, as a moment in time when society is shaken up but not settled down.

At the center of the model we are proposing is a punctum containing the socially transformative event in question. To the left of the punctum are two lines representing the antecedents of the transformative event. It is assumed that competing forces were operating in society prior to the event and that these competing forces eventually converged to produce the event. A wavy line represents the "march toward liberation," or, collectively, all those events and processes encompassing oppressed people's struggle against oppression and for liberation and full humanization.[3] The waviness of the line represents the ups and downs of that struggle. A jagged line represents maintenance of the status quo by those with oppressive power in society. Collectively, it includes all of those events and processes that created or maintained social inequality, generated violence, or prevented the full humanization of some members of society based on their group membership (race, class, gender, nationality, sexuality, etc.). The jaggedness of the line represents the harshness of the process and its wounding effect on those who were actively oppressed. Our model assumes that a punctum is produced when the competing antecedent forces converge at a point of direct human contact between representatives of the two processes and either a decision must be made about how to interrelate in the future or a notable shift in power relations occurs.

To the right of the punctum are two spiraling lines representing the historical consequences of the punctum. In an ideal scenario, the punctum would produce a single line representing the achievement of social justice and reconciliation between the people whose groups make up the competing forces. However, in reality, such a clear-cut and harmonious reconciliation is rarely achieved and social justice in the purest sense is not permanently established. Thus, the two spiraling lines represent partial victories for both sides, namely oppressed people seeking liberation and those in power wishing to maintain the status quo. As a result of the punctum, however, the life context has been changed significantly for both groups. The spiraling quality of the lines on the right side of the punctum represents the unpredictability of the outcomes that result from the shake-up of society. When things begin to settle down and new social processes begin to manifest, their exact nature cannot be known immediately. Outcomes spiral in all directions, often reconfiguring the internal dynamics of the groups in question and reordering the relations between the two factions. Thus, the spiraling lines warn us not to oversimplify the nature of the social change that has resulted from the punctum.

An important note about the punctum: Although it has been characterized as a single event or critical moment in history, that event or moment actually contains its own defined time line. Thus, the punctum is not a single moment in time, but rather an important, transformative event that took place over a relatively brief, identifiable period of time. This fact is important because microevents that take place within the punctum have the potential to influence the outcomes that emerge from the punctum. In a sense, the groundwork for the future is laid within the parameters of the punctum itself. Within the workings of the punctum, certain possibilities are enabled, while others are constrained.

To clarify the nature of the proposed model, we offer an example that relies upon a well-known transformative historical event, namely, the Supreme Court's 1954 *Brown v. Board of Education* decision that desegregated public schools in the United States. In this case, the Supreme Court's decision would be considered the punctum. This event represented the convergence of competing forces—those representing black liberation (which had, since the time of emancipation and even during slavery, organized and carried out a variety of resistance activities in the face of racism) and those representing maintenance of the racially discriminatory status quo (which had, beginning with slavery and continuing through the Jim Crow era, enforced racial discrimination and endorsed brutality toward black people). Representatives of these forces carried out face-to-face interactions in the context of a confined time (the time it took to hear and decide the *Brown v. Board of Education* case) and place (the Supreme Court of the United States). During the course of the case, different arguments were made and different pieces of evidence were offered to influence the outcome of the decision. Ultimately, a single, unanimous, and forceful decision was rendered that incorporated various aspects of the arguments and evidence presented by both sides. The most notable effect of the decision was the legally enforced racial desegregation of public schools in the

United States. An important by-product of the school desegregation process was the desegregation of other public facilities, which produced a massive change in the social context by increasing access for large numbers of previously disenfranchised people. This Supreme Court decision also sparked the most active phase of the civil rights movement.

A less well-known aspect of the Supreme Court's written decision, however, is its racially biased rationale for enforcing legal desegregation.[4] In an amicus brief submitted by the defense (spearheaded by Thurgood Marshall, who was then the attorney representing the African American defendants) and written by a racially integrated team of progressive social scientists (spearheaded by Kenneth B. Clark, then an up-and-coming social psychologist), the argument was advanced that segregation hurts children of both races. Black children were harmed, it was argued, because segregation led to low self-esteem and awareness that the black race was viewed by mainstream white society as inferior. White children were harmed, it was argued, because segregation gave them a false sense of racial superiority and dominance, possibly engendering an authoritarian personality. Yet, when the Supreme Court rendered its written decision, it acknowledged only that segregation hurt black children. This elision set the stage for those whose job it was to operationalize legally enforced segregation—that is, to make it happen—to do so in ways that allowed white educational institutions to remain largely unchanged except for the introduction of black pupils and, in some instances, black teachers, and black educational institutions to be effectively dismissed and dismantled. In the long run, this elision further allowed new and less obvious forms of segregation, such as ability tracking and racial isolation of students of color, to be reestablished within schools, thus undermining the social change objective of promoting integration and access and eliminating race-based discrimination and inequality. Thus, the events that took place within the confined parameters of the punctum itself influenced the quantity and quality of social change it produced.

Having provided a framework for thinking about historical events, let us now shift our focus to the Stonewall Rebellion.

THE STONEWALL REBELLION AS A
CRITICAL MOMENT IN HISTORY

At 1:20 a.m. on Saturday, June 28, 1969, a group of eight police officers, including one in uniform and seven in plain clothes—six men and two women—raided the Stonewall Inn and were resisted by patrons. The Stonewall Inn, located at 53 Christopher Street in the Greenwich Village section of New York City, was a popular gay bar. Like many gay bars in New York City during this period, the Stonewall Inn was owned and operated by members of the Mafia. Raids on gay bars during the 1950s and 1960s were common, but before the fateful night of June 27, 1969, patrons generally co-operated with police and dispersed quickly to avoid public exposure and arrest on morals charges.

Big cities like New York operated vice squads whose job it was to enforce laws that prohibited prostitution, gambling, racketeering, homosexual activity, and transvestitism. The enforcement of these laws, however, typically involved a highly choreographed script. Because the police often received pay-offs from the Mafia, police were sometimes disinclined from completely disabling or closing down the very businesses they raided. Thus, police or informants would provide tip-offs to bar operators in advance of a scheduled raid. Bar operators would then signal to patrons that a raid was about to occur. Patrons would then cease or mask illegal activity (for instance, in gay bars, same-sex couples would stop dancing or touching, women or men who were dressed like the opposite gender would leave or hide, and contraband would be concealed or removed from the premises) for the duration of the raid. Police would enter the premises, make a few symbolic arrests or rough a few people up, then leave—and the illegal activity would resume. Such events were considered "part of life" for gay men, lesbians, and transsexuals prior to the Stonewall Rebellion.

The night of Friday, June 27, 1969, was different. That night, the Stonewall Inn, which typically catered to gay men, was host to a diverse group of gay men, transsexuals, and even a few lesbians. Only a few days before, gay icon Judy Garland had died. Her funeral services had been held that very day in a funeral home on Madison Avenue and Eighty-first Street, drawing twenty thousand mourners and spectators. Large numbers of gay fans were out and about in the city that evening. In addition, Sheridan Square Park, adjacent to the Stonewall Inn, had become something of a campground for a multiracial coterie of gay homeless street youth, many of them transvestites and transsexuals. When the police began to assemble outside the Stonewall Inn late that night, spectators gathered and waited expectantly.

Things were also different inside the bar. Unlike most nights, the bar operators had not been tipped off about this night's planned raid. In addition, a different segment of the police force—officers of the First Division rather than the Sixth Precinct—was conducting the raid. There is also evidence that members of the federal government from the Bureau of Alcohol, Tobacco, and Firearms were indirectly involved. A new head of the First Division, Deputy Inspector Seymour Pine, had recently been hired and wanted to make his mark by getting serious about vice law enforcement. When police broke through the door, both the bar operators and the patrons were caught by surprise.

Sylvia Rivera was among the patrons at the bar that night. A raucous eighteen-year-old, she was in no mood to take the police interference with her night of merriment lying down. Although popular myth has it that Sylvia "threw the first grenade" of the evening, by her own account, she was actually the second person to resist the police in such a visible manner. Nevertheless, from that moment on, Sylvia Rivera was among the most active and vocal resisters in the rebellion[5] that followed. As a Puerto Rican drag queen, she was also one of the most easily identifiable participants. Along with many other people who participated in or witnessed the events of that night, Sylvia had a hunch that this night would later prove to be of great significance, an important turning point for the gay, lesbian, and transgender communities. She has been quoted as proclaiming, "I'm not missing a minute of this—it's the *revolution!*"[6] In another account, she recollected saying, "Oh Lord Jesus, the revolution is finally here! Hallelujah—it's time to go do your thing!"[7] In yet another account, she reports that her feeling was, "Oh my God, the revolution is here. Thank God. I'm here and I'm part of it."[8]

An excellent and detailed account of the events of June 27 and 28, 1969, as well as their aftermath, can be found in Martin Duberman's 1993 book *Stonewall* as well as in the PBS film series *The Question of Equality: Lesbian and Gay Politics in American Since Stonewall* produced by the Testing the Limits video collective and the accompanying 1995 book edited by David Deitcher. For purposes of this chapter, the most important events can be summarized as follows: After police entered the bar, patrons with IDs began to line up and file out. Those who were unruly or defiant were pulled aside by police. A paddy wagon pulled up and police began to load those people who had been pulled aside. Unlike usual, however, those patrons who had been released did not quickly disperse. In concert with onlookers who had already gathered outside and more who continued to gather, bar patrons began to boo and hiss at the officers. Boos and hisses escalated into a chorus of defiant shouts and taunts. People began to throw coins at the officers as a symbol for payoffs. As Sylvia Rivera remarked, "You could feel the electricity going through the people. You could actually feel it. People were getting really, really pissed and uptight."[9] Some members of the crowd began pressing against the paddy wagon. Police called for people to back up and, when they didn't, began prodding people with their clubs. By one account, a lesbian, singled out for dressing in men's clothing, was loaded into a waiting police car. When she immediately jumped out the other side, her action was read by the crowd and police alike as a turning point: the first act of open resistance. Almost simultaneously, a particular drag queen asked the police officers to stop pushing and, when they did not, began swinging. From there, a melee quickly ensued. To quote Craig Rodwell, another eyewitness and participant, "A number of incidents were happening simultaneously. There was no one thing that happened or person . . . a flash of group—of mass—anger."[10] According to Sylvia Rivera herself, "A lot of blood was shed, but people stood. . . . Nobody was afraid that night to die."[11] Eventually, cries of "Gay power!" could be heard rising from the din.

As the night wore on, police eventually had to take shelter within the Stonewall Inn, which they had previously cleared out. Barricading themselves inside, they prepared for the worst. As Seymour Pine subsequently recalled, "For some reason, things were different this night. As we were bringing the prisoners out, they were resisting."[12] Outside the bar, rioters were turning over cars, uprooting parking meters, setting fires, cutting phone wires, and throwing explosives. Sylvia Rivera reports being handed a Molotov cocktail and being told to throw it, which she did. Ultimately, the Stonewall Inn itself was bombarded and set aflame. The officers were forced out and placed a call for emergency backup. At around 2:55 a.m., the New York City Tactical Patrol Force (TPF)—a riot-control team of two dozen—appeared, complete with clubs, tear gas, and face masks. Protesters, who had by this time worked up a great deal of courage and zeal, were not intimidated. A chorus line of drag queens had formed, Rockette-style, and followed the TPF around the block, singing bawdy, resistant chants and intimidating the police. As Sylvia Rivera recounted, "It was street gay people from the Village out front—homeless people who lived in the park in Sheridan Square outside the bar—and then drag queens behind them and everybody behind us."[13] As another early activist later related, "Anyone with more to lose would never have stood up to the cops the way the drag queens and street kids did at the Stonewall that hot weekend in June 1969."[14] Members of the TPF singled out resisters to beat, but members of the crowd cooperated to rescue those being beaten. By 3:35 a.m., when police officially declared the situation over, it could be fairly stated that the police had lost and the gay, lesbian, and transsexual resisters had won.

Craig Rodwell, a gay man with professional connections with several New York City newspapers, placed phone calls during the event and had reporters on the scene on very short order. Running back to his apartment, he grabbed his camera and took pictures, insuring that the events of the night would appear in the next day's front-page news. As Sylvia Rivera later reminisced, "The movement was born that night, and we knew we had done something that everybody in the whole world would know about when the news came out."[15] And thus did the Stonewall Rebellion go down in history.

For several days and nights thereafter, crowds appeared at the scene. As Sylvia Rivera reported, "Even the next day there was an immediate change amongst the community—letting themselves be visible to the world. You saw lovers walking down the street holding hands and kissing in public."[16] In fact, resistance on the second night was arguably stronger and more organized. According to Bob Kohler, a prominent early participant in the Gay Liberation Front, "[D]uring that day, people started showing up with leaflets. The first leaflet I saw said, 'Are homosexuals revolting? You bet your ass they are!'"[17] He continued, "The second night you did have—and I use the word kindly—provocateurs. . . . Things were actually worse. More people got hurt. It was a rebellion. . . . [T]he second night was more planned. You had Trotskyites, you had crazies and yippies. You had almost every gay person that had ever had a radical thought turn out."[18] For the week thereafter, heightened activity around the Stonewall Inn was abundant. Pro-gay graffiti began to appear on surfaces all over the Village. Gay activists began forming new organizations and plotting new agendas. A new era of gay and lesbian visibility, pride, and activism had dawned.

Having described the punctum that will hereafter be referred to simply as Stonewall, we will now turn to a description and discussion of the antecedents and sequelae of the event, allowing us to relate the event to the civil rights movement and the larger context of liberation struggles occurring in the United States and globally during the 1950s, 1960s, and 1970s.

SOCIAL FORCES LEADING UP TO THE STONEWALL REBELLION

Many people falsely assume that gay and lesbian activism began with Stonewall. Like those who assume that African Americans did little to resist their oppression prior to the Emancipation Proclamation or prior to the time Rosa Parks sat down in the white section on the bus in Montgomery, Alabama, they fail to appreciate much of the groundwork that was laid prior to the "big event." Indeed, such groundwork constitutes the entire "march toward liberation" leading up to the punctum itself. In this section, we will briefly discuss some of the social forces that produced the punctum we know as Stonewall. In so doing, we will illustrate the larger context in which Stonewall was embedded as a historical event.

In the period after World War II, a number of social movements were gaining momentum. That the war had been fought, by the United States at least, to "make the world safe for democracy" animated a number of thinkers and activists who were concerned about the absence of democratic freedoms and effective citizenship for members of certain groups within supposedly free, democratic countries. For instance, in the United States, African Americans and their political allies at home and abroad began to question and contest institutionalized racial discrimination practices, leading to the emergence of the civil rights movement and later the Black Power movement. Anarchists, communists, socialists, and labor unionists had all developed well-articulated critiques of the U.S. class structure in the period since World War I and had developed dramatic and effective strategies for addressing issues related to workers' rights. Globally, Marxism and socialism were on the rise as colonized nations in Africa, Asia, Latin America, and the Caribbean looked for models that would help them throw off the colonial yoke and become economically and politically independent of the European nations that ruled and occupied them. As these events were unfolding, African Americans in the United States became more conscious of their links to other blacks outside the United States, particularly in Africa and the Caribbean, where black people were achieving self-rule, thus heightening their political fervor. Feminism was beginning to inspire women around the world, particularly white women in the United States and Europe, to question gender subordination and patriarchy. Similarly, gay and lesbian individuals were beginning to recognize that they formed a political interest group that had been subjected to systematic discrimination and oppression. Thus, organizations whose purpose was to advance the rights and dignity of gay and lesbian people began to form and operate.

During the middle part of the twentieth century, so-called homophile organizations such as the Mattachine Society and the Daughters of Bilitis (DOB) began to organize gay men and lesbians, respectively, for political action. One goal of these organizations was to demonstrate the human dignity of gay men and lesbians, who were often maligned within the wider mainstream society. Midcentury attitudes about homosexuality ranged from a belief that homosexuality was an illness to a belief that homosexuality was unnatural and a grave sin. Homosexual activities, whether social or sexual, were banned by law. Homosexual people were routinely barred from a variety of establishments, not hired or fired from jobs, blacklisted, publicly ridiculed, and subjected to interpersonal violence based on their sexuality. Often, the names of people picked up by the police during raids of gay bars and other places of congregation were published in the local newspaper as a way of alerting others in the community to ostracize the people. Another problem for gay and lesbian people during the midcentury period was the conflation of homosexuality and gender nonconformity. After World War II, a period during which U.S. women had been afforded some unusual freedoms, particularly in the vocational sphere, U.S. culture again reasserted fairly rigid gender norms. These norms pressured "women to be women" and "men to be men." As a way of enforcing these gender norms, men who were effeminate and women who were masculine were accused of being homosexual, whether or not they actually were. The interplay of gender in this process effectively doubled the stigma associated with homosexuality.

Some gay and lesbian people tried to survive by passing, that is, by manifesting no markers of gay or lesbian identity or gender nonconformity and even by functioning in heterosexual marriages and families. Other gay and lesbian people simply chose to maintain a low profile for survival, limiting their congregation with other gay and lesbian people and keeping their gay or lesbian relationships and social lives secret. A much smaller contingent of lesbian and gay people lived their lives openly, not hiding the fact of their homosexuality. Such people most often appeared at the extremes of the economic spectrum, where money or celebrity could offer some protection to people at the top, and anonymity and social marginality produced the situation of having "nothing to lose" for people at the bottom. Noted midcentury writer Truman Capote, for example, circulated at the highest echelons of New York society as an openly gay man. Sylvia Rivera, at the other extreme, lived most of her life as a homeless street hustler. She lived openly as a gay, transgender drag queen. While she was frequently subjected to taunts and violence, she found solidarity and aid among others who were similarly socially situated.

In addition to providing a sense of community to gay and lesbian people, organizations like Mattachine and DOB carried out public awareness campaigns designed to demonstrate that gay and lesbian people were "just like everybody else"—good workers, upstanding citizens, loyal patriots, members of families, and the like—with the exception of the minor fact of their sexual orientation. Their goals could be described as assimilationist, that is, geared toward achieving widespread acceptance and integrating gay and lesbian people into the mainstream of society. In this sense, early gay and lesbian activism bore some similarity to early civil rights activism. Homophile organizations favored methods that used orthodox channels of social change. Changing laws, policies, and attitudes through lobbying, letter writing, and public education were preferred techniques. In this way, the homophile organizations were also similar to many black civil rights organizations, like the NAACP. Some, although certainly not all, gay discourse during this period capitulated to the suggestion that homosexuality was an illness or a sin by arguing that gay people "couldn't help it" and were trying to live as decently as they could with their "problem." Although today we might consider these modes of gay and lesbian activism relatively conservative, it is important to remember that, at the time, they were bold and daring. It is also important to remember that not all individual members of organizations like Mattachine or DOB held the same opinions or were in agreement about the nature of homosexuality or the best approach to activism. Finally, it is important to note that organizations like Mattachine and DOB were not immune from forms of discrimination or exclusion that were unrelated to sexual orientation, such as race or class. Both organizations were predominantly white and composed of mostly middle- to upper-class members. Although these facts do not detract from the importance of the groundwork carried out by either Mattachine or DOB, they highlight the complex and ongoing nature of social justice work.

During the mid-to-late 1960s, radicalism began to infuse and transform a number of social justice movements in the United States. Numerous identity groups within U.S. society were assertively proclaiming their cultural distinctiveness, opposition to the status quo, and collective power and agency. For instance, the Black Power movement emerged out of the Student Nonviolent Coordinating Committee within the civil rights movement,[19] and feminism took a decidedly more radical turn with the emergence of the women's liberation movement,[20] including the formation of groups like the National Organization for Women and later Radicalesbians. In addition, the antiwar movement associated with the Vietnam War gathered widespread social currency and provided an entrée into radicalism for many Americans. Even the Catholic Church was expressing more liberal sentiments with the introduction of Vatican II during the early 1960s. This sea change in the overall political and cultural climate on the left eventually infused gay and lesbian activism, making an event like Stonewall thinkable and possible.

It is, of course, important to remember that the punctum, in this case Stonewall, was fueled by the intensification of forces that opposed liberation for the oppressed group, in this case lesbians and gays, just as much as it was enabled by the "march for liberation." While organizations like Mattachine and DOB were doing their work, other inimical social forces like McCarthyism and vice raids like those described above were intensifying both oppression and the desire for liberation among those oppressed. For people like Sylvia Rivera, exclusion from mainstream gay society further fueled the impulse to resist and rebel.

THE ROLE OF SYLVIA RIVERA IN THE
STONEWALL REBELLION: FROM PARTICIPANT TO ICON

So far, we have focused primarily on Stonewall as an event, describing what happened, why it was significant, and what led up to it. We will now turn our attention to the figure of Sylvia Rivera, addressing such questions as: Who was Sylvia Rivera? What was her role in Stonewall? What led up to her participation in this watershed event? What did she do after Stonewall? Why is it important that we memorialize her as a hero of both lesbian and gay liberation and transgender rights? What is her legacy today?

CRITICAL MOMENTS IN THE LIFE OF SYLVIA RIVERA

Sylvia Lee Rivera was born Ray Rivera Mendoza on July 2, 1951, outside the old Lincoln Hospital in the Bronx, New York. In the words of Rivera herself, "My moms wanted a Fourth of July baby, but the queen wanted to be born on July 2nd, so I was born feet first in a taxicab in the parking lot."[21] When Ray was three, his mother committed suicide by ingesting poison and attempted to kill Ray, too, by inducing him to drink a similarly laced concoction. Her second husband was a drug dealer, a fact that caused her great vexation. She wanted to spare herself and her son from the hard life she saw ahead. Ray refused to drink and thus survived. He was raised by his grandmother, known as Viejita, on the Lower East Side of Manhattan. He also had a half-sister, Sonia, who was two and a half years his junior.

Ray's transgenderism was evident early. As a very young child, he was both effeminate and rebellious. As a result, Ray's home life was particularly difficult. His grandmother would say to him, "I never wanted you, but I ended up with you and now I gotta deal with it."[22] Ray began wearing makeup to school in the fourth grade. Over time, Viejita sent Ray to various boarding schools and foster homes in the New York City area. In one home, the lady of the house asked Ray for sexual favors, which he refused. During this same period, he was molested on multiple occasions by an older man in the neighborhood. Such premature sexual exposures contributed to Ray's childhood difficulties and the deterioration of his relationship with his grandmother. But Ray also began having secret homosexual encounters with peers. By the time Ray was ten, neighbors had begun taunting his grand-mother by calling her a pimp because Ray had taken to hustling on Forty-second Street in New York, then a sleazy corridor for male and female pros-titutes, many of them homeless. As Sylvia stated in an interview, "When we used to go on the subway, the adults would always start laughing when we got to Forty-second Street. The queens would get on and they'd say, 'Oh, look at the patos'—which means 'faggot'—and 'This is where they all hang out.' . . . One day I was curious, so I went. . . . I saw that you can make money by having sex with men. I was ten years old. . . ."[23] Viejita's dismay over this discovery about Ray's activities precipitated a suicide attempt on the part of Ray at age ten. As a result of both the suicide attempt and Ray's homosexu-ality and effeminacy, Viejita committed Ray to Bellevue Hospital, a large, public mental hospital in New York City. From there, Ray was transferred to the state mental hospital. There, the doctors attempted to persuade Viejita to allow Ray to receive electroshock treatment, then a widely used, yet severe, treatment for various mental disorders. According to Rivera, "The only thing that saved me is that one of the woman attendants, that happened to be a gay woman, explained to her in Spanish that—'Look, it's not going to do any good for him. He is who he is. Don't let these doctors talk you into doing this to him.'"[24]

Eventually, Ray ran away from the mental hospital, ended up back on Forty-second Street, and joined the community of street people. There he met a black transgender drag queen by the name of Marsha P. (for "Pay It No Mind") Johnson, born Malcolm Michaels Jr., who became his mentor, care-taker, best friend, and fellow activist. Marsha was then sixteen or seventeen; Ray was eleven. Shortly thereafter, Ray Rivera Mendoza was rechristened Sylvia Lee Rivera—Sylvia because there were no other Sylvias on the strip at that time, and Lee because it was a name Ray had always liked. As was cus-tomary among queens, the former "he" would thereafter be referred to as a "she." The name change took place in an in-home ceremony of mostly black and Latino drag queens officiated by "an old, old lesbian and an old, old drag queen."[25] Sylvia was now the youngest member of a group of about forty to fifty drag queens who lived, worked, and took care of each other in the vicinity of Forty-second Street.

During this period, police would conduct random sweeps of hustlers, prostitutes, and transvestites on the streets of New York, particularly on and around Forty-second Street. As the result of one of these sweeps, Sylvia was picked up and sent to jail for the first time at age twelve. She recounted: "A lot of us were beaten up and raped [in jail]. When I ended up going to jail, to do 90 days, they tried to rape me."[26] At age fifteen, she was arrested for shooting a violent john, but due to her grandmother's intervention and the temporary adoption of a more traditional, masculine appearance, Sylvia was let off by the judge. Some years later, Sylvia was taken to jail again for seeking signatures for a gay rights petition in Times Square. It was in jail that Sylvia first became involved with, and eventually addicted to, drugs. She remembers Rikers Island Prison in particular as the place where she was first exposed to and ultimately became addicted to heroin in 1966. Periodic drug abuse would plague Sylvia for the rest of her life, causing periods of abject poverty, poor health, joblessness, and homelessness, ultimately having a negative impact on her activism and her public reputation.

During the mid-1960s, Sylvia considered a sex-change operation. After taking hormones for a period, she decided against the surgery. "I came to the conclusion that I don't want to be a woman. I just want to be me. I like to dress up and pretend, and let the world think about what I am. Is he, or isn't he? That's what I enjoy."[27] At various points in her life, Sylvia would be criticized both for being too feminine and for not conforming to female drag fastidiously enough. Often, Sylvia would be seen wearing articles of both male and female clothing, which often confused onlookers. By wearing what she liked, Sylvia confronted not only stereotypes about gender, but also stereotypes about transgender people. For similar reasons, Sylvia also chose not to perform as a drag queen. For her, drag was an identity and a way of life, not simply a costume or performance.

In 1969, at the age of eighteen, "Ray Silvera Mendoza" got notice to report to the local draft board in Jersey City, New Jersey, where Sylvia was living at the time. Opposed to the Vietnam War, Sylvia appeared before the board in full drag, wearing high heels, a miniskirt, and long red nails. The draft sergeants, assuming she was female, sent her with the women. Although Sylvia protested, announcing that she was "one of the boys," she was initially ignored. Once she arrived at the women's induction center, however, she was sent to the office of the psychiatrist, who asked, "Is there a problem with your sexuality?" Sylvia's reply was: "Is there? I don't know. I know I like men. I know I like to wear dresses. But I don't know what any *problem* is."[28] The psychiatrist then stamped "Homosexual" on Sylvia's papers and dismissed her from military service.

On the night of Stonewall, which Sylvia Rivera characterized as a hot, muggy night, Sylvia was supposed to go to the birthday party of her friend Marsha P. Johnson, but she felt too tired. At that time, she was working as an accounting clerk in a chain-store warehouse in Jersey City on an eleven-to-seven shift Mondays through Thursdays. That Friday night, her plan was to stay home and light prayer candles for the late Judy Garland. Later in the evening, however, she received a call from a friend inviting her to go to the Stonewall Inn. Her friend refused to take no for an answer, so Sylvia gave in.

Sylvia did not usually patronize the Stonewall Inn, as it did not cater to drag queens, but every once in a while, she and her friends would stop by for a drink on their way to the Washington Square Bar, an after-hours establishment that did cater to the transgender community. Thus it was that Sylvia, her lover at the time, and a few friends ended up there on that fateful evening.

When the police entered the bar, Sylvia was in a state of heightened emotion: fatigue, combined with her feelings of grief over the loss of Judy Garland, guilt over missing Marsha's party, and drug-induced ups and downs, had her on edge. By her own account, "I was just not in the mood. . . . It had got to the point where I didn't want to be bothered anymore."[29] In another account, she reported, "We were not taking any more of this shit. We had done so much for other movements. It was time [to fight]."[30] Although she managed to escape being nabbed by the police on her way out the door of the establishment, she immediately became caught up in the commotion outside the doors.

> Now everybody says that it was me who threw the first bottle. No. It was somebody that was behind me that threw the first bottle. But when the first bottle went by me, I said, "Oh Lord Jesus, the revolution is finally here! Hallelujah—it's time to go do your thing!" Then all kinds of things started flying! I broke out of the crowd trying to find something to throw, and someone handed me a Molotov cocktail. I don't know where it came from, I had never handled one in my life, but it was lit and they said, "Hurry up and throw it." So I did, and boom![31]

Sylvia later stated, "I enjoyed being there that night. Every outrageous thing that I did I did out of anger because society had fucked me over for so long. . . . It's hard to explain, except that it had to happen one day. . . ."[32]

From that point forward, Sylvia Rivera became very involved with organized gay and transgender activism. Always sassy and scrappy by temperament, Sylvia was a natural in the newly created context of gay visibility, and her loud, confident voice was needed as the newly emerged movement required intrepid spokespersons. She became active with the Gay Liberation Front (GLF), a newly formed radical gay rights organization from which many other activist organizations were later spawned, often "manning" the table at its fund-raising dances and famously maintaining a concealed knife just in case confrontation ensued or trouble broke out. A year later, she became involved with the Gay Activists Alliance (GAA), working tirelessly to pass a gay rights bill in New York City. One of her most memorable acts was to climb the walls of City Hall in a dress and high heels to crash a closed-door meeting on the bill. While collecting signatures for the petition in Times Square, Sylvia was arrested—the only GAA member to be arrested in the effort. Ironically, despite her valiant efforts on behalf of the bill, the GAA later dropped drag and transvestite concerns from the bill to make it more palatable to legislators and the general public. Despite these changes, the bill was voted down.

Unfortunately, this mainstreaming effort caused Sylvia Rivera and similarly gender-nonconforming activists to be ostracized by the more centrist elements of the gay liberation movement during the mid-1970s. Yet, according to Sylvia Rivera, "There were a lot of drag queens behind the scenes that could not be seen in the front lines. . . . the drag queens were doing a lot in the background,"[33] particularly in terms of planning the Christopher Street Liberation Day Parade, the original commemoration of Stonewall and precursor to today's Gay Pride events that fall in June. At the fourth annual commemorative event in 1973, Sylvia Rivera's scheduled speech was abruptly disrupted by Jean O'Leary, a founding member of the Radicalesbians, who held that the presence and participation of drag queens and transgender people was detrimental to "the movement." Her position has been quoted as follows: "Men dressing up as women to play out roles that men have created to entice and seduce men, has nothing to do with being female."[34] According to Perry Brass, a fellow Gay Liberation Front member, "the GLF women felt that drag queens were 'appropriating female' dress, but still had 'male privileges.'"[35] As Sylvia recounted it:

> Well, my dear girlfriend Jean O'Leary, a founder of Radicalesbians, decided that drag queens were insulting to women. In 1973 the 82 Club show queens were in the march. Side-by-side with the Queens Liberation Front banner and the S.T.A.R. banner. I had been told I was going to speak at the rally. And that's when things just got out of hand. I'm very militant when it comes to certain things, and I didn't appreciate what was going down with Jean O'Leary stating that we were insulting women. . . . She told Vito Russo to kick my ass onstage . . . but I still got up and I spoke my piece. I don't let too many people keep me down. Especially my own. . . .[36]

Although Rivera was famously quoted as saying in response, "Hell hath no fury like a drag queen scorned,"[37] this incident precipitated yet another suicide attempt on her part. Jean O'Leary later reversed her position, and she and Sylvia ultimately remained respectful peers, but the events of that day in 1973 ultimately took something out of Sylvia Rivera. In the succeeding years, Sylvia Rivera's participation in "the movement" waned. Although she attended every Christopher Street Liberation Day Parade (with the exception of two) until her death, Sylvia's formal participation in organizations like the GLF and the GAA came to a halt.

Another key event in Sylvia Rivera's activist career that took place on the heels of Stonewall was the founding of the Street Transvestite Action Revolutionaries, known as S.T.A.R., with her friend and comrade Marsha P. Johnson in 1970. This organization provided aid to transgender street youth and mobilized the transgender street community for various political actions. As part of the program, Sylvia and Marsha founded the S.T.A.R. House, a shelter for gay and transgender homeless street youth set up in an abandoned house at 213 E. Second Street that Sylvia and Marsha had gotten from the Mafia. To sustain the house and keep the young people off the streets, Sylvia and Marsha, then both in their twenties, hustled. Unfortunately, a lack of funds and problems with the certificate of occupancy forced Sylvia and Marsha to abandon the venture within a couple of years. Despite the formal loss of the site, Sylvia continued to sustain support activities for street youth. Some years later, as described below, both S.T.A.R. and S.T.A.R. House were resurrected and revitalized. According to Wicker, "She always considered her efforts with Marsha P. Johnson and others in establishing the first refuge for transgendered youth in East Village as the apex of her activist career."[38]

Sylvia Rivera's activism not only extended beyond gay and transgender concerns early on, but also built bridges between sexuality- and gender-based communities and racially or ethnically defined communities. In 1970, Sylvia built an alliance with the Young Lords, a radical Puerto Rican organization, by attending an East Harlem demonstration and representing the S.T.A.R. constituency. In 1970, she attended a Black Panther congress in Philadelphia with white yippie and GLF activist Jim Fouratt. Together and in concert with others, they challenged the Panthers on their homophobia and sexism, providing impetus to the then controversial but now famous statement of alliance that came from Panther leader Huey Newton. In it, he stated that gay and feminist radicals were true revolutionary allies and should be treated as such by members of the Black Panther Party.[39]

A similar spirit was also in evidence later. To quote Wicker, "Wherever and whenever there was an injustice, she would join with those demonstrating about it. When some angry Blacks who were marching to protest the brutalization of Abner Louima started calling NYPD officers 'faggots', Sylvia quickly reminded them that a lot of gay people were there supporting their protest. The shouts of 'faggot cops' ceased."[40] By this time Sylvia had built up quite a reputation as a voice to respect among progressives and a voice to suppress among the guardians of the status quo. For example, quoting Wicker again: "When the memorial march commemorating Matthew Sheppard took to Fifth Avenue, the officer in charge reportedly pointed at Sylvia and instructed his underling 'to get that one' because 'she is a real troublemaker.'"[41]

During the 1980s, Sylvia Rivera took food service jobs in Westchester, New York, and Tarrytown, New York. She lived and worked in these places for approximately a decade, until her drug habit again reemerged, this time around crack cocaine, taking its toll and forcing her back onto the streets of New York City and into hustling for survival. Over the years, in all the places she resided, one constant that remained was her continued "mothering" of gay and transgender street youth. Typically, she opened her home, wherever that might be (including, at one time, cardboard boxes) to needy youth, many of whom had been thrown away by their families.

The early 1990s was a period of both difficulty and transition for Sylvia. Returning to New York City addicted, Sylvia endured several years of homelessness, surviving on the Christopher Street piers where she had hustled as a youth. She reached a low point when, in 1992, her friend and mentor Marsha P. Johnson was found dead on those same piers. Although the cause of death—suicide or murder (a hate crime was suspected)—was unclear, the event cast Sylvia into a deep depression and precipitated yet another suicide attempt. Coming out of this emotional abyss, however, Sylvia reentered politics and activism, on the belief that Marsha would have wanted her to do so.

Sylvia's activities were diverse. She cofounded an organization called the Stonewall Riot Veterans. She agitated on behalf of homeless gay people who lived near the Gay and Lesbian Community Center in New York City, at one point being banned from the site for her activities. In 1994, she led the "illegal" march commemorating the twenty-fifth anniversary of Stonewall up Fifth Avenue. She helped plan the first Brooklyn Pride March in 1997 as well as the 2001 Transworld III conference for transgender people of color. She intentionally took arrests on behalf of a number of activist organizations, including Soul Force, the Irish Lesbian and Gay Organization, and the New York City Homeless Coalition, and events, including the Matthew Sheppard political funeral, the Amadou Diallo demonstration, and the 2000 St. Patrick's Day demonstration. She organized a rally to raise awareness of the case of slain transwoman Amanda Milan, who was murdered in front of several witnesses on a New York City street in broad daylight.

She joined the Transy House Collective—a group of transgender people committed to the principles of the S.T.A.R. House—in Park Slope, Brooklyn, living there during the last years of her life and providing financial assistance and counseling services for young people there until the time of her death. In 2000, she reactivated S.T.A.R., renaming it the Street Transgender Action Revolutionaries and fronting trans inclusion efforts before the Human Rights Campaign and the New York State Transgender Coalition. In a 2001 letter to the Human Rights Campaign leadership, she wrote, "Your people had no problem in 1969 from using the anger of our people who gave their all, who had nothing to lose, who brought you out of the closets you would still be in if it were not for us."[42] Although the Human Rights Campaign did not change their position while she was alive, the organization did recognize her upon her death.

A highlight of the "second wave" of Sylvia Rivera's activist career came in 1999 when she was invited by the Italian Transgender Organization to address the World Pride Rally at the World Pride Celebration in Rome. At this event, Sylvia was given tribute as the founder of the world's struggle for transgendered rights. During the 1990s until the time of her death, Sylvia was honored with numerous lifetime achievement awards from organizations such as the Puerto Rican Gay and Lesbian Association of New York, the Neutral Zone Youth Organization of New York, the National Transgender

Advocacy Coalition, the AmBoyz Organization, and the Metropolitan Community Church of New York. As Rivera stated in an interview with the *New York Times*, "The movement had put me on the shelf, but they took me down and dusted me off."[43] "I walked down 58th Street and the young ones were calling from the sidewalk, 'Sylvia, Sylvia, thank you, we know what you did,'"[44] she also reported.

Sylvia Rivera died at approximately 5 a.m. on February 19, 2002, in St. Vincent's Hospital in Greenwich Village. The cause of death was complications of liver cancer. She was fifty years old. Prior to her death, she served as coordinator of the food pantry at the Metropolitan Community Church of New York, of which she had become an active member and in which she had been baptized in 2002. On her deathbed, she met with a delegation from the Empire State Pride Agenda to negotiate for the inclusion of trans rights in a gay and lesbian rights bill, known as SONDA (the Sexual Orientation Nondiscrimination Ordinance), pending in the New York State legislature. Her funeral services were held at the Metropolitan Community Church of New York at 446 West Thirty-sixth Street. The service was followed by a memorial at the Stonewall Inn, from which her ashes were carried in a horse-drawn carriage (an idea she adopted from the film *Imitation of Life*) to the Christopher Street piers, where they were scattered and allowed to intermingle with those of Marsha P. Johnson. As part of the ceremony, a wreath was laid at the piers to commemorate Marsha. Sylvia was survived by her life partner and lover, Julia Murray, a transwoman whom she had met at Transy House; the hundreds of gay and transgender homeless street "children" whom she aided over the years; and numerous activists whom she had inspired across the course of her life.

INTERPRETING SYLVIA RIVERA'S LIFE AND WORK

Viewing the life of Sylvia Rivera through the lens introduced earlier in this chapter, we can observe antecedent forces that delivered her to the punctum that became known as Stonewall. Forces associated with race, class, gender, and sexuality yielded a particular consciousness and set of tactics in Sylvia that she was ultimately able to deploy toward a larger historical end when the opportunity arose. Following the work of Chela Sandoval, this consciousness and these methods could be characterized as "differential," insofar as they reflected multiple mind-sets and used multiple methods, taking advantage of whatever was on hand, whatever was needed, whatever was possible within the constraints of a situation and specific set of resources, to get the work of social change done.[45] Indeed, that moment in which Sylvia Rivera found herself a key actor was partially of her own making; there would have been no rebellion without rebels present at the moment of confrontation.

What could not be as readily anticipated and what must necessarily be characterized as only a partial victory for the gay and lesbian liberation movement is the way in which Sylvia Rivera as a gay transgender person was sidelined from the very movement she had helped to initiate. That many early leaders of the movement failed to "recognize the connections" between multiple forms of oppression, including the oppression of transgender people who might also be gay or lesbian as well as the oppression of poor people and, to a somewhat lesser extent (because it was more widely recognized, if not better enacted), people of color, allowed the movement to mimic and reproduce forms of oppression from outside and thus to splinter from within. On the one hand, such splintering attenuated the movement's transformative energy and momentum, but, on the other hand, it allowed new, more focused liberationist groups—such as those formed by trans people, people of color, poor people, women, men, radicals, conservatives, and, later, people with HIV—to form and articulate unique and valuable critical standpoints and activist tactics.

SYLVIA RIVERA'S LEGACY: UNANSWERED PLEAS AND BECKONING HORIZONS FOR SOCIAL CHANGE

In her lifetime, Sylvia Rivera fought for the rights and dignity of gay and transgendered people, poor and homeless people, people of color, and, more generally, marginalized people everywhere. As an outsider to many of the circles in which she circulated politically and socially, Sylvia Rivera knew firsthand the way in which the politics of discrimination and exclusion reproduce themselves in even the most well-intentioned and progressive places. For instance, she watched mainstream gay and lesbian activists abandon transgender concerns in their fight for gay and lesbian rights. She observed poor, black, and Latino drag queens and other street activists being ridiculed and silenced in gay and lesbian organizational circles. Despite experiencing such exclusion, ridicule, and abandonment herself, she kept fighting for the causes she believed in and speaking up for those less able to speak. In addition to keeping up the fight, she stayed true to her own self, her own identity, almost never attempting to fashion herself in some more "acceptable" way for the sake of expediency. She stands as a beacon of courage and a model of dedication for those facing similar obstacles and attempting to pursue a similar course. In the end, her causes were, like those of the larger civil rights movement, dignity, self-determination, and inclusion for all.

Today, we can pick up where Sylvia Rivera left off by conceiving of progressive social change not only as the struggle to attain inclusion for specific social groups, such as black people, women, gay and lesbian people, or people with disabilities, but also as the struggle to eradicate center-margin relations altogether. Sylvia Rivera proved that people are more than the sum of

their social categories—in her case, Puerto Rican, gay, transgender, and poor—
and that overly simplistic politics based on the achievement of liberation for
one group or another is never enough to create a truly just society. Today, we
can use the lesson of Sylvia Rivera's life to begin thinking about how to eliminate our tendency to normalize one group of people or one way of life over
another and promote a shared context in which we all can thrive.

An example of someone who has taken up the mantle of Sylvia Rivera's
activism is Dean Spade. Spade founded the Sylvia Rivera Law Project
(www.srlp.org), which, according to its own mission statement, "works to
guarantee that all people are free to self-determine our own gender identity
and expression, regardless of income, and without facing harassment, discrimination or violence." Based in New York City, the Sylvia Rivera Law Project advocates on behalf of and legally represents transgender people and
others whose nontraditional gender has met with negative outcomes. As the
project states on its website:

> Transgender, transsexual, intersex, and gender variant people face persistent
> and severe discrimination in employment, education, health care, social and le-
> gal services, criminal justice and many other realms. All low-income people are
> suffering from the severe cutbacks to anti-poverty programs, but low-income
> people who experience gender identity discrimination are particularly vulnera-
> ble in this climate. Many are turned away outright from essential services like
> homeless shelters, drug treatment or mental health services, while others expe-
> rience discrimination or violence in these settings because of their gender iden-
> tity or expression.
>
> Because so many of the systems in which low-income people are over-repre-
> sented or seek services are sex-segregated—such as prisons, group homes, shel-
> ters and detention facilities—many face serious problems of inaccessibility or
> violence if their gender identity does not conform to their birth sex. Further-
> more, those who seek legal and social services to help get on their feet or fight
> for entitlements often encounter ignorance or discrimination at the door. The re-
> sult is that transgender, transsexual, intersex and gender variant people are dis-
> proportionately poor, homeless, and incarcerated, and are 7–10 times more
> likely to be a victim of murder.[46]

While the Sylvia Rivera Law Project is but one example of how progressive
activists might carry on Sylvia Rivera's life work, it demonstrates that Sylvia
Rivera's legacy will be a prolific one.

SUMMARY AND CONCLUSIONS

> We used to sit around, just try to figure out when this harassment would
> come to an end. And we would always dream that one day it would come
> to an end. And we prayed and we looked for it. *We wanted to be human beings.*
>
> Sylvia Rivera

For those of us in Public Morals, after the Stonewall incident things were completely changed from what they had previously been. They suddenly were not submissive anymore. They now suddenly had gained a new type of courage. . . . *We were now dealing with human beings.*

Seymour Pine

Did the life of Sylvia Rivera make a difference? There is a reason that Sylvia Rivera has been called "the Rosa Parks of the modern transgender movement."[47] As one writer has penned, "I think that it is as if the history of the modern queer rights movement is written on her life."[48] Sylvia Rivera's contributions to the gay and lesbian liberation movement are by now self-evident, but in choosing to look only at this particular facet of her legacy, we run the risk of overlooking her contributions to an even grander socially transformative project, namely, full humanization.[49] Perhaps the most profound legacy of Sylvia Rivera's life is the way in which it forces us to affirm the value and agency of some of society's most rejected and dispossessed persons—the poor, the homeless, the addicted, the imprisoned, the nonconforming. As a society, we are often quick to assume that a person who lives on the street, who sells his or her body, who is or has been a prisoner, who struggles with heroin or crack addiction, who can't hold a job, or who wears clothes or adopts mannerisms associated with the "opposite" gender is little more than an unfortunate misfit, certainly not the stuff of heroism or historical significance. The life of Sylvia Rivera proves all of those myths wrong, forcing us to reconsider and reaffirm the worth and genius of those whom we as a society often struggle to make invisible or, worse, make disappear. The epigraphs above attest to what her life in some measure achieved, namely, the healing of a certain kind of blindness that keeps some people from seeing other people as human. That this same blindness is at the root of virtually all oppressions, particularly those oppressions that the civil rights movement and its progeny sought to address, makes her legacy that much more universal and monumental.

NOTES

1. David Isay and Sylvia Rivera, "I Never Thought I Was Going to Be a Part of Gay History," *New York Times Magazine,* June 27, 1999, 66.
2. Chela Sandoval, *Methodology of the Oppressed* (Minneapolis: University of Minnesota, 2000).
3. Paulo Freire, *Pedagogy of the Oppressed* (New York: Continuum, 1970).
4. See Layli Phillips, "Recontextualizing Kenneth Bancroft Clark: An Afrocentric Perspective on a Model Psychologist Activist," *History of Psychology* 3, no. 2 (2000): 142–67. See also Layli Phillips, "Anti-racist Work in the Desegregation Era: The Scientific Activism of Kenneth Bancroft Clark," in Andrew Winston, ed., *Defining Difference:*

Race and Racism in the History of Psychology (Washington, D.C.: American Psychologi-cal Association, 2002), 233–60.

5. There is debate among scholars about whether to use the term *riot* or *rebellion* in conjunction with historically notable events characterized by spontaneous crowd eruption of a resistant nature. The term *riot* implies unruly civil unrest without a clear agenda, whereas the term *rebellion* implies intentional political resistance. Consistent with a number of other writers, we decided to adopt the term *rebellion* in this chapter.

6. Martin Duberman, *Stonewall* (New York: Dutton, 1993), 198.

7. David Isay and Harvey Wang, *Holding On: Dreamers, Visionaries, Eccentrics, and Other American Heroes* (New York: Norton, 1997), 75.

8. David Deitcher, *The Question of Equality: Lesbian and Gay Politics in America Since Stonewall* (New York: Scribner, 1995), 67.

9. Duberman, *Stonewall*, 196.

10. Duberman, *Stonewall*, 197.

11. Isay and Wang, *Holding On*, 76.

12. David Isay and Michael Schirker, *Remembering Stonewall*, radio documentary by Sound Portraits, premiered July 1, 1989, on National Public Radio's *Weekend Edition*, updated July 5, 2001, available from www.soundportraits.org/on-air/remembering_stonewall/ (retrieved July 8, 2003).

13. Leslie Feinberg, "Leslie Feinberg Interviews Sylvia Rivera: 'I'm Glad I Was in the Stonewall Riot,'" *Worker's World*, July 2, 1998, 1, available from www.workers .org/ww/1998/sylvia0702.html (retrieved June 4, 2003).

14. Perry Brass, "Sylvia Ray Rivera (1951–2002)," *Gay Today*, February 25, 2002, available from gaytoday.com/garchive/people/022502pe.htm (retrieved July 9, 2003).

15. Isay and Wang, *Holding On*, 76.

16. Isay and Wang, *Holding On*, 76.

17. Deitcher, *Question of Equality*, 71.

18. Deitcher, *Question of Equality*, 71.

19. Kristin Anderson-Bricker, "'Triple Jeopardy': Black Women and the Growth of Feminist Consciousness in SNCC, 1964–1975," in Kimberly Springer, ed., *Still Lifting, Still Climbing: African American Women's Contemporary Activism* (New York: New York University Press, 1999), 49–69.

20. Radicalesbians, "The Woman-identified Woman," in Miriam Schnier, ed., *Feminism in Our Time: The Essential Writings, World War II to the Present* (New York: Vintage Books, 1994), 160–67.

21. Isay and Rivera, "I Never Thought," 66.

22. Isay and Wang, *Holding On*, 73.

23. Isay and Wang, *Holding On*, 73.

24. Isay and Wang, *Holding On*, 74.

25. Isay and Wang, *Holding On*, 73.

26. Feinberg, "Leslie Feinberg Interviews Sylvia Rivera," 1.

27. Duberman, *Stonewall*, 125.

28. Duberman, *Stonewall*, 128.

29. Duberman, *Stonewall*, 193.

30. Feinberg, "Leslie Feinberg Interviews Sylvia Rivera," 2.

31. Isay and Wang, *Holding On*, 76.

32. Deitcher, *Question of Equality*, 67.

33. Deitcher, *Question of Equality*, 68.

34. Duberman, *Stonewall*, 238.

35. Perry Brass, 2002. "Sylvia Ray Rivera (1951–2002)," available from gaytoday .com/garchive/people/022502pe.htm (retrieved June 4, 2003).

36. Deitcher, *Question of Equality*, 68.

37. David W. Dunlap, "Sylvia Rivera, 50, Figure in Birth of the Gay Liberation Movement" [obituary], *New York Times*, February 20, 2002, A19. See also Riki Wilchins, "A Woman for Her Time: In Memory of Stonewall Warrior Sylvia Rivera," *Village Voice*, February 27–March 5, 2002, available from www.villagevoice.com/issues/0209/wilchins.php (retrieved July 8, 2003).

38. Randolfe H. Wicker, "Sylvia Rivera in Life and Death—Legendary Figure Dies at 50," *Gay Today*, February 20, 2002, 1, available from gaytoday.com/garchive/events/022002ev.htm (retrieved June 4, 2003).

39. Huey P. Newton, "A Letter from Huey to the Revolutionary Brothers and Sisters about the Women's Liberation and Gay Liberation Movements," reprinted in Rudolph P. Byrd and Beverly Guy-Sheftall, eds., *Traps: African American Men on Gender and Sexuality* (Bloomington: Indiana University Press, 2001), 281–83.

40. Wicker, "Sylvia Rivera in Life and Death," 1–2.

41. Wicker, "Sylvia Rivera in Life and Death," 2.

42. *Gay Today*, n.d., 2.

43. Dunlap, "Sylvia Rivera, 50," A19.

44. Dunlap, "Sylvia Rivera, 50," A19.

45. Sandoval, *Methodology of the Oppressed*.

46. Sylvia Rivera Law Project, www.srlp.org (retrieved June 4, 2003), 1.

47. Wilchins, "A Woman for Her Time."

48. Unidentified guestbook entrant on the www.coyotecomics.com website (retrieved June 4, 2003).

49. Freire, *Pedagogy of the Oppressed*.

SUGGESTED READING

Books

Clendinen, Dudley, and Adam Nagourney. *Out for Good: The Struggle to Build a Gay Rights Movement in America*. New York: Simon & Schuster, 1999.

Deitcher, David. *The Question of Equality: Lesbian and Gay Politics in America Since Stonewall*. New York: Scribner, 1995.

Duberman, Martin. *Stonewall*. New York: Dutton, 1993.

Feinberg, Leslie. *Transgender Warriors: Making History from Joan of Arc to Dennis Rodman*. Boston: Beacon, 1997.

Isay, David, and Harvey Wang. *Holding On: Dreamers, Visionaries, Eccentrics, and Other American Heroes*. New York: Norton, 1997.

Articles

Bronski, Michael. "In Memory: Sylvia Rivera: 1951–2002." *Z Magazine* 15, no. 4 (April 2002): 2–3.

Dunlap, David W. "Sylvia Rivera, 50, Figure in Birth of the Gay Liberation Movement" [obituary]. *New York Times*, February 20, 2002, A19.

Feinberg, Leslie. "Leslie Feinberg Inteviews Sylvia Rivera: 'I'm Glad I Was in the Stonewall Riot.'" *Worker's World*, July 2, 1998. Available from www.workers.org/ww/1998/sylvia0702.html. Retrieved June 4, 2003.

Isay, David, and Sylvia Rivera. "I Never Thought I Was Going to Be a Part of Gay History." *New York Times Magazine*, June 27, 1999, 66.

Film

Finch, Nigel [Director]. *Stonewall*. Hollywood, Calif.: Fox Lorber, 1996.

Index

About the Editor and Contributors

Susan M. Glisson is a native of Evans, Georgia. She holds a doctorate in American studies from the College of William and Mary. Since 2002, she has directed the William Winter Institute for Racial Reconciliation at the University of Mississippi. She is the coauthor of *First Freedoms: A Documentary History of First Amendment Rights in America*.

Crystal S. Anderson is an assistant professor in the Department of American Studies at the University of Kansas, where she teaches courses on race and ethnicity in literature and visual culture. She has written several book chapters on comparative Afro-Asian American cultural interaction and is currently completing a book manuscript, *Trickster Discourses: African American and Asian/American Cultural Interaction in Fiction*. Dr. Anderson received her PhD in American studies from the College of William and Mary.

Eric Arnesen is professor of history and African American studies at the University of Illinois at Chicago, and is the author of *Waterfront Workers of New Orleans: Race, Class, and Politics, 1863–1923* (1991); *Brotherhoods of Color: Black Railroad Workers and the Struggle for Equality* (2001); and *Black Protest and the Great Migration: A Brief History with Documents* (2002). He is the editor of *The Human Tradition in American Labor History* (2003); *The Black Worker: Race, Labor, and Civil Rights since Emancipation* (2006); and *The Encyclopedia of U.S. Labor and Working-Class History* (2006); and coeditor of *Labor Histories: Class, Politics, and the Working-Class Experience* (1998). In 2006, he held the

Distinguished Fulbright Chair at the Swedish Institute for North American Studies at Uppsala University in Sweden. A regular contributor to the *Chicago Tribune*, Arnesen is currently writing a biography of A. Philip Randolph.

Paul R. Beezley is assistant professor of American history at Jacksonville State University in Jacksonville, Alabama. He holds a doctorate in history from the University of Mississippi. His primary research interest centers on Southern and cultural history in the late nineteenth and early twentieth centuries, including the political uses of Jefferson Davis's funerals, and Southern exhibits at World's Fairs.

David S. Cecelski is a native of the North Carolina coast. Historian and writer, he is the author of several award-winning books and more than a hundred articles about his native land's history and culture. His most recent books are *A Historian's Coast: Adventures into the Tidewater Past* and *The Waterman's Song: Slavery and Freedom in Maritime North Carolina*. His popular oral history series, "Listening to History," has been appearing in the Raleigh *News & Observer* since 1998. He has held several visiting professorships, including the Lehman Brady Chair at Duke University's Center for Documentary Studies and the Whichard Distinguished Chair in the Humanities at East Carolina University.

Constance Curry is a writer, an activist, and a fellow at the Institute for Women's Studies, Emory University, Atlanta, Georgia. From 1960 to 1964, she was the director of the Southern Student Human Relations Project of the U.S. National Student Association, Atlanta, Georgia, and served as adviser on the executive committee of the Student Nonviolent Coordinating Committee during its campus-based years. From 1964 to 1975, Curry was Southern field representative for the American Friends Service Committee (AFSC). Curry is the author of several works, including her award-winning book *Silver Rights*, which won the Lillian Smith Book Award for nonfiction in 1996. Curry coauthored *Deep in Our Hearts: Nine White Women in the Freedom Movement* and wrote, with Aaron Henry, *Aaron Henry: The Fire Ever Burning*. Her most recent book is *Mississippi Harmony*, with Ms. Winson Hudson.

Jay Driskell, a graduate student at Yale University, is writing a dissertation exploring the links between race-building and state-building through an examination of the electoral strategies of the NAACP and its competitors between 1887 and 1965. His experiences as a rank-and-file union organizer for the Graduate Employees and Students Organization (GESO) at Yale have taught him a great deal about the nature of power and resistance. He grew up in Chicago and currently lives in Phoenix, Arizona.

Carol Giardina was an early participant in the women's liberation movement and in 1968, with Judith Brown, cofounded Gainesville Women's Liberation, the first women's liberation group in the South. She was active in the civil rights movement and the New Left and was an ardent supporter of Black Power, and she continues to work for social justice today. She received her PhD in American history at the City University of New York and teaches at Queens College in New York.

David J. Libby taught history at Wake Forest University, Western Washington University, and the University of Texas at San Antonio. His research interests include the history of slavery in the United States and the history of borderland regions in the South and Southwest. He is author of *Slavery and Frontier Mississippi, 1720–1835* and coeditor of *Affect and Power Essays on Sex, Slavery, Race, and Religion in Appreciation of Winthrop D. Jordan*. He currently works for an educational publisher and lives in San Antonio, Texas.

Ernest M. Limbo is a native of Shelbyville, Tennessee. He holds a doctorate in history from the University of Mississippi. He is the dean of social sciences and associate professor of history at Tougaloo College in Jackson, Mississippi.

Robert E. Luckett Jr. graduated from Yale College in 1999 and is a PhD candidate in history at the University of Georgia. His focus is on the civil rights movement in Mississippi, and his dissertation will look at the life and career of Joe T. Patterson, attorney general of the state of Mississippi from 1956 until his death in 1969.

Shomari Olugbala earned his BA magna cum laude from Georgia State University, where he majored in African American studies. Currently he is working toward his MA in women's studies at the same institution. The tentative title of his forthcoming thesis is "Butch Queens, Femme Queens, and Realness: Performance and Gender in the Ballroom Community." As an interdisciplinary scholar, he has a variety of intersecting research interests, which include performance, culture, and liberation; African traditional spirituality and dance; and black queer studies.

Layli Phillips, PhD, is associate professor of women's studies and a member of the associated faculty of the Department of African American Studies at Georgia State University, where she teaches courses on womanism, black feminist thought, women and hip hop, and African American lesbian and gay activism and also serves as faculty adviser for GSU BlackOUT, a queer Africana student group. She is currently completing two books, *The Womanist Reader*, a retrospective on the first quarter century of womanist thought; and *Queer Africana Uprising*, an anthology of essays, poems, and other writings by emerging black Lesbian, Gay, Bisexual, Transgender, Queer (LGBTQ) writers.

Jennifer A. Stollman is chair of the Department of History and Political Science at Salem College in Winston-Salem, North Carolina and an assistant professor who specializes in the history of ideas and the contruction of identities. She specializes in social and intellectual history with an emphasis on the historical constructions of racial, gender, sexual, and religious identities.

Timothy B. Tyson teaches writing and history at the Center for Documentary Studies and the Divinity School at Duke University. His biography of Robert F. Williams, *Radio Free Dixie: Robert F. Williams and the Roots of Black Power* (1999), won the James Rawley Prize and the Frederick Jackson Turner Prize from the Organization of American Historians. His most recent book, *Blood Done Sign My Name* (2004), was a finalist for the National Book Critics Circle Award and won a Christopher Award, the North Carolina Book Award, and the Southern Book Critics Circle Award for nonfiction. He lives with his family in Chapel Hill, North Carolina.

Minoa Uffelman received her BS and MA from Austin Peay State University in Clarksville, Tennessee. She received her PhD from the University of Mississippi and is now an associate professor at Austin Peay.

Christopher Waldrep is Jamie and Phyllis Pasker Professor of American History at San Francisco State University. He received his PhD from Ohio State University in 1990 and is the author of *Roots of Disorder: Race and Criminal Justice in the American South, 1817–1880* (1998); *The Many Faces of Judge Lynch: Extralegal Violence and Punishment in America* (2004); and *Vicksburg's Long Shadow: The Civil War Legacy of Race and Remembrance* (2005).